Introduction

Just how do you define a great football match? What are the essential ingredients that cause Walsall's victory over Arsenal in 1933 to be discussed today by fans who were not even alive then? Why is England's defeat by the 'Wembley Wizards' of 1928 still regarded as Scotland's greatest moment? Just how significant was Colchester's defeat of Leeds United compared with other giant-killings.?

Here sixty experts reconstruct a carefully devised selection of the best games ever witnessed by British audiences. They range from the first-ever FA Cup final to Manchester United's European Cup success, from unashamedly parochial battles like Newcastle versus Sunderland and Liverpool versus Everton, to the European Cup final of 1960, tagged in Scotland as the best game ever seen in the British Isles.

Each of the games is carefully analysed to judge whether time has blurred or exaggerated what really happened. Is the legend of the Matthews final more myth than reality? Was it really a surprise when non-league Spurs won the Cup in 1901? How much does Joe Payne remember of the ten goals he scored for Luton in his first-ever game at centre-forward?

These are sixty cameos of unforgettable, history-making moments in British football. If you were not there – even if you were – then this book is the next best thing to have.

CONTENTS

Charles Lamb wrote: 'The key to understanding anything is to look at the people who do it.' When Scotland played her first international against England in 1870 one of their number was the son of the Prime Minister, another was Quintin Hogg, grandfather of the Lord Chancellor, yet another was Old Etonian A F Kinnaird, later High Commissioner for the Church of Scotland.

The first years of organized football are a history of the recreational activities of the children of the upper classes. The Football Association itself was founded by graduates of the public (meaning private) schools and the universities, and it remained remarkably exclusive until the advent of professionalism in the late 1870s. This should surprise no one.

Sport is a recreation that requires time, space and health. There was precious little of any of these commodities anywhere outside the country houses of the rich south.

In Nottingham, a typical provincial city of the period, half-day working on Saturdays was unheard of before 1861, local public transport, in the shape of horse-drawn trams, did not exist before 1874 and average weekly wages were still under £1 per week. Though compulsory elementary education—to the age of 11—had been introduced in 1870 it was still not uncommon to read of children working 12 hours a day in virtual sweat shops.

Hardly any dwellings—they could not be called homes or houses by any stretch of the imagination —had any sort of sanitation and, though Chadwick's efforts had virtually eliminated the virulent cholera epidemics after 1860, there was little medical aid for anyone but the very rich. For the masses life consisted of a short childhood, an exhausting manhood—or perpetual confinement for the female—and an early, and usually painful, death.

There was little time or capacity for organized sport for the 1870s saw the worst depression since the 'hungry forties' and most people were simply glad to have a job in which they could work themselves to death.

Yet the organizers of the very first Cup Final seemed blissfully unaware of all this. They set the entrance fee at 1/- (in an age when the average weekly wage was less than twenty times that amount) and still managed to persuade 2,000 people to come along. In subsequent years the event was held in the mornings to avoid clashing with the boat race—it was assumed that the sort of people who watched the one would wish to watch the other.

Spectators arrived in carriages and cabs to watch the officers of the Royal Engineers (there was not a single enlisted man in the side) and the old Harrovians who had formed The Wanderers, and the atmosphere could not have been far removed from a public school sports day.

The fact that the game was played at the Kennington Oval is not insignificant, for that arena is one of the great homes of the traditional pastime of the English upper classes—cricket—and the secretary of the FA, Charles Alcock, was later Secretary of the Surrey County Cricket Club.

It was to be ten years before a team composed of other than gentleman-amateurs was to win the FA Cup—in 1872 it must have seemed unlikely that the trophy would ever rest anywhere but in the genteel houses of the home counties.

The competition was unashamedly based on one organized annually at Alcock's old school—Harrow—where the winning house in a knockout tournament was known as the 'Cock House'.

The FA Cup competition had been conceived at a meeting in the *Sportsman* office London, on 20 July 1871. It was the brain-child of Alcock, who was concerned that there were still only thirty clubs in membership of the Association. He rightly assumed that a Cup competition would fire interest in a game that was then 'rather a

Top The team line-up of the Royal Engineers, the first team to suffer the disappointment of receiving runners-up medals 'of trifling value' for the FA Cup. The stirring red and blue hoops of the shirts and stockings made them look more like a rugby team, but this was fairly common in an age when the distinction between the two games was not as clear-cut as it is today.

Above left C W Alcock, the legendary secretary of the Football Association, played for The Wanderers, winners of the first Final—a happy result since he was the chief instigator of the FA Cup competition, conceived at a meeting in 1871.

Above right The first FA Challenge Cup, worth £20, which vanished in 1895 never to be seen again in its original form.

recreation and a means of exercise for a few public schoolboys than a truly National sport', as he wrote himself.

Charles Alcock was 29 at the time, 'a man of fine and commanding presence who had the happy knack of being able to persuade others to his way. He may not have been the most machine-like of officials, but he was essentially a leader,' as a contemporary wrote. He was a fine player himself and captained the side that first won the Cup—the celebrated Wanderers. He had a special love of dribbling which he regarded as the game's supreme art. In the *Football Annual* of 1873 he wrote: 'A really good player will not lose sight of the ball, at the same time keeping his attention employed in spying out the gaps in the enemy's ranks which may give him a favourable chance of arriving at the coveted goal. To see some players guide and steer a ball through a circle of opposing legs twisting and turning as occasion demands is a sight not to be forgotten.'

Priorities may have changed for, tactically, football must be a passing, and not a dribbling game. But the speed and skill of the accomplished dribbler is still its most spectacular art and the quickest way to the crowd's affection—as George Best can testify. It is nevertheless worth pointing out that dribbling was not just a result of selfishness. Before 1867 many soccer clubs had followed the traditional 'rugby' offside law which forbade passing the ball forward. There was often, therefore, little alternative but to dribble until dispossessed when playing under these rules, and the habit had tended to stick to the feet, even if the ball generally did not.

For that first year only 15 clubs entered the competition and only two—Donington Grammar School and Queen's Park, Glasgow—came from north of the Home Counties. Queen's Park were the most surprising participants—particularly as the one guinea entrance fee represented about one-sixth of the club's funds at the time.

The previous year Queen's Park had provided a player, Robert Smith, for a Scottish side selected to play a representative English side in London. Smith had reported in detail on the strange features of the English game, particularly the entire prohibition of the use of the hands; and the fact that while the ball was in play the practice was to run or dribble with the feet, instead of indulging in high or long kicks. He was warmly thanked for the information and his 'able and spirited play on behalf of Queen's Park and Scotland'.

When they were informed about the Cup Queen's Park were keen to take part but concerned about the problems of travel and expense. They therefore sent the minimum subscription until more was known and instructed: 'Mr Gardner and Mr Wotherspoon to forward suggestions to the Association that would place Queen's Park on an equal footing with other clubs.' It was in part their representations that led to Queen's Park being exempt until the semi-final. Arrangements were also made that the Final should be played the following day *if* Queen's Park won, so that only one journey to London would be necessary.

Queen's Park were later to refer to the Cup as the 'blessed pot' though it is uncertain whether this was out of respect for its success or exasperation at the problems it caused them. But their first match in the competition went off smoothly and happily and their club secretary, Mr A Rae, minuted this report:

'The funds which had been collected for a projected Border match were diverted to the London match and eleven men chosen, two resident in London (the brothers Smith), to represent the Club. The match was played at Kennington Oval on the afternoon of Monday, March 4th, at 3.30 pm. The day was fine and very favourable to the game. The turnout of spectators was large. The Wanderers having won the toss Queen's Park kicked off. After playing an hour and a half, the game, very much to the astonishment of the Londoners, who expected to carry it without much effort, ended in a draw. The game was pretty equal and very hard although the Queen's Park lost more chances at goal than their opponents. The match had created considerable interest both in England and Scotland and was perhaps the most prominent event in the annals of modern football.'

It was a pity the game was drawn as Queen's Park had to withdraw since neither the honour nor the rewards of medals 'of trifling value' were sufficient to justify the expenditure of a second trip to the capital.

The Wanderers were having a very fortunate run—having won only one game in four rounds. In the quarter-final they had drawn 0-0 with Crystal Palace, but progressed under rule 8 of the competition which stated: 'In the case of a drawn match the Clubs shall be drawn in the next round or compete again at the discretion of the Committee.' As there were only three quarter-finals, a sensible decision was taken to send Wanderers into one semi-final against Queen's Park, Glasgow, and Crystal Palace into the other against the Royal Engineers—who would otherwise have had no semi-final opposition.

The Royal Engineers won through 3-0 against Crystal Palace and, as has happened rarely since, the two Final contestants were probably the best of their day.

At that time betting was so much a part of sport that in cricket the MCC laws contained a section regulating it. So it was no surprise that the practice should extend to the new game of soccer and the Royal Engineers were made firm 7 to 4 favourites.

Many army officers had a public school background, which helps to explain the military presence. Success, however, was rooted in the character of an individual and the traditions of Chatham. In the 60 years since an Establishment—now the Royal School of Military Engineering—had been set up at Chatham for instruction in the duties of 'sapping, mining, and other Field Works', the Sappers had built a reputation for mental and physical fitness.

The man who developed their interest in Association Football was one Major Francis Marindin, Brigade Major at Chatham. He was one of the central characters in the development of the Cup and the game. In the year that the Cup competition began the Royal Engineers' diverse activities ranged from designing the Albert Hall to the development of the 'steam Sapper', a traction engine which pulled a train of vehicles across country and was the forerunner of the Army's mechanical transport. Marindin himself was fully imbued with this professional skill and personal resource and he was later to be President of the Football Association from 1874 to 1890.

His enthusiasm soon built up a fine football team at Chatham and in 1869 the Royal Engineers joined the Football Association. They were, without doubt, the best team in the country during the first four seasons of the Cup. All their matches were against leading clubs such as The Wanderers or the Universities, and their playing record was remarkable—of 86 games they won 74 and lost only three—two of these being the Cup Finals of 1872 and 1874. The magnificence of their record was matched only by the extravagance of their strip—though uniform would be a better word. They normally wore jerseys, 'night-caps' and stockings, all horizontally striped in regimental red and blue, with 'dark blue serge knickerbockers'. A fine and stirring sight.

The fitness and team spirit of the Sappers made them the most formidable and consistent opponents. From their style of play we can get a good picture of the tactics and formation in those early games. Their line-up was the fashionable one of a goalkeeper, one back, two half-backs, and seven forwards, three in the centre and two on either wing.

Lieutenant Ruck recalled that the 'centres were selected for weight, strength, and charging powers as well as their talent as dribblers, the game being perhaps a bit strenuous and many goals were got for RE by hustling goalkeepers through their own goal all ends up. The keynote of Royal Engineers' football was combination, not individuality, and that was the great advantage they possessed over their opponents.'

Opposing them in the Final were The Wanderers, who had grown out of the Forest Club which is usually regarded as the first of the southern clubs. All of Forest's members were Old Harrovians and the ground where they 'erected their posts' in 1859 was at Snaresbrook. For four years their ground and their success remained constant, though their rules were as varied as their opponents until they became one of the founder members of the Football Association in 1863. Charles Alcock enlarged the membership of Forest by no longer confining it to Old Harrovians and he abandoned Snaresbrook in favour of more convenient grounds in various parts of London. Some of the older members declared it impracticable to have an organization of ex-public schoolboys 'wandering from place to place'. As so often, opposition hardened resolve giving the club new impetus and a new name—The Wanderers.

The catholic composition of The Wanderers was now such that they had six future internationals in their side for the Final. Their best players were C H R Wollaston from Lancing, about to gain the first of his five winners medals, T C Hooman of Charterhouse and R W S Vidal, the 'Prince of Dribblers' from Westminster.

The odds in favour of the Royal Engineers were soon cancelled out by an injury to Lieutenant Cresswell who broke his collarbone after only ten minutes play. From then on the Royal Engineers were kept on the defensive and, before half-time, The Wanderers had scored what proved to be the decisive goal. M P Betts scored from an acute angle, sending the ball beneath the tape that then served in place of a cross-bar. Betts was listed on the programme as A H Chequer. This made little attempt to conceal the fact that he was a Harrow Chequer from the club which had scratched to Wanderers in the first round. Clearly rules about transfers and being cup-tied were more elastic in those days! The goal was made by the Reverend Vidal, a legendary soloist who had once scored three successive goals without a single opponent touching the ball (that was in the era when the team which scored kicked off immediately afterwards.) Thus The Wanderers won the very first Cup Final by the score which was to become so familiar of one goal to nil.

In the years to come Wanderers were to appear four more times in the Final and four more times they were to win, before drifting into dissolution as more of their members left to play for the old boys' clubs.

The Royal Engineers share with Old Carthusians the record of winning both the Challenge Cup and the Amateur Cup. Their Challenge Cup victory came in 1875 against Old Etonians, the Amateur Cup victory as late as 1908.

By the late 1870s the Lancastrian mill towns were beginning to stir. After a few years flexing their muscles, the newly formed northern clubs were to start paying their best players and so drive the gentlemen-amateurs of the south from the front ranks of football for ever.

The Wanderers: E E Bowen, C W Alcock, A G Bonsor, M P Betts, T C Hooman, W P Crake, E Lubbock, A C Thompson, R C de Welch, C H R Wollaston, R W S Vidal.
Royal Engineers: Captain Merriman, Captain Marindin, Lt Addison, Lt Cresswell, Lt Mitchell, Lt Renny-Tailyour, Lt Rich, Lt Goodwyn, Lt Muirhead, Lt Cotter, Lt Boyle.

Nice one, Tottenham

2

The appearance of a non-League club in the later stages of the FA Cup invariably excites national attention as well as the more partisan enthusiasm of the localities in question. Several clubs have produced some remarkable results in this respect —Yeovil Town's performance in reaching the fifth round of the Cup in 1949 at the expense of Sunderland was said to have reduced experienced sports journalists to states of profound shock— but some 48 years previously another non-League club had gone as far . . : and further. For in 1901 Tottenham Hotspur became the only non-League club to take the FA Cup since the foundation of the League when they beat Sheffield United in a replay.

At the turn of the century, the South was very much football's depressed area. Only one club, Woolwich Arsenal, were actually members of the League, most of the good players joining amateur or Southern League sides. It had been 20 years since a London side had actually won the Cup and all of 18 since one had even played in the Final. Southampton had restored the balance a little by reaching the Final in 1900 but they had lost 4-0 and there was little reason to suppose that Spurs would fare much better.

Even the most ardent of the Tottenham supporters would have admitted that their club's history had been no glory-trail. Their first honour had been the Southern League Championship in 1900 but their appearance at Crystal Palace the following year had been won on merit, for they had beaten three First Division sides on the way.

Sheffield United, Tottenham's opposition, had not entered the League until 1892 but they had won promotion in their first season, taken the League title in 1898, won the Cup in 1899 and had been runners-up in the League in 1900. Their side contained three of soccer's immortals —'Nudger' Needham, the wing-half, Fred Priest, the inside-left who scored in three Finals and played in both the 1901 games and 'Two-Ton' Foulke, the goalkeeper who weighed 22 stone. By all accounts Sheffield United were the more imposing combination.

The pre-match scene was vividly depicted by the correspondent of the *Daily Graphic*: 'From the Midlands, from Yorkshire, from the great towns that form the greater town of London, the army of footballers streamed along the lines of communication which led to Sydenham, until 114,000 were gathered around the big green board of turf where Sheffield and Tottenham were to play their Kriegspiel. . . . As for the general appearance of the spectators,' he went on, 'the southern bank, opposite the pavilion, was filled by that great pack of people whose involuntary move-ments, resembling the waving of a field of corn, look so dangerous and are so striking a token of intense interest. The western slope was filled to the skyline and, a circumstance never before observed, the Caryatids along the steps of the old cascade, had each their five or six tenants.' Comparisons were made with Derby Day, but the scene would perhaps have been more suggestive of a Test Match in the Caribbean, had not those perched precariously in the tree-tops been wearing bowler-hats.

The match itself obviously got off to a brisk start. The *Graphic* correspondent noted that the Sheffield team started 'as a crew sometimes does from Putney to Mortlake; to cut down their opponents'. Their dubious tactics paid quick dividends, for Sheffield scored after only ten minutes with a shot from Priest, sardonically described by the man from the *Graphic* as 'a daisy-cutter'. Sheffield were having much the better of the play in the early stages. Tottenham, however, managed to hold out against the pressure; as the half drew to a close, they were themselves taking the initiative and before half-time they scored a deserved equaliser through their centre-forward, Brown.

Tottenham started the second half where they had left off the first, and they were rewarded by a second goal by Brown, in which each forward played a part. If, as *The Times* correspondent remarked, Brown's goal was the best thing in the match, Sheffield's equalizer was certainly the most controversial. So contentious, indeed, that it occasioned one of the first sporting films ever made, a film, moreover, which seemed to show that the referee, a Mr Kingscott from Derby, had made a very grave error in awarding it. 20 April 1901 was indeed an unfortunate day to make such a mistake if only because it was done in view of 114,815 paying spectators, but the prospect of having his error both confirmed and publicized by film must have made the unfortunate Mr Kingscott consider the possibilities of swallowing his whistle.

Spurs' eventual triumph was hardly one for the South

The goal came out of a goal-mouth melee, whence the ball was kicked into the hands of Clawley, the Spurs goalkeeper. Clawley fumbled it, regained it and eventually cleared it, but he was astonished to find that both the referee and the linesman had judged him to have been over his own goal-line when the ball was cleared. 'This,' noted the man from the *Graphic*, 'was not the view of the spectators.' But he added with an objectivity that was a credit to his trade, 'The spectators are not the people who decide such points.' The match thereafter was devoid of goals if not incident, and the whistle blew on a drawn game. Sir Redvers Buller concluded the proceedings with a short speech, in which, by way of a joke, the shooting skills of a footballer were compared to those of an army rifleman, but attention was already turning to the subject of the replay in general and the capacity of Mr Kingscott to handle it in particular.

The FA, however, was not perturbed; the same referee was chosen to officiate at Bolton the following Saturday. There justice was seen to be done; Spurs won 3-0 with goals from Cameron, Smith and Brown, and Spurs became the only Southern League club ever to win the FA Cup. Yet perhaps it was not so much a triumph for the South as it might appear. More careful scrutiny of the records shows that five of the Spurs side were Scotsmen, two Welshmen, and one an Irishman; there were only three Englishmen, all of whom came from north of the Trent.

Tottenham Hotspur: Clawley, Erentz, Tait, Jones, Hughes, Morris, Smith, Cameron, Brown, Copeland, Kirwan.
Sheffield United: Foulke, Thicket, Boyle, Needham, Morren, Johnson, Bennett, Field, Hedley, Priest, Lipsham.

Bottom Brown, the Spurs No 9, kicks-off the 1901 Cup Final. He was to score Spurs' goals.
Below The condition of one's lumbar regions was an unimportant consideration for the 1901 fan.
Opposite The Daily Graphic *depicts the characters and incidents of the game.*

WILLIAM HEINEMANN

PRESS ASSOCIATION

THE DAILY GRAPHIC, APRIL 22, 1901.

DAILY GRAPHIC
ONE PENNY

NO. 3536.—Vol. XLVI.

LONDON : MONDAY, APRIL 22, 1901.

REGISTERED AS A NEWSPAPER.

THE WEATHER.

"FINE AND WARM GENERALLY."
(See page 3.)

Sun rises (at Greenwich), 4.53: sets 7.5.
Moon's age at noon, 3 days 14 hours.

THE ENGLISH CUP.

FINAL TIE AT THE PALACE.

A GOOD GAME AND A DRAW.

More than two army corps of the British public joined General Sir Redvers Buller at the Crystal Palace in watching a struggle that, for a day at least, obliterated the sterner interest of the fight which still harries South Africa. From Yorkshire, from the Midlands, from the great towns which make up the greater town of London, the army of footballers streamed along the lines of communication which led to Sydenham on Saturday, until 114,000 of them were gathered round the big green board of turf where Sheffield United and Tottenham Hotspur were to play their great Kriegspiel. Without exception, the days for final Cup ties at the Palace have been fine, but Saturday was the warmest and finest of them all, and this fact, added to the other that, for the first time in nearly twenty years, a London club's presence in the arena was giving ground for the hope that the Cup might come back South, made the numbers greater than have ever watched a final tie—or any football match—before. The nearest comparison to the numbers and the appearance of the crowd as it made its way through London would be the multitude that streams southwards on Derby day. No railway carriage that set out from Victoria or London Bridge or Holborn Viaduct held fewer than fifteen enthusiasts, and thousands of people—among them, no doubt, many who had suffered the tedious discomfort of the railways on previous occasions—went by the road. A long stream of brakes and buses, carriages, hansoms and coster-carts churned up the dust through Tulse Hill, Herne Hill and Dulwich; their progress making the resemblance to Derby day more marked than ever. Most of the brakes sported colours—blue

FOULKES IS MARVELLOUSLY AGILE FOR HIS TWENTY STONE

NEEDHAM FINDS TOM SMITH A GREAT HANDFUL

BROWN HEADS THROUGH AFTER A TUSSLE ROUND THE SHEFFIELD GOAL

GREAT SAVE BY CLAWLEY

TOTTENHAM'S SECOND GOAL

AN UNPOPULAR GOAL

LITTLE WILLIE'S LITTLE PUNCH WITH ALL HIS WEIGHT BEHIND IT

A DRAWN GAME: THE FINAL TIE FOR THE ASSOCIATION FOOTBALL CUP BETWEEN SHEFFIELD UNITED AND TOTTENHAM HOTSPUR AT THE CRYSTAL PALACE

9

Newcastle r el to Sunderland's one-over-the-eight

3

Local derbies have always been a special part of football; they produce a unique mixture of excitement and loyalty. Yet even the partisans never expect the absolute victory that Sunderland once achieved. On 5 December 1908, they beat Newcastle, at St James' Park, 9-1.

What made the result so incredible was that Newcastle were the premier club in Edwardian England. They had twice won the League championship and been losing FA Cup finalists three times in the previous five seasons. In that same season, despite that defeat by Sunderland, Newcastle were to win the League for the third time, and within the next two years they would appear in two more Cup Finals—winning the Cup for the first time in 1910.

Sunderland, beaten at home 4-2 by Newcastle the previous season, had, however, vastly improved in 1908-09 and were to finish third. As they travelled the 18 miles separating Roker Park and St James' Park they were in sixth position and United were second. Perhaps significantly, Sunderland had won 7 of the previous 10 games at Newcastle. It ought to have been a close match.

The week before the game had been wet; the pitch was greasy and soon likely to be treacherous. A quarter of an hour before the kick-off a fine rain began to fall.

There was nothing in the first half that made this a game apart. It was a closely contested, skilful and exciting tussle between two of the country's leading clubs of the time enjoyed by a capacity crowd of over 45,000. United were soon bombarding the Sunderland goal which escaped luckily when Higgins, the Newcastle inside-right took the ball upfield and crossed a great centre. Roose under pressure from Gosnell, United's outside-left, punched the ball away but the ball was promptly whipped back into the box and Shepherd, the centre-forward, forced it past Roose for what should have been the first goal. But it struck one of the full backs on the line and was scrambled away. If that one had gone in the game may have been completely different.

The reality, however, was that Sunderland made a sortie from their own half and were in front after only seven minutes. Mordue and Hogg sped away down the right and, with the backs caught square, Lawrence rushed from goal to narrow the angle. Hogg looked up long enough to pick his spot in the net before driving the ball home.

Newcastle retaliated fiercely and the Newcastle 'Evening Chronicle' reporter stated: 'No time was wasted in the pretty short-passing game, and for that there were two reasons. The hard-

ness of the game itself was partly responsible and the greasy surface of the turf was also a contributor.'

Newcastle were not playing badly on this first December Saturday of the dying year but somehow everything began to go right for Sunderland. It was their marksmanship that was so extraordinary. Brown and then Holley fired in two hard accurate shots that brought the best out of Lawrence. Back again came Sunderland to force a corner and after that it was the turn of Low and Bridgett to bring brilliant saves from Lawrence.

As the teams warmed to their work all the best in football was laid before the great Tyneside crowd. Both teams were reported as going all out for a goal 'and every possible opening seized and made the most of'. But there was plenty of science too and the spectacle on the Gallowgate pitch delighted and excited the crowd and probably frustrated the thousands who could not obtain admission and had to follow the game vicariously.

United's attempt to equalize was successful in the closing minutes of the half. In a truly desperate scramble in front of the Sunderland goal their centre-half Thompson handled. The referee consulted the linesman and awarded a penalty which Shepherd struck past Roose. The moment Brown restarted the game from the centre spot the referee blew for half-time.

Newcastle resumed full of confidence as was to be expected after scoring right on the stroke of half-time—traditionally the most crucial time to damage the morale of their opponents.

Shepherd was kept out by a despairing last second tackle and in another attack Gosnell shot just over the bar. Yet Sunderland's first real attack of this half regained them the lead. Bridgett tempted Whitson into a rash tackle and went past him as the full-back lunged. The outside-left held off Liddell until Holley was in a position to shoot. Then Bridgett turned a short

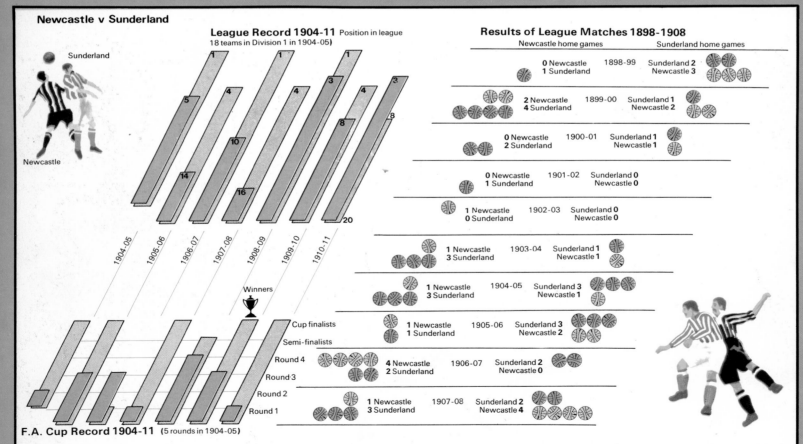

Newcastle v Sunderland

Sunderland

Newcastle

League Record 1904-11 Position in league
18 teams in Division 1 in 1904-05)

1904-05 · 1905-06 · 1906-07 · 1907-08 · 1908-09 · 1909-10 · 1910-11

Winners

Cup finalists
Semi-finalists
Round 4
Round 3
Round 2
Round 1

F.A. Cup Record 1904-11 (5 rounds in 1904-05)

Results of League Matches 1898-1908

Newcastle home games		Sunderland home games
0 Newcastle / 1 Sunderland	1898-99	Sunderland 2 / Newcastle 3
2 Newcastle / 4 Sunderland	1899-00	Sunderland 1 / Newcastle 2
0 Newcastle / 2 Sunderland	1900-01	Sunderland 1 / Newcastle 1
0 Newcastle / 1 Sunderland	1901-02	Sunderland 0 / Newcastle 0
1 Newcastle / 0 Sunderland	1902-03	Sunderland 0 / Newcastle 0
1 Newcastle / 3 Sunderland	1903-04	Sunderland 1 / Newcastle 1
1 Newcastle / 3 Sunderland	1904-05	Sunderland 3 / Newcastle 1
1 Newcastle / 1 Sunderland	1905-06	Sunderland 3 / Newcastle 2
4 Newcastle / 2 Sunderland	1906-07	Sunderland 2 / Newcastle 0
1 Newcastle / 3 Sunderland	1907-08	Sunderland 2 / Newcastle 4

When the two teams met for their local derby in December 1908 Newcastle had indisputably succeeded Aston Villa as the best team in England. In these pre-War years the club's reputation was established. But they had never been able to gain any real dominance over Sunderland who had, as the table shows, won 7 of their 10 previous League games at Newcastle and recorded twice as many League victories in these derby clashes as United. The table also records just how successful Newcastle were in this period and contrasts Sunderland's achievements in the First Division *and FA Cup during those years. Sunderland were obviously overshadowed by their neighbours but the Wearside club's golden era had been in the previous decade. They were League Champions in 1892, 1893, 1895 and 1902; and runners-up in 1894, 1898 and 1901.*

pass inside to his partner and the inside-left cleverly steered it past Lawrence.

It was a shock for the 'Magpies' and their supporters but in the minutes that followed there was absolutely no sign of a rout. Pulling themselves together after some uncertainty, Newcastle once more stormed at Sunderland for an equalizer. Both Shepherd and Higgins were within a fraction of making it 2-2. Roose made a superb save and kept out a fusilade of shots from Veitch, Higgins and Shepherd. It seemed United must score at any second but suddenly the ball was swept out to Mordue the right-winger, who beat Pudan and raced away at top speed. Chasing along beside him came his inside-forward, Hogg, the Sunderland captain, who accepted Pudan's pass, drew Lawrence from his line and slipped the ball adroitly between the posts.

Before Newcastle could recover Holley set off on a brazen solo dribble that took him right through United's demoralized ranks until he was confronted by only Lawrence, who was unable to prevent the fourth goal. The next time Holley got the ball he was between 30 and 40 yards out but he shot immediately. That one also rocketed into the net as if drawn by a magnet. Sunderland, by now completely irresistible, continued to attack. Once more Bridgett went past Whitson as if he was a mere wraith and shot on the run without, it seemed, even bothering to take aim, but all Lawrence could do was catch it as it came back off the net.

Poor Lawrence. Without making a real error he had conceded six goals at home. Some three minutes later Bridgett repeated his success, once more giving Lawrence no earthly chance to reach a shot of great power. The crowd, as well as the United players, was mesmerized. One old fan said, 'I was mentally still cheering Hogg's goal that put us 3-1 up and had given us the points when I realized we were winning 7-1. Every time our lads shot it was a goal.'

And soon it was 8-1. Hogg toyed with both

Willis and Pudan before shooting wide of Lawrence to complete, like Holley before him, a hat-trick.

By this time according to the local reporter only three Newcastle men were still really playing. The rest can surely be forgiven. The finest team in the land had been destroyed by a good side who probably on this day could not have lost had they tried. The local reporter, was so busy describing the unprecedented events and persuading his office he was not drunk that he completely missed the ninth Sunderland goal, Hogg's fourth, just before the end. Another of the legends that was popular on Wearside was

Above Sunderland's inside-left, Holley, who scored a second-half hat-trick. His first goal restored their lead; his second (4-1) and third (5-1) completely demoralized Newcastle.
Below The happier Newcastle team which won the FA Cup in 1910. Lawrence, the unfortunate goalkeeper, was one of the six survivors of the shock defeat.

that the sub-editor responsible for the story could not bear to show Newcastle as the home team and switched the result to read Sunderland 9 Newcastle 1.

Sunderland had scored eight times in 28 minutes and their last five came within the space of eight minutes—the quickest burst of goalscoring since Preston got six in seven minutes against Hyde in 1887. Newcastle admittedly had full-back Whitson off the field injured for the last quarter of an hour but it was still Newcastle's worst beating in their history. For 47 years it stood alone as the worst home defeat in the First Division until Cardiff City also shared the unwanted distinction after their 1-9 defeat at Ninian Park by Wolves in 1955.

The headline in the Newcastle 'Evening Chronicle' was simply 'A sensational game' which must surely have been the understatement of 1908.

Those Newcastle fans who wondered if this signalled the collapse of a great side were soon reassured. United went on to overhaul Everton and win the title by a margin of seven points. For neighbours Sunderland, Newcastle's triumph enhanced their own victory.

It was just one of those days, baffling, bewitching, beyond understanding. Perhaps the closing minute of the match makes the point. Duncan dashed away to conclude with at least a note of defiance in the face of a disaster too vast to comprehend. Not only was his shot so wide it nearly hit the corner flag but he fell and hurt himself and was carried off like a sack of coal on the back of the Newcastle trainer. It was a unique derby match, unlikely to ever be repeated.

Newcastle United: Lawrence, Whitson, Pudan, Liddel, Veitch, Willis, Duncan, Higgins, Shepherd, Wilson, Gosnell.
Sunderland: Roose, Forster, Milton, Daykin, Thompson, Low, Mordue, Hogg, Brown, Holley, Bridgett.

You can take a white horse anywhere

4

There are some moments which transcend parochialism, opinion or immediate impact, and become national legend. In sport Roger Bannister's four-minute mile was one such event; so was England's World Cup victory in 1966. But for sheer dramatic, myth-making effect it is unlikely that any single occasion has ever compared with the 1923 Cup Final.

That game was the inaugural event in a gleaming new Wembley Stadium—then the largest, grandest and most imposing arena anywhere in the world. No-one knows how many people were there that day. The official attendance was a mere 126,047. But some suggest that 250,000 got inside the vast bowl, making it the largest crowd to attend—they could not possibly all have 'watched'—any football match ever played. Others contend that half a million probably tried to make their way there for the game. Certainly there were traffic jams that make the Exeter by-pass on a Bank Holiday look like an Irish country lane; certainly the only surface visible in the stadium at any time was the pitch—and for much of the match large tracts of that disappeared under helpless feet.

The contestants on a day when the actual players seemed almost irrelevant were Bolton Wanderers and West Ham United. Bolton, one of the League's founder members, were just entering the most successful period in their history, one in which they won three Cup Finals and twice finished third in the League in the space of seven seasons.

West Ham had no such greatness to look forward to. They had not entered the League until 1919 and were still a Second Division club. The Monday after their Wembley appearance, the Hammers ensured entry to the First Division by winning 2-0 at Hillsborough, but there were few glories to follow. Within ten years they were back down again and had to wait until the Cup Final of 1964 before they won a major honour.

The real star of the 1923 Final was not to be found in the ranks of those two contrasting teams. Rather it was Wembley itself.

The Empire Stadium—to give it its more correct title—was only one part of a vast circus which went under the name of the British Empire Exhibition. While the Exhibition and its exotic sideshows came and went, the stadium was destined to remain and become to English football what Mecca is to the Moslem faith.

The Wembley site of Watkins' Folly—London's answer to the leaning tower of Pisa—had been chosen as the potential site for such an exhibition some ten years earlier. It was then in open country, six miles from Marble Arch as the crow flies when it is sober, and well served by the Metropolitan Railway, at Wembley Park. The ex-chairman of the Metropolitan Railway, incidentally, was the same Sir Edward Watkins who had built the folly as a supposedly lasting monument.

But it was not until the Football Association declared their interest in the sports stadium part of the exhibition plans that the whole idea really caught the imagination of the British people.

That was in 1921. At the time the Cup Final was being played at a woefully inadequate Stamford Bridge, the pre-War venue Crystal Palace still being in the hands of the Army. The Palace was due to become available again in 1923, but the FA appreciated that, if the vast crowds that attended the ritual of the Cup Final were ever to see anything, either the Palace would have to be rebuilt or the event would have to move elsewhere—which is precisely what happened.

In fact the stadium was completed long before the rest of the exhibition in only 300 working days. It cost a mere £800,000; a single Cup Final now takes a quarter of that sum. A battalion of infantry was marched round and round the stadium to test the strength of the 25,000 tons of concrete and 250,000 steel rivets before it was declared open.

It was estimated that 125,000 spectators could be accommodated, 23,000 of them seated. As the previous year's Final, at Stamford Bridge, had attracted only 53,000, this was thought adequate. Around lunch-time on Saturday, 28 April 1923, something like four times the maximum capacity were heading towards Wembley.

A later statement by the stadium's board of directors sums up what happened next: 'The turnstiles were opened before 11.30 am . . . and by 1.00 pm the pressure of the crowd became very great. At 1.45 pm, when the returns showed that the standing accommodation was nearly full, instructions were given for all gates to be closed . . . All London termini were informed that the stadium was now full but during the following half-hour thousands more people arrived and

Above *Before Wembley was built it was the site of Watkins' Folly—England's answer to the Eiffel Tower.*
Below *The white horse was not the only police horse at Wembley, but it was easily visible; it can be seen here directing the crowd behind the goal line.*
Right *The Daily Mirror saw the Cup Final as a contest between Police and Crowd.*

RADIO TIMES HULTON PICTURE LIBRARY

SPORT & GENERAL

CHAOS AT CUP-TIE FINAL: WHO WAS TO BLAME? SEE P. 7

The Daily Mirror

24 PAGES

NET SALE MUCH THE LARGEST OF ANY DAILY PICTURE NEWSPAPER

No. 6,079. Registered at the G.P.O. as a Newspaper. **MONDAY, APRIL 30, 1923** One Penny.

POLICE v. CROWD: WEMBLEY'S FIRST CUP FINAL

A remarkable photograph, taken from the air, of the Stadium at Wembley, with spectators swarming over the playing pitch, while hundreds more are clustered outside.

Robert Bruce at Willesden Hospital with a crushed chest.

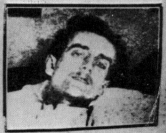

Mr. I. Hall, who was picked up unconscious, in Willesden Hospital.

Police pushing back part of the crowd on the pitch from the neighbourhood of one goal.

Official records will claim that the first contest to be staged at the Empire Stadium, Wembley, was the final for the Football Association Challenge Cup between West Ham United and Bolton Wanderers. The many thousands who journeyed to Wembley on Saturday will, however, long retain the memory of an earlier struggle in which the opposing elements were police and public, the ultimate victory resting with the force, whose efforts eventually produced order from utter chaos.—(See also pages 12 and 24.)

*At the first Wembley Cup Final those who could not get through the gates (**top left**) climbed over the walls (**centre left**). When the teams did come out they had to share the pitch with the crowd until the police cleared it (**bottom left**). Eventually, Bolton Wanderers played West Ham United (**top right**) and won 2-0 with goals from David Jack and John Smith. Smith's goal was disputed by West Ham fans*

milled around the entrances. At 2.00 pm Scotland Yard was asked for a large mounted force of police . . . at 2.15 pm the crowd broke through the barriers and it is estimated that another 100,000 got into the Stadium.'

The report ends phlegmatically with the comment that '. . . the total number who either paid for admission or broke the barriers may be estimated to have exceeded 200,000. Probably 150,000 got a good view of the match.'

Those are the bare bones. What was actually going on can be imagined. One West Ham fan, then a child, recounted his experiences nearly 50 years later: 'When we arrived at Wembley Park station I couldn't believe the crowds. They just carried us along. By the time you got within 50 yards of the stadium you could take your feet off the ground and just move with the crush. There didn't seem to be any barriers—I suppose they'd all gone by then. I remember we got into a staircase. My father wanted to go back, but it was impossible. The people behind were literally kicking us up the stairs. When we got inside we simply clambered over the heads of people until, somehow, we found an empty seat. I never thought the game would start then—you couldn't see a blade of grass.'

Looking back the most remarkable fact was that no-one was killed and very few were hurt. At 2.45 pm there seemed no chance that the game could possibly start. The Irish and Grenadier Guards' bands were somewhere on the pitch— like bad children they could be heard but not seen. Stadium officials suggested to King George V that he should leave, but he refused.

Bolton won the Cup but the star was Billy the horse

He showed remarkable foresight, for it was about then that the legendary white horse Billy started to play a part that was to earn him equine immortality. His rider, PC George Scorey, described what happened in a BBC interview.

'Before that day I'd helped control a lot of crowds, but I'd never seen anything like Wembley that afternoon . . . as my horse picked his way onto the field I saw nothing but a sea of heads. I thought "We can't do it. It's impossible." But I happened to see an opening near one of the goals and the horse was very good—easing them back with his nose and tail until we got a goal-line cleared. I told them in front to join hands and heave and they went back step by step until we reached the line. Then they sat down and we went on like that . . . . It was mainly due to the horse. Perhaps because he was white he commanded more attention. But, more than that, he seemed to understand what was required of him. The other helpful thing was the good temper of the crowd.'

The directors later stated their opinion that it was PC Scorey who had made it possible for the Final to proceed—and the box-office still gets half-a-dozen requests for Cup Final tickets most years from fans claiming to be the policeman. The irony is that PC Scorey was not, and never became, interested in football. 'I never went to another football match,' he admitted 30 years later.

After the players came out the pitch was cleared and, 40 minutes after the official kick-off time of 3 o'clock, Bolton won the toss and the game began. Within two minutes the Lancastrians' inside-forward David Jack had become the first man to score a goal at Wembley.

Jack Tresadern took a throw-in and gave the ball to West Ham team-mate Young. But Jack, who claimed a supporter on the left touchline used his feet to keep the ball in play for Vizard, who centred to Smith. So many people sat around the pitch it was quite possible (**centre right**). After it was all over officials were left to count the record £27,776 gate receipts, and (**bottom right**) clear up the inevitable mess. It surprised no one when the FA made the 1924 Final all-ticket.

one of three brothers (David, Donald and Robert) who all played for both Plymouth and Bolton, intercepted Young's clearance and hammered a shot so hard that goalkeeper Hufton stood no chance. Neither did the wall of spectators who had trampled down the netting behind Hufton. The ball hit one of them with such force that those behind him went down like a row of dominoes. At the time West Ham right-half Tresadern was trapped in the crowd, unable to get back on the field after his throw.

The half lasted for over an hour, the game having to be stopped now and again when sections of the crowd were forced over the lines, and the players were unable to leave the pitch for the interval.

Wembley's first goal knocked the spectators down like dominoes

Bolton started the second-half just as they had the first. After eight minutes Ted Vizard roared down the left-wing and centred for John Smith to volley on to the underside of the bar. The ball bounced down and came out again—in the manner of Geoff Hurst's goal in 1966—but the referee awarded a goal in what were obviously trying circumstances. The goal is famous for an even more controversial incident, for Vizard's run is reputed to have been assisted by a friendly spectator who stuck his foot over the line to prevent the ball going out of play.

West Ham captain George Kay, who had once played for Bolton, apparently asked the referee to call the game off some time during the second-half, but received as much sympathy from that quarter as he did from his former club. Bolton captain Joe Smith declared that he would be happy to play till dusk. Exactly 30 years later Smith was to manage Blackpool to a famous victory over Bolton in a Cup Final almost as renowned as this one.

Though most of them had to report the game from wherever they could find standing space, the pressmen agreed that Bolton had played the better football and were well worth their two-goal win. George Kay disagreed—he always contended that West Ham would have won in any other circumstances.

It was the first time in Bolton's history that they had won a major honour, and their supporters allowed no-one to forget it. Some were still clambering over the stadium at seven o'clock that evening.

When the money was finally counted the following week it came to a staggering £27,776—easily a record for any sporting event. Over half was in florins, the admission price to the terraces for the game. West Ham and Bolton took over £6,000 each for their troubles, a hefty sum at the time, the rest going to the FA, the Exhibition and the Government. The latter's cut was over £4,000 in entertainment tax.

At the end of it all the FA returned £2,797 to ticket holders who claimed not to have reached their seats, though how the FA checked whether they had or not is unclear. And the Association's own report commented that: 'Arrangements are being made for next year's Challenge Cup Final to be organized on an all-ticket basis.' And it has stayed that way ever since.

Bolton Wanderers: Pym, Haworth, Finney, Nuttall, Seddon, Jennings, Butler, Jack, Smith (J R), Smith (J), Vizard.
West Ham United: Hufton, Henderson, Young, Bishop, Kay, Tresadern, Richards, Brown, Watson (V), Moore, Ruffell.

TOPIX

RADIO TIMES HULTON PICTURE LIBRARY

TOPIX

15

Casting a spell over Wembley

5

Jimmy Dunn was one of only three players (Harkness and Morton were the others) from Scottish clubs in the Wembley team. The small Hibernian forward was later transferred to Everton.

For many years Scotland's only interest in international football was that they should defeat England. It was rather like Liverpool being content to be twenty-first in Division One as long as Everton were bottom. Even that limited ambition has not always been accomplished but there was one occasion when the Scottish team fulfilled all that Scotsmen have ever dreamed of. On 31 March 1928, and at Wembley, an unrated Scottish team humbled England 5-1 and created the legend of the Wembley Wizards which, ever since, has been used (by Scots) as irrefutable evidence that Scottish football is superior and naturally more skilful.

The myth still persists that a side of near

Above *Alec Jackson, hat-trick wizard and at 5ft 7in the tallest Scottish forward.*
Right *Signing a Cup Final souvenir. He also scored in that match but Blackburn won 3-1.*

midgets from a small country showed the English precisely what the game was all about. They proved that football was not a game of slogging and sweat, but a contest of science and skill.

Like most myths it has some validity but a closer inspection of the legend's antecedents shows that this match was a triumph in spite of popular opinion and typical non-planning.

When that team was first selected it was greeted with derision. It was criticized for containing too many 'Anglos'. It was given no

chance of winning, even though England's recent record (they had scored only one goal in the Home International Championship) was no better than that of the Scots, who had taken one point from their games with Wales and Ireland. Against Scotland's unusual and diminutive side, and with the home advantage, England had Dixie Dean, Roy Goodall, Joe Bradford and West Ham's Ted Hufton, who was reckoned to be the best goalkeeper in the world.

It was the Scottish custom between the wars to proclaim their sides to the populace. Police would bring traffic to a halt around the offices in Glasgow's Carleton Place, then the home of the SFA. An official would appear on the steps and read out the team to fans standing on the pavements. A crowd of several thousand was waiting on 21 March.

As the names were read out they were astonished that Meiklejohn, McPhail and McGrory were omitted. Instead they heard the official read out the names of eight players from English clubs and soon they realized that the forward line—Jackson, Dunn, Gallacher, James and Morton—would be the smallest ever fielded. Even Gallacher's name was not greeted with any enthusiasm. Injury had kept him out of the Newcastle United team for two months. And at centre-half, to mark the great Dixie Dean, was Bury's Tom Bradshaw, who had no previous international experience. 'Yon team's nae chance,' they said and the Glasgow newspapers had a field day criticizing the selectors. The *Daily Record*'s terse verdict was, 'It's not a great side'.

But the Scottish team that settled into their London hotel was in good spirits and determined to avenge the 2-1 defeat at Hampden of the previous year. They also knew that the losers in this match would suffer the further disgrace of finishing bottom of the home international table. After dinner a Scottish selector suggested to captain Jimmy McMullan that he should give the side a tactical talk. He looked at his forwards, not one of whom stood over 5ft 7in, and said 'Go to bed and pray for rain.' It may have been the shortest lecture on record. It was certainly the most efficacious.

For the next morning it rained. By the time the team arrived at Wembley there was a downpour. These conditions gave the small Scots a priceless advantage on a slippery pitch over their bulkier English opponents.

Wembley was largely uncovered then but the

80,868 crowd spent two full hours in community singing before the game. Inside the Scottish dressing-room there was one moment of panic: Alex James tried on his Scottish strip and complained about his mini shorts. An official was sent out to find a larger pair, more in keeping with the wee man's image as the player with baggy pants. Meanwhile, McMullan spent most of the time telling nineteen-year-old full-back Tony Law not to worry.

But the international was effectively won and lost within the first three minutes. England made the opening attack which ended when Huddersfield winger Smith shot past Harkness and the ball cannoned back into play off the post. McMullan picked up the rebound and started a move between James and Dunn. James played the ball to Alan Morton who took it almost to the line before crossing it precisely into the goalmouth where Alec Jackson dashed in from the other wing to head the ball past a bemused Ted Hufton.

The downpour was increasing and England tried to equalize but poor finishing and three good saves by Harkness maintained Scotland's lead. As the game progressed it seemed that Scotland

Hughie Gallacher, the great Newcastle centre-forward, had only recently recovered from injury before the international. His inclusion in Scotland's team was far from popular.

Alex James, whose meagre total of caps was unrepresentative of his ability. His two goals and excellent distribution certainly instilled much of the magic into the Wizards' performance.

must score again and it was Hufton's turn to deny Scotland's forwards. But a minute before half-time Alex James received a bad clearance from Smith and dribbled past Wilson, Healless and Jones before releasing, from outside the penalty area, a fast low shot that beat the England goalkeeper.

But it was in the second half that Scotland made this an immortal victory. In bad conditions they played almost perfect football. They teased the English with their nippiness and cheek, frequently leaving them stranded on the turf. With a complete command of midfield and the brilliance of the small forwards, more goals were inevitable. James shot against the bar; Hufton held another of his fierce drives. Then a replica of the first goal took them further into the lead after 65 minutes: Morton again crossed and Jackson again headed past Hufton. Almost immediately, Gallacher, surging forward, was tackled heavily but James, following up behind him, shot the fourth goal.

England were no longer in contention; despite their stars they were only stooges for the certain genius of the Scots. The Scottish defence had time to admire their forwards who were intuitively combining their talents into a magical blend of inspired football. So this was a great team after all. But it was not time for reflection; this was an occasion, despite the rain, to relish Morton's studious play, Gallacher's swerving runs, James' distribution and Jackson's decisive finishing.

Five minutes before the end Morton again sprinted through the England defence, crossed a ball that lured Hufton off his line, and there, almost inevitably, was Jackson who met the ball with a mid-air kick that ended the Scottish scoring, gave him his hat-trick, and supplied the game with its most spectacular moment: 5-0. The humiliation was complete. Yet England did finally score, in the last minute of the game, when Bob Kelly hit a forty-yard free-kick past Harkness. Like all consolation goals it only emphasized how completely the team was outplayed; Scotland could afford to give them a goal.

The whole display had been full of high speed grace. At one stage Scotland strung eleven passes together without an English touch. Frequently they strung seven and eight passes together around the English players.

The crowd applauded it all. They were in no doubt that they had witnessed a great football occasion and supreme skill. The Scottish newspapers also forgot their previous criticism and joined in the praise. The *Glasgow Herald* expressed the euphoria that swept through Scotland after this triumph.

'The success of the Scots was primarily another demonstration that Scottish skill, science and trickery will prevail against the less attractive and simpler methods of the English style in which

Alan Morton, the 'Wee Blue Devil' who was the Scottish equivalent of Stanley Matthews. His studious wing-play destroyed England's defence and created all of Jackson's goals.

speed is relied upon as a major factor. This is provided that the Scottish side chosen is speedy.

'Want of height was looked upon as a handicap to the Scots attack but the Scottish forwards had ability and skill of such high degree as to make their physical shortcomings of little consequence.'

The *Daily Record* emphasized that it was the manner of victory that counted—that it was the Scottish style that had been vindicated: 'Came the second half and an exhibition of football that was as perfect as football can be. Every man touched his highest pinnacle. Every man became part of an efficient machine that moved with a rhythm, power and speed that crushed the Saxons. There was never any sign of selfishness. Their power and virility were amazing.'

The game has passed into the folklore of British football and has comforted Scots after many disappointments. But was that team really comparable with the Brazilian or Hungarian sides of later years? It was certainly an excellent performance but even goalkeeper Harkness admitted that 'But for the goalpost there might never have been any Wembley Wizards'. England's critics blamed the selectors for choosing six players who had to play in the Blackburn-Huddersfield Cup Final.

Jimmy McMullan had a more technical point to make. 'I want to emphasize that all our forwards are inherently clever, but I wish to say that the English tactics were wrong. The Saxon wing-halves paid more attention to the wingers than the inside-forwards. Therefore the latter were given a lot of space. It is a common thing in England to let wing-halves and not full-backs mark the wingers. It doesn't pay and I don't know why they pursue it.'

McMullan's explanation may well be the most valid. England exposed themselves to the skill of the nimble Scottish forwards; the rain made England's heavy defence even more vulnerable. It was certainly no freak result, for Scotland again won, 1-0, in Glasgow the following year, when they won the international championship for the seventh time in the decade.

Unfortunately for Scotland the selectors could never repeat the magical recipe. Not that it mattered; the Wembley Wizards had 'proved' that Scottish football was inherently superior to the more robust English style. The truth, though, was that a Scottish team played exceptionally well to beat an English side that played badly. It was no proof that Scottish football was the best in the world: legends, and even wizards, are not enough to win World Cups.

England: Hufton, Goodall, Jones, Edwards, Wilson, Healless, Hulme, Kelly, Dean, Bradford, Smith.
Scotland: Harkness, Nelson, Law, Gibson, Bradshaw, McMullan, Jackson, Dunn, Gallacher, James, Morton.

17

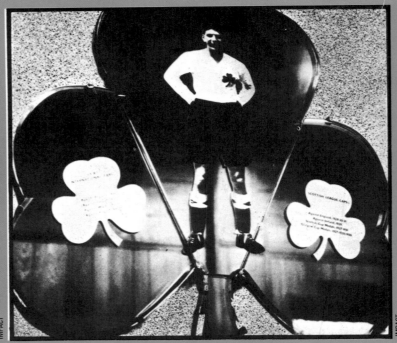

The making of a martyr

6

At 3.55 pm on 5 September 1931, Ibrox Park was filled with the atmosphere of hatred and bigotry that is a tradition of Glasgow's derby matches between Rangers and Celtic. Five minutes later it was completely subdued as the 75,000 crowd witnessed the tragic end to the career of one of the city's best loved heroes. The songs, jeers, insults and flag-waving all ceased as John Thomson, the young Celtic and Scotland goalkeeper, was carried from the field on a stretcher.

The game had been a poor one until half time. Like most of the great Glasgow derbies, there had been too much tension, too much thought of safety, for the Celtic and Rangers rivalry had reached a critical stage. Rangers, managed by Bill Struth, had won the League Championship in the previous five seasons and were after Celtic's record of six successive championships. Celtic, who had beaten the superb Motherwell team in the Scottish Cup final the previous season and who were being described as the team of the year, were determined to end Rangers' domination.

Thus the players had forgotten about winning, so concerned were they over not losing. The wing halves David Meiklejohn and George Brown of Rangers and Peter Wilson and Chic Geatons of Celtic were the best attacking midfield players of their day, but they were pulled back apprehensively on top of their defences. The fanatical supporters, segregated behind opposite goals, did not resent the lack of goals because that too meant that their favourites were not losing.

Play continued to be cautious into the second half but after five minutes the quality of it was to become irrelevant. Another Celtic attack broke down and they lost possession as they had done many times before. This time Celtic's defence had followed the play upfield and when the ball went to the young medical student, Doc Marshall, Celtic's half was thinly guarded. He pushed the ball square to his captain David Meiklejohn and out on the right Rangers powerful winger, Jimmy Fleming, was already galloping forward in anticipation of a through pass.

It was a typical Rangers raid, and when the ball was sent in front of Fleming that redoubtable Celt, Peter McGonagle, raced to challenge. Fleming dodged him and, seeing Sam English uncovered in the middle, pushed a pass through and ahead for English to run onto. That was the fateful moment.

Sam English, a fair crinkly-haired Irishman, was new to the Rangers team. There had been doubts about him playing because of injury and only a late fitness test freed him for a match he was always to regret.

With only Thomson to beat a Rangers' goal seemed certain at last

But there was the ball running in front of him, ahead was the exposed goal and behind it the mass of Rangers supporters were cheering him on. At last a goal seemed sure as Sam English sped to catch the ball. John Thomson, a lithe figure in a red jersey, saw the threat and glided out in that athletic way of his. He was balanced and watchful, trying to anticipate English's attempt to score.

On came Sam English nearing the penalty spot with the ball running perfectly for a shot and it was then that John Thomson made his move. He dived forward, his body parallel with the ground as Sam English's leg drove into the ball. There was a clash and both fell to the ground. The ball passed Thomson's right hand post. He had made yet another great save but it was to be his last and he was to know nothing of it.

Sam English grimaced with the pain in his knee where John Thomson's skull had struck it. He limped to the prone goalkeeper and then ignored his own pain as he saw the blood pouring from Thomson's ear, and forming a pool on the pitch. He waved frantically for help. The other players gathered round anxiously, their rivalry forgotten in their concern.

One young Rangers player made some disparaging remark about getting the injured man moved but Alan Morton sternly silenced him. Behind the goal the Rangers horde had watched an opponent go down and they howled with exultation and danced savagely in the factional tradition of Glasgow religion. But David Meiklejohn, the most noble of Rangers captains and the hero of their supporters, advanced sternly towards them and with a hand raised demanded silence and respect.

As the tumult was stilled everybody knew that the young keeper was seriously hurt and in the stand his fiancée screamed as that realization hit her. With his brother she rushed to the dressing room where the stretcher bearers had laid him. A doctor quickly diagnosed a depressed fracture of the skull and he was taken to the Victoria Infirmary nearby. He never regained consciousness and died at 9.25 that night.

The crowd was shocked, its own violence exorcised by the accident on the pitch. They had forgotten their obsessions with William of Orange, the Pope and Irish republicanism. The game had previously been dull but after it restarted its tension had disappeared. It had become irrelevant and neither side had any interest in the result. The players merely imitated the actions of footballers. They and the crowd were waiting for the end of a game that would be no credit to win. When the final whistle officially concluded a match that had ended just after half-time there was still no score.

There had been other deaths in football but the immensity of the emotion roused by the death of John Thomson was due, in part at least, to the fact that he was but 23 years old when he died and at the time was so clean and athletic and skilful that already there were those to argue that he was the greatest goalkeeper of all time. Had he lived he could well have substantiated such a claim.

His was extraordinary courage in an era when goalkeepers had little protection and were more vulnerable to physical challenge. His dive into Sam English's knee was not a new experience for him. He knew well what the consequences might be for the previous February at Celtic Park, against Airdrie, he had made another such dive and had to be carried from the field with a broken shoulder and shattered jaw.

He had joined Celtic as a 17-year-old from the Fife mining village of Cardenden and quickly shown that he was not only a great goalkeeper but also a natural athlete with a rich competence

in all games. He was slim and slightly below the ideal height at 5 ft 9½ in but adequately compensated for that by an extraordinary speed and agility and the absolute certainty with which he caught the ball.

There is a true story that he hesitated about signing a professional form for Celtic because his mother had told him, without knowing that he had been approached, that she had dreamed he had been badly injured playing in goal.

He had gone to Celtic Park a raw lad from a mining village but possessed a certain refinement which showed in politeness, and in making his confidence pure and unspoiled. He was soon in the first team and demanding that every ball in the penalty area was his and demonstrating that when he touched the ball he held it. His clutching has never been surpassed.

By the time he played in that 1931 match at Ibrox he was established as Scotland's goalkeeper and, even in partisan Glasgow, there was no-one to dispute that he was the best there was. His skill and his clean athletic appearance lifted him above all sectarian squabbling.

There was a public enquiry into Thomson's death when it was confirmed that it had been a complete accident and that Sam English had in no way fouled the goalkeeper. But the enquiry brought no comfort to English, who had continued to play after Thomson had been carried off when he surely wished he had never been playing at all. For the rest of his life he remained disturbed by that collision and was never forgiven by some Celtic supporters who inevitably blamed him for Thomson's death.

Thomson's mother dreamt that he would be badly injured playing in goal

Religious differences were forgotten for a time in Glasgow and life stood still there until he was buried and laid to rest like a prince. It was reckoned that thirty thousand mourners attended the funeral, trying to crush into the little cemetery at Bowhill, near his home in Cardenden. Two special trains carried mourners from Glasgow and there were two coaches filled with flowers. There were twenty thousand at Queen Street station to see the train away and crowds at all the stations along the route. All denominations held memorial services and a football match which had started in an atmosphere of hatred finished a week later in sadness but in a spirit that approached brotherliness.

All matches between Celtic and Rangers cause concern to the police in Glasgow but that one in 1931 particularly. There are cycles in these meetings, as there are in other matters, and the confrontations had moved into a violent phase the previous season. There had been ill-feeling among the players as well as the supporters. The leading Glasgow commentator had written on the morning of the match, 'The stage is set. The crowd will be there all right. Let's hope they are entertained with a clean sporting contest.' Until Thomson was injured there was little chance of the match being peaceful.

After that tragic incident Glasgow people remained grieved by his death for some months. Yet by the time of the next clash between the two clubs the sympathy had ended and the attitudes of the rival supporters were as hostile as ever. Rangers-Celtic matches were once more battles between implacable religious antagonists. It is the saddest of ironies that Thomson, a man who has since become the martyr of Celtic's Catholic fans, was himself a Protestant. If there was a lesson to be learnt from his death, its meaning has obviously eluded much of Glasgow.

Opposite page Two of Scotland's tributes to the dead goalkeeper, John Thomson: **left** the memorial on his grave at Bowhill, Fife, and **right** the cut-glass plaque at Parkhead.
Top and *centre* A sequence clearly illustrating Thomson's fatal accident. Sam English (left) had broken through and was about to shoot when Thomson dived. Instead of falling across the shot as most goalkeepers do, Thomson dived headfirst along the line of the ball and straight at English's feet. The pictures were used as evidence at the subsequent enquiry and proved beyond any doubt that English was totally blameless. Many Celtic supporters claimed that the Irishman had kicked Thomson; the evidence shows that his right foot could only have connected with the ball.
Bottom Surrounded by attendants and players, Thomson is carried from the Ibrox field.

Rangers: Dawson, Gray, McAulay, Meiklejohn, Simpson, Brown, Fleming, Marshall, English, McPhail, Morton.
Celtic: Thomson (J), Cook, McGonagle, Wilson, McStay, Geatons, Thomson (R), Thomson (A), McGrory, Scarff, Napier.

Left Jimmy Hampson, the Blackpool centre-forward who scored two of England's goals, challenging Rudi Hiden the Austrian 'keeper.
Above *Captains Billy Walker and Walter Nausch with the famous Belgian referee John Langenus before the kick-off. It was Walker's first international for five years.*
Right *Hampson's first goal which gave England an early lead. In Vienna the Austrian committee were listening to the radio commentary and anticipated a heavy defeat. But their pessimism was premature: the Austrian team recovered to play well and lost only 4-3.*

7

If only England had lost...

On 7 December 1932, Austria's international team, the so-called Wunderteam, came to Stamford Bridge and gave England the fright of their lives. Had they won, as they might so easily have done, their victory could have changed the whole course of British soccer. As long as England remained unbeaten at home they were popularly regarded as invincible. Until they were so decisively defeated by the Hungarians in 1953 English football remained complacent; so convinced of its superiority that it did not believe in change. It was no coincidence that Jimmy Hogan, the little English coach who brought Austria so successfully to London, should sit in the Royal Box as the Hungarians' honoured guest in 1953.

Hogan and Hugo Meisl, the wealthy Jewish businessman who was the virtual father of Austrian football, had founded the Wienerschule (the Vienna School) of play. Skill, technique and a great deal of short passing was its basis. The Austrian team, still playing with a brilliant attacking centre-half, Smistik, while England had long since gone over to the negative third back stopper, was acknowledged the most skilful in Europe. A couple of years earlier, they had held England to a 0-0 draw in Vienna, but this was the real test.

England's soccer prestige at that time was immense. No visiting European country had as much as managed to force a draw on English soil and when Spain, after a narrow 4-3 win in Madrid in 1929, came for the return at Highbury in 1931, they were thrashed 7-1. The Austrians knew how difficult it would be.

Hugo Meisl expected bodily contact to upset his Wunderteam

Two weeks before the game, Austria played a trial match against a Viennese side on a damp and foggy day, scraping through by only 2-1. It looked bad. Even their marvellous centre-forward, Mathias Sindelar, 'the Man of Paper', fantastically elusive and skilled, continually shot over the bar; though it was true that he had recently been ill. People in Vienna began to say that it was going to be a case of England versus Rudi Hiden, a Viennese baker who was Austria's spectacular goalkeeper. Hugo Meisl, admittedly a renowned and perhaps superstitious pessimist before international games, wrote in a Berlin paper that the Austrians were well below form, lacked key forwards, and would be upset by 'the abundant use the English make of their bodies'.

Each Austrian player, before the team set off, was issued with a dark suit and a book of instruc-tions, which warned him not to boast before the match. Not all the players were pessimistic. Schall, an inside-left with an untypically thundering shot —Viennese players liked to walk it in—predicted that if the weather was good, they would win. Vogl, his left wing partner, ebulliently predicted victory by two goals. Smistik said Austria would not die of fright, but Walter Nausch, captain and left-half, believed that this would happen only if the forwards found their old form. At Vienna railway station, hundreds of fans turned up to cheer them on their journey.

England, who in those days had no team manager and chopped and changed the side continually, nevertheless fielded some impressive players. There was Billy Walker of Aston Villa, recalled to captain the team at inside-forward after a five year absence. His partner was the hard-shooting Villa left winger Eric Houghton, while on the other wing played the elusive Sammy Crooks of Derby. The great Harry Hibbs was in goal, in front of him the celebrated full-back partnership of Roy Goodall and Ernie Blenkinsop; a team by and large to make anyone tremble.

Billy Walker won the toss, Sindelar kicked off, and a remarkable game had begun. In the very first minute, David Jack, the Arsenal inside-right, famous for his individual goals, moved out to the right wing, tacked inwards, and crossed. Houghton had a good chance, but he failed to make proper contact. Austria went to the other end, Goodall missed his kick, but Hibbs came rushing out of goal to take the ball, while Vogl chivalrously stood aside. Most un-English.

Within seconds, England had scored. Hibbs booted the ball upfield, where David Jack controlled it and sent Hampson, the Blackpool centre-forward, through the Austrian defence. Hampson retained the ball under heavy pressure, and when he at last lost it, it only ran loose to Walker. Walker found Jack, Jack found Hampson again, and the centre-forward's fast, low shot beat Hiden. In Vienna, the Austrian committee, listening to the radio commentary, gasped with

horror. They were quite convinced that the Austrian team would now fall apart; but it did nothing of the sort.

The retreating defence was clearly puzzling the English forwards, while the Austrians began to use longer passes in attack. It was 26 minutes before Hampson, later to die tragically in a boating accident, made it 2-0, but by this time the Austrians were playing as well as England. Besides the superb skills of Smistik and Sindelar, there was the muscular competence of the left-back Szesta, who was playing as a stopper, and the dangerous running of young Zischek, 'the Ghost', at outside-right.

Perhaps if Vogl had scored at a vital psychological moment, just before half-time, all might have been very different, but with only Hibbs to beat, he miskicked hopelessly, allowing Roy Goodall to clear. So Austria went in a couple down, and it seemed much more than they could hope to retrieve.

After the interval, the skilful Austrians began to move the ball much more quickly, yet only a superb recovery by Hiden prevented a third English goal. He pushed the ball right to the eager feet of Eric Houghton, but when the young winger released one of his famous shots, Hiden jumped to turn it over the bar, to great applause.

Six minutes into the half, Austria were able to reduce the lead. It was the consummation of a lovely, lucid movement which shattered the English defence. Sindelar found Schall, who sent a square pass to Zischek the right winger. Zischek promptly drove the ball past Hibbs: 2-1.

It was a new Austria, now, and their red shirts, donned for the occasion, buzzed around the English goal. They forced four corners, then Schall had one of his renowned shots, which Hibbs managed to block. Walter Nausch beat him with a dive, but it hit the post and bounced out. No team had thus far bearded the lion in its lair as Austria were now doing. But England managed to get off the hook, and their powerful, talented attack began to assault the visiting defence, again.

Hiden had to dive to a shot from Houghton, push out another from David Jack; then England were given a free kick, just outside the Austrian box. Eric Houghton, a famed kicker of a dead ball, took it. The shot sped towards the Austrian wall, where all might have been well had not Schall ducked; understandably but expensively. The ball hit him on the side of the head, and skidded past Hiden to make the score 3-1 for England. On play, it was cruel, for the passing of the Austrian forwards was now much more subtle and precise, and their half-backs were gaining control of the English forward-line. They came swarming forward in their efforts to save the game, and when Sindelar received the ball in front of goal, he had the cool head and the masterly technique to control it in his own time, and slip it past Hibbs.

Austria were unlucky to be losing 3-1 when they were playing so well

Unfortunately for the Austrians, however, England kept countering their splendid team work with flashes of individual virtuosity and power. When Walker passed to Crooks, the little Derby winger shot strongly from far out, and beat Hiden to make the score 4-2.

Austria did not give up, and their final goal, five minutes from the end, was infinitely deserved, if somewhat doubtful in its nature. Hibbs was badly impeded at a corner kick, but the famous Belgian referee, John Langenus, he of the plus-fours, allowed play to continue and Zischek was able to run the ball home.

Two more alarms were left for the final seconds of this dramatic match. First, a fine attempt by Schall was frustrated by Hibbs. Then a fraction of a second after the final whistle blew, England got the ball in the Austrian net a fifth time, but it was disallowed.

Inevitably, there were some who brushed the closeness of the result aside as a mere freak. One critic accused the Austrians of being predictable. Billy Walker said publicly that were the teams to meet again, England would score eight or nine. This was not the view of one national correspondent who wrote of the Austrian football as 'first class Corinthian with a kick in it, and played at twice the pace'. Nausch was voted the best half-back on the field, Vogl and Szesta were also praised. The most pertinent criticism was of the Austrian finishing; they made chances beautifully but they just could not take them. Nevertheless, Austria's first appearance in England had produced an excellent game and technically Austria had been superior.

This, indeed, was probably what had saved England from defeat, and would do so on many occasions until the Hungarians riddled their defence, in 1953. The Austrians visited Glasgow a year after the Chelsea game, drew 2-2, then came to London to play Arsenal, Titans of the time. Arsenal beat them 4-2. 'It looks fine,' wrote one London reporter, 'it is fine: when the Austrians have learned to turn all their cleverness into something that counts: when, in a few words, they have organised the winning of football matches as highly as they have organised the taming of a football, they will make [everyone] sit up and take notice.'

Austria, in fact, succeeded in beating England 2-1 in Vienna in May, 1936, and the memory of their display at Chelsea lingered on for years. Long afterwards, when Hugo Meisl's brother, Willy, came to collect a Press pass at Stamford Bridge, the big commissionaire found his envelope with no trouble. 'I shall never forget that name,' he said, simply.

England: Hibbs, Goodall, Blenkinsop, Strange, Hart, Keen, Crooks, Jack, Hampson, Walker, Houghton.
Austria: Hiden, Rainer, Szesta, Gall, Smistik, Nausch, Zischek, Gschweidl, Sindelar, Schall, Vogl.

Arsenal's black day in the Black Country

8

There may have been greater FA Cup giant-killing deeds than Walsall's 2-0 defeat of Arsenal on 14 January 1933, but none made a more lasting impact. The context of the match gives greater significance to Walsall's triumph—or to be more accurate to Arsenal's humiliation—than perhaps finer achievements elsewhere.

Arsenal were the upstarts from the South, the first side to break the monopoly the North and Midlands held over the Football League Championship. They won the title in 1930-31, and were now on the way not merely to regaining it but also to the start of a Championship hat-trick.

Walsall, though founded 18 years before these newcomers from London, in 1868, had nevertheless been left behind in the development of football. They shuttled between the Third Division North and the Third Division South between the Wars and eventually had to seek re-election a record number of seven times before the Fourth Division was created. Arsenal's record could not have been more different.

The rise of Arsenal to the position of outstanding club in the country was based on a tactical revolution. The centre-half was changed from an aggressive unit in midfield to an out and out stopper or 'policeman', with Herbie Roberts filling the role.

The defence retreated under pressure and there was an abrupt switch to a devastating counter-attack by means of a shrewd midfield general, Alex James. The way Arsenal won matches, by snatching goals after encouraging opponents to come at them, aroused resentment. The tactics were considered ugly and negative, and the club became known as 'lucky Arsenal'.

Arsenal were managed by Herbert Chapman, the magician who transformed the club from Cinderellas struggling to stay in the First Division. His professionalism lifted not only Arsenal, but football as a whole, taking it from a semi-amateur organization to a top entertainment industry.

But command of the headlines and love of controversy caused jealousy which, in turn, was reflected in attitudes to the club. The revolutionary ideas would have been tolerated had they originated from Aston Villa, Everton or Newcastle, but not when they came from the newcomers of London.

Yet Chapman made a mistake for the Walsall match. He made the cardinal error of underestimating his opposition. It was understandable. In the previous year Arsenal had met another minnow, Darwen from the Lancashire Combination, and annihilated them 11-1 for the club's record win in the competition proper. A few days before the tie, Arsenal met Sheffield United, a leading First Division club, at Highbury, and won 9-2 to strengthen their Championship challenge.

With usual thoroughness Chapman checked the form of Walsall and was lulled by the results—three draws and a 5-0 defeat in the four matches before the Cup-tie.

One newspaper became almost lyrical about the differences between the teams: 'Arsenal, the Rich, the Confident, the League leaders, the £30,000 aristocrats, against the little Midland Third Division team that cost £69 all-in. Arsenal train on ozone, brine-baths, champagne, golf and electrical massage in an atmosphere of prima donna preciousness. They own £87 worth of football boots. Walsall men eat fish and chips and drink beer, and the entire running expenses of the club this season have been £75.'

When England left-back Eddie Hapgood was ruled out by injury, Chapman was not worried. He was more concerned when 'flu struck the club and claimed left-half Bob John, a Welsh international, and centre-forwards Jack Lambert and Tim Coleman.

At least one of the 'flu victims could have played, but Chapman decided not to rush anyone back. Nor did he recall England winger Joe Hulme, who had been dropped because of loss of form, and whose experience would have been invaluable.

After all, Chapman reasoned, Arsenal had the assurance of a First Division club and even with reserves the quality of their game should see them through. So he confidently promoted four 'unknowns', of whom only one, Norman Sidey, had had first-team experience, and that was limited to one game. The others were left-back Tommy Black, a former Scottish Junior, and recruits from London amateur soccer, outside-right Billy Warnes and centre-forward Charlie Walsh.

However, Arsenal still fielded seven internationals. Elegant David Jack cost the first £10,000 fee when signed from Bolton, Alex James cost nearly as much to join the club from Preston and Cliff Bastin was an ice-cold executioner of goals who had won all the game's honours by the age of 21.

These were world-class forwards, and behind them were Frank Moss, George Male, Frank Hill and Herbie Roberts who had helped to make the defence the most feared in the game.

The first warning signal was in the dressing-room before the kick-off. Walsh was so nervous that he put on his boots before his stockings.

Walsall began with a rush, as was expected, but even when the early enthusiasm waned, they refused to allow Arsenal to settle down and take command.

Some of the tackling, especially on the little Scot, James, was very grim and Walsall were aided by the narrow ground, which was made more cramped by the encroachment of the spectators up to the touchlines.

Walsall were going to meet the ball, while the Londoners were waiting for it, and tackled quickly and vigorously whenever an Arsenal man was in possession. Backs Bennett and Bird and centre-half Leslie were magnificent as Arsenal strove to repeat the sophisticated moves which had taken them to the top of the First Division.

As their confidence increased, so the shortcomings of Arsenal's newcomers were exposed. Walsh had a great chance in the first half from an inviting centre by Bastin, and shaped at it so tentatively that he hit the ball with a shoulder

Right *The greatest Cup shock of all time? Many of the newspapers of the day certainly thought so.* ***Below*** *The victorious Walsall team pose with the Lady Mayoress. The two goalscorers were* ***left inset*** *Sheppard and* ***right inset*** *Alsop.*

instead of the head. Warnes clearly did not relish the tough tackling, while Black became increasingly irritated, although he produced Arsenal's one shot of note in the first half.

Bastin was the only forward to show glimpses of his real form, and he lacked support. With no score at half-time, Arsenal felt they could at least hold out for a replay at Highbury. But 15 minutes after the restart centre-forward Gilbert Alsop became the hero of the Black Country by heading in Lee's corner kick.

Chapman went to the touchline and ordered a switch—Jack to lead the attack. The move looked like succeeding when Jack manoeuvred into a scoring position but, as he drew a leg back, Walsh intervened—and he lost the ball! Jack turned away, not a little displeased.

Five minutes after Alsop's goal Black's simmering anger boiled over and he badly fouled Alsop in the penalty area. Sheppard scored from the spot and the cheers of the 20,000 crowd were heard two miles away.

The match was as good as over. Arsenal were rattled and although they pressed desperately they never looked like penetrating the cock-a-hoop Walsall defence. Before the end Walsall took command again and were chaired off the field by their supporters.

Arsenal's defeat has gone down as the biggest shock in Cup history

The effects on Arsenal were immense. To this day they would rather be drawn against a top First Division club than an outsider. Defeats by Peterborough, Rotherham, Northampton, Norwich and Bradford, and uneasy performances against Colchester, Bedford Town and Carlisle, heightened the dread.

Chapman felt the humiliation more than anyone, because of his part in it. In order to obliterate the memory as quickly as possible, he transferred Black to Plymouth less than a week after the tie. In fact, Chapman was so disgusted with Black's behaviour on the pitch that, immediately after the match, he said he would never play for Arsenal again. Walsh moved on to Brentford before the month was out. In May Warnes was transferred to Norwich, and only Sidey remained of the four Arsenal newcomers to give loyal service for several seasons.

In the event, the result had little effect on the positions of the two clubs for the rest of the season—apart, of course, from eliminating Arsenal from the Cup. Walsall were knocked out in the next round by Manchester City, losing 2-3, and they finished a respectable third in the Third Division North. Undismayed by their shock defeat, Arsenal surged ahead in the League to take the Championship for the first of three successive times. Arsenal the unbeatable were born.

There were Cup upsets before that game and there have been many since. Colchester beat Leeds 3-2 in 1971 and, in 1959, Third Division Norwich eliminated Manchester United, Spurs and Sheffield United before unluckily going down to Luton in the semi-final. There will be more, too, because that is what the Cup is all about. But there was something different about Walsall's win that day.

For the match was played in the hungry thirties. It was played between a traditional—and poor—provincial club and a rich Southern one. And the provinces, rightly or wrongly, resented the fact that it was they, who produced the great wealth of the country, who were suffering more from the effects of the Depression than the unseeing and condescending South. Arsenal symbolized this presumed arrogance. So the result was more than just a triumph for the football underdogs—it came to be seen as a victory for the have-nots over the haves.

Walsall: Cunningham, Bird, Bennett, Reed, Leslie, Salt, Coward, Ball, Alsop, Sheppard, Lee.
Arsenal: Moss, Male, Black, Hill, Roberts, Sidey, Warnes, Jack, Walsh, James, Bastin.

SUNDAY · PICTORIAL
SALE VASTLY IN EXCESS OF ANY OTHER PICTURE NEWSPAPER
931   Registered at the G.P.O. as a Newspaper.   SUNDAY, JANUARY 15, 1933   Twopence

ARSENAL'S SENSATIONAL CUP-TIE DEFEAT

Cunningham picking up the ball to save for Walsall, the Third Division team who provided the sensation of yesterday's Cup-tie by beating Arsenal, the League leaders, by two goals to none. The Walsall team cost less than £100, whereas Arsenal represents several thousands, but the result fairly reflects the play. See also page 32.

Bride and bridegroom leaving the church after the wedding at St. Columba's, Pont-street, yesterday, of Miss Bunty Paterson, only child of Mr. and M—— William P——son, w—— Hunty Gordon son R——

Page 22   THE DAILY MIRROR   Monday, January 16,

THE (F.A.) CUP THAT CHEERS—SOMETIMES

Walsall on Top o' the World

Play round the Walsall goal during the sensational Cup-tie against the Arsenal.

Pearson, Oldham goalkeeper, rushing o— clear against the Spurs, who won 6—

ARSENAL'S

Brighton and Che——
Goalkeepe——

SUNDAY PICTORIAL

When 'FLU is suspected —take GENASPRIN The SAFE BRAND

'GENE CORRI'S MEMORIES—P. 15

WALSALL'S WONDER WIN

Saturday may have been a dream to the small teams in the Cup-ties, but it was something akin to a nightmare for the "big" noises.

Walsall led the way and gave the Arsenal the shock of their lives in defeating them by two goals to none.

The Londoners were completely unsettled and their craft failed against the bustle and energy of the Black Country men.

Jack and James tried desperately hard to set the "machine" going, but always the Arsenal found themselves robbed of the ball.

Alsop, Walsall's leading goalscorer, drove the first nail into Arsenal's coffin and Sheppard, with a penalty, completed the job.

The crowd were almost mad with excitement and the players were carried shoulder high off the field. Thus a struggling Third Division team created a sensation of the century

Brighton and Chesterfield also hit the high-spots. The Southern Third Division side actually ousted Chelsea from the Cup, while the Second Division men astounded Sheffield Wednesday, at Hillsborough, by thoroughly earning a replay.

Brighton largely owe their success to Attwood, who, I think, was once understudy to

Hedley.   Attwood.

Dixie Dean at Everton. This player got a snap goal in the opening minute, and after this Chelsea never had a look in.

Brett saw to it that Gallacher would not be a dangerous force, and, truthfully speaking, the Londoners' weakened eleven never looked like scoring.

Actually Barber, at full back, got Chelsea's point after Wilson had put Brighton two up.

I would not like to have been in the unhappy position of Ball, the Sheffield Wednesday centre, against Chesterfield. He had given his side a two-goal lead—which was later nullified—and then with seven minutes to go he was trusted with a penalty—the result was that Chesterfield live to fight again, for Ball missed.

I consider Chester's 3—0 win at home against Fulham at one of the finest feats of the round.

NO FLUKE RESULT

Chester struck their best form, the forwards combined perfectly and their speedy attacks thoroughly bewildered the Fulham defence.

Hedley pierced the Fulham rearguard four times, but, I am sure, he will be the first to say that much of his success was due to the fine support he received from Armes, Cresswell and Mercer—the last-named player of the——

A miserable day for the London Cup sides was brightened by the fact that the Spurs went to Oldham and won 6—0 a performance that was accomplished without the help of Poynton, left back, in the second half.

Are the Spurs going to do what West Brom—— did a couple of seasons ago—gain pro—— —tion and win the Cup?

I will dismiss the other London sides' efforts with: Charlton got lost in the fog against Bolton at the Valley; the Rangers roved at Darlington and missed their way to the fourth round; Corinth bid adieu in a timorous fashion to the advantage of West Ham, and Millwall meet Reading once again because the fog robbed them of success at New Cross when the game was abandoned.

If Folkestone had possessed ten other players with the ability of their twenty-year-old inside-keeper, Goodman, they would be in the Cup now!

This youth, I am told, fielded all manner of shots with the confidence of a veteran until three-quarter-time; then, just a couple of slips in judgment allowed Luke and Willingham to scrape Huddersfield through.

Huddersfield's attack had almost battered itself to pieces in attempting to beat Goodman, whose work, says my correspondent, seemed to have earned a replay.

Newcastle, the Cupholders, are out! Leeds did the trick at St. James's Park, thanks mainly to a hat-trick by Hydes.

DEFENCE ALL AT SEA

Newcastle's side, that included three reserves, started well but faded out and their defence was all at sea against a keen set of forwards.

Burns, in the Newcastle goal, was the hero of the home team. He saved his side time and again when a score seemed certain.

Aston Villa live to fight another day, but they must be wondering how they came away from Bradford sharing honours with the City.

They lost Talbot, their centre half, who damaged a shin, a quarter of an hour after the interval, but even when at full strength they were at times overplayed by a team that combined punch with skill.

I am not going to suggest that the Villa did not have polish. They did, and Houghton, Walker and Beresford, backed by Gibson, contributed neat efforts which, however, were spoiled by over-keenness.

The Villa's defence, Morton, Mort and Blair, undoubtedly saved them. Peel and Watmough were Bradford's shining lights in attack, while Barkas was an outstanding back.

Nine goals were scored at Wolverhampton, but the home side, under a double handicap, could claim only three of them against Derby. Wolves had to call upon two reserves, Farrow and Smelley, in attack, and after only ten minutes the former forward was lamed and became a passenger.

FABIAN'S FINE GAME

Derby gradually outplayed the Wolves despite a shock goal from Crook in the opening minutes.

A. H. Fabian, Derby's much-discussed Corinthian forward, caused a lot of mischief to Wolverhampton's defence.

Those great Cup-fighting forces, Blackburn and Sheffield United, were through.

The Yorkshiremen's feat in winning by an odd goal at Swansea, where only one other side has been successful this season, was a great performance.

Jimmy Dunne, the United's Irish international centre forward, was in his element on the small Swansea ground.

He made rings round three opponents to open the Sheffield score, and after Martin equalised he put on another.

Martin once again found his way through the Sheffield defence to equalise, but only three minutes elapsed before Oswald put the United in the fourth round with a good goal.

Only Kendall's goalkeeping kept Swansea out after this.

At Lincoln, Blackburn met a side that the reserves in five positions because the 'flu demic had taken its toll in the City o—

(Continued in next column)

Arsenal forward caught between two Walsall defenders during yesterday's sational game. Alsop and Sheppard were the scorers of Walsall's two goals. The home team stood up wonderfully to the Arsenal attacks, and the visitors allowed themselves to become rattled. Walsall took their chances brilliantly.

SYNDICATION INTERNATIONAL

Pr sti t st k - and battle raged

In November 1934, Italy, new holders of the World Cup, a tournament whose very name then provoked a sneer in Britain, came to Highbury to play England. England, the acknowledged masters of football, still refused to enter the World Cup competition. Instead, they arrogantly let the contenders fight it out amongst each other. Then, when a winner emerged, England would challenge this upstart of a nation to a contest on English soil, win the match, and promptly claim to be the World Champions.

This was the reason for Italy's visit to London in 1934. At England's invitation, the two countries were to join battle for the unofficial championship of the world.

The consequent, confused melodrama of the game has gone down in the annals of British football as the Battle of Highbury, while the Italians still regard it as a moral victory, a kind of footballing Dunkirk. It could and should have been one of the most exciting and distinguished international matches of all time. Instead, with its ill temper, its persistent violence and its welter of prone bodies, its football was in fact the very last thing for which it is remembered.

Yet football there was, among the fouling. Ted Drake, the Arsenal centre-forward, said that England, for the first twenty minutes, 'were playing the best football it was possible to play. You could not play any better,' while Italy, in the second half, suddenly forgot about kicking people and came to life to score two admirable goals, though not even these could salvage the occasion as a game of football.

England, then, had never failed to beat foreign opposition on their own soil. Italy had won the World Cup, played in Italy itself, with a brand of football which had won them few friends. As the famous Belgian referee, John Langenus, who always officiated in plus-fours, remarked: 'It was natural that Italy should want to win the trophy, but they made it a little too obvious.' Ruthlessness was the keynote of their football, never more evident than in the quarter-final matches in Florence, when Spain, and the veteran Zamora in goal, bravely defied them, and forced them to an unexpected replay.

There were many fascinating sidelights on the Italy-England game. In the first place, the inspiration, the very soul of the Italian team, was their manager, Vittorio Pozzo; no man could have been more pro-English than Pozzo. As a poor student working in England before the Great War, Pozzo had evolved his theory of the game by watching such teams as Manchester United, holding conversations with such as their great attacking centre-half, Charlie Roberts, and with Derby County's legendary goal scorer, Steve Bloomer. Thus when England had gone over lock, stock and barrel to the third-back game and the 'W' formation, Pozzo and Italy were still playing with a roving centre-half.

At that time it was the notorious Luisito Monti, an Argentinian nicknamed 'The Man Who Strolls', who played in that position for Italy. Heavy, powerful, talented and relentless, Monti had been involved in a deplorable incident when playing for a Buenos Aires XI against Chelsea, on tour five years earlier. He approached a Chelsea player, Rogers, stretched out his hand as though to greet him, then kicked him. Two Buenos Aires players promptly rushed him off the field, and it was promised that he would be suspended; which did not stop him appearing against Chelsea in their very next game. Estudiantes were certainly no sudden phenomenon in Argentinian football.

Italy just then was in the florid throes of Fascism, and Pozzo used the inflated bombast of the time to give his players morale and gain

The Italians were determined to prove they were the best in the world

their loyalty. He was nicknamed by a French journalist 'the poor captain of a company of millionaires.' He was an egotist and an autocrat, but his players loved him, and he them.

So for Pozzo and the Italians, this was a chance to prove that despite the absence of England, they were the true world champions. For England, well endowed at the time with fine players, but haphazardly prepared, without even the benefit of a team manager or a regular team doctor, it was simply one more game. While Italy prepared studiously and secretively in the Tuscan watering place of Roveta, the English players trained with their clubs; and, on the Saturday before the game, fell victim one after another to injuries in League games.

It was amusing that the late Emilion Martino, an Italian journalist, in his book, *Roveta to London*, should write that England had deliberately chosen Arsenal Stadium as the venue, because there were so many Arsenal players in their team! Quite apart from the fact that at the time the match was made the English selectors could have had little idea of whom they would choose, the last two Arsenal men picked to play, George Male and Ted Drake, came in only at the eleventh hour, after injuries to Cooper and Tilson. That made seven Arsenal men in all in the

PRESS ASSOCIATION

English side, and Eddie Hapgood, the young left-back, was made captain for the first of many times.

Martino made further capital out of the fact that Italy were refused permission to train on the Arsenal ground, though at that time of year, with grounds so heavy, it was common and quite explicable practice on the part of the Football Association.

The incident which determined, in fact sabotaged, the whole game took place as early as the second minute. Monti, now centre-half for Juventus of Turin, challenged the powerful Drake for a ball, was kicked on the foot, and broke a toe. It was several minutes before Pozzo could persuade him to come off, for Monti was tough as well as violent. Pozzo had first to move him to right-half, then to outside-right, before he could withdraw him to the dressing-room; and in those days there were no substitutes. 'He kicked me deliberately!' Monti cried, as he came off, and there is no doubt that the whole of the Italian team thought the same thing. From that point on, as far as they were concerned, they were merely 'retaliating'.

Since it is scarcely likely that Drake even knew about what had happened to Rogers five years ago in Buenos Aires, and inconceivable that the selectors of that epoch would have dreamed of encouraging such tactics (if only on the grounds that things were simply not taken so seriously, then!), Monti's complaint seems quite unfounded. What mattered was that the rest of his team believed it. Later explanations, which became more fanciful as time progressed, suggested that the Italians had been offered huge bonuses for winning—a car and exemption from military service—but were wide of the mark. It was purely a question of jumping to conclusions—then jumping on the opposition often quite literally.

Another, lesser, bone of contention was the English habit of charging the goalkeeper; a custom which was despised on the Continent. Drake, tired of watching the acrobatic but self-indulgent Ceresoli, successor to the famous Combi in the Italian goal, bounce the ball constantly to the edge of the area, charged him. The result was instant pandemonium, Drake being seized

Football was the very last thing for which the game is remembered

round the neck by the Italian right-back Monzeglio.

But in those opening fifteen minutes, England scored three times; and that after missing a penalty-kick in the first minute. This was taken by Eric Brook, the blond, muscular left-winger from Manchester City. His shot was ferocious, but the excellent Ceresoli reacted superbly, reaching the ball with both hands. Brook was to have his revenge, however.

For it was Brook who headed England into the lead from Britton's free kick. Then, when he shaped to take another free kick, Ceresoli, over-confident after his penalty save, majestically waved his covering 'wall' away. Brook took advantage of this with a 20-yard shot of stupendous power. An Italian back kicked the ball four times into the goal, then Ceresoli sat on the ball and would not surrender it. After only a quarter of an hour, with Hapgood off the field, Drake pivoted to get the third.

England's forwards were now being shamefully maltreated, and the lack of a strong referee did not help matters. The original nominee had been Dr Pecos Bauwens of Germany, rejected by the Italians on the grounds that he could speak English but not Italian; an ironic move, given that in Milan five years later, he would allow Italy a goal blatantly punched by Piola! Olsen, the Swedish referee who eventually took charge of the game, spoke neither language, and had little control. After the rough fiasco, he was to say in the inevitable interview by the press, 'The Italians were very excitable. When they learn to control themselves, they will be a great side. I had

to warn two of the defenders repeatedly, but whether they understood me or not, I do not know. I hope they did.'

It seems very doubtful, especially as one of them smashed Eddie Hapgood's nose with a deliberate blow of the elbow, as they went up to head the ball at a throw-in. At the banquet that evening, where Hapgood's maltreated nose was strapped and plastered, the Italian laughed in his face. Hapgood later remarked that it was just as well that he was a pretty even-tempered fellow, or he would quite easily have gone across the table at him.

In the second half, however, Italy forgot for a while to kick people and Meazza, their fine centre-forward, scored two elegant goals. The goalkeeping of Frank Moss and the centre-half-back play of Jack Barker prevented others.

'When England were allowed to play anything,' one newspaper wrote, 'it was football from the copybook. Yet Italy remain the football champions of the world. If, in order to win such a title, it is necessary to acquire an outlook revealed by some of the Italians playing against England, I prefer that we should remain among the less exalted football people . . . If a man goes into a tackle expecting that he may get a punch in

'There were numerous English bodies lying all over the field . . .'

the jaw, an elbow in his ribs, or meet a raised knee, it is not to be expected that he will face it with confidence. If a man with the ball at his feet knows, because of what has already happened, that it is even money he will be tripped from behind, then the natural tendency is obviously to get rid of the ball as soon as possible.'

Stanley Matthews, then only nineteen years old and playing in only his second international, was certainly among those of the England side thus affected. In retrospect, the observations of one football correspondent have a superb, unconscious irony to them. 'I saw Matthews play just as moderately in the recent inter-League match,' he wrote, 'exhibiting the same slowness and hesitation. Perhaps he lacks the big match temperament.' Perhaps . . .

The English player who truly relished the situation was the Yorkshire born left-half, Wilf Copping, whose muscular tackling was more than the Italians could take. The following day his partner at wing-half in Arsenal's team, Jack Crayston, walked into his manager's office and remarked, 'If we play Italy again tomorrow, there's only one half-back line to pick: Copping, Copping and Copping.' Copping had certainly come off better than the Italians he tackled.

One cartoonist drew a tiny spectator cowering away from a huge football boot. 'With England three up,' he wrote, 'the good old Latin temperament exerted itself, and soon there were numerous English bodies lying all over the field, so many in fact that our selectors must have wondered if they had picked more than eleven players. In conclusion, we were very glad when the whistle blew because you never know when this Latin temperament is going to leave the field and set about the spectators.'

'Can I go now?' the tiny spectator was enquiring. 'You've kicked me twice.' Seven England players needed treatment after a match which even Pozzo saw as 'a little bit of a battle', and the Football Association seriously considered abandoning matches against foreign teams. Luckily, however, they relented, and for 19 further years England remained invincible at home. Though Italy had damaged England's players, she could not damage her deserved reputation as football's true masters.

England: Moss, Male, Hapgood, Britton, Barker, Copping, Matthews, Bowden, Drake, Bastin, Brook.
Italy: Ceresoli, Monzeglio, Allemandi, Ferraris, Monti, Bertolini, Guaita, Serantoni, Meazza, Ferrari, Orsi.

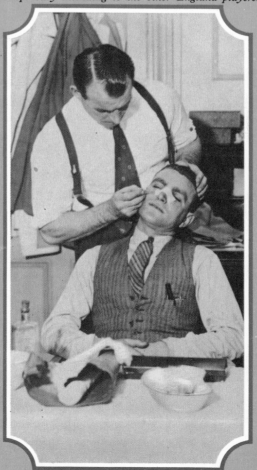

Below left The seven Arsenal players who formed the nucleus of the England team that faced Italy, the new World Champions, in 1934. From the left, Copping, Bowden, Male, Moss, Drake, Hapgood, Bastin. **Above** Wilf Copping's muscular tackling made him exactly the kind of defender needed for this match. **Below** Eddie Hapgood had his nose broken by a deliberate blow from an Italian elbow. Here he receives treatment from the Arsenal trainer, who was kept busy attending to the other England players.

Eight shots, seven goals

Shortly before 2.15 pm on 14 December 1935 the band of the 5th Battalion Royal Warwickshire Regiment finished its final number and the huge Villa Park crowd began to concentrate upon the likely outcome of the afternoon's game between Aston Villa and Arsenal. Their anticipation was an ambivalent mixture of excitement and apprehension, for although this fixture was one of the highlights of British football in the thirties and had attracted the largest crowd of the season—nearly 70,000—there was nothing in the recent records of the two teams to suggest the parity that had been characteristic of earlier years.

Arsenal, the pre-eminent club of the period, were eight points behind Sunderland, but still hoping to win their fifth Championship in six years. Villa were at the bottom of the division, had already conceded 52 goals in 18 games, and had lost to Manchester City 5-0 the previous week.

Unlike Arsenal, they had allowed a good team to decline and were desperately attempting to avert disaster by spending a fortune on new players: between November 1935 and the end of January 1936 they spent £35,500. Within the month preceding the Arsenal match they bought five players, three of them internationals. The latest of these, Alex Massie, Scotland's cultured wing-half who cost £6,000 from Hearts, was making his home debut, and it was the first time all the new players were appearing together: Tommy Griffiths, the Welsh international centre-half bought from Middlesbrough for £5,000; George Cummings, the Scottish international left-back from Partick Thistle for £8,000; Jack Palethorpe, a £2,500 centre-forward from Sheffield Wednesday; Jackie Williams, a winger signed from Huddersfield for £2,000; and Massie. Villa had also replaced Young and McLuckie with Blair and Wood. Would this be the team to save the great Aston Villa from the disgrace of their first-ever relegation?

Certainly Arsenal were no team to experiment against. Even without Alex James they looked formidable. The defence was near impregnable with England's George Male and Eddie Hapgood, Jack Crayston, Herbie Roberts and Wilf Copping. At the end of the season—although they were to finish only in sixth position—they had conceded just 48 goals, almost 30 less than champions Sunderland. Before this daunting barrier were other England colleagues, Cliff Bastin and Ted Drake, whom Arsenal manager George Allison had described as 'the best centre-forward in the world' when he purchased him from Southampton for £6,000 in 1933.

Recently, however, Drake had lost form and had been put in the reserves. He was also suffering from a knee injury that was to cause a lot of trouble; when he played at Villa Park it was strapped for the first time. Drake was certainly one of the great centre-forwards of his time—but after this day he was to be remembered in Birmingham simply as the man who scored seven goals against Aston Villa.

Yet, as Dai Astley won the toss and chose to

play with the wind behind his side, there was no reason for Villa supporters to panic. There were 14 internationals on the field (the total value of the two teams exceeded £100,000) and six of them were wearing claret and blue. And if Villa were going to save themselves, then this was an appropriate game to begin the revival.

There was no apparent disparity between the sides during the opening minutes. Arsenal, wearing unfamiliar white shirts and black shorts, kicked off, but Blair checked their two immediate attacks down the left-wing and Villa commenced a period of sustained pressure.

First Wood's shot passed wide of the post. Then Massie soon impressed his new home crowd when he trapped the ball in midfield, swerved to send Bastin dashing in the wrong direction, and passed to Williams. The right-winger's centre came back to Massie who created a chance for Dix, but he, instead of shooting, passed out to Williams. Shots in quick succession from Dix, Astley and Massie raised the hopes of Villa's fans; to their delight it was Arsenal who

were on the defensive and Male was forced to concede a corner to relieve his defence.

When Arsenal did attack it provided the home crowd with a moment of slapstick comedy—the only light relief of the afternoon. Drake was optimistically chasing a ball over the Villa goal-line and, because he was wearing long studs, skidded on the surrounding track. To the amusement of the crowd he fell over in a manner worthy of Buster Keaton; he arose unharmed but angry.

At the other end Villa should have taken the lead after ten minutes when George Cummings put a long clearance at Palethorpe's feet; yet he too passed cautiously to the wing. In retrospect that incident was to epitomise the difference between the teams: by a combination of skill and confidence Arsenal were able to take their chances, whereas Villa's finishing was inept. But in that early period, far from having to contain the champions, Villa looked on top.

So the crowd were quite surprised when, after 15 minutes, Arsenal scored. Pat Beasley beat Danny Blair and sent a long, diagonal pass down the left where Drake was running to receive the ball. Tommy Griffiths was following him but Drake pushed the ball between the centre-half's legs and ran on to score with a straight shot that Morton had little chance of holding.

Another quarter of an hour later Drake, in the middle of the field, received a long pass from Bastin and sprinted towards the Villa goal. Cummings and Griffiths converged upon him in the penalty area but he used all of his 11st 10lb to resist their united challenge and shoot past Morton for his second goal. The crowd sank under a weighty cloud of injustice: two breakaways and 'lucky Arsenal'—the cry that carried

PAGE 34

PLAIN MR. DRAKE

SUNDAY

Goal... Was

SEVEN
GUN
SINKS

Cruising R
Off the "

Palethorpe.

" SUNDAY PICTO

Aston Villa

IN the days of good Queen Bess a certain man named Drake—Sir Francis of that ilk—smashed up the luxury Spanish Armada. Yesterday at Villa Park plain Mr. Drake—[scor]ed this time—smashed the Villa's team of stars on which something like £30,000 has been spent in the last month or so.

Morton, the home goalkeeper, must have thought the spheres which flashed past him with monotonous regularity were cannon balls, with such force and accuracy were they directed.

Drake broke all records by scoring the whole of his side's seven goals, and the way he played it would not have been surprising if he had reached double figures, though it must be admitted that at times he was smiled on by Dame Fortune.

Faced with Griffiths, captain of Wales and regarded as a fine stopper, Drake did not keep to the middle of the field, but wandered right out on to the wings.

Time after time he would bear down on the home goal with the defence wondering just where he had come from. His shooting was remarkable and he had really few likely openings except for the seven which he converted.

It was not a one-man victory, for Arsenal played as a team, showing combination in general and covering in defence that were sadly lacking about the Villa

Drake's sensational performance naturally made the headlines, although the Sunday Pictorial only printed pictures of two new Villa players.
Right *Ted Drake, as Arsenal's centre-forward.*
Far right *Ted Drake, some twenty years later during a successful period as Chelsea manager.*

across the thirties—were winning 2-0.

Five minutes later Drake completed the first of his two hat-tricks. Possibly he was in an offside position when Beasley's shot rebounded to him off Blair, but the centre-forward did not hesitate and promptly struck the ball hard and low into the net: 3-0.

Such success could hardly now be attributed solely to luck, yet everyone felt the score was a false reflection of the play. Believing this, but no longer confident, Villa continued to attack—there was little alternative—but failed to realise any of the half-chances they created, except a disallowed goal by Palethorpe, who had fouled Arsenal goalkeeper Wilson. A goal before half-time was an essential encouragement, but the famous Arsenal defence confidently countered all the opposing forwards could devise and the score at the interval was unchanged.

As play resumed the fans were still discussing the exorbitant margin of Arsenal's lead and passionately remembering the half-back line of Gibson, Talbot and Tate that had so recently kept Arsenal forwards in check, when the result was conclusively settled. Griffiths, keeping himself between Drake and the goal, judged the ball was going out for a goal-kick. Instead it rebounded from the post to Drake who skilfully screwed it between Morton's legs. The crowd was silent. Only the final score was now in doubt. There was to be no redemption, no legendary come-back to be related to future generations. But what was wrong with the Villa?

What was wrong, apart from Drake's excellence, was a basic tactical inadequacy. Prominent though they were in the early thirties Villa had failed to adapt. The London team, under Chapman, had made famous the defensive centre-

half, or stopper third-back. Villa had belatedly tried to adjust to this new system and 18 months before had bought Jimmy Allen from Portsmouth for this role. But Allen, or the club, could not settle; Villa's defence was no longer reliable.

Arsenal's achievements, however, were the consequence of more than that limited strategy. The real strength of their teams was the ability of their midfield players. The wing-halves and inside-forwards had the skill to convert immediately to defence or attack whenever they lost or won possession. The inside-forwards lay deep and were quite prepared to concede the midfield to the opposition and retreat into defence when they did not have the ball. Villa fell into the trap of carrying the ball to the Arsenal penalty area and leaving their own rear exposed. Against Arsenal's defence most forward lines were dispossessed and then Arsenal also had the astute players who could swiftly send long passes to the wings—to forwards who were capable of taking the chances that had been created directly from defence. Villa may have appeared to have territorial superiority, but it was Arsenal who were always in command.

If Villa's forwards had been more effective in front of goal Arsenal would have been less certain of dominating the game. As it was they were hesitant and inaccurate, and Ted Drake was able to translate Arsenal's tactical superiority into the more tangible evidence of goals.

The attention of the crowd, the result having been decided, was changing from Villa's plight to Drake's remarkable performance. No one was surprised when Arsenal scored again, since by this time the home team were demoralised. Once more Bowden and Bastin created the opportunity: another Bastin pass to Drake hit immediately

into the net. Five shots—five goals. Drake was famous for his strength, courage and opportunism, but here he displayed fine control, an ability to beat defenders at will, and superlative finishing that defeated Morton by accuracy rather than force. Few people had witnessed such a complete exhibition of striking power.

His sixth goal, from his sixth shot—whenever Drake had the ball in the Villa half a goal seemed imminent—came in the 58th minute, when he took a bad clearance at the edge of the penalty area and put a first-time shot in the back of the net before Griffiths could tackle. This was not the type of memorable game Villa supporters had hoped for, but for Drake it was complete retribution for their earlier derision, and really the crowd were privileged to see one of the greatest individual performances in the history of English football. By now Massie, Wood and Griffiths were fully occupied trying to suppress the Arsenal centre-forward; it was only that which kept the score below double figures. Their attentions were probably responsible for Drake missing with his next shot: not a wild drive but one which rebounded from the underside of the bar to be cleared by a defender.

Why did Ted Drake's seventh shot only hit the Villa crossbar?

That was the first chance Drake missed. After 65 minutes one of Villa's finally counted. Houghton, the only forward to consistently use the ball well, crossed another good centre into the penalty area and Palethorpe headed past Wilson. It was hardly any consolation—only emphasising Drake's greater ability—but it provoked a belated rally and Palethorpe almost scored again in the next attack. Attack, though, had hardly proved the best means of defence.

But the last gesture appropriately belonged to Ted Drake and, in the final minute, after the longest period in the game without a goal, he scored his seventh. He accepted yet another crossfield pass from Cliff Bastin and a goal was inevitable. On that darkening December afternoon Drake only once 'almost scored'.

Villa's heavy defeat, in their circumstances, did not surprise the world. But for Drake to score all seven goals was a remarkable achievement, equalling the total of Preston's James Ross against Stoke way back on 6 October 1888, and creating an individual record aggregate away from home. Not suprisingly he received most of the credit for Arsenal's triumph. To commemorate his performance all 22 players autographed the ball and presented it to him.

For much of the remainder of that season injury interrupted his football but the game at Villa Park was not Drake's only highlight. Arsenal missed the Championship but finally won the FA Cup, Drake (who else?) scoring the only goal at Wembley against Sheffield United.

Nor had he completely finished tormenting Aston Villa. The week before the Cup Final, playing to prove his fitness a few weeks after a cartilage operation, he scored once more against them at Highbury—a final nail in their relegation coffin.

Yet it was his performance at Villa Park that had almost condemned the club to the Second Division. He had ruthlessly exposed the team's frailities and destroyed the slender faith of the players and supporters. The popular impression did less than justice to the merits of the whole Arsenal team but Ted Drake had, to all intents and purposes, humbled Villa single-handed. If one player could score seven goals against Aston Villa at Villa Park they could hardly claim some divine prerogative to remain in the First Division.

Aston Villa: Morton, Blair, Cummings, Massie, Griffiths, Wood, Williams, Astley, Palethorpe, Dix, Houghton.

Arsenal: Wilson, Male, Hapgood, Crayston, Roberts, Copping, Rogers, Bowden, Drake, Bastin, Beasley.

ICTORIAL   DECEMBER 15, 1935

E'S ARMADA ACT

SHOT
NER
VILLA

ole Holds
Stopper"

IAL" SPECIAL

Arsenal 7

Massie.

Spot...bout

Remarkable as it may seem, play was fairly ven from a territorial point of view. But Villa's ttack was shipwrecked on the rock-like de-ence of the champions.

Wilson did not have an idle time in goal, bu most of the shots with which he had to deal ere of a hopeless variety. He was covered so well by the rest of the defence and the Villa were such poor finishers that one goal for the ome side was about their due.

There was one weak link in the Arsenal attack. owden, playing a singularly in-and-out game. e would make a brilliant move and then muff he next hopelessly, while his shooting was retched.

Drake scored a hat-trick in the first half, but n one occasion he appeared to be off-side when he ball was deflected to him by a Villa defender. In the first five minutes of the second half e added another two, and had scored a sixth hen Palethorpe headed in Villa's solitary one. ate in the game the Arsenal centre forward eaded number seven.

Palethorpe deserved a goal for his whole-earted work in face of a most difficult task. or he got little support from the other members f the line with the exception of Astley.

Massie, the Scottish international, made his ebut at Villa Park, but he, too, had a most difficult job. His defence did not impress, but e did show some nice touches constructively.

The ... game were Wa... practically ... ck, who left wing tr... Charlton's The war ... d Welsh.

BEDS & HERTS
Evening Telegraph

RADIO—PAGE 4

FINAL

No. 1161 Registered at the GPO as a Newspaper · MONDAY, APRIL 13, 1936 · Sun Rises 5.11 a.m. Sets 6.51 p.m. Lighting-up Time 7.21 p.m. London · ONE PENNY

TOWN FIND A GOAL-GETTER AT LAST

MASTERS SAY WOMAN'S CANINGS MAKE BOYS LAUGH

A demand that all boys above infant age should be taught by men teachers was unanimously made by the Schoolmasters' Conference at Sheffield to-day.

Mr. A. H. Russell, Bristol said that if the State refused the demand of the boy's ?ul for the control of a man, the State ? definitely injuring the boy's develop ?t.

?n the schools where headmistresses in ?d corporal punishment on boys, the ?

PAYNE'S AMAZING FIRST APPEARANCE AS CENTRE

Luton Run Into Double Figures Against Bristol Rovers

By CRUSADER

There was nothing very spring-like about the weather ?his afternoon and Luton Town football ground was a very cold and cheerless place ? for the brightness ?
? was ver ?

The Town r.?h? w.?g put in some pretty work but Payne was pulled up for push ing Mackey rather wildly conceded a corner when both Smith and Dolman had the ball covered and from the flag kick Crisp headed over
Widsen th sent ?
pas.? ?

Crisp got away to force a corner. Mackey clearing.

Dolman had to save a long shot from the right. Crisp got over a good centre but there was no one up to tackle Smith
Roberts made a sharp run through the middle and drove in a hard shot that Ellis brilliantly turned round the upright
From the flag kick Payne headed over

PAYNE'S HALF DOZEN

Earley got through to centre but Mackey cleared.

Godfrey paved the way for the next goal with a clever pass to Stephenson, who raced straight through and then gave PAYNE a perfect pass. The goalkeeper again had no chance with the drive.

A free kick to the Rovers brought a header from Hartul but Dolman was at home for .t, and in another visit by the Rovers Crisp was offside.

Along pass up the left wing sent Stephenson clean through.
He centred grandly for PAYNE to head another fine goal, Ellis being hopelessly placed.

Roberts had another chance to reach double figures bol doing clever work by Martin, but he managed to lift the ball over from a very difficult angle
A nice ? ?me to ?tephen ?

JOE PAYNE

before the interval, when PAYNE completed his hat trick.

The move originated on the left wing and when Roberts shot in Payne collared the ball and gave Ellis no chance from close range.
Half-time came

?TON TOWN
? ROV?

The reserve who made 10-goal history

Wages of £4 a week and a £2 bonus for a win: that was the price of a record that is likely to stand for all time. Six pounds for cracking in 10 goals in a 12-0 victory: scarcely a fortune, but Joe Payne, the man who did just that, was well satisfied. For he set that record in 1936, and football in the pre-War thirties was a far cry from today's sophisticated world of agents and managers, of syndicated articles and television appearances.

In today's game of massed defences, of 4-2-4 and 4-3-3, any player who scored 10 times in one game—though an unlikely event—would be whisked off to the nearest television studio and headlines would scream of his triumph.

But it was not like that in 1936. In those days men played the game because it offered a fair

> **23 minutes:** Seized on long punt upfield that McArthur (Bristol) missed, and beat advancing goalkeeper Ellis.
> Ellis pushed out ?

living when fair livings were not that easy to find. There were few frills for the stalwarts of the Third Division; no sun lamps or sauna baths. Those were the days, too, of maximum wages. Footballers did their best and were more than content to earn a regular first-team place with the prospect of a modest retirement.

Joe Payne was such a footballer. A Derbyshire lad, a coalminer with a flair for football, he arrived at Luton after being spotted as a bustling centre-forward with his local colliery team in Bolsover.

By Easter, 1936, it seemed that it had not been such a good idea. Payne had been tried at centre-forward in Luton's reserves and had been rejected. Luton's manager Ned Liddell, sizing up Payne's muscular physique, had decided to

Luton's manager, Ned Liddell, whose shrewd guidance kept Luton near the top of their division, decided to give Payne another chance when both his recognized centre-forwards were injured.

convert him into a defender. By April of that year Payne had made only three first-team appearances, none of them in the attack, and was considered a reserve wing-half of no more than average ability.

At that time only one team went up from each section of the Third Division. Luton, who had a useful side, were challenging for the Third Division South championship. Luton were among the front-runners by sheer endeavour and shrewd management, fighting it out with Coventry City and Reading. Their chances looked good.

For teams challenging for promotion or trying to stave off relegation, Easter was a hectic time. So when Easter Monday arrived and Ned Liddell had a long list of injured players, he was confronted with serious problems. For example, both the recognized first-team centre-forwards, Ball and Boyd, were out of action. Who could Liddell play in that position? He weighed the possible permutations, and decided that with Bristol Rovers having a difficult time and not expected to present a particularly severe challenge, why not give Payne another chance, this time as leader of the attack? After all, he had been signed to score goals and, anyway, it was really a case of Hobson's choice.

Payne, 22, was in the dressing-room. He had reported to the ground, as a reserve wing-half, little thinking that he would be asked to play. Liddell approached him, tossed a shirt into his hands and said: 'You're in, lad. At centre-

> **40 minutes:** Ellis pushed out a shot by Stephenson. Ball went to Payne, who easily scored.

forward. Do your best. Get a couple of goals if you can.'

So the teams jogged out on to the well-worn Kenilworth Road pitch. A crowd of some 13,000 holiday fans had turned up, braving the unseasonable icy cold. Thin, stinging rain fell, later to turn to sleet.

Payne was determined to take his big chance, but for the first half-hour or so he saw little of the ball and when he did, he was seldom able to elude the hard tackles of Murray, the Bristol centre-half.

But Luton were completely on top. Their forwards, prompted by outside-left Stephenson and canny inside-right George Martin, later to manage the club, regularly beat the defence and

Ellis, in the Rovers' goal, was a very busy man.

He was also becoming somewhat disheartened. For every time he punted the ball clear of his box one or other of the home attackers would return it, zig-zagging a way through an unimaginative defence. Rich and Roberts for Luton, had brilliant efforts parried. The example of his colleagues gave Payne new confidence.

Twelve minutes or so before the interval the Bolsover boy broke his duck. The ball came over from the left, Payne soared higher than his

43 minutes: Close-range shot after Roberts had centred from the left.

challengers and it was in the back of the net. Between then and the half-time whistle Luton added another three goals, two of them from the man who was playing only because his manager had been forced to take a chance on an unproved reserve!

In the warmth of the dressing-room Payne was elated. Colleagues congratulated and kidded him. 'If you're not careful you'll break Bob Bell's record,' they joked.

The previous Boxing Day Bell, Tranmere Rovers' centre-forward, had scored nine times against Oldham Athletic in a fantastic 13-4 victory. This was a match the statisticians said, with some justification, would forever hold its place in the record books. Nine goals from one player—and he had also missed a penalty!

49 minutes: Roberts-Stephenson run on left wing. Payne met Stephenson's centre and crashed the ball into the net.

Payne joined in the laughter. That record, he knew, could be in no danger. Yet he was certain he had more goals in him, more to give to the crowd that buzzed with excitement as they talked about the young man who, after such an ordinary start, had so suddenly set the game alight.

They forgot the sleet. Could Payne, they asked, add to his tally? Even if he did not they were at least satisfied that the club had unearthed a new star. They knew, too, that their favourites, in this mood, were going to give Rovers a thrashing

55 minutes: Centre from Rich. Payne headed the ball down to his feet and beat Ellis.

that would be long remembered in those parts.

Luton trotted out buoyantly to a great cheer, with Payne receiving a special ovation, the sort reserved for the youngster who has suddenly made good.

Rovers were more chastened. Their steps were heavy as they took up their positions. They knew they could not win. Their job now was the mundane one of checking a side heady with the smell of success, and to put in his place the russet-haired leader who had been transformed from clumsy novice into a deadly marksman in 12 eventful minutes.

But how could they shackle Payne? The man thrown in at the deep end by Liddell was now totally elusive. Far from being the weak link, Payne was the driving force of an attack that

57 minutes: That who-scored-it scramble goal awarded to Payne after his header.

could afford to play cheeky, almost exhibition, football. Nothing they tried failed. Every move had the stamp of success.

The hapless Ellis threw himself this way and that. He leaped and dived and, in fact, played a reasonable game; the catastrophe was certainly not of his making. But he was living through a nightmare that was to haunt him for months.

Inevitably, Payne was soon on the mark again. With Stephenson repeatedly ghosting his way through the Rovers' defence and then sending the ball accurately into the Bristol Rovers goalmouth, more goals just had to come. After the game, Payne was quoted by Frank Poxon, sports writer of the late *News Chronicle*, as saying 'It would be silly on my part to say that it was all

A reserve wing-half, Joe Payne was suddenly chosen as Luton's centre-forward against Bristol Rovers. Payne responded by scoring ten goals and securing a place in football history.

luck, for I do believe I played well. I am a very happy fellow. But please give praise to Stephenson, who made nearly all our goals.'

Poxon himself wrote: 'Payne proved that when a chance comes along his brain is packed with ice.' Packed with ice it seemed as he struck three times to complete his second hat-trick, taking his chances coolly and with all the prudence of a man with years of experience.

For Ellis, the Bristol Rovers goalkeeper, the game against Luton became a nightmare that was to haunt him for months. In fact, Ellis was not to blame for the devastating scoreline.

Then, with Rovers in utter chaos, he outjumped the defence and headed the ball down. The ball seemed to have been partially stopped by Ellis but Martin thundered in and bundled ball and goalkeeper into the back of the net. Who had scored? The crowd did not know until afterwards that the referee had judged the ball already over the line before Martin's challenge. And Martin never dreamed of claiming the goal for himself, especially after Payne went on to score three more.

65 minutes: Godfrey passed to Stephenson. He cut through, and his centre to Payne was perfectly made and perfectly taken.

Luton did not let up and Payne inexplicably could do no wrong. Each time he touched the ball the crowd stilled momentarily, but more often than not it was only to take breath to roar their appreciation of yet another goal.

The 90 memorable minutes flew by all too quickly. Ninety minutes in which Dolman, in the Luton goal, had little to do but watch after the first, preliminary skirmishes, and in which 'Ten-Goal Payne' was conceived, born and matured into a goal-scoring machine who was later to play for Chelsea and England.

Against Bristol he scored with headers and shots and once, from a sitting position in which he turned round on his muddy backside and converted a half-chance into a goal by sticking out a leg.

76 minutes: Another Stephenson centre and another fine header left Ellis helpless.

Even after that, though, Luton did not win promotion. They were pipped by Coventry who went up with 57 points, one more than the Town. But promotion was not long delayed. Luton made it the following year, beating Torquay United in their final match to clinch their place in Division Two. The winning goals were scored by Payne.

In 1938 Payne was transferred to Chelsea. The fee was a ridiculous one by today's standards: £2,000. But war was just around the corner, and in 1939 it came. League football was aban-

84 minutes: Stephenson forced a corner, took it himself, and Payne headed his ninth.

doned and the stars were called up. Payne still played as often as he could but twice broke his right ankle in 1942—ironically in matches that meant nothing. He was later to play for West Ham and Millwall, but he was never quite the same again.

His 10-goal feat has faded in Payne's memory. He recalls the match that made him a star only patchily and is more concerned with golf. He would have liked, he says, to have concentrated on it 'and maybe made a bit of a name for myself at that'. He was an accomplished cricketer, too, but football is the game for which he will forever be remembered.

Joe Payne is somewhat critical of modern football. 'Too much defensive play, too many petty fouls and too much money for the players.'

86 minutes: Payne fell, but shot as he lay on the ground.

It is easy to understand his condemnation of massed defences. For Payne was a footballer with only one mission—to get the ball past the enemy. It was a mission he accomplished to perfection, as the football records testify to this day. And 'Too much money for the players'? Bearing in mind the £6 he earned on his greatest day it is not really too difficult to understand why Joe Payne says that, too.

Luton Town: Dolman, Mackey, Smith, Finlayson, Nelson, Godfrey, Rich, Martin, Payne, Roberts, Stephenson.
Bristol Rovers: Ellis, Pickering, Preece, Wallington, Murray, Young, Barley, Hartill, Harris, Houghton, Crisp.

ALBERT WILKES

ALBERT WILKES

COURTESY BRISTOL EVENING POST/ARTWORK ROY FLOOKS

Hitler 3 England 6

During the late sixties the South Africans discovered to their cost that politics cannot be separated from sport—and they were not the first. In May 1938, with Europe moving to the verge of the Second World War, England met Nazi Germany in the huge Olympic Stadium in Berlin. Everyone, not least the England players, was well aware that it was to be far more than a mere football match—that the Nazis would use victory as propaganda for the master-race.

Only three years earlier, Germany had gone down 1-0 to England at Tottenham without putting up much of a resistance—with the exception of the left-back, Muezenberg, who had done surprisingly well against the brilliantly elusive Stanley Matthews. But to play in Berlin in front of 110,000 fanatical spectators was wholly another matter. Besides, the Germans had significantly widened their catchment area. The Anschluss had taken place, Austria was technically part of 'Greater Germany', and this in turn meant that the Germans could call on Austrian star players, though in this match it was only Pesser who played.

Eddie Hapgood, then the elegant, highly patriotic left-back and captain of England, has written about his own feelings on the approaching game. 'All who were likely to be connected with the forthcoming German trip', he says in his autobiography, *Football Ambassador*, 'and many others besides, sensed that this was not merely a football match but something deeper, a challenge from Germany which England had to answer, and not only to answer, but to defeat.'

The England party, which included no fewer than five players from London clubs, all of them picked for the Berlin team, left cheerfully from Harwich to sail for the Hook of Holland, and thence to travel overland to Berlin. Air travel, for footballers at least, was still a rare experience. The wing-halves, stocky Ken Willingham of Huddersfield Town, and burly Don Welsh of Charlton Athletic, were in especially buoyant spirits.

Cliff Bastin, typically phlegmatic, would make up a left-wing partnership with brisk little Len Goulden, of West Ham United. The only previous occasion on which they had played together was 12 years previously, for the England schoolboys' team. Bastin, who had been much impressed by the profusion of uniforms when he played in Fascist Rome against Italy in 1933—Hapgood's first international—was this time surprised by the relative lack of them in Berlin.

Tom Whittaker, Arsenal's celebrated trainer, was England's trainer once again, though the team travelled, as usual, without either a manager . . . or a doctor. The players found the immense Olympic Stadium, where the Games themselves had taken place two years before, impressive. 'The pitch,' Hapgood wrote, 'was if anything slightly better even than Wembley's famous Cumberland turf.' The only negative aspect was that the team's dressing-rooms were set high up in the very roof of the main stand. It took a long weary climb to get there.

When British athletes refused to salute, the Nazi crowd was furious

The German team had been away for special training in the Black Forest. 'Sun-bronzed giants', Hapgood called them, and the English players knew when they met them, in all their Aryan splendour, that they would have a tough job ahead of them. Matthews, however, remarked with satisfaction that Muenzenberg, his stumbling-block at Tottenham, looked measurably older.

And so to the question of the Nazi salute. Two years earlier, at the opening ceremony of the Olympic Games, the Great Britain team had caused Nazi resentment by refusing to give either the Nazi or the Olympic salute—the right arm held outwards, rather than upwards. Simply, as they went by Adolf Hitler, they gave the Fuhrer an 'eyes right'—which may well have gone unnoticed.

There have been controversial accounts about who first suggested that the England team should give the Nazi salute at that match in 1938. According to Eddie Hapgood, it was the secretary of the Football Association, then plain Mr Stanley Rous, who proposed it to Sir Nevile Henderson, the pro-appeasement British ambassador to Nazi Germany. The story continues that Henderson

thankfully agreed with the suggestion.

In fact, what really seems to have happened was this. Stanley Rous and Charles Wreford Brown, the distinguished Corinthian who was senior FA official on the tour, consulted Henderson on what was the best thing to do. Rous says that Henderson asked that the team give the 'heil Hitler' sign. He and Wreford Brown agreed, mainly because they had been present at the Olympics and Sir Stanley had also seen a further athletics meeting when the French had remained with their arms obstinately at their sides. 'It seemed foolish to create such antagonism from the crowd,' he said. He added, 'Also, at that time, it seemed more of a courtesy gesture to the host country, rather than an endorsement of the Nazi regime.' Henderson had told him that he himself was in the habit of saluting the Fuhrer in this manner whenever he had an audience with him in his capacity as British ambassador.

Accounts about the English team's reception of the decision also differ. In Hapgood's eyes, the team was from the British Empire, and he could see no reason for giving the Nazi salute. 'They should understand that we always stand to attention for every national anthem.' He says that, when he told the rest of the players, 'there was much muttering in the ranks.'

But Rous refutes this. 'They all accepted it at the time. The row really started later.' And there certainly was a row. Leading articles in all the papers, letters to *The Times*—everyone seemed to have something to say about it. But pictures of the team's salute, showing them with their arms held out straight and true, certainly seem to show that Rous's account is the correct one. Indeed, Cliff Bastin, self-contained as always, wrote in his book *Cliff Bastin Remembers*: 'I did not feel very strongly about the incident.... We gave our own salute immediately afterwards, and it seemed to me that this palliated any indignity there might have been in stretching out our right arms in the Nazi fashion.'

It is also worth recording that, despite the scandal of the salute, the Football Association the following year obliged the England team playing Italy in Milan to give the Fascist salute to all four corners of the ground.

However, when the match began, all thought of politics was forgotten—and this was an extremely good match.

The England team was interesting, not least for the fact that it flung a 19-year-old inside-right, Jackie Robinson, in at the deep end for his first international match. It was also a

Above left Chancellor Adolf Hitler stands proudly in the new stadium he built in Berlin for the 1936 Olympic Games. Nazi Germany was going to show the world what the master-race could do. But, as the greatest athletes of the world marched past the rostrum with their arms held out in the Nazi salute, his pride turned to fury as the British contingent obstinately kept their arms at their sides. The crowd, too, howled with anger, so loudly that the officials on the FA tour two years later, Stanley Rous and Charles Wreford Brown, were happy to fall in with the British ambassador's suggestion that the team give a Nazi salute before the match left—mainly to pacify the crowd. The salute may have pleased the German fans, but back home it stirred up one of the biggest rows in the history of football. Though the football was exciting enough—the picture on the right shows a brave save from goalkeeper Woodley—it was the politics that took the limelight. Captain Eddie Hapgood top right wrote later that when he told the rest of the players about the decision, 'there was much muttering in the ranks'. Sir Stanley Rous centre right refutes this. 'They all accepted it at the time,' he said. 'The row really started later.' Cliff Bastin bottom right, phlegmatic as always, backed up Sir Stanley's account by saying, 'I did not feel very strongly about the incident. . . . We gave our own salute immediately afterwards.' The stiff and correct salutes of the team seem to show no objection to the decision.

bold piece of selection, in those days of the dreadnought centre-forward, to prefer a small, quick, subtle player like Frankie Broome, who had just finished an excellent season with Villa.

It was a roasting hot day and Stanley Rous was proved right in at least one respect, when the huge German crowd gave an ecstatic response to England's Nazi salute. A few English voices managed to make themselves heard out of the bedlam: 'Let them have it, England!' they pleaded, and their appeal was heeded.

It soon became clear that whatever had happened in 1935 at Tottenham, Matthews now had the beating of Muezenberg. After 16 minutes, he put over a centre. Jakob, the German goalkeeper, could only punch it out, and Bastin silenced the crowd with a powerful right-footed volley into the net. Hitler was not present to see this—he was out of Berlin—but the Chancellor's deputy Herman Goering watched the match resplendent in a cream uniform, weighed down by a panoply of medals. To assist him, he had brought along an immense pair of field glasses, which at one point he was focusing on the English goal while England were scoring at the other end; a fact which Nevile Henderson gently pointed out to him.

Bad marking at a corner allowed Germany to equalize only three minutes later, and the crowd's hopes were alive again. But, despite the heat and the noisy partisanship, England took firm hold of the game. Jackie Robinson, totally unaffected by the nature of the occasion, was having a splendid match. He put England back into the lead again, Frankie Broome made it 3-1 and, before half-time, Stanley Matthews got one of his beautiful goals to send England up to their remote dressing-room 4-1 ahead.

Despite the presence of Austrian talent, Germany were showing their familiar inability to produce the unexpected. One of the first continental teams to embrace the third-back game with its stopper centre-half, they had excellent footballers such as Szepan, the captain, and Kitzinger, who later that year would play for the Rest of Europe against England at Tottenham. But it was many years before they began to breed the kind of individualists who would make them a real power in world football.

Len Goulden's goal— a fitting climax to an impressive victory

England's lead had clearly ended the game as a contest, and in the second half, each team scored a couple more goals. No doubt England would have done better had Bastin not been hurt, and obliged to limp through the rest of the game—there were no substitutes in those days.

Jackie Robinson, whom Bastin described as 'the sensation of the match, running circles round the German defenders', got another goal for England, Gauchel, the centre-forward, the second for Germany when Vic Woodley missed the ball at a corner. The third German goal arrived when the ball bounced off Ken Willingham's studs to Germany's left-winger. But England had a last, highly spectacular, shot left in their locker.

It came from Len Goulden, their little Cockney inside-left; a gloriously powerful left-footed volley from outside the penalty area which flashed past Jakob virtually before he could move. It was a fitting climax to an impressive victory.

Whatever the rights and wrongs of the famous Nazi salute, there is little doubt that it gave some of the English players a burning will to win.

Germany: Jakob, Janes, Muezenberg, Kupfer, Goldbrunner, Kitzinger, Lehner, Gellesch, Gauchel, Szepan, Pesser.
England: Woodley, Sproston, Hapgood, Willingham, Young, Welsh, Matthews, Robinson, Broome, Goulden, Bastin.

Wolves sign away the FA Cup

Below *Freddie Worrall, Portsmouth's outside-right, fastens his manager's 'lucky spats'. Jack Tinn was a colourful figure who realized the value of publicity and psychology in getting his team into a relaxed frame of mind for the Final with Wolves.*
Right top *Two minutes from half-time, Anderson beats Scott to put unfancied Pompey two goals up.*
Right centre *Sixty seconds into the second half, Scott fails to prevent Parker forcing a third goal.*
Right bottom *After a crisp centre from Worrall, Parker headed Portsmouth's fourth, only the second time a club had scored that many in a Wembley Final.*

The scoreline of the 1939 Cup Final reads Portsmouth 4 Wolverhampton Wanderers 1. As a cold fact, that suggests nothing more than a convincing Portsmouth victory. But at the time, it meant sensation, for just about the strongest favourites ever to contest a Cup Final had been soundly drubbed.

It was an enormous upset—for Wolves, their supporters, and for the general public. For Portsmouth, it was the success they deserved after years of footballing endeavour that had brought them little if any reward.

Through the threadbare years of the thirties, through the years of economic disaster, and the slide to a second World War, Portsmouth FC battled without success. They had ended the twenties by losing 2-0 at Wembley, in the FA Cup Final, after holding Bolton Wanderers, the greatest Cup fighters of the decade, for 78 minutes.

In 1934 Portsmouth were back at Wembley. They had fought their way past Manchester United, Grimsby, Swansea, Bolton and Leicester City, and there were many who fancied they could beat Manchester City in the Final. When Rutherford put Portsmouth ahead after 26 minutes they seemed on their way to victory but, with less than 20 minutes to go, an injury to centre-half Jimmy Allen saw the dream explode in their faces. While Portsmouth officials worked desperately on Allen, lying injured beside one of the goals, Fred Tilson, the Manchester No 9, scored twice in the last 17 minutes to give Lancashire another Cup triumph. So Portsmouth had again failed the last hurdle.

Now, in 1939, despite a poor League record, Portsmouth were again in the Final. But there was little to suggest that they would fare any better than the last time, especially as their opponents were to be Wolves, runners-up to Everton for the Championship. These were the Wolves of Major Frank Buckley—Stan Cullis, Dizzy Burton, Denis Westcott—the glamour team of the Midlands, all Molineux, long ball and old gold. Wolves powered to Wembley with the irresistible surge of an express train. Bradford went down 3-1, Leicester City 5-1, Liverpool 4-1. In the sixth round Wolves became racing certainties for the Cup when they put out Everton, the League champions, 2-0. All Wolves' ties had so far been at Molineux. But they showed how little ground advantage counted when, with Westcott hammering four goals in the semi-final at Old Trafford, they routed Grimsby Town 5-0, a Grimsby then in the top half of Division One.

Portsmouth, too, were favoured with four ties at home. Third Division Lincoln City presented no difficulty and were beaten 4-0, and two mid-table Second Division clubs, West Bromwich and West Ham, were seen off by two goals to nil. In the sixth round, Portsmouth faced Preston North End, eight places above them in the League. Ground advantage just swung it for Pompey who got the only goal. Then, in the semi-final at Highbury, they moved on past the beaten finalists of the previous season, Huddersfield Town, by the odd goal in three.

And so Portsmouth returned to Wembley for their third Cup Final in ten years. No one gave them a chance, however, against the young and brilliant Wolverhampton team built around Cullis. Perhaps it was their youth, that vibrant quality which had swept them triumphantly through the season, which let Wolves down at the crucial moment. Certainly no one could have foreseen the

KEYSTONE

TOPIX

Above *Jack Tinn leads Portsmouth out. In those days Wembley stadium was without its now familiar tunnel.*

lush turf made slippery by steady rain began to hinder them as much as the nimble Portsmouth players did.

With 29 minutes gone Wolves paid for their surprising slackness in marking. Anderson, the Portsmouth centre-forward, found himself in possession with yards of room to move about and he was able to measure his pass to Barlow waiting 12 yards from the Wolves' goal. Bert Barlow had been transferred from Molineux to Fratton Park in February and he did not play in Pompey's Cup side until the semi-final. Then he scored the first goal and now he did it again—this time against his old club—with a carefully placed shot dead into the corner of the net.

The first goal has always meant a great deal at Wembley. There was then no thought of going on the defensive. Portsmouth attacked harder than before and showed the speed on the ball that had been expected of the dithering Wolves. Two minutes from half-time the unfancied team from the south coast went further ahead. Centre-forward Anderson outwitted Cullis who was fatally late with his tackle. Scott flung himself at a swift shot, got his finger-tips to the ball, but that was all. In between the posts it went—Anderson's seventh goal in the competition.

Anderson had now scored in every round except the fifth. Westcott scored for Wolves in every tie except the Final, his tally being eleven. Imagine the sensation it would create to-day if the rival leaders in a Cup Final could claim 18 goals between them!

Portsmouth, three goals up, were just toying with the mighty Wolves...

So Wolves were two down. This was a shattering blow to them, made worse by the withering blast which they received less than 60 seconds after the restart. Barlow let fly from the edge of the penalty area and Scott allowed the greasy ball to slip from his grasp. He might have prevented it rolling over the line but Parker, Pompey's outside-left, was too quick for him, forcing the ball home as Scott made an agonized, convulsive jerk to check it.

Wolves retained a flicker of interest in the game when eight minutes later Dicky Dorsett took a short pass from Westcott and drove it past Walker.

With just 19 minutes remaining Portsmouth became only the second club to score four goals in a Wembley Final. It was this goal that finally killed the odds-on favourites and fittingly it was the goal of the day. The flying heels of Worrall took him clear on the right and Parker, tearing in at full speed from the opposite flank, put his cross wide of Scott with a beautifully judged header that flew into Wolves' net.

For the rest of the game Portsmouth toyed with Wolves. When the referee sounded the end of the game, Portsmouth had four goals to Wolves' one. As that most remarkable of women, Helen Keller, once said, 'You can do anything you want if you stick at it long enough.' In Portsmouth's case it took ten years, but when Jimmy Guthrie, later to become the militant post-War spokesman of a rapidly-emerging Players' Union, fulfilled his final duty for the season as captain of Portsmouth by accepting the Cup from King George VI, those years seemed well worth it.

Guthrie turned, showed the Cup to the crowd, looked at the rain and refused to take it on the customary triumphal parade to the dressing-room. It was probably one of the few moments in his life that he was at a loss for words, but he felt that he could not allow a single drop of rain to fall upon this symbol of the near unattainable.

Portsmouth: Walker, Morgan, Rochford, Guthrie, Rowe, Wharton, Worrall, McAlinden, Anderson, Barlow, Parker.

Wolverhampton Wanderers: Scott, Morris, Taylor, Gailey, Cullis, Gardiner, Burton, McIntosh, Westcott, Dorsett, Maguire.

way in which their mental anguish was revealed to Portsmouth before the game.

Half-an-hour before the kick-off, the official autograph book arrived in the Portsmouth dressing-room after going the rounds of the Wolves' dressing-room. The signatures of the Wolves players were such shaky scrawls that the Portsmouth players were unable to recognize them.

As soon as Jack Tinn, the Portsmouth manager, saw those Wolves signatures, he gave a great shout of mingled glee and triumph. 'You've got 'em lads. They're paralyzed with fright; look at these signatures. And you've drawn No 1 dressing-room, the lucky dressing-room at Wembley. All the omens are right. It's your day, it's got to be.'

And while Wolves sat white-faced, watching the minutes drag away, there was noise and hilarity in the Portsmouth dressing-room. For besides the boost that autograph book had given their morale, Tinn had got a show business pal to come along and play court jester.

Jack Tinn was a shrewd, indestructible manager, a kind of forerunner to Bill Shankly.

Once when travelling to a Cup replay at Norwich, he was wearing an actor's-type overcoat—somewhat on the flamboyant side. In it Tinn had put a label which said 'Stolen from Bud Flanagan.'

In many ways, Tinn was ahead of his time as a football manager. He realized the value of psychology, of publicity, of kidology, of colour. Countering Major Buckley's 'monkey gland' treatment—very much a press fabrication—was a very real 'Jack Tinn and his lucky spats'—two of the early gimmicks of big-time professional football.

So Tinn got his team into a relaxed, confident frame of mind. They went out and set about Wolves like a bunch of sailors on their first shore-going spree after a six-month voyage.

Early on, Scott, the Wolves goalkeeper, running out to intercept a cross, was bundled off the ball near the penalty-spot, and when Worrall lobbed it quickly into the goalmouth, there had to be desperate work by the other Wolves defenders to prevent a shock goal. That disquieting moment did nothing to improve Wolves' nerves, and the

Unlucky thirteen

It must be difficult for most football followers to visualize Newport County as a Second Division club. Their post-War history has seen them totter from one disaster to another and their ground, Somerton Park, has taken on the identity of a 'Hard Times Hall' of soccer. For the most part their pre-War story was distressingly similar, and as someone once said 'Newport is like Naples—it lives permanently on the edge of a volcano.' Yet just once this club which has known every unpleasant experience that can befall a first class outfit won national acclaim as the No. 1 club of Wales.

The biggest win in the League's history— after a missed penalty

Their moment of glory came in 1938-39 season when they won the Third Division South, finishing three points clear of runners-up Crystal Palace. Their rise had been quick, but so was their fall. And on the way down, they created history of a bitter kind. On October 5 1946 they met Newcastle United at Gallowgate and lost 13-0—the record defeat for the division, and only once equalled in any other League match.

But all this was the unseen future in 1937 when Newport were one of the traditional strugglers of the Third Division South. Their manager, Jimmy Hindmarsh, was typical of the unsung men who, because of their love of game and club, help football survive against all the probable odds. Hindmarsh gave over 20 years of his life and some of his wages to keep Newport County alive and then walked out into obscurity to, as he said, 'give someone else a chance to turn the club's luck.'

County then got that 'someone else', and he turned the luck in a fashion which in two years had the football world shaking its head in disbelief. His name was Billy McCandless, a tough, sawn-off, little Irishman who as a full-back with Linfield and Glasgow Rangers had collected many international caps. In 1938 Newport finished with six teams below them. This was the highest position the club had occupied since 1928! Against this embarrassing background of sustained non-success Newport County came up to the starting line for season 1938-39—the last nationally competitive campaign for seven years. It was as if the side's 'success' of the previous season had been greatly magnified, for they stormed through to win the championship of the Third Division South—a moment without parallel in the history of the Monmouthshire rugby stronghold.

'I didn't start from rock-bottom; I started 100 yards below it'

But history played a cruel trick on Newport in their moment of triumph. Just seven days after they began their Division Two career the Second World War began and, unable to use Somerton Park, the club became inactive. Even so, in those seven days Newport County played Southampton at Somerton Park and beat them 3-1. In midweek, Tottenham Hotspur appeared there and were held to a 1-1 draw and on the following Saturday, less than 24 hours before Neville Chamberlain's voice coming through on radio sets told the nation 'We are once again at War with Germany', Newport lost 1-2 away to Nottingham Forest.

It was a start which suggested that this fine

Left above Charlie Wayman scored four times for Newcastle but, had he not missed a penalty, they might have established a new record win.
Far left 'Wor' Jackie Milburn who scored twice and *left* Roy Bentley (in stripes on right) who claimed the thirteenth and final goal.
Opposite page Len Shackleton who, in his debut game for Newcastle, scored six times. His comment afterwards was that 'the game could not have been more successful for me had I planned the whole 90 minutes.'

Avenue for £13,000, at that time the third biggest fee ever paid. What they saw far surpassed their hopes. With the game only two minutes old Newcastle were awarded a penalty-kick which was shot wide. For some strange reason it was later widely believed that the man who missed that spot-kick was Shackleton when in fact the guilty party was Newcastle's No. 9 Charlie Wayman.

But who among the vast crowd would, at that moment, have taken a bet that before half-time not one but two Newcastle forwards would register hat-tricks? Within three minutes of his miss, Wayman had put United in front and before the game was a quarter of an hour old had added another. In between, Shackleton had joined the select band of players who can say they scored on debut. Before the game was a third over Wayman had completed his hat-trick and 'Shack' had missed an absolute sitter. (Was this possibly the reason over the confusion of memory regarding that missed penalty?) By that time Newport's hotch-potch of veterans and inexperienced players were completely demoralized and with a display of dazzling individual virtuosity Shackleton now scored three times in the space of six minutes. Newport reeled off at half-time seven down with Shackleton having scored four and Wayman three.

Though Newcastle's defence did not match the brilliance of their attack—and this was to cost them no fewer than 13 defeats that season—on this day they had no problems.

The second half continued in the same vein as the first. Poor, sadly outclassed Newport could not live on the same pitch as United's gifted attackers and they conceded another six goals. Shackleton hit two more to bring his personal total to six in his first game in the black and white stripes of 'The Magpies', Jackie Milburn swooped in from the wing to grab a couple of goals, Wayman netted his fourth and Roy Bentley put his name on the scorers' list, leaving Pearson the only forward who failed to score. Some gallant saves by Newport keeper Turner and a string of near misses were the only reason Newcastle United did not get 20 goals that day.

Instead the final score was Newcastle United 13, Newport County 0, and Wayman's miss from the penalty spot denied his side the distinction of becoming the only team in over 80 years of Football League history to score 14 in one match. It was, however, the largest margin separating two teams in the history of the First and Second Divisions, equalling the 13-0 victory of Stockport County over Halifax Town in the Third Division North in 1934.

Yet the last laugh belonged to Newport and not to United

But there was a somewhat ironic epilogue to the annihilation of Newport County by Newcastle United. The first post-War season had to be extended until June 14 1947 due to the severe winter plus a Government ban on mid-week football for economic reasons and on June 7 Newport County staged their final match as members of the Second Division. It was at Somerton Park and their opponents were Newcastle United. County, all hopes and all cares gone, turned on their best display of the season and finding the gaps in that shaky United defence, won 4-2. On the same day Chesterfield beat Sheffield Wednesday at Saltergate by the same score when George Milburn scored a hat-trick of penalties in the space of 22 minutes. These results meant that Chesterfield pushed Newcastle into fifth place and so at the death United not only missed promotion but failed to qualify for talent money which was then paid to the first four teams in the table. It was a wry revenge for Newport.

Newcastle United: Garbutt, Cowell, Graham, Harvey, Brennan, Wright, Milburn, Bentley, Wayman, Shackleton, Pearson.
Newport County: Turner, Hodge, Oldham, Rawcliffe, Low, Cabrie, Davies, Wookey, Craddock, McNab, Bowen.

side built up in a couple of seasons by McCandless could have easily held its own in Division Two. Then suddenly there was nothing. The Army took over Somerton Park and Newport County were forced to accept six years of idleness, six years which destroyed the 1939 side.

When Newport competed in the first Second Division programme after the war they were taken over by Tom Bromilow, the former England and Liverpool half-back. Said Tom: 'I didn't start from rock-bottom but a hundred yards below it.' The pitch, always one of the muddiest in Britain, was derelict, the chicken coop of a stand dilapidated—he could not even find equipment for the players to wear. There could only be one outcome. County, with 133 goals shot past them, were relegated. Another nine points would not have saved them. When they travelled to Tyneside on the first Saturday in October they were already bottom and three points behind the next side.

Their opponents Newcastle United were already being called the new Bank of England side and tipped everywhere to regain their rightful place in Division One. The value of their forward line in the 1970s would, at a conservative estimate, have been around three-quarters of a million.

A crowd of 52,137 assembled in anticipation of a big win by United and to run the rule over Len Shackleton, just signed from Bradford Park

Aston Villa rally failed

Aston Villa 4, Manchester United 6

EVERYTHING which gives drama to football happened at Villa Park . . . a goal in the first 13 seconds; unexcelled attacking play by Manchester United which made five goals before half-time seem child's play; a fighting come-back by Villa; a penalty with nine minutes to go which gave Villa a chance of forcing a replay, and a goal two minutes from the end to make Manchester United's entry into the fourth round certain.

On their first-half form, no side in the country oculd have checked Manchester United. The ball was pushed along the ground into open spaces, feints suddenly changed the direction of attack, and a man was always left unmarked with a clear shot at goal.

Four goals down against this super-side, Villa surprised even their own crowd by their second-half display. Quick tackling took the smoothness out of the United attacks, and instead it was the Villa forwards who, without the same method as their opponents, started to get goals.

A penalty goal by Dorsett in the 81st minute brought United out of their lethargy—and only just in time. The last five minutes again saw the perfect football machine in action, and two minutes from time Pearson scored their sixth goal almost nonchalantly.

Goalscorers were: Edwards (Villa), 13½ secs.; Rowley (United), 6 mins.; Morris (United), 17 mins.; Pearson (United), 29 mins.; Morris (United), 31 mins.; Delaney (United), 42 mins.; Edwards (Villa), 46 mins.; Smith (Villa), 70 mins.; Dorsett (Villa), penalty, 81 mins.; Pearson (United), 88 mins.

Alec, team 1—5 down, said: 'Just do your best'

By HENRY ROSE

I WORKED much harder yesterday trying to get 8—1 against Manchester United winning the F.A. Cup than on writing the rest of this column.

The wonder 6—4 win at Villa Park has made Matt Busby's lads the hottest favourites on record at this stage of the competition.

There will be a readjustment after today's fourth-round draw.

A warning note to you fortune seekers—don't forget that United's defence conceded four goals.

If you were a manager and your side were 1—5 down at half-time in a 60,000 crowded Cup-tie, what, if you trusted yourself to go to the dressing-room at half-time and speak, would you say to your team?

I'll tell you verbatim exactly what Alec Massie, one of Scotland's most cultured players ever and now Villa manager, said to the depressed room:—

"Keep your chins up, lads. They've had the run of the ball. Your task is not impossible. Just go out there for the next 45 minutes and do your best. That's all I ask of you."

No recriminations. No harsh words.

Thus encouraged, out went the Villa team. Within two minutes Edwards, direct from a corner kick, made it 5—2. Les Smith seized a charged-down jet-propelled free-kick from Dorsett to make it 5—3. Dorsett made it 5—4 from the penalty spot, the kick being given ...lton..... ...ul on Ford

the way down the Villa centre in the 1920's when he was good enough to play for his country.

Frank, senior, now an hotel-keeper in Worcester, has seen his son play five times. Each time Villa have lost. On Saturday he made the journey from Worcester to see them for the first time this season.

United in the first half gave the greatest display of Soccer I have ever seen. Even old-timers said that it was the best ever. Certain it is no side could have stood up to such devastatingly brilliant play.

GREAT MOVE

It had everything from the Soccer text-book. The stuff every side does at practice, when there are no opponents to beat. Villa might not have been there, and they were not playing badly in those pulse-throbbing, blood-warming 45 minutes.

● In one move that charmed even the Villa fans the ball went along the carpet swiftly and surely in front of the foot of the man it was meant for, from Cockburn to Morris, to Pearson, to Rowley to M....... ...k ...

Villa—valiant in vain

15

In the austere years after the Second World War many of the small luxuries which make life tolerable were rationed. Luckily, football was an exception; the post-War years were distinguished by some excellent players and outstanding matches.

One of these games, probably the best of them, occurred on a wintery January Saturday at Villa Park in 1948 when Manchester United came to contest the third round of the FA Cup. Despite the damp weather over 60,000 people crowded into the ground and were rewarded with a most exciting and remarkable match. Despite the stimulus of a very early goal, Aston Villa were completely outclassed in a sensational first half and trudged into the dressing-room 5-1 down at the interval and apparently in danger of losing by a record score.

Yet ten minutes later Villa were fighting back and came within one goal of saving the tie before United scored once more to win 6-4. Of all the games between these two celebrated clubs, this was undoubtedly the best.

After the War there was tremendous public interest in football, interest that was increased by the special appeal of the Cup. But the crowd at Villa Park were also attracted by the teams, both of which were considered likely Cup winners. Villa had the blend of strength, skill and experience which were regarded as traditional

Cup attributes. To the overall competence of the Villa team had been added the scoring power of centre-forward Trevor Ford, signed from Swansea the year before for £9,500, and at outside-left there was another international match-winner, Leslie Smith.

Yet it was the Manchester United team that was more generally admired. It was the first of Matt Busby's great sides. Around centre-half Chilton were clustered such men as Carey, Aston and Cockburn, while the names of the forward line tripped off the tongue of every schoolboy more easily than any mathematical formula—Delaney, Morris, Rowley, Pearson, Mitten.

Clear indication that it was to be no ordinary game came while many of the spectators were still jostling for vantage points on the high terraces. From Ford's kick-off 'Sailor' Brown beat Morris and Anderson and passed out to Smith on the left, and before United realized serious exchanges had begun, the pale-faced, slender George Edwards had slipped in from the right to meet Smith's cross with an unstoppable shot. Only 13½ seconds had passed and no United player had touched the ball. Yet the Villa fans' exultation was premature; it was an optimistic start but, as Edwards recalled: 'It set United alight.'

The United players were men of character, utterly confident in their own considerable skills,

and they brushed off the attacks with which Villa supported their encouraging opening and established their own rhythm. Before long United were in control and that brilliant front line was displaying its skills.

Delaney and Mitten brought immense problems to the Villa defence with the kind of wing-play youngsters of the seventies only read about. After six minutes Villa were forced to concede a corner-kick; a centre from Mitten fell straight to Jack Rowley, and he scored the first of five consecutive Manchester goals.

Nearly all those goals were to come from movements inspired by superb wing play. Until half-time, United, playing in blue shirts, tormented Villa with their own very unique style of football. Nor did the heavy ground disrupt the natural sophistication of their play. The long pass was used with increasing efficiency, and to the perpetual embarrassment of the Villa defenders, Frank Moss, son of a famous father, Harry Parkes, later to become a Villa director, and the stout-thighed Dicky Dorsett tried to stop the gaps. But United's wingers, well-supplied by their inside-forwards, were irresistible.

In the 17th minute Delaney made yet another of those exacting centres and Moss robbed Rowley only at the price of a corner-kick. It was no relief—Morris headed Delaney's corner into the net.

United, having taken the lead, began to exhibit their brilliance, and Villa were able to venture only occasionally into attack. Martin dropped one shot just over the Manchester crossbar, and Ford shot into the side netting after breaking clear in the inside-right position. Then with half an hour gone, United scored a third goal. Rowley's free-kick ten yards outside the penalty area was deflected off Villa's defenders, and Pearson shot in without difficulty.

From free-kicks, from corner-kicks, from the straightforward wing cross, United created—and took—their chances. Two more goals in a particularly disastrous eleven minutes for Villa saw their lead increased to 5-1. Just a couple of min-

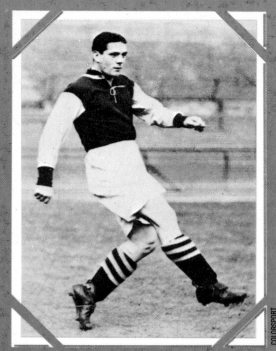

Above *Dickie Dorsett, who was signed from Wolverhampton Wanderers. His goal, from the penalty spot, gave Villa a real chance of saving the game.*

utes after Pearson had scored, Morris headed Mitten's pass into the net and, after a bout of short passing with Morris and Pearson, Delaney added the fifth moments before half-time.

United retired to the dressing-room well content; Villa were left to ponder on the probability of further discomfort and the chances of saving some self-respect. Incredibly, they very nearly saved the game.

United, resting a little nonchalantly on their laurels, were almost as unprepared at the start of the second half as they had been at the beginning of the first, and Villa sneaked another early goal which changed the match. Brown forced Carey to concede a corner-kick, and Edwards flighted it over a crowd of players into the net. This was only the first minute of the second half and the crowd revived in appreciation of Villa's challenge. They were not disappointed. Ford put the ball past Crompton, but the goal was disallowed and

Below *George Edwards, who scored a goal within the first minute of each half, encouraged Villa's remarkable second-half revival.*

then he missed another chance.

But Aston Villa were now in command. They had changed their tactics, keeping the ball in the air, away from United's brilliant ball-players and isolating their defenders on the ground. No longer were Villa trying to match the skill and style of their opponents but using their own strength to play and chase long passes. Moss, Parkes and Dorsett were now composed in Villa's defence as the pitch became more muddy. United's accomplished interpassing, so beautiful to watch, was no longer effective.

Another goal seemed inevitable and United, alert to Villa's ability to rescue the game, attempted to settle the outcome by scoring that goal themselves. A quick thrust upfield ended with Moss bringing down Mitten, and in the subsequent turmoil Parkes cleared off the goal-line. Villa resumed their pressure, yet Martin and Brown were not able to pull the defence out of position in the same way that Manchester's midfield players had done earlier. So although the Villa reaction to adversity had been spirited enough, and the crowd were quick to praise their determination, it did not, after all, appear that Aston Villa would force a draw.

With 20 minutes left, the score resting at 5-2 and Villa apparently checked, United were marking time again. They were playing well

Above *Leslie Smith, the ex-Brentford winger who was Aston Villa's first big signing after the War, scored their third goal against United.*

within themselves, going only occasionally for goal in the devastating style which had created so much havoc in the first half. They were to regret the lack of maximum effort. Villa, pressed forward by Dorsett and Lowe, forced United to concede a free-kick.

Dorsett, a very powerful kicker of a dead ball, took it and the ball spun off a defender to Smith, who scored the goal Villa had been seeking since the first minute of the second half.

The cheers of an enthusiastic crowd now swelled into a paean of encouragement for the inspired Villa team. The yelling fans were willing the Villa to score, attacking United with a passionate roar. But United, being Manchester United, used attack as the best means of defence. Delaney and Mitten were brought into the match again, with Delaney heading just over from Mitten's centre. The Villa revival might have stopped had he scored. But, leaving gaps at the back, Villa forced forward and in the 80th minute narrowed the score to 5-4. Chilton fouled Ford as he was about to shoot and conceded a penalty. It was not the easiest shot to make in those circumstances but Dorsett fired the ball past Crompton into the net.

Above *Centre-forward Jack Rowley, whose sixth-minute equalizer was the first of five consecutive Manchester United goals before half-time.*

Only ten short minutes remained; but time enough for Villa to save the game. Ford hit the bar. How could those few United players resist the fervour of Villa Park? The answer, naturally, was by attack. With only two minutes left a Manchester counter-attack found Villa unprepared and goalkeeper Keith Jones conceded a corner-kick in saving from Mitten. When the ball came over Pearson shot in to make the score 6-4. There was no longer time for Villa to equalize—United had won. The fans, breathless, hoarse and shocked, were left to applaud two fine teams and disperse into the wet side-streets, to retire from magnificence back into the world of the ration book.

Aston Villa: Jones, Potts, Parkes, Dorsett, Moss (F), Lowe (E), Edwards, Martin, Ford, Brown, Smith. *Manchester United*: Crompton, Carey, Aston, Anderson, Chilton, Cockburn, Delaney, Morris, Rowley, Pearson, Mitten.

Below *Charlie Mitten, United's outside-left and one of the main causes of Villa's defeat. He and Delaney tormented Villa on the wings.*

At last— The 1948 Show

All FA Cup Finals are unforgettable. Most are remembered for a memorable winning goal, for a victory against all the odds and expectations, for a dramatic come-back or a gallant failure. Few, however, are recalled for the quality of the football. Perhaps it is because of the importance of the occasion or the prospect of defeat with the stakes so high that Cup Final teams have consistently failed to produce their true form at Wembley.

An exception to the rule came on a lovely late April afternoon in 1948, when Manchester United won the Cup after a lapse of 39 years. By general consent the 1948 match was the most attractive and exhilarating Final since Sheffield Wednesday beat West Bromwich Albion, also by 4-2, 13 years earlier. Later matches, notably the Matthews Final of 1953 and the Leeds-Chelsea marathon of 1970, have claims to have been as exciting, but from the point of view of footballing quality, the 1948 classic is likely to remain unsurpassed.

All the circumstances indicated a game that, for the first time in many years, would match the occasion. The teams, both liberally studded with famous names and potential stars, were leading First Division sides. They were popular everywhere because they played a choice brand of attacking football, no matter whether they were playing home or away. Both managers wanted their players to make the most of their ability and to enjoy giving their admirers pleasure.

United had already delighted 300,000 fans in the Cup that year

Of these there were no shortage. Next to Arsenal, Blackpool were the best crowd-drawing team in the League away from home, while in five FA Cup ties without a replay, Manchester United had already played before 300,000 spectators.

Their passage to the Final would have been difficult enough had all their ties been at Old Trafford; of their six opponents none had finished below 13th in the First Division. Yet United had risen magnificently to their task; including the Final, their goal return in the competition had been 22-8. Only Aston Villa, in a spectacular third-round tie at Villa Park, had scored against United in the second half.

Blackpool's five pre-Final tasks were less demanding and they, too, had prevailed each time at the first attempt, ousting Leeds United (home 4-0), Chester (home 4-0), giant-killing, non-League Colchester (home 5-0, with a goalless second half), Fulham (away 2-0) and Tottenham Hotspur (Villa Park 3-1). They did not meet a First Division side until the semi-final with Spurs and then they had only been saved by a late equalizer by Mortensen, who had gone on to score two more in extra time.

The formbook made Manchester United clear favourites. They had finished their League programme as runners-up to Arsenal and eight points above Blackpool. Matt Busby had only been in charge of the team for two seasons but he had already fashioned an exceptional team. He had known the players' names when he took over but little of their capacity. He realized quickly enough that he had the right material, also that far-reaching measures were needed to get the blend and teamwork he wanted. Players had been switched around like the pieces of a difficult jigsaw until at last they had all dovetailed to form an exciting and balanced combination.

The team was full of outstanding footballers. Johnny Carey, who was capped 36 times for Northern Ireland and Eire, in his new position as full-back, Allenby Chilton, a wing-half until Busby visualized him as another Herbie Roberts, Celtic reject Jimmy Delaney, a shrewd right-winger, and Jack Rowley, a penetrative centre-forward with a tremendous shot. Rowley and Delaney were exceptional as individualists; in combination they were even more devastating and their rapid positional interchanges had proved constant match-winners for United. The inside-forwards, Morris and Pearson—the latter sharp and full of surprises, the former as subtle as he was clever—were the perfect foils for each other. There was scoring power in every position. All five forwards had shared in the Cup scoring spree—Delaney one, Morris three, Rowley five, Pear-son eight and Charlie Mitten three.

If Blackpool were the less fancied team few were writing off their chances. With Matthews, in his first season with Blackpool, and Mortensen amongst the forwards, they could be expected to score at least once. In defence they had the redoubtable Eddie Shimwell, while Harry Johnstone at right-half would ensure a good measure of control in midfield. Their manager, Joe Smith, a forthright individual, completely without frills, was no lover of tactical talks and special planning. His pre-match instructions were blunt but clear—to get on with the game, give 100 per cent effort and play to a purpose. It was good advice. Smith, himself, had won two FA Cup winners medals with Bolton, and Blackpool had enjoyed a successful period under his guidance.

With so many of the game's gods on view, the ticket touts were clearly out for a killing. Outside the ground, 3/6d tickets were on offer at £20 —and still finding takers. Inside, the pitch looked immaculate as the Grenadier Guards set about the

they were a goal down, United's were perhaps the more closely linked and their personalities better defined. United, wrote the *Observer* correspondent 'did not seem unspirited by the surprise of Blackpool's goal—like a master perplexed yet pleased by the unexpected excellence of a pupil.' For Blackpool, Matthews, increasingly tightly held by Johnny Aston, was being slightly outshone by Walter Rickett, Blackpool's left-winger who had a fine game against Carey.

Jack Rowley hurled himself forward to head a wonderful goal

In the 28th minute, United equalized. Hayward and Robinson misjudged a centre from Delaney and left Rowley with a simple chance which was duly accepted. Within a few minutes Crosland headed out from under the bar to deny Rowley a second goal, but United's attack, with Mortensen setting Chilton all sorts of problems, restored the balance of play. Before half-time Blackpool regained the lead from a free-kick. Matthews put the ball in the goal area, Kelly headed it on and Mortensen scored a characteristic goal with a quick turn and instant shot. In so doing he joined the select band of players who have scored in every round of the Cup.

The overall pattern of much of the second half was more or less like that of the first, with the play fairly even as the match ebbed and flowed. Yet the scoresheet was to be radically transformed. Midway through the half, United equalized with a goal that foreshadowed England's first in the World Cup final. The goal stemmed from a disputed free-kick given against Kelly for pushing Morris. As Kelly argued his case with the referee, Morris's sharp mind was at work. With the Blackpool defence unprepared, he crossed the ball unerringly to Rowley, practically unmarked in the penalty area. Rowley, moving faster than Shimwell and Hayward, hurled himself forward to head a wonderful goal; the speed of it was astonishing.

Blackpool were annoyed by the ruse but, for the moment at least, it did not appear to unsettle them. In a swift recoil thrust Mortensen would have scored again—this time at speed from an angle—it was only a slight error of judgement that gave Crompton the chance to make a fine save. Yet it was United who scored next and the goal was the outcome of Crompton's judicious clearance.

The ball was cleared to Anderson who, in turn, found Pearson. With a deft feint the inside-forward removed his marker from the game, before firing a crisp, deliberate shot onto the post and into the net. ('At this third goal', the *Observer* correspondent remarked, 'several hitherto staid Mancunians expressed an agreeable insanity.') There were only 12 minutes left and Matthews' hopes of a Cup winners medal were fading fast. They disappeared completely when Anderson scored a fourth goal with a shot that plummeted into the far corner of Robinson's goal with the help of a deflection off the head of Kelly.

On these sort of occasions people often lament the fact that one side has to lose, and Blackpool indeed deserved more than the bitter taste of defeat, all the more sour for having been so close to victory. It can have been little consolation for them to know that King George VI remarked to Johnny Carey, the winning captain, how much he had enjoyed the game. Yet even in the moment of United's victory they were as spontaneous and whole-hearted in their applause for the team to whom they had so narrowly lost, as they had been in their play. It was a match that would be remembered for years.

Blackpool: Robinson, Shimwell, Crosland, Johnstone, Hayward, Kelly, Matthews, Munro, Mortensen, Dick, Rickett.
Manchester United: Crompton, Carey, Aston, Anderson, Chilton, Cockburn, Delaney, Morris, Rowley, Pearson, Mitten.

last few bars of 'Abide with Me' and the teams lined up—United in blue, Blackpool in white.

Both managers had made late changes on the eve of the match. Busby decided to recall Johnny Anderson to right-half in place of the more experienced Warner—the only change in the United's line-up throughout the tournament. For Blackpool, Johnny Crosland, normally a centre-half and untried at full-back, replaced the injured right-back, Ron Suart. Smith also took a gamble with his forwards. He dropped Jimmy McIntosh, who scored five Cup goals, moved Mortensen to centre-forward in the hope that his speed would unsettle Chilton, and put Alec Munro, the team's outside-right before Matthews was signed, at inside-right. Both the newcomers were to play fine games. Munro in particular was to be described as 'the hardest worker on the field—and nearly the most intelligent in the anticipation of events'.

In the early stages it soon became clear that both teams saw that the greatest hope of victory

lay in constant pressure on their opponent's defence. Each set of forwards set about probing the weak joints of the other's rearguard, testing defenders for mobility and speed, prising open gaps, searching for openings. There can be few Cup Finals in which both teams were more committed to attack, and throughout the match, the forward play was balanced and controlled, clockwork in its precision.

At first the ball ran for Blackpool. In the seventh minute, Matthews left Aston reclining on the Wembley turf before squaring the ball to Munro. Taken aback by the chance of so easy a breakthrough Munro miskicked and the chance was gone. In the 14th minute Mortensen tore through. His path was clear but for Chilton who brought him down on the edge of the penalty area. The penalty, which Shimwell converted, was disputed and caused controversy, but there was no hesitation in Mr Barrick's decision and he was nearer the incident than the cameras.

Both attacks were penetrative yet, even though

Yeovil Town win their place in history

No club can afford so clear an example of the unpredictability of football as Yeovil Town. For nearly forty years this small Somerset county town has been producing teams that have consistently shown that in football, the reputation counts for nothing, the performance on the day for everything.

The list of League clubs to whom Yeovil have played hosts is long and often impressive. Crystal Palace, Exeter City, Liverpool, Manchester United (twice), Sheffield Wednesday, Bury, Bournemouth, Colchester, Chesterfield, Oxford United, Southend and Shrewsbury have all played against Yeovil. Yet only a few have overcome the combination of the celebrated Yeovil slope—in reality less marked than its reputation suggests—and the ability of Yeovil Town, or Yeovil and Petters United, as they were called before the Second World War, to rise to the occasion of the FA Cup.

Yeovil's supreme achievement came in an FA Cup tie played on 29 January, 1949 when, lying sixth from the bottom of the Southern League they met Sunderland of the First Division of the Football League, a team eighth in their class and studded with great names of the period—Shackleton, Robinson, Watson, Turnbull, Hall and Mapson. The result? Yeovil Town 2 Sunderland 1. The prize was a tie with Manchester United in Round 5. There can have been few more dramatic matches in all soccer history.

The slope, Sunderland thought, had been greatly exaggerated

A remarkable feature about Yeovil's greatest season was that they reached the third round without a line of publicity in the national press. Coming into the competition in the fourth qualifying round they beat Lovells Athletic, a Welsh works team from Newport, Monmouthshire, Romford in Round One and then Weymouth in Round Two.

The meagreness of Yeovil's previous opposition may have given Bury, their next opponents, a false sense of complacency. Certainly Bury never got into a game that Yeovil won 3-1 and could have won 5-1 without being flattered. Prior to this match, Bob Keeton, the Yeovil Number 4 had gone to the local public library where he happened to drop on a quotation from the poet Dryden. He pointed it out to a London sports journalist; 'They can conquer who believe they can.'

Keeton's maxim worked well enough against Bury but only the foolhardy could give a team, low in the Southern League and with a total weekly wage bill of £70 per week, any kind of chance against one of the country's most glamorous clubs. The chance of victory looked even slighter when Hall, the regular goalkeeper, who had once been with Orient, cut his knee on a bottle-top in the pre-match training. The injury was serious; Hall needed five stitches and he failed to pass the fitness test. His place was taken by Dickie Dyke, a 23-year-old solicitor's clerk who had played only one game in Yeovil's senior team.

The match was played on one of those fine, cold, diamond-bright winter afternoons. The population of Yeovil at the time was around 19,000 and inside this country cousin of a ground were jammed 15,000. Outside, with no hope of getting in, at least another 5,000 milled around,

making entry difficult for the lucky ones who had tickets. Local reporters occupied the four-seater press box, which created an emergency that the Yeovil club solved in two ways.

The 150-odd journalists from all over Britain and some parts of Europe were accommodated in the front row of the stand to which planks of fresh timber had been nailed to give them a writing surface and in desks borrowed from the junior school adjoining the ground and put on the touch-line. It was an incredible sight to see distinguished soccer columnists squeezed into desks usually occupied by six year olds.

Sunderland's official party had inspected the ground on Friday and announced themselves satisfied. The slope, they thought, like the reported death of Mark Twain, had been greatly exaggerated.

'If we should happen to get beaten, there will be no complaints about the pitch, or the slope, from Sunderland,' announced their chairman Colonel Joseph Pryor and manager Bill Murray. Less than twenty-four hours later they had to stand by those words.

Yeovil Town lined up in green jerseys and white shorts. The team was made up of an assortment of publicans, glove-cutters, clerks, warehousemen and labourers. Only the player-manager Alec Stock, later to manage Roma, Queen's Park Rangers and Luton, could boast any experience of League football!

Referee W F Smith of Aldershot set the long awaited match in motion and from the first whistle Yeovil went into the attack. When Mapson had to go down quickly to a curling drive from Eric Bryant, who spent his weekdays humping corn for a Yeovil chandler, the locals felt the chance of a Yeovil win become more than a possibility.

With ten minutes gone Yeovil suffered a second disaster to match the loss of their goalkeeper Hall. A pulled muscle made the winger Hargreaves a virtual passenger for the rest of the game; no substitutes, of course, were then allowed. The match as a contest seemed certain to curl up and die. Yet the injury, if anything, forced Yeovil to greater efforts and tighter cohesion. Mapson conceded a corner and Keeton put a vicious drive only inches high. Alec Stock spoke no more than the truth when, asked about the Hargreaves handicap, said 'We simply ignored it.'

Fate was to give Yeovil another kidney punch. Mapson, holding the ball, was bundled over the line by the burly Bryant. Instead of giving the goal the referee awarded Sunderland a free-kick. In the 28th minute, however, Yeovil put the ball in the Sunderland net again and this time the goal stood.

Centre-half Les Blizzard lobbed a mid-field free kick to inside-left Alex Wright. He slipped a waist-high ball to player-manager Alec Stock who swivelled on his right leg and smashed a fine shot well to the left of Mapson.

From the kick-off, whereas Sunderland had waited for the ball to come to them, Yeovil had gone to meet it. But now they had to face Sunderland's reprisals. The main anxiety was Dyke, but although obviously raw he was a big, fearless fellow with an equable temperament.

He made a succession of fine saves until, with 62 minutes played and the score unchanged he missed a long pass into the goalmouth by full-back Barney Ramsden and Robinson tapped it over the line for what he later described as 'the

easiest goal of my life'.

At the end of ninety minutes the score stood at 1-1 and normally, that would have meant a replay at Roker Park and a very different story. But this was the final post-War season when extra-time applied to original ties if they were drawn—part of the Government's austerity campaign to avoid unnecessary journeys and loss of working days in the years just after the War.

So the capacity crowd already emotionally limp settled down to a further half hour and most must have felt convinced the superior stamina of the First Division stars would decide things. As the extra period began, thick mist enveloped the ground. Now there was a new matter to consider, the distinct possibility that this historic match would be abandoned on a heart-breaking note of anti-climax for Yeovil. Suddenly with only seconds remaining to the end of the first period of extra time, the mist lifted and clearly revealed Shackleton with the ball on the halfway line.

He stood juggling the ball up on his instep, facing his own goal. He was faced with a number of alternatives; he could turn it and dribble or pass; he could hook it out to either wing; he could pass back or even bang it into the crowd for safety. Any one of these things he could have done and Sunderland would probably have escaped with a replay. Being 'Shack' he tried an overhead kick to his centre-forward. Being 'Shack'

Right Dyke, the Yeovil goalkeeper clears a Sunderland attack; a solicitor's clerk, he played brilliantly after being drafted into the side to replace the regular goalkeeper Hall, who had cut his knee in pre-match training.
Below Hall was back in the team for the fifth round tie against Manchester United; he saved this shot but could do little to prevent United's 8-0 win.
Opposite below right Alec Stock, the Yeovil player-manager and captain described his job at Yeovil as 'one of many parts'; here he completes his desk-work, prepared for more physical activities.
Opposite below left An air of geniality pervades the pre-match formalities; after their defeat Sunderland's smiles turned to scowls as they locked themselves in their railway carriage.

PRESS ASSOCIATION

ninety-nine times out of a hundred he would have pulled it off but this was the exception. He caught the ball with the toe of his boot and it flew straight up the middle towards his own goal—a perfect through pass for Wright, the Yeovil inside-left. Wright gathered it to him greedily, paused and then pushed it into the path of the onrushing Bryant. Mapson started to come out but Bryant hit the ball swiftly and truly into the net.

Yet the match was far from over. A further 15 minutes of extra-time had to be played and that quarter of an hour seemed almost as bad as being roasted over a slow fire. At last Sunderland shook off their lethargy and Yeovil, physically handicapped and spent, reeled back in the face of withering attacks. Then the mist rolled down again. For Yeovil it was a race against time whichever way they looked at it. Three minutes left and one final piece of irony threatened to rob Yeovil of their victory.

The referee blew for a free-kick to Sunderland just outside the Yeovil penalty area. The crowd thought it was the final whistle and over the railings they came in their thousands. Within seconds the pitch looked like one of those 1923 photographs of the first Wembley Final when the public stormed the gates. It seemed Yeovil might be robbed of their triumph by the hysteria of their own supporters.

Somehow, the Yeovil players, arms waving like maniacs, pleading, cajoling, threatening, persuaded the crowd to return behind the barriers and the last three minutes were played out.

Only when the final whistle blew did the full impact of Yeovil's sensational win make itself felt. A great many people remained in their seats, drained of all emotion, simply staring in front of them as if hypnotised. Reaction hit Sunderland on the express from Yeovil Junction to Waterloo. The players did not come into the dining car. Their manager, Bill Murray however, was not so shattered as to miss his dinner. With a sour grin he jerked his thumb behind him and said to press acquaintances—'they've locked themselves in'. Meanwhile a dance had been laid on for the Yeovil players but Alec Stock recalls that the Yeovil team was too tired to celebrate.

A couple of weeks later Yeovil Town's band of part-time footballers travelled North to take on the Cup holders Manchester United at Maine Road, home of Manchester City at a time when Old Trafford had to be restored from the ravages of wartime bombing. This time there was no miracle. United won 8-0. Yet even so the West Country team attracted a gate of 80,000. And certainly the defeat against Manchester United did nothing to tarnish the achievement against Sunderland that established a permanent place for Yeovil in the annals of football.

Yeovil Town: Dyke, Hickman, Davis, Keeton, Blizzard, Collins, Hamilton, Stock, Bryant, Wright, Hargreaves.
Sunderland: Mapson, Stelling, Ramsden, Watson, Hall, Wright, Duns, Robinson, Turnbull, Shackleton, Reynolds.

Did the Irish spoil England's record?

18

When Eire played England at Goodison Park on Wednesday, 21 September 1949, most of the 51,000 crowd were anticipating a football massacre.

The media unanimously predicted an easy England victory. Henry Rose of the *Daily Express* suggested a 'brains test' for anybody who considered the Irish to have a chance of bearding the British lion in its own den. Generally, the affair was looked upon as a pleasant social occasion. It would be an opportunity for the FA to royally entertain the visiting officials—it was Eire's first visit—and England would offer an exhibition of their renowned skill.

There were, of course, solid reasons for England to be well fancied. England had never lost at home to anybody except its fellow members of the International Board—Scotland, Wales, and Northern Ireland. Two world wars had occurred since, in 1914 at Middlesbrough, the Irish Football Association, with a team representative of all Ireland, had made history with a 3-0 victory.

Nobody gave Eire a chance of beating England at Goodison

The 1949 Eire side, moreover, was entirely composed of natives of the Republic of Ireland and included two part-timers from Shamrock Rovers of the League of Ireland: the goalkeeper, Tommy Godwin, a carpenter, and the outside-left Tommy O'Connor, a printer with a Dublin daily newspaper. Also the inside-left, Peter Desmond, had been a close season transfer from Shelbourne to Middlesbrough and had yet to play for Middlesbrough's League team.

Nor had Eire played very impressively that year. They had been beaten by both Belgium (2-0) and Spain (4-1) in Dublin, and had gone down 3-1 to Sweden in Stockholm in a qualifying match for the 1950 World Cup.

On the credit side, there had been a single goal success against a pedestrian Portugal at Dalymount Park and a 3-0 World Cup preliminary round win over Finland's amateurs, also at Dalymount. This match was played just 13 days before the Goodison commitment and the margin of success did not blind the Eire selectors to certain limitations.

Four changes, in fact, were made for the England match. At right-half Eddie Gannon of Sheffield Wednesday was replaced by Billy Walsh of Manchester City. In attack Johnny Gavin (Norwich City), Arthur Fitzsimons (Middlesbrough) and Brendan Carroll (Shelbourne) were replaced respectively by Peter Corr (Everton), Peter Farrell (Everton) and Dave Walsh (West Bromwich Albion).

Dave Walsh, for all his success in League football, had previously been an international disappointment and won recall mainly because of his experience. It was felt that Corr and Farrell—though Farrell, an established Everton wing-half, had not played inside-forward for some years—would be worth playing on their club ground. Also Fitzsimons, for all his skills and pace, was only 19 and thought likely, because of his light frame, to be tackled out of the match.

England, possibly in anticipation of an easy fixture, called in three new caps. One was Bert Mozley, the Derby County right-back. The others were Peter Harris, a goalscoring Portsmouth right-winger with tremendous pace, and Jesse Pye, the Wolves centre-forward. To accommodate the new forwards the selectors had dropped Stanley Matthews and Stan Mortensen.

Yet with Johnny Morris, at the time England's highest priced player at £24,000, to feed Harris, and Tom Finney playing outside Wilf Mannion on the left, it looked, with Pye, an attack well capable of goals.

Mozley apart, England were well established in defence with Bert Williams, Johnny Aston and Neil Franklin there to deal with anything that escaped the wing-half pair, Billy Wright and Jimmy Dickinson.

The Irish did not even select any reserves, trusting that neither illness nor injury would befall the team before the match.

On the Sunday night Godwin, O'Connor and the trainer, Billy Lord, journeyed to Liverpool on the boat and on Monday evening more players checked in at Birkdale. There was Bud Aherne, the left-back from Luton, Tommy Moroney, the left-half from West Ham, Billy Walsh, Desmond and the man who was to play the most vital role of them all—Manchester United and Eire captain and right-back Johnny Carey.

Remarkably, only those seven took part in the Eire training session at Haig Avenue, Southport, the following afternoon: Corr and Farrell trained

2

4

instead with Everton and Dave Walsh and the centre-half, Con Martin of Aston Villa, arrived too late from Birmingham to join in the Haig Avenue workout. In those days Eire didn't have a team manager and tactics were left to Carey.

At the practice he worked on Godwin, who had been having a rough time with club and country. Carey now prepared his goalkeeper for the morrow by standing inside the box at one end of the Southport pitch and throwing a hundred balls at him. He had Godwin showering perspiration after testing him with every kind of ball. But Godwin hadn't looked good.

Eire kicked off with the wind, what there was of it, at their backs. The match began, as expected, with an England attack, from which Pye was just wide; and it went on that way for some time as Finney carved holes in Carey. Pye had a likely shot charged down by Aherne, Godwin saved a shot from Finney. Pye, who was receiving a lot of support, headed an easy chance wide.

The siege went on unabated through the opening quarter. England, superbly driven on by Wright, had 75 per cent of the ball and were only kept out by a lot of courage. Eire had five men in a line across the field tackling furiously and, behind them, Godwin was defiant.

The game changed when Carey altered his tactics. He now committed himself less to tackling Finney. Instead he laid off and, as Finney continued to attempt to beat a man before passing, England's tempo slowed. By the time the crosses came Eire had marshalled extra players at the back. Gradually Eire emerged from grim defence and in a sudden raid Williams was stretched to stop Dave Walsh. From that single thrust it seemed Eire grew in confidence.

After 32 minutes O'Connor appeared almost for the first time and pushed inside to Desmond; he broke into the box at the angle and Mozley tripped him. It was a penalty. The vital kick was entrusted to Martin, so well seasoned internationally.

Martin relied on power when taking penalties. He simply galloped up and banged the ball. This one sped at Williams, just a yard to his right. The goalkeeper got a hand to the ball, but the force of the shot bent his fingers and the ball dropped gently over the line.

It was now a different game. Eire were winning possession more frequently and Moroney, with

For the match with Eire, England stars Matthews (1) and Mortensen (2) were dropped and replaced by Peter Harris (3) and Jesse Pye (4)—whose missed chances were to prove costly. Yet England dominated the game until (5) Johnny Carey (right) mastered Tom Finney (left). As Eire's attack grew more confident, Bert Mozley (6), England's other new cap, tripped Desmond in the penalty area and Con Martin (7) scored decisively from the spot in the 32nd minute. Eire, controlled by Carey and inspired by goalkeeper Tommy Godwin (8), retained their slender lead until, with five minutes left, Peter Farrell (9) scored to give Eire an astonishing 2-0 victory.

more time, was pushing Eire forward. Finney sniped a shot just on the break, but Godwin always had it covered.

England began the second half as they had the first with Pye in the clear and Godwin stopping his shot with his chest. Wright continued to play beautifully and Godwin went full length to Harris. When a header from Morris left Godwin stranded Billy Walsh seemed to come out of the ground to clear. Godwin kicked away a shot from Morris that a full-back might have handled and soon made the most remarkable of his many good saves: Harris curled the ball towards the goal but Godwin quickly raised a hand and jammed the ball against the underside of the bar. For seconds it seemed he stood there like a soccer statue of liberty before getting back to business.

Farrell's late goal killed England's last hopes of a draw

That save may have broken England. They began to fade and Eire, with Carey now controlling and coaxing his men, were revealing that they had skill as well as strength.

Five minutes were left when the thing was finally settled. Dave Walsh passed to O'Connor and Farrell was quickly on the move. England were caught outrageously square. Williams tore from his posts but Farrell calmly waited until the lob was possible and it was 2-0. England tried to save face but Godwin added to England's despair with another fine save from Mannion.

Within a week Godwin had been sold to Leicester City, while Desmond was immediately promoted to Middlesbrough's first eleven.

This was the first time that England had ever played a home fixture against the Republic of Ireland and the Irish claimed their victory as the first foreign team to beat England on English soil. Shocked though the English public were, they did not share that view. After all, not only was Ireland part of the British Isles, only two of the Eire team did not play for English League clubs. How could players such as Carey and Martin be regarded as 'foreign'? That distinction remained for the Hungarians to claim at Wembley in 1953.

England had been unlucky in the sense that Godwin had been in excellent form, but they had also underrated the opposition and failed to take early chances when Eire were still settling. Yet, in retrospect, Eire had deserved more respect from the critics. In 1946 they had lost to England by only one goal in Dublin and the following year, also at Goodison, both Walshes, Carey, Farrell and Martin had helped Northern Ireland hold England to 2-2.

England: Williams, Mozley, Aston, Wright, Franklin, Dickinson, Harris, Morris, Pye, Mannion, Finney.
Eire: Godwin, Carey, Aherne, Walsh (W), Martin, Moroney, Corr, Farrell, Walsh (D), Desmond, O'Connor.

8

9

The Great American disaster

Ever since England's World Cup triumph in 1966 there has been ample scope to criticize the organization of the national team. But, compared with the circumstances of England's World Cup debut in 1950, England's preparations are almost perfect.

Consider that, in 1950, there was not only the perennial problem of securing the release of players from League clubs and the considerable disadvantage of a team manager who was not allowed to select his own team, but the FA had even arranged a simultaneous tour of Canada. And England's difficulties were only a part of Britain's cautious entry into this championship.

None of the four home countries had previously competed in the World Cup, partly because of the disputes with FIFA, but Stanley Rous, then secretary of the FA, had devoted a lot of effort to encourage them to participate in the first post-War tournament. The British Championship had been classified as a qualifying group with *two* qualifiers, but the Scottish FA refused to send a team to the finals in Brazil unless Scotland were British champions. A victory by England at Hampden Park prevented that, and so England became Britain's only representatives.

Such petty behaviour distracted attention from England's other problems. FIFA had demanded that each country name 22 players twenty-one days before the finals, and no competing country could deviate from this list. But the FA had included Stanley Matthews and Jim Taylor, of Fulham, in the party to tour Canada. Manchester United, due to tour the USA, had requested the release of Aston and Cockburn. Another handicap was that Neil Franklin, the automatic choice at centre-half, left the World Cup squad for the financial benefits offered by Santa Fe of Colombia —a country not then a member of FIFA.

Enough talent remained in the England party, however, for them to be rated favourites with Brazil, the hosts. Matthews and Taylor, though not available for the first game against Chile in Rio de Janeiro, were to join the squad in Rio later. Even without Matthews, there were also Stan Mortensen, Wilf Mannion, Tom Finney, Billy Wright, Alf Ramsey and Bert Williams. Unfortunately, the quality of the players was not matched by the management. A group of selectors chose the team which was then surrendered to the guidance of Walter Winterbottom, the FA's Director of Coaching. It was a complicated system of planning England's first attempt on the World Cup.

Nevertheless, goals by Mortensen and Mannion gave England a 2-0 victory. It was an adequate start, especially considering that the other two teams in England's group were USA and Spain. The USA team was rare proof that that country even played the game, and Spain had only beaten them 3-1. Even if the World Cup (which was arranged on a league basis) was unfamiliar to England, they could be reasonably confident of finishing top of their group and qualifying for the final four.

The next match, against the USA, was to take place at Belo Horizonte and the English party retired to the British-owned Morro Velho gold mine in the mountains, sixteen miles above the city. In such congenial surroundings, with the company and encouragement of the mine's British and Canadian employees, England were entitled to feel relaxed. Even Bill Jeffrey, the American's Scottish coach from Pennsylvania

State University, expected his team to be defeated; they were allowed to stay up into the early hours of the morning before the match. The only unanswered question seemed to be the size of their defeat.

Yet it was in these happy conditions that the decision was taken which was to have such far reaching effects. Walter Winterbottom wanted to rest some of his players and give some of the other eleven a game, before choosing his strongest team for what was obviously going to be the big match against Spain. But the FA member in charge, the

late Mr Arthur Drewry, who was to become President of FIFA, did not agree with his team manager. He said in effect that the players would have an easy game against USA which would count as match practice.

So Winterbottom's professional judgement was over-ruled, because he had not been granted the sort of authority which was given to his successor Alf Ramsey. The same team that had played against Chile, apparently regarded as England's strongest side, was made to play against the weakest team in the competition.

By contrast, there was only one selector from the United States' FA, and his eleven players who had settled, either temporarily or permanently, in the US originated from six different countries. They included, as captain, Eddie McIlvenny, a Scottish-born player who had been given a free-transfer by Wrexham only 18 months previously and who later signed for Manchester United.

An early inspection of the narrow ground revealed that it was completely unsuitable for a World Cup match. Yet Winterbottom did not protest; after all England were supposed to be capable of beating most countries and certainly the USA, whom England had never met in a full international before. But he did refuse to allow his players to change in the minute, dimly-lit, rat-infested dressing rooms. Instead, the team changed at the Minas Athletic Club, ten minutes coach drive away.

But the ground was not merely cramped, but also rutted and stony, which was probably the reason why the American centre-half, Colombo, wore strong leather gloves throughout the match! Yet for England it still should have been a fiesta. From the start it was one-way traffic towards Borghi's goal. Seconds after the kick-off, the England forwards surged through the American defence and Mullen was all set to score, when the ball bobbled and he lifted his shot over the bar. The players strolled back laughing.

Laughter became frustration, however, as the game continued. The pitch was small. Accurate passing was impossible on the bumpy surface. The genius of Mannion was reduced as the ball bounced around erratically. Even so, continuous effort kept England surging on to the American goal. But so often did the ball deflect unexpectedly that the skill of England's best players was annulled, and often their movements were

reduced to the level of the opposing team.

The pressure began to tell, but chance after chance was struck over or past the goal. Then Tom Finney hit a post with goalkeeper Borghi sprawling well clear of the ball. And Mannion, with what on a reasonable surface would have been an easy goal, smashed the ball goalwards only to see it rebound far upfield, again from an upright.

The 20,000 crowd, jammed into the terraces of this tiny ground, could hardly believe that England were not sailing supremely through the game. And the hundreds of workers from the gold mine grew more and more anxious as the ball just would not go into the net. There were arguments with the local aficionados who, like the rest of Brazil, were apprehensive of the power of England and who were delighted to see the 100-1 outsiders still in the game.

Then, of course, America scored, and the Reuters representative, the only man among eight pressmen with a phone link to Rio and the outside world, was able to transmit the extraordinary news that England were a goal down to a 'team I never knew played football'.

The goal was appropriate to the whole bizarre situation. Left-half Bahr tried a shot, or rather a clearance out of danger. The ball was sailing straight to goalkeeper Bert Williams, when the Belgian-born centre-forward, Gaetjens, trying to duck out of the way, got a stinging blow on his left ear, and the ball shot into the English net at a point furthest from the goalkeeper.

The locals, understandably, went wild. The England team smiled sheepishly, and the only American journalist there, who was on holiday in Brazil with a brief to file if there was anything interesting, started to enquire where the nearest cable office was. The English players spent half-time standing up, or sitting on the grass listening to the excited chatter of the fans, and trying to sort themselves out. Quick directions from team manager Walter Winterbottom took Bentley to outside-right, Finney and Mortensen, the man the Rio crowd had named the Flying Bandit, into the middle. Things were bad but not yet desperate.

But although the only times that Bert Williams touched the ball were from long back passes or far flung clearances from the other end, in the gathering darkness it became obvious that England were going to lose. The longer the game went on the more composed the Americans became. After all, as one of the England players said afterwards: 'They are used to playing on Hackney Wick. The pitch suited them.' But there were other reasons; Colombo, of the leather gloves, was equal to Mortensen, and the Souza

brothers started to play a victory march down the England right flank, despite Alf Ramsey and Billy Wright. Borghi, in goal, was playing well.

Bad luck still afflicted the England forward-line. Mullen crashed a shot against the upright. Mortensen hit the bar, the ball bounced down and an American fist punched it away for a throw-in. But no penalty was awarded. Then Mortensen broke clear only to be rugby-tackled to the ground, well inside the penalty area. This time a free-kick was given—outside the box. Still, Ramsey hit the ball hard and true towards the top corner of the net. For a moment England's supporters felt that perhaps, after all, England would salvage a draw. But Borghi, making the save of his life, clawed the ball away. And suddenly it was over. The referee's whistle confirmed what must rate as the most unexpected result in the history of international soccer.

It was soon dark. No sooner had the crowd gone, no sooner had the England players climbed

And win is a 'must'

England's defeat has led to a tense situation in Group "B" of the World Cup competition.

Spain now head the Group with two wins from two games, and they meet England on Sunday. Spain need only to avoid defeat in that game to shatter all hope of England going forward to the final pool. United States, by beating Chile could, in the event of an English win, force a triple tie in this pool.

Italy, holders of the Jules Rimet World Cup, have failed to survive for the final because of Sweden's draw yesterday with Paraguay. Sweden top Group C with one game to be played.

ENGLAND FALL TO U.S. AMATEURS

From JOHN THOMPSON
BELO HORIZONTE (Brazil), Thursday.

ENGLISH Soccer was humbled as it never has been before in the little stadium here today, when America beat us 1—0 in the World Cup match. The Americans, who entered the competition on a "hiding-to-nothing" basis and completely unfancied, were the better team, and fully deserved their victory.

England		USA	
		○	29 June 1950
○○○○○		○○○	8 June 1953
○○○○		○	28 May 1959
○○○○○			27 May 1964
○○○○○○○○○○ 24		○○○○ 5	Aggregate

Top *The* Daily Mirror's *verdict was that: 'It was a pathetic show from a team expected to do so much.' But that ignored the gross inadequacies in the organization of the England team.*
Centre *This diagram displays the true superiority of English football. Unfortunately, in the only match that mattered between the teams the 'inferior' United States football team won.*
Bottom *A new World Cup hero: Gaetjens, whose goal humbled England in their first World Cup.*

aboard their bus, still in the clothes they had worn in defeat, than the gates were locked, and the handful of English pressmen were left to fend for themselves with the telephone which had been handed over by the Reuters correspondent. For the next hour Maurice Smith of *The People* phoned back to Rio, for cabling to London, page after page of copy for the *Daily Mail, Daily Express, News Chronicle* and *Allied Newspapers.* For light he burnt newspapers. Many would do the same in England the next day. And as each sheet of typescript was read, so it was ignited to make sure that the next page could also be seen.

The American journalist had also gone to find his cable station, and the English journalists had subscribed dollars to help him pay the cost of the cable.

Meanwhile, the England party, less Mr Drewry whose only comment had been, 'This leaves me speechless', and who had decided to stay in the town before returning to Rio, had climbed the sixteen lonely miles to the gold mines. There was sympathy for Walter Winterbottom. Ever a gentleman, he was as near to breaking-point as he could be. He shrugged his shoulders in complaint, asking: 'What can you say about a result like that? It just was not possible. If one of those shots had counted, it could have been a massacre. Now we have got to beat Spain to gain a play-off.'

Wilf Mannion commented: 'Bloody ridiculous. Can't we play them again tomorrow . . . on a proper pitch? Stan Mortensen, who as always had run himself into the ground, was slightly more objective as he said: 'When we beat Chile last Saturday I thought we were going to win the World Cup. It's made it just that little bit harder.'

But there was never a word of criticism against Arthur Drewry, whose decision had allowed England's best team to be humiliated. There was no obvious reason for blaming him; if the USA had defeated England's best team, what would they have done to the reserves? Football rarely follows such logic however. There were good reasons for Winterbottom's desire to change some of the team. Key players could have been rested for the harder matches later in the competition and there would have been no unnecessary risk of injuries. Also, what was the use of having reserves if they could not be used; and what better opportunity to give them match practice than against the USA. Perhaps they too would have been unable to prevent England's defeat; but perhaps also they would have been more determined from the beginning, if they had been playing for their places in the team.

Still, the defeat was irrevocable. All that could be done to mitigate it was to beat Spain the following Sunday. But, as they tried to relax amidst the music, the food, and the drink supplied by hospitable British employees of the gold mine, the overall feeling was one of despair. To have tried so hard, to have come so far, to be among, and hope to defeat the best footballers in the world, made the international ridicule harder to bear. Nor was it only the players who had to endure the humiliation; England's supporters at the mine would have to remain among the local people after the England team had returned home.

Only a convincing victory over Spain could have repaired the damage to England's pride and prestige. But on the Sunday and despite four changes—including Matthews—England lost to a second-half goal by Zarra. Again England could claim to have been unlucky for an apparently good Jackie Milburn goal was ruled offside. Yet it was not a convincing excuse for the whole purpose of thorough organization is to avoid having to rely on luck. That was the lesson England should have learnt from their disastrous World Cup debut. But further humiliation—by the Hungarians—and three more World Cup failures occurred before England finally understood.

England: Williams, Ramsey, Aston, Wright, Hughes, Dickinson, Finney, Mortensen, Bentley, Mannion, Mullen.
United States: Borghi, Keough, Maca, McIlvenny, Colombo, Bahr, Wallace, Pariani, Gaetjens, Souza (J), Souza (E).

Forward go the Centaurs

Below Brown, the Pegasus goalkeeper, watches a Bishop Auckland shot go past the post.
Bottom Pegasus defenders (white shirts) watch anxiously as another Bishop Auckland attack, by left-winger Edwards, threatens their first Cup win.
Right In the first-half Pegasus had been forced to defend, but six minutes after the interval they scored the first goal of the match. Left-winger Jimmy Potts, who rarely headed the ball, leapt forward to nod Dutchman's centre into the top corner of the net.
Bottom right Two goals later and Pegasus had won the Amateur Cup 2-1 a remarkable achievement for a club that was only three years old and a great stimulus to amateur football.

In 1971 only 45,000 spectators watched the Amateur Cup final at Wembley. They looked lost in the vast expanse of that concrete bowl, and no-one could remember when it had been any different. Yet twenty years earlier 100,000 people were packed into Wembley for an Amateur Cup final between two teams, one of which had been founded of Oxford and Cambridge University players in 1889 and the other by recruits of the same universities in 1948. The country was fascinated by two teams with pedigrees more characteristic of mid-nineteenth century football than the game as it was played in the 1950s. They seemed complete anomalies in the professional era.

Not that there was anything anomalous about the success of Bishop Auckland, who had won seven of their previous thirteen finals and were to be the most successful amateur team of the fifties. They were the most experienced team in amateur football. By contrast to their northern opponents, Pegasus were only in their third year of existence, did not have the benefit of regular league competition, had no ground of their own, did not play more than 16 matches in a season, and had only played as a team since Christmas. Given the peculiar genesis of the club, Pegasus invested the final with a David versus Goliath appeal.

In the few years of its existence, Pegasus had attracted a great following, many of whom saw the club as latter-day Corinthians. People enjoyed their happy, carefree approach to football.

Within three years of their foundation Pegasus were at Wembley

The new club was the brainchild of Dr H W Thomson, later as Professor Sir Harold Thomson to be Vice-Chairman of the Football Association. He was aware of the urgent need to give amateur football some prestigious encouragement if it was to compete with rugby in the schools and universities. Many schools were changing to rugby because headmasters felt that game had more status and social significance. Dr Thomson knew that a striking success for university soccer could change this trend.

In 1948 many of the undergraduates at Oxford and Cambridge were older than normal, having come out of the forces at the end of the War and having had an opportunity for their playing skill to mature. As a not untypical example winger Tony Pawson was 27 and he had played regularly in Army teams in Italy and Austria with Tom Finney and others of similar calibre.

The name Pegasus was proposed by Dr Thomson's wife, Penelope. The leading Oxford football club was called the Centaurs and its Cambridge opposite, the Falcons. The winged horse, Pegasus, was the aptest of descriptions for the joint venture. Before it could take to the air, however, Pegasus had administrative battles to win. Initially the club was limited to those at either university or who had graduated the year before. Corinthian-Casuals gave the club firm support at its initiation and it was hoped that Pegasus would provide them with players. But since it was impossible for the team to play together as a side before the annual University match in December, the club needed exemption to the later rounds of the Amateur Cup. Only if it could enter the Cup could Pegasus make any worthwhile impact. This exemption was

CENTRAL PRESS

PRESS ASSOCIATION

finally granted for one year on the basis that in future it had to be won on merit.

So the club could have died still-born had it lost its first Cup game against Enfield. The match had to be postponed to enable Pegasus to play and Enfield agreed on condition that Pegasus played on their ground, rather than, as drawn, at home at Oxford. The powerful Enfield side gave them a hard, anxious game, but Pegasus rallied to win 2-1. On a rising tide of success they surged through to the quarter-final. Their opponents were Bromley, then the most powerful side in the South, and the match at Oxford was perhaps the most exciting in their history. But it was Bromley who won by the odd goal in seven and who eventually won the Cup in the first Amateur final to be staged at Wembley.

But Pegasus had earned their exemption. After the success of the first year their rules were amended to allow graduates of two years standing to play and, later, even this limitation was abolished. The club was open to all graduates and

undergraduates but with the understanding that selection preference should be given to undergraduates. This caused problems between Pegasus and Corinthian-Casuals, but it allowed the club to maintain its impetus and twice win the Amateur Cup.

On the way to Wembley in 1951 Pegasus beat Gosport Borough Athletic, Slough Town, Brentwood, and Oxford City before they narrowly survived two breathless semi-finals with Hendon. In the first, at Highbury, Hendon went ahead in the final half-hour when Stroud's shot from the far post arrowed past Brown. A somewhat fortunate deflection gave Pegasus the equalizer in a grim struggle in the wind and rain. Then, with barely four minutes to play, Hendon were awarded a penalty. Dexter Adams hit the shot true and hard, high to Brown's left. Hats, coats and umbrellas went flying in the air as Brown arched across his goal to palm the ball over the bar. But that was a tame finish compared to the replay. With less time than five minutes to go Hendon

and Cowan never lost their poise or control in defence and their competent covering gave Pegasus ever-growing confidence.

Pegasus quickly adjusted to playing at Wembley. The presence of the large crowd did not have the distracting impact of smaller, homelier grounds. The pithy comments of Durham miners beside the touchline at Willington came over much clearer than that vast impersonal gathering at Wembley.

Just before the interval Pegasus should have taken the lead. The ball ran loose in the Bishops' penalty area and the eager Jimmy Potts, the left-winger, pounced on it. But his hasty shot was smothered by White. Yet it encouraged Pegasus—made them realize they could win.

It was with that stimulus that Pegasus stormed at the Bishop Auckland goal at the start of the second half. A close shot by Pawson flew up off the goalkeeper's elbow over the bar. From the corner the ball almost crept over the line but Hardisty stretched out an elastic leg to knock it away. Six minutes into the half the goal came. Some swift interpassing down the right drew the Bishop Auckland defenders out of position and Dutchman's deep centre was met by Jimmy Potts, diving forward to head into the far corner of the net. Potts, who rarely headed the ball, had chosen the ideal moment to give a perfect demonstration of the art.

Bishop Auckland desperately sought an equalizer but were unable to disturb the well-organized Pegasus team, whose long-ball tactics were proving superior. In the 80th minute Pegasus went further ahead through John Tanner, an amateur international later to play in the First Division with Huddersfield. Pawson cut inside, beat Hardisty and passed to Dutchman on the right-wing. He passed precisely to Tanner who raced past Davison to stick the shot into the corner of the net.

The Flying Dutchman and the Centaur-forward win the Cup for Pegasus

Yet with three minutes left Auckland's Nimmins put the ball just under the bar with a remarkable overhead kick from a corner. The shot dipped into the net just over the head of Ralph Cowan. It had needed something unusual to beat the Pegasus defence.

Those last seconds dragged interminably with the great prize so near. But there was only one more brief moment of expectation for Bishop Auckland as they forced a corner on the right. The response was a nonchalant dribble in his own area by Dennis Saunders and a precise pass that set the Pegasus forwards flying into a final assault before the final whistle. Even under mounting tension Pegasus had continued to enjoy their football and now they were free to hug their happiness in the warm spring sunshine. An impossible dream had become reality.

It was a dream that recurred again two years later when another capacity crowd at Wembley saw Pegasus beat Harwich and Parkeston by a crushing 6-0, their highest score until then in any Amateur Cup game. But that was the climax of a club that in a few years startled and enthused the world of amateur football and did as much for football in the schools. Pegasus' triumph had been one for genuinely amateur football, but the problems of co-ordinating Oxford and Cambridge, of maintaining a supply of top-class players in an ever-changing team, and of competing as true amateurs proved too difficult to sustain. Pegasus now is just a memory of a club that achieved swift and spectacular success with old-fashioned ideals. Perhaps they were fifty years behind their time, but their demise was sad nevertheless.

Pegasus: Brown, Cowan, Maughan, Platt, Shearwood, Saunders, Pawson, Dutchman, Tanner, Carr, Potts.
Bishop Auckland: White, Marshall, Farmer, Hardisty, Davison, Nimmins, Taylor, Anderson, McIlvenney, Williamson, Edwards.

were leading 2-1. Then Dutchman—the flying Dutchman as the papers inevitably christened him—snatched two decisive goals in the hectic closing minutes.

None of the team could quite credit that they were really to play at Wembley or that they had any chance against the formidable Bishop Auckland. The correspondents agreed. But the Pegasus coach was Vic Buckingham, the former Tottenham Hotspur player who was later to lead West Bromwich Albion to victory in the Cup. He arranged special practices with the Spurs team, and Arthur Rowe taught Pegasus their art of playing the game simply and with speed. Buckingham's pre-match instruction was confined to just three points: 'Don't worry about what they will do, make them worry about what you are doing. However you are playing want the ball all the time and help each other get it. And if you can run off the field at the end of ninety minutes you haven't been trying.'

Well, Pegasus tried and they also went out to enjoy themselves. Perhaps it was this that made the team's play so attractive to the spectators and critics. The cool, constructive play at wing-half of Pegasus' captain Dennis Saunders set the example. Alongside him was Ken Shearwood, who coped so effectively with McIlvenney, Bishop Auckland's amateur-international centre-forward. It was 57 minutes before he had a shot—and to make it worse he had to listen to a constant monologue from his tormentor.

Bishop Auckland had most of the game in the opening 20 minutes, but with inside-forward Anderson injured after five minutes their forwards were never as dangerous as Pegasus had expected. Bishop Auckland's captain, Bob Hardisty, was a tall, commanding player and one of the great names of amateur football. Without appearing to hurry he moved effortlessly over Wembley's lush and clinging turf, contributing well in midfield with Nimmins, a terrier of a player. Their styles contrasted but their matched effectiveness won the Bishops much of the ball. But Shearwood

Wh n Lofthous became the Lion

In bald fact Nat Lofthouse earned his nickname, 'the Lion of Vienna', by scoring two goals against Austria in the Prater Stadium on 25 May 1952. Like many bald facts, this statement conceals more than it conveys. The bare statistics, considered in isolation, seem unexceptional, but when seen in the context of all the circumstances, they take on a new importance. The FA member in charge of the England party perhaps put the matter into its true perspective, when he said after the game, 'I have had the pleasure of seeing a great team in their finest hour.'

To savour the full excitement of the climax, it is necessary to understand the anxiety which preceded it. This again is something not apparent from the record books. England arrived in Vienna unbeaten in their last eight games; they were returning to a city where they had only lost once (1936) and where, in pioneering days, they had been accustomed to winning with ease.

The Austrians clearly had plenty of old scores to square and, despite the impressive nature of England's record over the last few years, the most recent form of both teams suggested that the Austrians would have every chance to settle up at the Prater stadium. For England had begun their close-season tour with a 1-1 draw with Italy in Florence in which, after an early goal by Broadis, there had been a sad capitulation by the forwards.

Reporters had complained of lack of effort and spirit. Reuter's correspondent called the game 'one of the poorest internationals seen for years'. In the *Daily Express*, Peter Wilson struck at what was perhaps the root of the problem in terms to become familiar in more modern times: 'Each year we hear from the players complaints that the season is getting more and more congested and that the strain of the domestic season is becoming more excoriating.'

After the match in Florence, the party went to a retreat near Siena where team-manager Walter Winterbottom set about healing wounds with hard work. Clearly there had to be changes in the attack. But what changes? Not on the flanks, for the squad contained only two orthodox wingers; the 30-year-old Finney and the internationally inexperienced Elliott.

In the event, the inside-forwards Broadis and Pearson were replaced by Sewell and Baily, and one change was made in the defence which had performed stoutly in Florence—Eckersley for Garrett at left-back. One school of thought also favoured dropping Lofthouse, but the alternative was Allen of West Bromwich Albion, at that time uncapped.

The line-up as announced raised few hopes. In the League season just ended, the five chosen forwards—Finney, Sewell, Lofthouse, Baily and Elliott—had totalled fewer than sixty goals (against a yardstick of 46 by Dooley). Whatever confidence may have been building up at the training camp was not reflected elsewhere.

The lack of conviction in England's strength was well illustrated in a story that made the rounds of the service messes and canteens in Vienna. When the ball was kicked out of play in the match against Italy, the tale went, someone on England's bench dropped it in the trainer's bucket to reduce the bounce. The story is of doubtful authenticity, but the fact that it gained any credence at all is some indication of the general feeling about England's ball-skill.

In Vienna, the large British community waited with feelings not improved by news of England's 7-1 defeat at the hands of France in a 'B' international. At that time Austria's capital was still an occupied city. British servicemen and their families who would have to live on there with the result preferred not to contemplate what might be the aftermath of defeat for England.

Twelve months earlier, Scotland had been visitors to the Prater stadium. Outclassed by a team more gifted in every respect, the Scots had lost 4-0. To add to the ignominy, Steel had been sent off. At one stage, with the Austrians leading 3-0, a large section of the crowd, noticing a uniformed broadcaster commentating for the British Forces Network listeners, immediately made him the object of their derision; their grins were likely to be a good deal wider if their team could topple England as well.

Austria had scored 57 goals in their previous 16 matches

The performance of British teams in general had aroused a good deal of patriotic indignation in the Austrian capital. The strength of feeling was made plain in a letter to a newspaper from a member of the British Embassy staff. Disillusioned by clubs whose performances suggested that their close-season tours were no more than casual holidays, he attacked one team for showing 'no plan, no co-ordination and very little fighting instinct. . . . It really makes me feel ashamed to cheer British players.'

National pride was also at stake for the Austrians. Politically and economically their country had become a doormat for much of Europe. Vienna, in particular, still occupied by the troops of four nations, had found the end of hostilities and 'liberation' somewhat hollow. How sweet, then, to enjoy the reflected glory of a soccer team whose recent record suggested that they might be the best in Europe.

Austrian supporters, moreover, had every reason to be optimistic about the outcome of the match against England. Of their last 16 games ten had been won and four drawn. They had amassed a total of 57 goals in these games including eight against Belgium, seven against Yugoslavia, six against Eire and five against Yugoslavia, Hungary and Denmark.

Best of all, they had gone to Britain, and become the first continental side to win in Scotland before, eleven months later, holding England to a two-all draw at Wembley.

May 25th, a Sunday, was fine but overcast. The Prater stadium was an open bowl with a capacity of about 65,000. Although black market and other sources had supplemented the services' allocation of 1,400 tickets, English supporters were heavily outnumbered.

Austria wore their customary white so it was a red-shirted England that Billy Wright led on to the field. It was the Wolverhampton player's forty-second international, equalling the record set by Bob Crompton, the Blackburn full-back, between 1902 and 1914.

For the first 20 minutes, Wright found himself almost exclusively occupied in defence. In a series of fluent raids, the Austrians revealed the style that had dominated Europe, a style based on fast, hard-running wingers and strong mid-

Top *Jackie Sewell, in the dark shirt, almost evades the covering tackle of the Austrian full-back. The Austrians, with centre-half Ocwirk in midfield and left-back Happel marking Lofthouse, were often vulnerable to England's quick breaks.*

Above *Dienst, the Austrian centre-forward in the white shirt, races alongside Froggatt, the England centre-half. Dienst won the penalty from which Austria scored their first goal before scoring their second himself.*

field players with intuitive understanding. The team had been chosen from only four clubs, all based in Vienna; Rapid and F.K. Austria Vienna each contributed four men.

Much of the inspiration stemmed from Ernst Ocwirk, a tall, powerfully built man who played in the number five shirt. Some observers, used to the English style, gazed in wonderment at this attacking 'centre-half' but the Austrian formation was not as unorthodox as it might have appeared, for Happel, wearing three, was marking Lofthouse, the England centre-forward. Ocwirk's role was essentially in midfield. Ramsey, England's right-back that day, who also faced Ocwirk in club games, recalls him still as 'a player of genuine world class'.

In this opening phase, England resumed where they had left off in Florence, the defence tackling and covering stubbornly, the forwards struggling

to get into the game. But before the half-hour came three goals—two of them for England.

First, in the 21st minute, Baily broke up an Austrian raid on the half-way line. His pass to Elliott was pushed on to Sewell for a centre that found Lofthouse with his left foot poised. The volley sank deep into the netting.

England's followers have rarely known such a rapid turnabout of emotions as was packed into the next few seconds. English jubilation was immediately stilled as Froggatt brought down Dienst and Huber sidefooted home the penalty. But when England rose from the floor to hit back it was, appropriately, Froggatt who launched the counterpunch.

The Portsmouth centre-half began a move that was carried on by Wright and taken up by Sewell. With one wriggle the Sheffield Wednesday star showed why he had cost a record £34,000 from Notts County eighteen months earlier and thus became the first footballer worth his weight in gold. Feinting to go left, he swung right and restored England's lead with a hard, low shot that left Musil, the Austrian goalkeeper, prostrate.

In other days this might have been enough to destroy the morale of many a continental team, but these Austrians were a new breed. Melchior, a tall, direct winger, burst through and looked certain to score when Wright's brilliant interception saved England—but the respite was short-lived.

'If the goalkeeper had not checked as he came, I'd never have scored'

Three minutes before half-time, Dienst, who had been menacing throughout, collected a rebound from Froggatt's tackle and set off for goal. This time Wright's challenge was thrust aside and Merrick was left helpless. Two-all at the interval.

The second-half became a rugged struggle in which, for the most part, good football ran a disappointing second. The memorable, decisive break occurred eight minutes from the end. From a corner conceded by Elliott, Merrick caught the ball and threw out to Finney. Few shrewder readers of the game have worn an England shirt, and now the Preston winger saw Austria still exposed by their all-out attack.

A superbly judged through ball beat Happel. Into the empty half strode Lofthouse. As he advanced on the goalkeeper, the scene was reminiscent of the Roman amphitheatre—man against man in an atmosphere suddenly still. They met in an explosive collision. Lofthouse was prostrate but he had struck first. The ball rolled slowly into a vacant net.

Subsequently, England might have scored again as Lofthouse, after treatment on the touchline from Jimmy Trotter, returned to drive a shot against the post. Austria counter-attacked but time—and England's defence—beat them.

As the last minutes dragged by, uniformed servicemen began to infiltrate towards the running track, like sand trickling down the sides of the vast concrete bowl. At the final whistle, the pitch became a mass of khaki, the red-shirted English players lifted like wind-tossed poppies in a cornfield.

Today, Lofthouse recalls his crucial goal modestly. 'If Musil had not come, then checked before coming again', he says, 'I'd never have got there first.' On such a slender chance an imperishable reputation was made.

That night service messes held open house. And if the Lion of Vienna drank deep at the pool there was none to deny that he had earned the right.

Austria: Musil, Roeckl, Happel, Schleger, Ocwirk, Brink, Melchior, Hanappi, Dienst, Huber, Haummer.
England: Merrick, Ramsey, Eckersley, Wright, Froggatt, Dickinson, Finney, Sewell, Lofthouse, Baily, Elliott.

Above centre *Billy Wright and Alf Ramsey keep a close watch on Haummer, the Austrian winger. Ramsey and Wright were set many more demanding problems by a forward line that was amongst the best in Europe at the time.*

Above *Musil, the Austrian goalkeeper, dives in vain as Sewell (out of picture) scores England's second goal. Following up is Lofthouse, whose two goals won the match and established his nickname, 'the Lion of Vienna'.*

Did Bolton make Matthews a gift of that medal?

The 1953 FA Cup Final has gone into history as perhaps the most famous of them all, a Final of such drama, with such a remarkable ending, that an author writing for a children's comic would have the story rejected for allowing his imagination to run too wild.

Scoring twice in the last three minutes, Blackpool won 4-3 after Bolton had led 3-1 with three-quarters of the game gone. Blackpool's exceptional recovery—no other team had come back from being two goals down in any of the previous 71 Finals—won them the Cup and gained them some consolation for their defeats in the 1948 and 1951 Finals. It gave Wembley's crowd a match to remember.

But, more, this Final is remembered as the one which gave Stanley Matthews the winners medal that had been his lifelong ambition.

Matthews, a brilliant if inconsistent winger with Stoke before the War, came to greatness in the unofficial internationals played between 1940 and 1946. After the war he moved to Blackpool where he further extended his reputation, destroying defence after defence with his unique combination of speed off the mark, ball control, and supreme fitness—fitness that enabled him to go on playing at the age of 50.

Matthews was a great entertainer, and spectators everywhere admired him. When Blackpool reached the Cup Final, thousands of people who had never even been to a football match wanted Blackpool to win, not because it was their third attempt to win a Cup Final, not because skipper Harry Johnston and team mates Shimwell and Mortensen had two losers medals apiece, but simply because of Matthews' presence.

And so Blackpool, seventh in the League and with the legendary Matthews in their side, went into the Final as favourites—in every sense—over Bolton, who had ended the season in 14th place. As both teams had somewhat porous defences, plenty of goals seemed likely, and a devastating solo performance was expected from Matthews who, at 38, was surely faced with his last chance of a Cup winners medal.

But when the match began, it was Bolton, not Blackpool and Matthews, who took command. After just 75 seconds, Blackpool goalkeeper George Farm let a long, low drive from Nat Lofthouse, the Bolton centre-forward, slip through his grasp and into the net to put Bolton one goal ahead.

Bolton very nearly went two up after 20 minutes when Lofthouse again beat Farm. Unluckily, his shot hit the post. But there was worse to come for Bolton. Left-half Eric Bell pulled a muscle, an injury that had been troubling him before the game, and with no substitutes allowed he moved to the left wing. Bolton were forced to reshuffle their side and, as a result, Blackpool continually won possession in midfield. Blackpool began to threaten an equalizer, and with ten minutes to go to half-time, they got it. Mortensen sped past the defence, and his left-foot shot cannoned into the net off inside-left Hassall's outstretched foot.

The effect of this somewhat freak goal was immediately cancelled as Farm in the Blackpool goal blundered again. Bolton, reduced to ten fit men, and once more on even terms with Blackpool, reacted determinedly to the crisis and within four minutes of Blackpool's equalizing goal regained the initiative. Farm was slow to come off his line when Langton lobbed the ball forward, and inside-right Willie Moir dived across him to divert the

ball past him with his head, and into the net for Bolton's second goal.

Ten minutes into the second half, Matthews' hopes of a winners medal seemed dashed beyond repair as Bolton, shrugging off their handicap, went further ahead. It was the injured Bell who scored. Defying the pain from his leg, he leapt to head a ball centred by Holden into the Blackpool goal. The ball now having been there three times, Bolton looked safe.

So Blackpool's defence had again proved suspect, and with but 35 minutes of playing time remaining, it seemed impossible that the forwards could make good the damage, especially as Matthews had not figured much in the match so far.

But then began the Matthews half-hour, thirty minutes which made such an impact on the course of the game that the Final is popularly known as the Matthews Final. In that period he was unstoppable, his control and amazing speed tearing Bolton apart. Surpassing anything he had done in his long career, the Blackpool outside-right dominated Wembley as no individual had before, or has done since.

Matthews received pass after pass from his team mates, Taylor in particular. With Ralph Banks, his immediate opponent, handicapped by cramp, Matthews swept through Bolton's now weakened left flank, and gradually Blackpool swung the game. In the 68th minute, a high Matthews centre was dropped by Hanson, the Bolton goalkeeper, and despite colliding with an upright, Mortensen forced the ball in.

'The notion that it was a one-man match is sentimental nonsense . . .'

Twenty-two minutes were left for Blackpool to get another goal. Was that enough time? Bolton reeled as Matthews tormented and punished the defence. He continually shuffled past Banks, fooling him with his famous feint and body swerve. As Johnny Wheeler said afterwards, 'That last half-hour was sheer hell. We all knew the way Matthews operated—the shuffle up to the defender, the feint, the dart past. But knowing it and doing something about it were two different things!'

And so Matthews, determined to avoid another losers medal, swayed down the right wing, bewildering the defenders, equally determined in their efforts to contain him. Yet as the ninetieth minute loomed up, it seemed that for all Matthews' endeavour, he was again going to be unlucky. The chances he had created for Mudie and Perry had been wasted. Hanson had saved well from Mortensen on one occasion. And Bolton still clung to their lead.

According to referee Mervyn Griffiths, there were only two seconds left for play when Blackpool equalized. Mortensen, taking a free kick on the edge of the penalty area, thumped the ball high into the net. Ernie Taylor normally took those kicks, but he judged there to be no way through the 'wall' of Bolton defenders. Mortensen, fortunately for Blackpool, proved him wrong.

In injury time, Blackpool continued to give Matthews a stream of passes and Matthews continued to make good use of them. As he had done so often, he cut down the right wing, and inevitably dribbled inside the unhappy Banks. Round one more defender, centre-half Barrass,

and from the goal line he hooked the ball back to Bill Perry who crashed it into the net. 4-3 to Blackpool. Less than a minute later, referee Griffiths signalled the end of the game. Matthews had his medal after all, to the enthusiastic acclaim of Wembley.

Over the years, a mystique has surrounded this unforgettable match. That it was Blackpool's first FA Cup win in three Final appearances, that it was Mortensen's, Shimwell's and Johnston's third attempt at a winners medal, that Mortensen scored the first Cup Final hat-trick this century, that the seven goals was the highest aggregate in a Wembley Final—all this is forgotten. What is remembered is Matthews' tremendous display in the last leg of the match that led to his at last winning the prize he had wanted before retiring, a winners medal.

Not surprisingly, in the climate of the era and with the passing of time, the part Matthews played has been given even greater prominence. Television flashbacks to the match—the film must be almost threadbare through so much showing—concentrate almost entirely on the closing stages, adding to the aura of one man's invincibility. Mention Wembley 1953 and the reaction is usually one of ecstatic rapture—and an immediate reference to Matthews. Thus the legend has grown and fed upon itself.

But what did those involved, players and managers, think of the Final? Did Bolton throw the game away with the wrong tactics?

Ernie Taylor, Blackpool's midfield schemer, was later scathingly critical of the tactical switch that led to Harry Hassall, Bolton's inside-left, moving to left-half. 'They gave it to us,' he said. 'They should have switched their team around differently when Bell was hurt. They should have moved Johnny Wheeler across from right-half. Wheeler was a good defender. Taking Hassall out of the attack left them short of punch. I don't know what their manager was playing at.'

Hassall's place in the forward line was taken by Langton, a player who had made his debut 16 years earlier. Langton found it too strenuous a role on a hot afternoon on the most tiring of pitches.

Taylor was not the only person to criticize Bolton's tactics when Bell was injured. His manager, Joe Smith—a Bolton player for 16 years—maintained that right-winger Doug Holden should have gone to the left, to do the harrying that Langton could not manage, and that the full-backs should have been exchanged as well.

And Bolton's attempts to protect their 3-1 lead would be viewed with scorn were they to be used in a modern Cup Final. Long kicks upfield were promptly returned. (Lofthouse was badly shaken in a fall, and was extremely well handled by skipper Harry Johnston.) And although Lofthouse and other Bolton players repeatedly kicked into touch, there was none of the possession play now so evident. Nor—to Bolton's credit—was there any 'professional fouling' of Matthews. Indeed, Bolton's players acted throughout with commendable sportsmanship, never more so than in the last desperate stages.

Bolton manager Bill Ridding admitted in a radio interview that he had not given special instructions to his players on how to deal with Matthews. According to Lofthouse, the gist of Ridding's pre-match talk was, 'I'm not going to tell you how to play, but try to dictate the game.' Ridding was perhaps in step with the rest of his managerial colleagues of the time. The game was different then. The examination of opponents, the study and exploitation of weaknesses, these were not considered on the scale they are today. The players were simply left to play as they saw fit.

In fact, of the six popular daily papers, only one made any reference in the after-match reports to Bolton's tactics. Accounts of the game consisted mainly of sympathy for the losers and indulgent praise for the winners—Matthews in particular, 'scribbling with his fantastic feet the greatest Cup Final story of all time', as one newspaper wrote. The same paper devoted a leading article to Stanley, referring to 'the personal triumph that

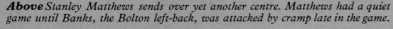

Above *Stanley Matthews sends over yet another centre. Matthews had a quiet game until Banks, the Bolton left-back, was attacked by cramp late in the game.*

Above *Mortensen pulls Blackpool back to 2-3. A high Matthews cross is dropped by Hanson and, despite colliding with an upright, Mortensen scores.*

has delighted and thrilled the whole country.'

But is even this true? Did Matthews really win the game on his own?

Looking back, the facts suggest not. Banks, the defender marking Matthews, was little more than a cripple who would have been unable to stop any winger. 'Once Banks was limping,' Matthews told reporters after the match, 'I knew our chance was to keep hammering away at the weak spot.' Yet Matthews failed to take complete advantage of this opportunity, most of his crosses dropping harmlessly over the bar. And his pass to Perry in injury time was a miskick delivered as he lost his balance and fell.

Matthews himself later said, 'It was my greatest day, but I didn't win the match on my own.' Ernie Taylor certainly agrees with that. 'Our hero was Morty,' he says. (Mortensen scored three of Blackpool's goals.) 'The notion that it was a one-man match is sentimental nonsense. The idea has grown over the years. I know how well Stan played—for part of the match. But he needed others to back him up.'

Perhaps Mortensen should have the last words.

'The match could have been a lot different,' he says. 'There were so many turning-points in it.'

Could a modern Cup Final be won by a team two down? 'Of course. Manchester United could do it, with Best. Spurs could do it, with Chivers and Peters. West Ham could do it, with Hurst. Everton did it in 1966. Any team could do it, provided they had a player, like we had in Stan, who was prepared to go at a defence and keep going at them. Bolton didn't know how to stop him— simply because he was who he was. It's bad enough for a team to find some inspiration when an ordinary opponent hits a spell and keeps making trouble. When it's a player who is a legend, like Stan, then the pressure is all the greater.

'I know that recoveries like ours are rare nowadays, with defences so well organized. But they aren't impossible, if you *believe* you can do it. That's the secret. That—and having someone like Matthews.'

Mortensen pinpoints the value of having a player like Matthews in your team. For when a player is a legend, it does not matter how well he plays, his mere presence can terrorize the opposition. And this was certainly what happened in the 1953 FA Cup Final. Matthews did not have a great game, but he scared Bolton, and in those last desperate moments, when the tension and the struggle were at their height, it was his reputation that finally swung the match Blackpool's way, his last-minute pass to Perry securing the FA Cup for his club and that precious winners medal for himself.

Blackpool: Farm, Shimwell, Garrett, Fenton, Johnston, Robinson, Matthews, Taylor, Mortensen, Mudie, Perry.
Bolton Wanderers: Hanson, Ball, Banks, Wheeler, Barrass, Bell, Holden, Moir, Lofthouse, Hassall, Langton.

Right *The Blackpool players celebrate the first FA Cup win in the club's history, chairing skipper Johnston and right-winger Matthews. Blackpool came from two goals behind to overhaul Bolton 4-3. Three of Blackpool's goals were scored by Mortensen (far right), here enjoying the moment with Matthews.*

THE match to remember

23

When Hungary defeated England at Wembley in 1953 they closed the door on an era that had lasted 81 years. The side's 6-3 home defeat on that dank November day was her first ever by foreign opposition. But it was less the fact of Hungary's victory than its manner which gave the game its renowned place in soccer folklore.

Twenty years later those ninety minutes can still be fairly called the most significant and memorable ever played on an English football field. Much has been written about the match since. Every attempt to analyse tactical evolution in the following decades inevitably referred to it as a vital turning point. But how did the game appear at the time? The following day The Times *published this report by Geoffrey Green, which* Sixty Memorable Matches *prints with its permission. Even with years of hindsight, there seems little need for addition.*

Yesterday by 4 o'clock on a grey winter's afternoon within the bowl of Wembley Stadium the inevitable had happened. To those who had seen the shadows of the recent years creeping closer and closer there was perhaps no real surprise. England at last were beaten by the foreign invader on solid English soil. And it was to a great side from Hungary, the Olympic champions, that the final honour fell. They have won a most precious prize by their rich, overflowing, and to English patriots, unbelievable victory of six goals to three over an England side that was cut to ribbons for most of an astonishing afternoon. Here, indeed, did we attend, all 100,000 of us, the twilight of the gods.

England—strangers in a strange world of flitting red spirits

There is no sense in writing that England were a poor side. Everything in this world is comparative. Taken within the framework of British football they were acceptable. This same combination—with the addition of the absent Finney—could probably win against Scotland at Hampden Park next April. But here, on Wembley's velvet turf, they found themselves strangers in a strange world, a world of flitting red spirits, for such did the Hungarians seem as they moved at devastating pace with superb skill and powerful finish in their cherry bright shirts.

One has talked about the new conception of football as developed by the continentals and South Americans. Always the main criticism against the style has been its lack of a final punch near goal. One has thought at times, too, that perhaps the perfection of football was to be found somewhere between the hard hitting, open British method and this other, more subtle, probing infiltration.

Yesterday the Hungarians, with perfect team work, demonstrated this midway point to perfection. Their's was a mixture of exquisite short passing and the long English game. The whole of it was knit by exact ball control and mounted by a speed of movement and surprise of thought that had an English team ground into Wembley's pitch a long way from the end. The Hungarians, in fact, moved the ball swiftly along the ground with delicate flicks or used the long pass in the air. And the point was that they used these variations as they wished, changing the point of attack at remarkable speed. To round it off—this was the real point—they shot with the accuracy and speed of archers. It was Agincourt in reverse.

One has always said that the day the continental learned to shoot would be the moment British football would have to wake up. That moment has come at last. In truth, it has been around the corner for some time, but there can no longer be any doubt. England's sad end on the national stage now proclaims it to the skies.

Outpaced and outmanoeuvred by this intelligent exposition of football, England never were truly in the match. There were odd moments certainly when a fitful hope spurted up, such as when Sewell put us level at one all at the quarter hour and later during a brave rally that took England to half-time 2-4 down. Yet these were merely the stirrings of a patriot who clung jealously to the past. The cold voice of reason always pressed home the truth.

Indeed from the very first minute the writing loomed large on Wembley's steep and tight-packed banks. Within sixty seconds Hungary took the lead when a quick central thrust by Bozsik, Zakarias, and Hidegkuti left the cenfre-forward to sell a perfect dummy and lash home, right foot, a swift rising shot to the top corner of Merrick's net. The ball was white and gleaming. It could have been a dove of peace. Rather it was a bird of ill-omen, for from that moment the Hungarians shot ten times to every once of England.

Just before England drew level a sharp move of fascinating beauty, both in conception and execution, between Czibor and Puskas was finished off by Hidegkuti. But the Dutch referee gave the centre-forward offside, which perhaps was charitable as things ended. Yet the English reply when it did come also arrived excitingly, for Johnston, intercepting in his own penalty area, ran forward to send Mortensen through. A quick pass to the left next set Sewell free and that was one-all as a low left-foot shot beat Grosics.

But hope was quickly stilled. Within twenty-eight minutes Hungary led 4-1. However disturbing it might have been, it was breathtaking. At the twentieth minute, for instance, Puskas sent Czibor racing down the left and from Kocsis's flick Hidegkuti put Hungary ahead again at close range, the ball hitting Eckersley as he tried a desperate interception. Almost at once Kocsis sent the fast-moving Czibor, who entered the attack time after time down the right flank, past Eckersley. A diagonal ground pass was pulled back by Puskas, evading a tackle in an inside-right position—sheer jugglery, this—and finished off with a fizzing left-foot shot inside the near post: 1-3.

Minutes later a free kick by the progressive Bozsik was diverted by Puskas's heel past the diving Merrick, and England, 4-1 down with the half-hour not yet struck, were an army in retreat and disorder. Certainly some flagging courage was whipped in that rally up to half-time by Matthews and Mortensen, both of whom played their hearts out, crowded as they were, but though it brought a goal it could no more turn back the tide of elusive red shirts than if a fly had settled on the centre circle.

After an acrobatic save by Grosics to a great header by Robb it was Mortensen, dashing away from a throw-in, losing then recovering the ball and calling up some of his dynamic past, who now set Wembley roaring as he sped through like a whippet to shoot England's second goal. But 2-4 down at half-time clearly demanded a miracle in the space left after some of the desperate escapes at Merrick's end that had gone hand in hand with the telling Hungarian thrusts and overall authority.

Within ten minutes of the interval the past was dead and buried for ever. A great rising shot by Bozsik as the ball was caressed back to him on the edge of the penalty area after Merrick had turned Czibor's header on to the post made it 5-2, and moments later Hidegkuti brought his personal contribution to three within a perfect performance as he volleyed home Hungary's sixth goal from a lob by Puskas. It was too much. Though Ramsey said the last word of all for England with a penalty kick when Mortensen was brought down half an hour from the end the crucial lines had been written and declaimed long since by Hungary in the sunshine of the early afternoon. Ten minutes before the end Grosics, with an injured arm, surrendered his charge to Geller, his substitute, but by now a Hungarian goalkeeper was but a formal requirement.

England were beaten on the ground, in the air, and tactically

So was history made. England were beaten at all points, on the ground, in the air, and tactically. Hidegkuti, a centre-forward who played deep in the rear supplying the midfield link to probing and brilliant inside-forwards and fast wingers, not only left Johnston a lonely, detached figure on the edge of England's penalty area but also scored three goals completely to beat the English defensive retreat. But Johnston was not to blame: the whole side was unhinged. The speed, cunning, and shooting power of the Hungarian forwards provided a spectacle not to be forgotten.

Long passes out of defence to five forwards who showed football dressed in new colours was something not seen before in this country. We have our Matthews and our Finney certainly, but they are alone. Taylor and Sewell, hard as they and the whole side now fought to the last drop, were by comparison mere workers with scarcely a shot between them at the side of progressive, dangerous artists who seemed able to adjust themselves at will to any demand. When extreme skill was needed it was there. When some fire and bite entered the battle after half-time it made no difference.

English football can be proud of its past. But it must awake to a new future.

England: Merrick, Ramsey, Eckersley, Wright, Johnston, Dickinson, Matthews, Taylor, Mortensen, Sewell, Robb.
Hungary: Grosics, Buazanszky, Lantos, Bozsik, Lorant, Zakarias, Budai, Kocsis, Hidegkuti, Puskas, Czibor. Sub: Geller.

In 1953 England were not only beaten by the magnificent Hungarian team, they were completely outclassed. It was the end of an era for English football. 1 Billy Wright smiled confidently as he led England out at Wembley, but then England had never been beaten at home by a foreign side. Yet after sixty seconds England were losing 1-0 and 4 and 5 within sixty minutes Hidegkuti had scored his third and Hungary's sixth goal which Grosics 6, the Hungarian goalkeeper celebrated by performing somersaults in the deserted Hungarian half.

The following year England visited Hungary, to discover in Budapest, as these rare Hungarian pictures 2 and 3 show, that their Wembley defeat was not an accident. Both the scoreboard and the expression of England team-manager Walter Winterbottom (glasses) clearly display England's further humiliation. The complete defeat in Budapest only confirmed the verdict after the previous result at Wembley: England were no longer the dominant force in football; the past no longer guaranteed British supremacy.

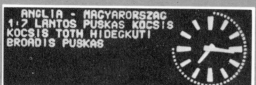

ANGLIA – MAGYARORSZÁG
1:7 LANTOS PUSKAS KOCSIS
KOCSIS TOTH HIDEGKUTI
BROADIS PUSKAS

Little Port Vale upset the odds — and the fans

On a blustery March afternoon in 1954, Port Vale, an undistinguished football team from among the slag heaps and grimy streets to the north of Burslem in Staffordshire, went close to establishing themselves as the most notable giant-killers of all time.

They very nearly became the first Third Division side to get to Wembley. They almost beat mighty West Bromwich Albion, then the League leaders, in the semi-finals of the FA Cup. Yet what Port Vale achieved was not the acclaim that usually accompanies great footballing feats, but notoriety.

The reason for Port Vale's unpopularity—outside their home town—was the way they played their football. They overcame opponents with a method that kept seven or eight men in the penalty area, with the others never very far away. It was defensive football, a style that by the 1970s had been accepted as commonplace. But in 1954 it was considered grotesque, even unfair. The fear of the British public was that if Port Vale continued to gain famous victories with this dour, extremely dull style, other teams might see it as a way to achieve success. Events have proved that fear fully justified.

'I can remember people saying that Port Vale were killing the game'

'I can remember, even at this distance, that people were saying that we were killing the game' recalls Basil Hayward, centre-forward for Port Vale throughout that memorable season. 'But we were simply well-organized, that's all. We all worked and ran for each other. We defended in great numbers, broke to attack quickly, and we developed the habit of restricting opponents to a minimum of chances while making the most of those that came our way. We just worked at it all the time.'

There was other evidence of the efficient way that Port Vale, guided by the thoughtful managership of Freddie Steele, harnessed their skill. They conceded just 21 goals in 46 League games, a defensive record that no team in the Football League has bettered. And besides reaching the semi-finals of the FA Cup, they carried off the Championship of the old Third Division (North) by eleven points.

But their well-organized method was before its time. While it brought them success, it brought them infamy too. Port Vale alienated most of the neutral footballing public. The dogged win-at-all-costs policy, whether or not it brought rewards, then counted for nothing; the public demanded open, attacking football.

If Port Vale had beaten West Bromwich, if they had reached the Cup Final, it would have been considered a moral injustice. As it happened, before a vocal and passionate crowd of 68,221 at Villa Park, West Bromwich, then two points out in front in the First Division, scored twice in the last half-hour to overhaul Port Vale.

Order, it was felt, had been restored and the good of football had been protected from this onslaught of a Third Division side impertinent enough to attempt to show their betters a better way to play.

West Bromwich Albion, of course, were formidable and talented opponents. But Port Vale's confidence was not dented by thoughts of

Right *After a rare Port Vale counter-attack, only a fine save by Heath, the West Bromwich goalkeeper, prevented the Third Division side from stealing ahead. Vale's emphasis on defence certainly brought them success, but it made them few friends.*
Below left *Port Vale's defence was at its famous best when, early on, WBA put them under considerable pressure. Here, inside-left Nicholls almost forces his way through the Port Vale rearguard.*
Below right *When Albion finally scored, it shattered Vale. Dudley sent over what was meant to be a cross, it was deflected, and the scores were level.*
Bottom *The issue was settled in WBA's favour when Allen slotted home this disputed penalty.*

TOPIX

meeting the finest opposition in the land. When Ken Griffiths, their diminutive inside-left, was declared unfit, not even the necessary team-change, their first in eight Cup ties, could destroy their belief in themselves.

Their self-confidence had been built up by a demanding run to the semi-finals, which made them the first Third Division side to reach that stage since Millwall in 1937. Port Vale started at Darlington, where they pulled back from a one-goal deficit at half-time to win 3-1. In the second round they were grateful for a 1-1 draw after an uncomfortable struggle at Southport, though they had an easier time in the replay, winning 2-0.

After two testing away matches, Port Vale's luck was still out in the next round. They had to travel to Queen's Park Rangers, then in the bottom six of the Third Division (South). Rangers, on their compact Loftus Road ground, did not submit easily, but Vale took the only goal of the match in the second half.

In the fourth round Vale were again on their travels, this time to Cardiff. The Welsh side were comfortably placed in the First Division and Port Vale's run was expected to end at Ninian Park. But with goals either side of half-time from Leake and Griffiths, Port Vale pulled off the shock result of the round.

Fate was kinder to them in the fifth round of the Cup. At last they had a home tie—and what a tie. Blackpool, the Cup holders, complete with Stanley Matthews, made a sentimental journey back to the area where it all began. Small wonder that a crowd of 42,000 turned up to watch.

Not even Blackpool and Stanley Matthews could beat Vale's defence

They saw only one flash of the authentic Matthews skill before Blackpool found themselves two down. Leake headed the first after 14 minutes, Hayward laid the second on for him 11 minutes later, and Port Vale never looked back.

In the sixth round Port Vale were paired with the only remaining club from the Third Division, Leyton Orient. Orient had ground advantage in a game which attracted 30,000 to see which unfashionable club would go through to the semi-finals. After 19 minutes it was again Leake who rounded off a move between Askey and Griffiths. Vale's magnificent defence made sure that was the end of the scoring.

In sharp contrast, West Bromwich had a much more straightforward route to Villa Park, with the expected victories over Chelsea (1-0), Rotherham (4-0), Newcastle (3-2) and Tottenham (3-0).

Griffiths had been expected to be a key component in Vale's system, a darting inside-forward who picked up the bits and pieces caused by the more belligerent style of Hayward. Vale's dressing-room spirit that season was so strong that many players turned out less than 100 per cent fit rather than risk the side's chances. On semi-final day, Hayward for instance had to have a pain-killing injection. But Griffiths, keen though he was, was forced to make way for Derek Tomkinson because of a knee injury.

The pitch had made a good recovery from heavy rain earlier in the week and, although only sparsely grassed, was firm and dry, the sort of conditions a skilled side like Albion would be expected to enjoy. Indeed, Port Vale's much-vaunted defence had to be at its best right from the start as Albion, switching the point of attack brilliantly, probed them mercilessly.

In the 20th minute only a post saved Port Vale when Griffin left two defenders in his wake and put in a shot that beat King's dive. For half-an-hour or so, Albion continued to surge forward, but when it came to breaking down Vale's defence, they fared no better than all the teams that had gone before them.

Suddenly Port Vale, having absorbed the early pressure according to plan, surged forward, increasingly encouraged by the crowd's traditional feeling for the less-fancied side as much as by Albion's frustration. Dugdale, under growing pressure, almost put the ball into his own net. It came as no surprise when Vale stole in front three minutes before half-time.

From a centre by Askey, whose ability to take the ball to the bye-line continually turned Albion's defence, a wild scrimmage developed in the goalmouth. Three Vale forwards lunged at the ball and missed before Leake finally forced it past Heath. Half-time beckoned, but Vale might have gone in two up if Heath had not left his line quickly to throw himself bravely at the feet of Hayward, who had gone clear. Vale were still attacking when the whistle went.

The start of the second half saw a similar pattern. The early poise and composure that had flowed through the Albion side ebbed away as Askey 'roasted' left-back Millard, and Hayward continued to torment Dugdale in the middle.

Albion, it seemed, had nothing left to offer. Their dream of the League and Cup double would remain, it seemed, just a dream. Then, with the match drifting towards three-quarter time, the afternoon turned sour for the little-known heroes from the Third Division as they conceded two goals with Wembley's twin towers less than thirty minutes away.

In the 66th minute Dudley hit over a long high ball from the right touchline. King made the fatal error of taking his eye off the cross to watch Nicholls and Allen as they raced in. None of the trio reached the ball and any hopes Vale had of clearing it were ended by a fractional deflection off centre-half Cheadle. The cross ended in the net and Dudley was credited with the goal.

That goal gave West Bromwich the injection of confidence and urgency they needed. Now, as in the opening half-hour, they again pinned the Third Division side back. For the second time a post stood between Albion and a goal and they appealed in vain for a penalty when Lee was brought down.

With 20 minutes left, Lee was once again sent sprawling and this time referee Webb, of Leeds, did award a penalty. It was to be the end of a long and seemingly impossible road for Vale and was made even more bitter for the team and its followers when the man who strode up to administer the *coup de grace* from the penalty spot was Ronnie Allen, the player they had started on his way to stardom as an unknown teenager, a few years after he had been a school rugby player.

Ronnie Allen, once a Port Vale player, scored West Brom's winning goal

Controversy over the two penalty incidents raged loud and long after the match and, no doubt, still crops up to-day in the Potteries. Hayward's version of the incidents was: 'I would say that the second time Lee was outside the area, but earlier, although I wasn't in such a good position to judge, Albion certainly seemed to have a case. Some people felt the ref gave the second because he realized he was wrong about the first—but who knows?'

Six weeks later Albion took the Cup when Frank Griffin scored in the dying moments at Wembley to give his side a 3-2 win over Preston. It was Albion's consolation for narrowly losing the League title to their neighbours Wolverhampton Wanderers. Port Vale's disappointment was soon submerged when they returned to Division Two after an absence of 18 years. They took with them the brand of football that had made them so unpopular, but that was in fact a foretaste of the method-play almost every modern side was later to adopt.

West Bromwich Albion: Heath, Rickaby, Millard, Dudley, Dugdale, Barlow, Griffin, Ryan, Allen, Nicholls, Lee.
Port Vale: King, Turner, Potts, Mullward, Cheadle, Sproson, Askey, Leake, Hayward, Tomkinson, Cunliffe.

Revenge for England, a Cup for Europe

25

European football, like a space shot to the moon, no longer startles the interest with its originality, but in the 1950s, when Wolverhampton Wanderers were exploring new football worlds, it was all fresh and tremendously exciting. The first floodlit matches were giving a glimpse of the soccer of the future, and Wolves had begun pioneering the new era with highly dramatic games at Molineux against First Vienna, Maccabi (from Israel) and Spartak from Moscow, a team they honoured by training on a Sunday for the very first time, and then emphatically defeated 4-0. But all this was merely the aperitif for the greatest match of them all—Wolves against Honved of Hungary under the Molineux floodlights on 13 December 1954.

The whole of Britain was fascinated by these exotic teams coming to play in such strange, flood-lit, almost magical, conditions. It was also slightly surprised that these foreigners played this *British* game so well. People half-expected some hybrid version of football and certainly did not anticipate the high level of skill that these teams displayed; they could have been scarcely more astonished if a team of Eskimos had arrived to play Test cricket.

Admittedly the public was not quite as ignorant since the Hungarian national team had humiliated England 6-3 at Wembley just over a year before, but they were eager to learn anything about the strangers that would reveal the secret of their success. What did they eat? How did they behave? Were they really the same as us? They expected some bizarre, 'foreign' reason for their excellence and there were even television cameras present at Molineux, ready to provide some explanation.

Honved arrived with no less than five players who were in the Hungarian national side in the 1954 World Cup final: Boszik, Lorant, Kocsis, Czibor, and the legendary Puskas. Wolves, the English Champions, countered with a good deal of local talent. England captain Billy Wright was the kingpin of a defence which included Bert Williams in goal, and Ron Flowers and Bill Slater. A forward-line led by Roy Swinbourne appeared handicapped by lack of height, but Johnny Hancocks had the speed, and Peter Broadbent the craft, to overcome this disadvantage. Above all, Wolves had the resolute spirit which enabled them to recover from being two goals down and win the game in an unforgettable climax.

Before play began, the Hungarians toured the perimeter of the pitch, throwing flowers to the crowd. It was an endearing gesture, but the roaring thousands found Wolves' gift of victory even more satisfying. Yet the first portents suggested an evening of disaster, not triumph.

The Hungarians began by probing for weaknesses down the wings and then confused Wolves with a switch to short-passing. Puskas, Kocsis and Budai interpassed through the defence so effectively that only a courageous plunge out of goal by Williams prevented an early setback.

Wolves were not allowed to compose themselves. Errors multiplied, each Hungarian attack became more dangerous, and in the eleventh minute even the brave Williams was beaten. Reg Leafe, the Nottingham referee, judged that Flowers had handled the ball. From the free-kick, Puskas jabbed the ball on to the head of Kocsis, who placed it into the net away from Williams.

Steeling themselves, Wolves retaliated strongly, and should have equalized. Swinbourne suddenly found himself with only the Honved goalkeeper to beat after he had eluded the attentive Lorant.

But he shot against the goalkeeper, and the crowd swayed back in disappointment.

By contrast, Honved were well-controlled. Three minutes after their first goal, they demonstrated just how chances had to be taken in top-class football. Kocsis sent Machos speeding through Wolves' defence and, with the ball under almost hypnotic control, he came quickly to the Wolverhampton goal. Williams came out with the appropriate desperation of the unarmed and deserted but, as the whole of Molineux feared, to no avail. Machos put the ball into goal as if it was a practice shot in a deserted stadium.

Honved rested a little on their laurels, though it was difficult to estimate how much the change of fortune before half-time was due to self-complacency or to fatigue and how much to Wolves' relentless pressure. Goalkeeper Farago came into the limelight as a succession of attacks fully stretched the Hungarian defence.

Swinbourne was by now determinedly seeking a goal, although it was Smith, on the left wing, who had the outstanding chance to score a deserved goal. Farago punched out from Wilshaw and the ball came temptingly to Smith. He hesitated, however, and a desperate Hungarian swept the ball away from him. The Honved goalkeeper saved magnificently from Flowers, Broadbent and Swinbourne before Smith, obviously keen to make amends for his mistake, forced the goalkeeper to turn his shot round the goalpost.

By now, perhaps, a less determined side than Wolves would have relaxed in disappointment. But with the support of Molineux and England's honour to retrieve, Wolves pressed forward constantly.

Smith had another chance when the goalkeeper was forced to push another shot out to him. Again the opportunity was lost. Wolves had already missed enough chances to have won the game and, keeping up this constant pressure, they risked a breakaway goal by Honved. The Hungarians tried to sieze such a chance near half-time. With a disconcerting use of the long pass inside the full-back, they brought some consternation to the Wolverhampton defence. Williams brought off another fine save just when another goal would have been disastrous, and so Wolves resumed the second-half still with a chance of saving the match.

A slim one it looked. Honved, proving that they were one of the mightiest sides in Europe, were two goals ahead despite all Wolves' efforts. Yet Wolves took inspiration from the incredible atmosphere at Molineux that night and, from the start of the second-half, pounded away at the Honved goal. Farago also seemed inspired, beating away shots, clutching centres, punching away those cunningly-flighted crosses from little Hancocks.

It was the Wolverhampton winger who was the centre of the incident which brought Wolves their first goal; he was fouled by Kovaks, and a penalty kick was the inevitable result. For a long moment the crowd was hushed. Hancocks was one of the best penalty kickers in the country, and he did not fail the Wolves at this crucial moment. The shot was hard and true; the crowd roared in joyous acclaim.

Honved, now more anxious, tried to halt the flow of attacks in midfield but Wolves' pressure forced a number of corner-kicks. Most of them brought some kind of scoring opportunity in the Hungarian penalty area, but were squandered by

ES THE GREAT!

Y HAD THE NELSON SPIRIT

By BOB FERRIER

IT AGAIN! AFTER SPARTAK, HONVED. WOLVES BEAT
LAST NIGHT.

that for a moment. Wolves beat Honved, champions of Hun-
greatest club side in the world, in one of the most glorious
ever seen.

rything—furious speed, blinding skill, pounding power, super-
eping, and something more.

It had, from Wolves, a strange,
scarcely describable bulldog spirit, the
Nelson spirit, that unquenchable moral
courage and faith in themselves that
now seems to be Wolves' copyright.

After the greatest first half I have ever
seen, in which the Hungarians played
brilliantly and proved themselves master
footballers, Wolves summoned up
apparently superhuman reserves of
strength and courage to grind Honved
into the Molineux mud.

It was a truly magnificent performance
in one of the greatest matches ever
played anywhere.

Now Wolves, who have clearly become
the Arsenal of the mid-century, can
rightly claim themselves club champions of the world.

Penalty Incident

The match turned on an incident four
minutes after half-time, when referee Reg
Leafe gave Wolves a penalty.

Left back Kovacs ran Hancocks off the
ball in the penalty area. To me it
merited nothing more than an indirect
kick for obstruction.

The decision horrified Honved, but not
Hancocks, who hammered the goal at fiery
pace past Farago to make the score 2 -1.

Molineux was a morass of mud. Surely
the Hungarian artistry would be drowned
in it, but it took them five minutes to
refute that . . . only ten minutes to
score. Mathos tried to cross a ball which
hit Flowers. The referee said "foul."
Puskas took the free kick and there was
Kocsis, best header of a ball in football,
sending it true and bullet-like past
Williams.

And two minutes later, Kocsis was
sending centre forward Mathos through
on a brilliant pass to hit a screaming,
swerving shot past Williams.

Defeat Spurned

But with a majesty that spurned de-
featism, Wolves plunged into furious
attack. Farago made fabulous saves from
Hancocks, Broadbent, Swinbourne, Wilshaw, Smith and Flowers from all angles.
Then came Hancocks's penalty goal.
Wolves were back in the game with a
bang and Honved failed temperamentally,
often kicking wildly to touch.

With fifteen minutes left, with Puskas
worried, the peak point of the drama was
reached.

Wilshaw made a long, determined
thrust down the left wing, crossed to
Swinbourne. The young centre forward's header beat Farago all the way.
Within two minutes, Shorthouse sent
down the wing to Smith, a perfect pass
inside, and then a blistering shot from
Swinbourne.

What a golden double for Wolves!
With these results, Wolves have made
English football once again a power in
the world game.

hits home.

urne scores the winner.

umps in vain.

game like it

inevitably

reat-hearted
Wright and
the Wolver-
ence to
under pres-
core as low
r forty-five

y

an defence
shakily
val. There
or it.
playing no
ertainly no
ey had been

of the ball
white jersey
y, with the
in by a split
were kick-

came the
and panic

stations for the Hun-
garians.

The football was not so
good as it had been, but
Honved never got their
domination back again and
were guilty of the most
childish attempts at time-
wasting.

It was like two strong
men trying to grip each
other's hands hard enough
to make the other beg for
mercy.

And suddenly you
realised that it was the
Hungarians who were
wriggling and shifting
and trying to get out of
the hold.

no, you KNEW . . . THAT
THE WOLVES HAD GOT
'EM.

The equaliser came from
Swinbourne's head but the
back-room architects had
been Wilshaw and Slater.

And before you could get
your breath back, or the
sweat out of your eyes—
yes, despite this raw,
clammy night you were
sweating now—Swinbourne
had done it again.

There was still nearly
ten minutes to go and with
less than two Honved
nearly—oh! so very nearly
—equalised through Csibor.

But somehow you
couldn't believe that
these titanic Wolves
could lose it now.

I may never live to see a
greater thriller than this.
And if I see many more as
thrilling I may not live
much longer anyway

over-excitement. Each near-miss was fresh
encouragement, however. The mighty Hungarians
could be harassed, it seemed, and forced into
desperate retreat. So, with Honved increasingly
nervous, Wolves now swelling with ambition, the
equalizing goal came in the 76th minute.

Swinbourne had been leading the Wolverhampton attacks so splendidly and it was
appropriate he should be the scorer. In the best
Wolves style, Slater sent a long, strong ball up
the left to Wilshaw, who made a sharp, twisting
run before sending a centre once more into the
ferment of the Honved goalmouth. This time
Swinbourne reached the ball first, and nodded it
past Farago to equalize.

By this time the spectators in the stands were
on their feet stamping and roaring. Wolves could
not just defend what they had gained and settle
for an honourable draw. They had no choice, the
crowd and their own fervour compelled them to
attack.

Wilshaw went clear again, and his centre came
to the middle just as Swinbourne was reaching
his full stride there. The centre-forward met the
ball on the volley to give the match an almost
fictional conclusion.

Yet, not quite the end, as Honved tried to
regain control. They still felt that there was a
slight chance that Wolves could be forced to yield
once more on their flanks. Czibor slipped through,
and with the crowd holding its breath, Williams
plunged out to smother his shot. A couple more minutes of suspense, and then Billy Wright and his
men were engulfed in the tumultuous acclamation.

It had been a marvellous game of football
which fully justified its publicity, but in retrospect one narrow home victory against a tired
touring side that had almost completed its own
league programme hardly marked a renaissance
in English football. Even if Wolves had attacked
incessantly it was, in part, because of the
Hungarians' tactic of retreating into defence. But
at the time Wolves' victory was hailed as a
vindication of English football; it was the popular
opinion that Wolves had beaten what was
practically the Hungarian national team and
proved that whatever was wrong with the
national team there was nothing wrong with
English football.

However, the most important consequence of
this excellent match was not the reassurance
derived by English chauvinists but its impetus
to the movement for international club football.
Gabriel Hanot, the editor of L'Equipe, the French
sports magazine, properly declared that: 'We must
wait for Wolves to visit Moscow or Budapest
before we proclaim their invincibility' but rightly
judged that if the British were confident of their
own superiority then it was the appropriate
moment to launch a European tournament.
Immediately L'Equipe published its plans for
what was to become the European Cup. Initially
FIFA and EUFA were not enthusiastic but they
could no more stop the tide than Canute and
eventually approved the scheme. More typically,
the Football League, perhaps more conscious of
their descent from that king, refused to permit
this contact with these foreign teams, apparently
fearing a congestion of fixtures.

So although it was English enthusiasm for
European football that had provided the ignition
for this new venture, Chelsea, the nominees for
the first competition, were refused entry by the
Football League. Perhaps the League could not
have been as autocratic if Wolves had been
England's representatives, but there again Wolves
could have easily lost their British reputation of
invincibility if they had had to compete away from
Molineux. Certainly, when they later participated
in the European Cup they were hardly equal to
such teams as Barcelona and Real Madrid. It was
their home victories over Spartak and Honved that
made their reputation.

Wolverhampton Wanderers: Williams, Stuart,
Shorthouse, Slater, Wright, Flowers, Hancocks,
Broadbent, Swinbourne, Wilshaw, Smith.
Honved: Farago, Sarosi, Kovaks, Boszik, Lorant,
Banyai, Budai, Kocsis, Machos, Puskas, Czibor.

SYNDICATION INTERNATIONAL

DERBY EVENING TELEGRAPH. DECEMBER 10, 1955

DERBY EVENING TELEGRAPH
FOOTBALL SPECIAL

No. 23,171   III   SATURDAY, DECEMBER 10, 1955   TWOPENCE

BURTON ALBION FORCE REPLAY WITH HALIFAX

SENSATIONAL 6–1 CUP DEFEAT OF THE RAMS

Chesterfield go out

HARTLEPOOLS UNITED were unfortunate not to be leading at the end of a goalless, cut and thrust first half at Chesterfield. Both goals had narrow escapes. Chesterfield were still full of fight after the interval and Smith scored for them in the 70th minute.

Luke scored two for Hartlepools.

HARTLEPOOLS UNITED visited Chesterfield this afternoon for their second round F.A. Cup-tie with an impressive run of victories behind them—seven wins from their last eight games—plus the knowledge of a 3–0 League win over Chesterfield at West Hartlepool last month, and the comfort of a

In the 13th minute Luke had to receive attention off the field for a few minutes when he skidded in chasing the ball out near the touchline and fell head first against the concrete surrounds.

Robinson was again the danger man, flashing across a high centre which Richardson did The

F.A. CUP — Second Round

Bedford ...	3	Watford ..	2
Half-time: 2–1.			
Bishop A. .	0	Scunthorpe	0
Bradford ..	4	Work'gt'n.	3
Half-time: 1–1.			
Bradford C	2	Worksop ..	2
Half-time: 1–2.			
Brighton ..	1	Norwich C.	2
Chesterf'ld	1	Hartlep'ls .	2
Half-time: 0–0.			
Darlington	0	Accrington	1
Half-time: 0–0.			
Derby C. .	1	Boston U.	6
Half-time: 1–3.			
Exeter C. .	6	Hendon ...	2
Halifax	0	Burton A .	0
Half-time: 0–0.			
Leyton O.	4	Brentford .	1
Half-time: 4–1.			
N'th'mpt'n	4	Hastings ..	1
Half-time: 0–1.			
Reading ...	2	Aldershot .	2
Shrewsb'ry	0	Torquay U	0
Southport .	0	Grimsby T	0
Swindon ..	1	Peterboro'	1
Tranmere .	0	Barrow	0
Half-time: 0–1.			
Walsall ...	2	South'pt'n	1
Half-time: 2–1.			
Weymouth	0	Southend .	1
York C. ...	2	Mansfield .	1
Half-time: 1–1.			

BOSTON UNITED gave Derby County a lesson in making and taking goal-scoring opportunities, when the two clubs met in the second round of the F.A. Cup at the Baseball Ground this afternoon.

Wilkins's goal in the 26th minute inspired Boston and following good work by Wilkins, Geoff Hazledine increased the United's lead in the 33rd minute.

Pye reduced the arrears from a penalty in the 38th minute, but three minutes later Birkbeck scored to give Boston a 3–1 interval lead.

Playing with only ten men in the second half—McDonnell was injured—the Rams proved no match for Boston and Geoff Hazledine scored in the 67th and 70th minutes and Wilkins in the 78th.

To-day's defeat was the Rams' heaviest of the season—and their first at the Baseball Ground this season.

(vertical, right margin) DERBY EVENING TELEGRAPH

26

The Boston team party

On the evening of Saturday 10 December 1955 a group of reporters stood waiting for a connection on Derby's dreary Midland Station. They had just seen Nottingham Forest defeat Swansea Town 2–1, but had yet to hear the result of a second round FA Cup tie between Forest's local rivals Derby and Midland League part-timers, Boston United.

Seeing a group of Boston supporters, they went up and asked the score. 'Six-one mate,' came the reply. It was no surprise; less than ten years earlier Derby had won the Cup and, though they were now in the Third Division, they were undefeated at home that season and good candidates for promotion at the first attempt.

It was not until these complacent journalists

26 mins.: Wilkins—from a Reg Harrison shot that was passing across the front of the Rams' goal.

picked up their Sunday papers the following morning that they discovered the truth. The score was correct, the assumed result completely wrong. Boston United had recorded the greatest ever victory by a non-League club over one of their League brethren. The margin equalled Wigan's defeat of Carlisle in 1934 and Walthamstow's performance against Northampton two years later, and it has not been surpassed since. Considering that Boston were away from home,

and that Derby were much better placed than any of the other clubs which have lost to non-League opposition by similar scores, Boston probably have a right to regard this performance as the greatest giant-killing feat of all time.

For Derby it was an unsurpassed humiliation. They attempted no explanation at the time and none has emerged since. So, nearly twenty years later, whenever Derby are drawn against undistinguished competition in a Cup tie, the local paper always prints the same warning—remember Boston!

Boston United had been members of the relatively insignificant Midland League since 1921. They had been worthy competitors, but never actually won the title. 1955–56, in fact, was to be their best season; they finished second behind fellow Fenland giant-killers Peterborough.

The small Lincolnshire port, famous only for the 'Stump'—the second tallest church tower in England—and a New England town named after it, had tasted little of soccer success. Memories had to go back to 1926, when a forward called 'Pint-sized' Porter had scored at Roker Park in the third round to find anything worthy of celebration. And that was to conveniently forget that Sunderland had scored eight by way of reply. In 1955 Boston were not regarded as giant-killers and a *News Chronicle* reporter judged that of all the tiny clubs fighting for Cup glory 'none

(vertical) COLORSPORT

Above Tommy Powell, Derby's left-winger, was the only player who satisfied the team's many critics after that match. His son, Steve, was later to play for Derby when they were League Champions. Curiously, both played alongside men named Todd.

33 mins.: Geoff. Hazledine—following good work by Wilkins and a Howlett shot that Webster held for a second before allowing the ball to slip from his grasp.

has a dimmer chance than Boston'.

But what Boston did have in 1955 was the luck of the draw. 'When Boston came out of the hat after Derby in the second round we were delighted,' says the man who both managed and played in goal for them, Ray Middleton. The reason was both simple and significant—Boston had seven ex-Derby County players on their books.

Middleton himself, after a career at Chesterfield and Derby during which he had picked up an England 'B' cap, had arrived at Boston in 1954. But five of the others, Ray Wilkins, Dave Miller, Reg Harrison and the Hazeldine brothers Don and Geoff, had all been bought virtually as a job lot at the end of the previous season.

The manager at Derby at that time was Jack Barker—and the mass exodus was part of his response to Derby's descent to the Third Division, for the first time in their history, in 1955. Nine years earlier they had won the Cup, and in 1949 had finished as high as third in the First Division. Their startling decline during the fifties was as mysterious as their subsequent collapse to Boston.

The disappearances of Doherty and Carter is not explanation enough as these two men, who had led them to the 1946 Cup Final, were expertly replaced with Billy Steel and Johnny Morris. At the start of the 1950s Derby were get-

> 38 mins.. Pye—from the penalty spot after one of three defenders who were crowding him away from goal had been penalised for hands.

ting crowds and results comparable with those at any time in their history. But the decline happened quickly enough, and manager Barker outlasted the five men he had sold to Boston by only a few months, making way for Harry Storer in October 1955.

Storer, who had won two caps when playing with Derby in the 1920s, was the archetype Sergeant-Major of a manager. He was also the Shankly of his time and 'Storerisms' abound. One of the best involves the twenty minutes he spent one Monday morning walking round the pitch with the club's centre-forward. 'What are we doing here boss?' asked the player when he tired of the meaningless behaviour. 'Looking for the hole you hid in all Saturday afternoon,' replied Storer. The whole of his team must have wished for the appearance of a cavity the size of the Baseball Ground when they had to face him at the end of that game against Boston.

'We expected to win to be honest,' said Middleton. 'Actually I couldn't see much of the game from between the posts where I was standing. Most of the action was at the other end. We had a good little side; we liked to attack and the team knew each other because it picked itself. The stars were the lads from Derby. When I'd heard they were coming free, I got in quickly to sign them. Having played with them all I knew they were good and it helped to make the team work as a unit.

'Naturally they were all delighted when we

> 41 mins.: Birkbeck—from a Howlett centre that appeared to produce momentary misunderstanding between McDonnell and Webster.

drew Derby. We didn't make any special plans. But we knew their weaknesses of course and played on them—especially down the wings.' Wingers Howlett, rejected by Forest at the beginning of the season, and Harrison, who had won a Cup winners medal with Derby in the 1946 Final against Charlton, ran riot. 'Harrison was as effective as young Cresswell was lacking in stature,' said the *Derby Evening Telegraph*. But the real Boston hero was centre-forward Wilkins, a schoolteacher during the week, who scored two goals and made three more. And Boston had even dropped their other ex-Derby player, Steve Wheatley, to make way for Howlett.

'It was all very simple really. There's no hidden excuse except that we were the better team, much the better team. Another 20 minutes and we would have won 10-0.' The *Telegraph* was more precise: 'Boston reached round 3 deservedly because they were much the better football unit. They had no time for kick and rush or unnecessary vigour. Just a good ration of football ability to which was allied 100 per cent endeavour.' They also scored more goals.

The crowd reacted to the game with either complete disbelief or total ecstasy. It had been

a big attendance, 23,757, but, as Middleton remembers: 'Most of them must have come from Boston the support we were getting. The town looked completely closed down when we left. Course, it was a local derby for us. And it was something of a topic of conversation for a few days afterwards as well.' No doubt also something of an understatement.

A Derby journalist who saw the game remembers the home fans' reactions, or lack of them. 'As it went on they just got more and more incredulous. There wasn't any trouble—heaven knows how many windows would be smashed if it happened today. But there didn't seem to be any post-mortems. Storer wasn't exactly pleased but it

Opposite page Derby's first home defeat of the season would have been headline news any week, but to be beaten 6-1 by a Midland League side was a sensational way to lose their undefeated record. Derby supporters came to regard the result as a fluke, which was less than fair to Boston.
Above Webster was unfortunate to be Derby's goalkeeper against Boston. His happier counterpart, Middleton, was one of six ex-County players who were in the successful Boston United team.

didn't finish anyone's career. After a while the fans just began to treat it as one of those one-in-a-million flukes. It is still looked on as a joke in Derby. Before the game we had billed it as Derby versus Derby Old Boys, though most people preferred Derby Rejects. It really was those six old Rams who did it. They played their hearts out.'

The press was uniformly scathing about Derby. The *Telegraph* said simply: 'You don't win Cup ties if your defence can't tackle and your forwards lack the spirit of aggression . . . the right-flank weakness had to be seen to be believed . . . Mays' misuse of the ball in midfield led directly to two goals. The whole team was tarred with the same lack of resolution. There was only one exception—Tommy Powell. He was always constructive, often artistic, always fighting for possession. A vital pass in the early moments to Todd might have turned the whole game, but the

> 67 mins.: Geoff. Hazledine—from a well-timed pass and solo run by Wilkins.

latter lacked the speed to beat Middleton and take the chance.'

When Derby took the field as Champions some 17 years later, Tommy Powell's son Steve, born just a few months before the humiliation, would take his place in the back-line alongside another man called Todd.

The game itself followed a simple pattern. Wilkins scored within half-an-hour and Geoff Hazledine got the first of his hat-trick soon after-

wards. Jesse Pye, an England international, pulled one back for Derby, but that, which was to be their only goal of the match, was scored from the penalty spot. 'I don't reckon to stop those,' Middleton recalls about the only blot on an otherwise flawless performance. The goalkeeper had in fact an injured right shoulder and had settled local speculation and anxiety only at the last moment when he decided to play. With so much of the action taking place at the opposite end it was a decision he never regretted.

With hardly any more time before the interval Derby's centre-half McDonnell had to go off with a knee injury, but this could not be used as an excuse. Boston's inside-left Birkbeck had already added a third and Derby were 3-1 down at half-time. As the *Nottingham Evening Post* observed, the Rams were unlucky to lose McDonnell 'But they had never displayed real confidence; they

> 70 mins.: Geoff. Hazledine—from a headed Wilkins pass after Reg Harrison had started the move.

were rarely together as a constructive force; they had far less skill than Boston'.

The second half was one-way traffic. Hazledine completed his hat-trick and Wilkins just missed his when a vicious shot almost broke the crossbar. Towards the end the Baseball Ground was in danger of witnessing a cricket score. The *Post*, possibly with one eye on Derby's League future, said of Derby: 'They will want to forget this exit, and the loss of their undefeated home record, in a hurry.'

It was Derby's biggest defeat since 29 January 1938 when Manchester City had won 7-1 at the Baseball Ground, and their biggest in the Cup since 1922 when they lost 6-1 away to Aston Villa. Still, they heeded the *Post*'s advice and did forget it. In retrospect, in fact, that day was the lowest point in a very low period for the club. It marked the end of Derby's rapid decline and the beginning of a much longer period of recovery. The fact that no one panicked after that humiliation may have prevented a total collapse. Derby finished second in the Third Division North in 1955–56 with 63 points; the following year the same number proved enough to win them the title and a place in the Second Division. A decade and a half later they were champions of the Football League.

In the meantime Boston United had tried their hand in the Southern and Northern Premier Leagues, leaving their more humble neighbours Boston FC as members of the Midland Counties

> 78 mins.: Wilkins—he dribbled the ball away from the advancing Webster before side-footing it into the net. Another move made by Reg Harrison.

League. There was a reminder of past glories in 1971–72 when they beat Hartlepool and lost by a single goal to Portsmouth in the third round.

Sixteen years earlier their third round display had not been quite so creditable. Drawn at White Hart Lane, they pulled in a healthy 46,185 gate but lost 4-0. Against First Division opponents and away from the Midlands Boston were not as potent, although they were hardly disgraced. Ray Middleton, now a Boston director, explains: 'We were caught on the heavy ground. They were fitter, got two kicks to every one of ours. It was Bobby Smith's first match. I like to think they had to sign him to be sure of beating us.'

At least there was no crushing defeat to detract from the glamour and glory of their historic victory over Derby. And who knows, if the rest of the side had been ex-Spurs players perhaps Boston would have won at White Hart Lane as well.

Derby County: Webster, Barrowcliffe, Upton, Mays, McDonnell, Ryan, Cresswell, Parry, Todd, Pye, Powell.
Boston United: Middleton, Robinson, Snade, Hazledine (D), Miller, Lowder, Harrison, Hazledine (G), Wilkins, Birkbeck, Howlett.

A Summers day at Charlton

27

Thirteen goals in one match. It sounds like one of the greatest team efforts in football history, and especially when the result was in doubt up to the last moment of the match. Yet, as the fans surged down from all parts of the terraces and stood in a cheering, waving, hilarious mass, once the players had been chaired off, it was one man they were calling for. 'We want Summers! WE WANT SUMMERS!' was the cry.

For this run of the mill Second Division meeting between Charlton Athletic and Huddersfield Town at The Valley four days before Christmas 1957, which drew only a moderate crowd of 12,000, turned into the triumph of Johnny Summers, the scorer of five of those Charlton goals.

Charlton had won by seven goals to six and never before or since had any side scored six times in a League game and left the field beaten. But the story is really two stories for, to savour the event fully, it is necessary to know of the remarkable but tragically short life of the player whom the delirious spectators singled out for boisterous acclaim on that memorable day in 1957.

Anyone who has played a game in new boots knows how Johnny felt that day

Fiction would never dare try to emulate the facts now to be recorded. With only a quarter of an hour played Derek Ufton, Charlton's captain and No 5, was carried from the field with a dislocated shoulder after a collision in a tackle. Substitutes were still nine years in the future so Charlton were doomed to play ten men for the remaining 75 minutes. They fought valiantly but by the interval Huddersfield had established a two-goal lead. In a subdued Charlton dressing-room Summers changed out of an old pair of boots held together with sticking plaster into a new pair not properly broken in. Every man who has ever played football at any level will know the blisters and discomfort arising from using new boots like this.

When the game was over and Summers was quietly sipping a drink he said to the journalists interviewing him: 'I'm going to keep these boots for the rest of my life. I shall probably give them to my son.' The rest of my life . . . .

John Summers, six feet, well built, handsome, with a head of dark, waving hair and a smile to charm the most frigid heart was the authentic hero figure that cold, dark December evening— a prototype of the successful professional footballer in his late twenties. Four and a half years later he would be dead, victim at 33 of the scourge of cancer.

He was born near Hammersmith, the best type of Londoner, quick-witted, humorous, brave, never prepared to admit defeat in any circumstances on the football field or off it. And when the disease struck he displayed consideration for the feelings of others and lived out his last days with dignity away from those who knew and liked him.

Before he established himself as a League star he prudently served a long apprenticeship in the printing trade. He was 21 when he made his debut for Fulham against Bolton Wanderers at Craven Cottage in November 1949. In the summer of 1950 Norwich City bought him and took him off to East Anglia but Johnny was a

spirit who could never be anything but a fish out of water away from London and it was not long before he joined Millwall. It was in November 1956, and Charlton paid what now seems the ridiculous sum of £6,000 for him in the vain hope —as it turned out—that his scoring flair would keep them in the First Division. Johnny did not fail his new club but Charlton had waited too long before getting out their chequebook. Less than a month after he left the Third Division Summers hit a magnificent hat-trick against Preston at The Valley, but North End won 4-3 and bottom of the table Charlton lurched nearer to the Second Division.

In the bath Johnny gasped: 'Three goals like that and not a stiver in bonus. There's no justice, is there?' But it was not the moan of a born whiner but the cheerful aside of a man who took everything fate could throw at him. Johnny could extract a laugh from any situation. There was the time he broke his leg playing for Fulham and the first occasion he appeared with it in plaster he tried to make a book with the rest of the staff, wanting to back himself that he would make the fastest return to action from such an injury. There was a morning in 1957 when a sportswriter called at The Valley to see the manager and the Charlton players were lined up in the corridor under the stand drawing their pay envelopes. Johnny grabbed him and said: 'If you slip off those specs, mate, and get behind me in the queue you've got a fair chance of copping a pay packet.' He was born a joker but he never gave offence and into the bargain he was a very nice person. Youngsters seeking autographs were never turned away, and when they asked for programmes—as they frequently did—he used to give what he had away and when they ran out he would take the names and addresses of the disappointed and put programmes in the post.

Most important of all, Summers scored 100

goals for Charlton, 10 of them in two games. Early in October 1960 Charlton met Portsmouth at The Valley. Summers, as he had against Huddersfield, wore the No 11 shirt and long before the final whistle the talk was of the famous match nearly three years earlier. Charlton won 7-4 and Summers scored five times. Here is how Johnny got his second nap hand: two with his right foot, two with his left and one with his head. 27 minutes—left-back Townsend's clearance helped on by inside-right Edwards whose pass eludes Gunter for Summers to slip it home. 46 minutes—Summers bobs up at inside-right and snaps the ball into goal when Townsend centres from the left. 56 minutes—Werge passes and Summers scores with a crisp left-foot drive. 70 minutes—Summers scores with a glorious header from a Werge corner. 88 minutes—Leary centres from the right and Summers slams it in. It was an amazing performance.

Although none at The Valley that day knew it, the sands were about to run out for Johnny Summers. This was to be his last season. The following season Charlton Athletic paid him a benefit cheque of £750 although they knew he was seriously ill. Soon they knew he would never play again.

Johnny knew it too and he kept away because he did not want to distress his mates or embarrass them, but on match days he would struggle to the ground from his Catford home and pay at

'Johnny's heart must have been breaking . . . he loved football'

the turnstiles. He could have had the run of The Valley, but he preferred it this way. One of the last of his old colleagues to see him was Stuart Leary, the great South African footballer-cricketer whose scoring had matched Summers. Johnny, still the lion-heart, still irrepressible, made light of his terrible situation. 'He did it to try and stop me feeling bad,' said Stuart, recalling the incident one day as he waited to go to the wicket and bat for Kent. 'Johnny's heart must have been breaking because he loved football but he said, "I'm not bothered, Stew. If I can't go back to the game I can always get a good job in the printing trade."'

He never did. On 2 June 1962 John Summers died at his home. If the foregoing demonstrates —as it surely must—that this man combined talent and character of a remarkably high order, it helps to understand more easily how Charlton

did the impossible with ten men against Huddersfield.

Two up at half time the Yorkshire side bored in mercilessly in the opening minutes of the second half and, in an astonishing spell that brought four goals in seven minutes, claimed three of them to lead Charlton by five goals to one. It was in this impossible situation that greatness arose in the heart and mind of Johnny Summers. Twice in a single minute he struck, scoring a goal himself (his second) and laying on another for John Ryan. It was 5-3 now and the crowd had begun to roar.

Summers, lifted above himself, tore all over the field. For half an hour he was no ordinary mortal. Sixteen minutes left and a scorching drive hit the back of the Huddersfield net. Summers had made it 5-4. Another six minutes it was 5-5 and then 6-5! Handicapped Charlton were actually in front and Summers had got five, including a six-minute hat-trick. Johnny had ripped Huddersfield to shreds, a one-man tornado, but now, as reaction set in, Charlton's timing relaxed and with two minutes left Town slipped away to make it six-all.

A fantastic end to a fantastic match—but there was more to come!

A fantastic end to a fantastic match but it was not over yet. Summers went off in one final, swashbuckling raid and, as the strength went from his legs and he saw the referee raise his whistle in readiness to blow full-time, Johnny Summers realized he couldn't make it. Out of the corner of his eye he saw John Ryan steaming up alongside in support. He passed the ball and responsibility to Ryan who belted it into the Huddersfield goal with the last shot of the match —the winning goal and the eleventh since half-time!

There still remains one scarcely creditable fact to hand on to posterity. Summers, a natural left-footer, scored all five goals in his new boots with his right foot.

There was just one way to describe this match —unique.

Charlton Athletic: Duff, Edwards, Townsend, Hewie, Ufton, Kiernan, White, Lucas, Ryan, Leary, Summers.
Huddersfield Town: Kennon, Conwell, Wilson, Taylor, Connor, McGarry, Ledger, Howard, Bain, Massie, Simpson.

Left *Johnny Summers, undisputed hero of the match, died tragically only four and half years later.*
Below left *One of the rare pictures of that Second Division match shows Huddersfield's first goal as Charlton's keeper Willie Duff dives despairingly.*
Below *Left-back Townsend (No 3) heads away from Huddersfield's Massie (No 10).*

PRESS ASSOCIATION

28

Epitaph for the Busby Babes

Sometimes an event is branded indelibly on the minds of those present. Such an example occurred on 1 February 1958. The occasion was a League match between Arsenal and Manchester United at Highbury. The final score that Saturday read: Arsenal 4, Manchester United 5. In itself the match was a classic, but it is as an epitaph above all else that it now stands. Within a week five of the side that helped fashion that victory were numbered among the United players who died in the snow and ice of Munich. The Highbury match was to be the last played on British soil by a young Manchester side that arguably contained more potential than any other to play for the club.

The Manchester side on that day read as follows; Gregg, Foulkes, Byrne, Colman, Jones, Edwards, Morgans, Bobby Charlton, Taylor, Viollet, Scanlon. With Jackie Blanchflower, the centre-half, Berry and Pegg, the wingers, and the inside-forward Billy Whelan, all being rested, this was the side that held Red Star to a 3-3 draw in Belgrade the following Wednesday night.

At Highbury, Manchester United gained a quick ascendancy. After only ten minutes they

snatched the lead through their powerful wing-half Duncan Edwards. A neatly laid-off pass from Viollet found Edwards a few yards outside the penalty box. In this position he was irresistible. His shot was driven too powerfully for Kelsey to handle and United were a goal up. The goal was typical of Edwards' shooting power. He had scored in much the same way against Scotland at Wembley; a similar goal also won the match against the German World Cup holders, captained by Fritz Walter at the Olympic Stadium in Berlin.

Next, on the half-hour, United were two up with a goal that was a model for the quick counter-attack. At one moment Gregg was saving superbly under the United crossbar, seconds later, straight from the clearance, Scanlon sprinted seventy yards down the left flank and Bobby Charlton crashed in the centre with all the explosive power that was to become his hall-mark. The goal prompted the *Guardian* correspondent into what was perhaps a rather belated acknowledgement of Charlton's genius. 'R Charlton', he noted, 'has grown from a limited left-sided player of little

pace into a brilliant inside-forward.'

United's magnificent performance was, of course, a team effort, but the contribution of their wing-halves stood out above all else. There can have been few pairs of wing-halves with more contrasting styles and appearances as Edwards and Colman, but both shared a belief in the old dictum that attack is the best form of defence. Each complemented the other to perfection; the one the aggressive dreadnought, the other the pocket Napoleon, they prompted and prodded the forwards into unceasing action. As the rhythms and directions of the attack were changed in midfield, the attack itself blossomed in response. Morgans, Charlton, Taylor, Viollet and Scanlon moved like one man.

A third goal was to come before half-time. Scanlon crossed from the one wing, Morgans returned the ball from the other, and Tommy Taylor slotted the ball past Kelsey in the centre to complete a goal of symmetrical precision. At half-time the rest of the game looked to be a formality. Up to that point the Manchester side, reigning Champions and Cup Finalists of the previous season and European Cup semi-finalists had revelled in all-out attack as natural to them as breathing itself.

The second half did indeed look to be a formality, but football was then a good deal less predictable than it is now. For it was an era when even the players with the technique and know-how of 'putting up the shutters' invariably lacked the inclination to do so when the alternative was to move on yet again with attack. The unexpected was in store. With half-an-hour left, phase two of the game exploded on the crowded scene. In a dazzling space of two and a half minutes, Arsenal were level. One moment United

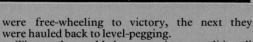

Far left Tommy Taylor, United's centre-forward, scores his team's third goal as Arsenal defenders lie prostrate like fallen skittles.
Above left Herd, the Arsenal centre-forward, scores the first of Arsenal's three goals in three minutes. Yet Arsenal's comeback was matched by United who went on to win 5-4.
Below left Evans, the Arsenal left-back, dramatically saves what seemed a certain United goal.
Above Duncan Edwards and Harry Gregg; the match at Highbury was Edwards' last in England. Gregg not only survived the crash but attempted to save his team-mates by returning to the wreckage.

were free-wheeling to victory, the next they were hauled back to level-pegging.

The goals tumbled out against a solid wall of noise. The breathless recovery was started by Herd, when he volleyed in a clever lob by Bowen. Gregg could only have heard that one. In another minute the score was 2-3 as Groves headed down Nutt's centre for Bloomfield to score. The cheers were still ringing as the match became all-square. Nutt's cross was low and precise and there was Bloomfield, diving forward to glance the ball into the net off his eyebrows. Highbury was a big top spinning madly; the stands nearly took off in the pandemonium.

Having turned the game on its head, Arsenal burst every blood-vessel to push home their initiative. At that point Bowen had become an inspiration at wing-half; Tapscott, Herd and Groves threatened danger every time the stylish Bloomfield threaded the ball through to them with pinpoint passes.

Where others would have sagged and died, United, however, as so often over the years, refused to wilt at the crisis. They trimmed their sails, steadied the boat with a firm hand on the tiller and rode out the storm. Step by step over the last twenty minutes they took charge again like Champions. By sheer force of character and will-power they superimposed their skill to dominate events once more.

A flowing passage between Charlton and Scanlon saw Viollet, an exceptional player before the Munich crash, head the ball sharply past Kelsey to give United a 4-3 lead. Yet another sinuous attack by Colman and Morgans sent in Taylor to score a remarkable goal from an acute angle. Even then Arsenal refused to admit defeat. Tapscott, always a great competitive spirit, burst clean through United's middle to score from a clever opening by Bowen and Herd, and a see-saw match of nine goals finally drew to a close, with the score at 4-5.

By the end of the game the thermometer was doing a war-dance

By the end the thermometer was doing a war-dance. Spectators and players alike were breathless as the teams left the field arm in arm. They knew instinctively that they had created something for the pride and the memory. Yet in the event the match was to become an epitaph.

It was the last time most spectators were to see the great Duncan Edwards. He had made his debut for United at the age of 15; at 18 he was the youngest player to win an international cap. He was a player of immense stature; the embodiment of all that was best in professional football. Jimmy Murphy, assistant manager of Manchester United, felt that he was 'the one player who, had he survived, would have made the rebuilding of the United side so much easier.' Murphy also pertinently asked where England would have played Bobby Moore had Edwards come away from Munich unscathed. Beside Edwards four others were killed: Tommy Taylor, a remarkable centre-forward who, with his unselfish running off the ball anticipated the likes of Hurst at a time when the battering-ram role of the centre-forward was only just beginning to lose ground; defenders Roger Byrne and Mark Jones and the midfield player Eddie 'Snake-hips' Colman, of whom Harry Gregg said, 'When he waggled his hips, he made the stanchions in the grandstand sway'.

This is merely to underline the quality of that United side that was still in the throes of development. But the real joy of that swaying Highbury battle was a sense, felt throughout the ground, of the pleasure and enjoyment which the players drew from a game into which they had put so much. The accent was always on attack. Passes were sent along the lines of longitude and not endlessly sideways as decreed by more modern strategists whose obsessions with numbers has at times threatened to turn football into a kind of bingo between the goalposts.

There perhaps lies a fundamental difference between the game today and that of yesterday. The contemporary player might equal his predecessor in dedication, but his enjoyment of the game seems often to have been turned sour by the pressures of modern football. If this is a matter of opinion, Joe Mercer for one has often emphasized the point. 'To see some players going down the tunnel nowadays', he has often said, 'one would think they were heading for Vietnam.' If in the light of subsequent events the match at Highbury was a tragic one, it will also be remembered by many as one that was enjoyed by all concerned with it. At any rate when Manchester United and Bobby Charlton returned to Highbury in 1970, the programme reproduced a full-page account of the match. After so many years its echoes still run around the marble halls of Highbury.

Arsenal: Kelsey, Charlton (S), Evans, Ward, Fotheringham, Bowen, Groves, Tapscott, Herd, Bloomfield, Nutt.
Manchester United: Gregg, Foulkes, Byrne, Colman, Jones, Edwards, Morgans, Charlton (R), Taylor, Viollet, Scanlon.

Northern Ireland joins the super-powers

29

There are moments when glory, like grief, needs no audience. That was why the door of the No 1 dressing-room at Malmo Stadium, Sweden, stayed locked on Tuesday 17 June, 1958. Inside that room, a dozen Irish footballers sat alone and savoured the greatest moment their national team has had to remember.

Northern Ireland, as little-rated a competitor for a World Cup final as North Korea in 1966 and El Salvador in 1970, had just beaten Czechoslovakia 2-1 after extra time in a Group One play-off. Now unbelievably they were through to the last eight of the 1958 competition.

Flame-haired Peter Doherty, brilliant inside-forward with Manchester City and Derby County, and then the manager who had inspired this Northern Ireland side, lifted an empty lemonade bottle and rapped it against the massage table for silence. The babble of excited chatter among the battered and bruised but happy players stopped.

The scene was set for a Churchillian speech. But Doherty, close to tears and with his voice filled with emotion, made no dramatic pronouncement. Simply and sincerely he said: 'Well done boys, you were magnificent.' It was a tribute from the heart—and it reflected the way every Ulster football follower felt about that team.

The Cinderella nation arrived in Sweden unsung and unheralded

Four weeks earlier the Northern Ireland squad had set up headquarters in a luxury hotel over-looking a sandy beach at Tylosand, near the small town of Halmstad. They had arrived unsung and unheralded—in contrast to the vast publicity afforded England, Scotland, Brazil, 1954 winners West Germany and, of course, host country Sweden.

Arriving in Sweden as the Cinderella nation, Northern Ireland were soon demanding re-appraisal. In their opening tie they showed their determination and skill by beating Czechoslovakia 1-0 with a goal from inside-forward Wilbur Cush. Emphasis had been very much on defence with lightening breakaways.

They were brought back to earth however with a 3-1 defeat by South American champions Argentina, who had hurriedly re-introduced veteran experience into their side by bringing in the 40-year-old Angel Labruna at inside-left and the equally ageing Nestor Rossi at centre-half.

Next came the 2-2 draw with West Germany at Malmo. Ireland were twice in the lead with goals from Peter McParland, but 11 minutes from the finish Harry Gregg, the Manchester United goalkeeper, who had turned in the performance of his life, was beaten by Uwe Seeler, a comparative newcomer at centre-forward. That draw saw the Germans through to the quarter-finals; the other place would go to the winner of a play-off between Ireland and Czechoslovakia, who had defeated Argentina 6-1.

Ireland's efforts to take up residence in Malmo until the decider failed: the team had to make a tiring 100-mile trip back to Tylosand where their supporters—two of whom arrived from Ireland on a motor scooter—had set up tents in the grounds of the hotel. After each match the local night club the 'Norre Kat' was taken over by the Irish with the celebrations carefree and

good-humoured whether in triumph or defeat. In fact, one local newspaper described the Irish team as 'the joker in the pack'. The Swedes, especially the citizens of Halmstad, had taken them to their hearts.

Gregg, his ankle swollen three times its normal size after twisting it against the Germans, hobbled with the aid of a stick. 'I bathed it for hours in cool water. For two days that process was repeated. I wanted so much to play in the decider but I couldn't make it,' said Gregg.

Centre-forward had been a problem position. Grimsby Town outside-left Jackie Scott was nominated to wear the No 9 jersey; Derek Dougan (Portsmouth), Fay Coyle (Nottingham Forest) and Tommy Casey (Newcastle United), the previous occupants, had not made a decisive impact. Scott's selection was really a tactical ploy by Doherty who ordered him to switch to the left wing after the kick-off with the long-striding, powerful McParland moving into the centre.

Northern Ireland had to win, for the Czechs, as a result of that 6-1 success over Argentina, were ahead on goal average. There could not have been a more vital setting.

With Gregg ruled out, Norman Uprichard (Portsmouth) took over as goalkeeper on that warm summer's evening. The flags of the nations fluttered at the top of the half-empty terracing. The Ulster supporters sang, cheered and waved a huge Union Jack.

As the players left the tranquility of the dressing-rooms they looked taut, tension-filled and tired, the Irish especially so after their exhausting and heroic efforts against West Germany only 48 hours earlier in that same stadium.

Within minutes of the start tragedy struck. Uprichard, going for a ball, twisted his ankle almost in the same manner as Gregg. But Northern Ireland played on with determination, spirit and understanding. They were inspired, too, by the captaincy of Blanchflower, who had not impressed in the previous three fixtures.

After 17 minutes, though, Czech centre-half Popluhar hooked a ball 20 yards for outside-left Zikan to head it into the net. From a team unable to find their rhythm or control, Czechoslovakia were emerging as one with confidence.

The Irish needed a goal to lift them. It came only seconds before the referee Maurice Guige, a French gendarme, blew his whistle for half-time. Billy Bingham broke on the right and slipped the ball to Cush who had three shots at goal, all of which were blocked by the defensive wall. He decided not to take a fourth and instead flicked a pass to McParland who hammered it into the net. One-all.

The second half proved almost a disaster for the Irish. In the opening minutes Uprichard dived to stop a shot from outside-right Dvorak; the ball travelled so fast and with such power that the impact smashed Uprichard's hand against the post. The goalkeeper's hand swelled up and each time he grasped the ball his face twisted with the excruciating pain. Only when the match was over and he was rushed to hospital was it discovered that a bone had been broken.

With both a hand and an ankle injured, Uprichard swallow-dived to cut off another shot but he could not hold the ball. In raced Bertie Peacock in an attempt to hook the ball clear. Uprichard dived again. Zikan challenged him

and both crashed into Peacock who had one leg in the air.

'I felt my knee go but after treatment from trainer Gerry Morgan I limped on the left wing' said Peacock, then with Glasgow Celtic. That injury sidelined him for three months the following season but, luckily, a cartilage operation was not necessary.

At the end of 90 minutes the teams were still level. During the interval before extra time, Peter Doherty suggested to Uprichard that he should come off and go to hospital for an X-ray but Uprichard refused.

'I asked Danny Blanchflower if I could play out with someone else in the goal but he urged me to stay,' said Uprichard.

The Doherty-Blanchflower psychology paid off at this crucial moment. 'We are tired but look at them—they are a lot tireder. Go at them,' urged Doherty, who had given the team a sense of unity and a fantastic belief in themselves. Never more so than during that interval.

Dusk fell on the stadium as the match went into extra time. Although Northern Ireland made most of the running they just could not get that winning goal. Inevitably, it seemed they would be eliminated from the series on goal average—a disappointing way to depart after such a glorious performance.

But in the 100th minute Blanchflower took a free kick on the right; the ball homed in on the waiting McParland, who hit it past the Czech keeper Dolejsi; left-back Mraz stood paralysed

PRESSENS BILD

PRESSENS BILD

PRESSENS BILD

in bewilderment as it smashed into the net.

But there were 20 minutes remaining. 'When Irish Eyes are Smiling' sang the Ulster fans. 'Come on lads keep at them,' shouted Doherty until he was hoarse. They responded to his every command. They fought until their legs could barely carry them. They used crunching but fair tackles which rattled the Czechs. So much so that right-half Bubernik, an ice hockey international, complained to the referee of being pushed in the back. Mr Guige contemptuously brushed him aside, Bubernik spat in his face and was sent off.

Czechoslovakia, reduced to 10 players, realized it was all or nothing. They brought everyone except the goalkeeper up into the Irish half. Irish Football Association officials came down from their seats and stood beside the trainers bench with backs to the play. 'We simply could not look at the game. Our hearts pounded. Our faces were white with anxiety,' said Harry Cavan, later IFA president and FIFA vice-president and then one of the selectors.

There was a roar as Ireland went into attack. Peacock, limping gamely, hit a Scott pass into the net but it was ruled offside. The agony continued for 10 minutes more. The single goal lead was wafer thin.

Then at 9.21 it was all over. Dozens of press photographers lined up in front of the trainer's bench where the supporters had gathered. They danced with joy and even the selectors did a jig when Blanchflower led his players in a round of

applause for the Czechs. As those Irish football immortals left the field they were cheered all the way along the tunnel by the jubilant fans. As they entered the dressing-rooms Alfie McMichael, the Newcastle United left-back, noticed two Czechs, Novak and Masopust, behind him. He stopped, shook them by the hand and said: 'Hard luck fellows.' The Czechs forced a smile in that moment of disappointment and dejection.

Northern Ireland had reached the quarter-finals but the limitation of players and the mounting injury list proved insurmountable handicaps. That night they drove back to Tylosand and the next day travelled 10 hours in a bus across Sweden to Norrkopping. There, on Thursday, June 19, they lost 4-0 to France.

Gregg, still not fully recovered, was drafted into the side in place of Uprichard whose hand was encased in plaster. Tommy Casey had stitches in a gaping leg wound and finished with the blood seeping through his stocking. It was asking too much of a team which had reached a peak beyond wildest dreams—a standard too high to maintain with so few players of required calibre from which to build a World Cup squad.

Irish hearts were heavy that night; so too was that of 13-year-old Bengt Jonasson from Tylosand who had been adopted as the team's mascot.

Players thought so much of Bengt they brought him to Belfast the following October for the British Championship game with Scotland and he was given the full VIP treatment.

'It was an achievement to qualify for the final series and more remarkable that we should finish in the top eight,' said Doherty. 'We played against terrific odds, odds that lengthened with every injury which hit us. No country in the history of world soccer earned such glory from ultimate defeat as we did.'

The people of Sweden will always remember Northern Ireland and that night in Malmo when they made history against the Czechs. For Irish football it was the pinnacle—and an unforgettable era.

Northern Ireland—Uprichard; Keith; McMichael; Blanchflower; Cunningham; Peacock; Bingham; Cush; Scott; McIlroy; McParland.
Czechoslovakia—Dolejsi; Mraz; Novak; Bubernik; Popluhar; Masopust; Dvorak; Borovicka; Feureisl; Molnar; Zikan.

Top *Caught off his line, Northern Ireland goalkeeper Norman Uprichard stands no chance against Zikan's precision header and Czechoslovakia take the lead.*
Left *Peter McParland scores Ireland's first goal to bring them level with the Czechs. McParland went on to score the winner in the first half of extra time.*
Above *A toothy grin from Billy Bingham as the jubilant Northern Ireland players leave the field at Sweden's Malmo stadium.*

GERRY CRANHAM

KEYSTONE

Spurs' 10-goal salute for Nicholson

30

Some great soccer occasions can be spotted a month ahead, and at the very least there is usually a few days' notice of most of them. A World Cup final in Mexico City, a European Cup final in Lisbon, an FA Cup Final at Wembley or even a decisive League encounter at Highbury or Old Trafford: the pre-match tension is built up in advance by newspapers and television as players and managers voice their hopes and doubts in interviews.

But there are memorable games when it is not like that at all. When what appears in prospect to be a run-of-the-mill fixture explodes out of the ordinary and into the memory and the record-books for no foreseeable reason.

That is the way it was at White Hart Lane when Tottenham Hotspur met Everton in a First Division match on Saturday, 11 October 1958, a routine affair which did not command the presence of all the uncommitted London-based football fans: some preferred Stamford Bridge for the clash of Chelsea and Bolton Wanderers, while others went to Upton Park where West Ham were playing Birmingham City. Even the newspapers showed little, if any, interest in the fixture at White Hart Lane.

And for those fans who supported neither Spurs nor Everton, it was a logical selection to watch one of the other London games. After all, both Chelsea and West Ham stood higher in the First Division table than Spurs, who were 16th with just nine points from 11 games, only a point clear of the bottom three clubs. And Everton were one of those bottom three.

How could those who ventured elsewhere have possibly guessed that at White Hart Lane Spurs would defeat Everton 10-4 to equal the record aggregate of 14 goals in a Division One fixture— a record set up in the previous century when Aston Villa thrashed Accrington Stanley 12-2 in March 1892.

It was a season which neither club had begun with any great expectations. Everton were still re-establishing themselves in the First Division four years after ending a humiliating spell in the lower division. Spurs were in a period of transition between the triumphant push-and-run side of the early fifties and the 'double' winning team of 1960-61: a team which at that stage had hardly started to take shape. Only three members of the eleven which shattered Everton were to be regulars in the 'double' line-up; full-back Peter Baker, wing-half Danny Blanchflower and centre-forward Bobby Smith.

What then sparked the goal avalanche? Did the Spurs players sense in the hours before the kick-off on 11 October 1958, that they were preparing for a match of headline potential?

'All I can remember is feeling miserable that morning,' says Tommy Harmer, Spurs inside-right. 'I had been dropped for the previous four games and knew it was in the balance whether I'd get my place back. When I reported to the ground I was apprehensive, half-afraid I'd find I had been left out again.'

Yet Harmer was to emerge as the star of the match, harnessing all his skills to devastate the Everton defence. From start to finish he

bedevilled opponents with his jinking runs, the ease with which he side-stepped lunging tackles and the accuracy of his final passes. It was a vintage display even by Harmer's own high standards, a demonstration of all the talents which— to the lasting shame of those concerned—were never rewarded by a full England 'cap'.

One Sunday newspaper columnist was so carried away that next morning he recorded, 'Harmer scored one goal and made the other nine.' If that was an exaggeration, it was not really so sweeping. And certainly Harmer's goal, the tenth of the day to make the score 8-2 to Spurs, was one he can still describe as faithfully as though he was seeing every detail in a slow-action TV replay.

'Everton's Bobby Collins had dropped back to the edge of their penalty area and robbed our right-winger Terry Medwin. But Collins lost control as he went to dribble the ball clear, and it bounced towards me . . . I hit the ball first time, on the half-volley, from 20 yards and it flew into

'Even though I was on the losing side, I'm glad I played in that match'

the top corner of the net. I never scored many goals from that kind of range, and I suppose it was one of those days when everything was going in,' he says. 'Like a rocket, it went, like a rocket,' adds Harmer with relish as he sees it all again in his mind's eye.

There were other notable individual performances in the game besides Harmer's. Bobby Smith, who at that time was preferred to Blanchflower as Spurs' captain, scored four. Jimmy Harris countered with a hat-trick for Everton to salvage personal pride from his team's resounding crash.

All the Spurs forwards—this was an era when each team had five—scored. It was a formation full of goal-power. In fact, of the attackers— Medwin, Harmer, Smith, Alfie Stokes and George Robb—all but Harmer were aggressive, forward-running players with reputations as marksmen.

Everton, for their part, had the tearaway Dave Hickson in a No 9 shirt alongside Jimmy Harris. Quite likely Hickson is still rueful about his failure to get a goal from a match in which 14

Inset far left *Before the game, the Spurs players were told of the appointment of Bill Nicholson (right) as manager of the team. Nicholson was no stranger to White Hart Lane. Under previous manager Jimmy Anderson he had been the club's coach.*

Far left *After ten minutes of the match, Everton equalize Spurs' early goal. Hollowbread, the Spurs goalkeeper, and Baker, the right-back, watch as Jimmy Harris's shot trickles over the line.*

Left *Having scored three goals in four minutes, Spurs were comfortably ahead by 6-1 at half-time. In the second half, Everton began promisingly with a quick goal, but Bobby Smith almost immediately scored the third of his four goals. Here his powerful header beats Dunlop to take the score to 7-2.*

Above *Tommy Harmer (right, pictured in another match) had an outstanding game for Spurs. One paper said, 'He scored one goal and made nine.'*

were scored. With Bobby Collins as the 'general', Everton also paraded Eddie O'Hara, an orthodox Scottish winger, at outside-left and the veteran Wally Fielding at outside-right—lacking in pace, but nevertheless a ball-player to be compared with Harmer and Collins, still able to create a space and pinpoint a pass with the best of them.

Fielding says of that game, 'My memory of that match is not only that so many goals were scored, but of how many more there might have been. There were a number of near misses at both ends and quite a few good saves by the goalkeepers. No professional footballer enjoys being on the losing side, and who wants to play in a team beaten by six goals? Yet I'm glad I played in that game.'

One man who was glad he missed playing was Everton's first-choice goalkeeper Jimmy O'Neill. Injured the previous Sunday when on international duty for the Republic of Ireland, his place was taken by Albert Dunlop.

Poor Dunlop! In mid-week he had made his come-back in a friendly fixture with the South African touring team at Goodison Park. Everton won that match 7-4, so by the time the final whistle sounded at Tottenham he had conceded 14 goals in the space of 180 minutes; his one consolation was that even the harshest critic could blame him for only two or three of them.

Dunlop soon had a taste of what was to come against Spurs. Harmer's through ball split the Everton defence in the second minute, Smith's shot was stopped on the line by left-back Bramwell—only for Stokes to follow up and put Spurs ahead. Everton's response was an all-out onslaught, and Hollowbread made spectacular saves from Hickson and Fielding before Jimmy Harris swept in a tenth-minute equalizer from a Hickson cross.

Another accurate Harmer pass enabled Smith to restore Spurs' lead. But such was the ebb and flow of the game that until the half-hour it was impossible to predict which side would win. Then Spurs dispelled all doubts with three goals in a spell of four minutes.

The Everton bewilderment began as Harmer sent Robb away to weave a path through a crowded penalty area and smash his shot wide of Dunlop; it continued as Smith scored from a careful Blanchflower centre; and it reached a climax when Stokes ran in Spurs' fifth goal after Dunlop only half-stopped a Robb header.

With Harmer and Blanchflower linking up as perfectly as though some off-field puppet-master was pulling their strings, it seemed futile for the Everton players to try to stop them. So it occasioned no surprise at all when Medwin shot in off a post to make it 6-1 by half-time.

'We won't win 10-4 every week' one Spurs player told the new manager

There were Everton hopes of the start of a revival soon after the interval when Jimmy Harris headed a Fielding corner-kick into Spurs' goal. And though a powerful Smith header soon pushed the score to 7-2, Spurs were relatively subdued until the final ten minutes when Harmer's successful shot renewed the taste for goals in an amazing finish.

Straight from the kick-off, Everton burst downfield en masse and Jimmy Harris completed his hat-trick from Hickson's left-wing centre. But Smith, seeming to take that as a personal affront, quickly took his own tally to four (and the overall statistics to 9-3) when he headed in a looping centre from Stokes.

By now a new record defeat in a League game had passed into the Everton records, but they were not prepared to let it go at that. Collins collected the ball 25 yards out and blasted a drive past the diving Hollowbread.

Up to that point all 13 goals had been credited to forwards, but Spurs' centre-half Ryden—who had been limping, injured, along the left touchline for 15 minutes—had the very last say. When a free-kick from the right sparked off a scramble in Everton's goalmouth, Ryden got into the act to direct the ball wide of Dunlop. It was the final agony for the stand-in goalkeeper. Minutes later referee Gilbert Pullin signalled the end.

But all the drama had not been acted out on the field. In the dressing-room before the game, the Spurs players had learned of the appointment of Bill Nicholson as manager, taking over from Jimmy Anderson, who had resigned because

of ill-health. The change had brought no great tactical upheaval, since Nicholson had been coaching the first team since his own playing days had ended. And the stolid Nicholson certainly was not the type to send the team out with a corny phrase like, 'Win this one for me, lads.'

Even so, it must rate as the most remarkable start by any manager in the long history of League football. In fact, Nicholson acknowledged it as such when shortly after the game his appointment was announced and he called a Press conference. 'Nobody could have wished for a more memorable beginning,' he said. Then, as his natural caution caught up with his buoyant mood, he added, 'I've been in football long enough to know you can be up in the clouds one minute, then down to earth the next.'

He soon had warning of this. When Nicholson congratulated his team as they left the field, Harmer had turned to his new boss and said what hardly needed saying—'We won't win 10-4 every week, y'know.'

For it was obvious to everybody—especially those who had seen the match or read of it the next day—that this had been an epic football occasion. What was less obvious was the reason for it being so. Why should two teams from the lower reaches of their division suddenly produce 14 goals in the space of 90 minutes?

To this day there is no real answer to that question. In the absence of a logical reason for this fantastic game, the only satisfactory explanation is that everything freakishly went right. It was one of those days when the half chances were taken, when the first-time shots found the goal instead of the crowd behind, and the ball ran for the attackers rather than the defenders.

And when play ended, and the unbelievable scoreline made its way round the country's pubs, those who had witnessed the goal-rush gave up trying to understand it, and contented themselves instead with re-living each of those 14 goals.

Spurs: Hollowbread, Baker, Hopkins, Blanchflower, Ryden, Iley, Medwin, Harmer, Smith, Stokes, Robb.

Everton: Dunlop, Sanders, Bramwell, King, Jones, Harris (B), Fielding, Harris (J), Hickson, Collins, O'Hara.

31

When the Canaries outcrowed the Cock

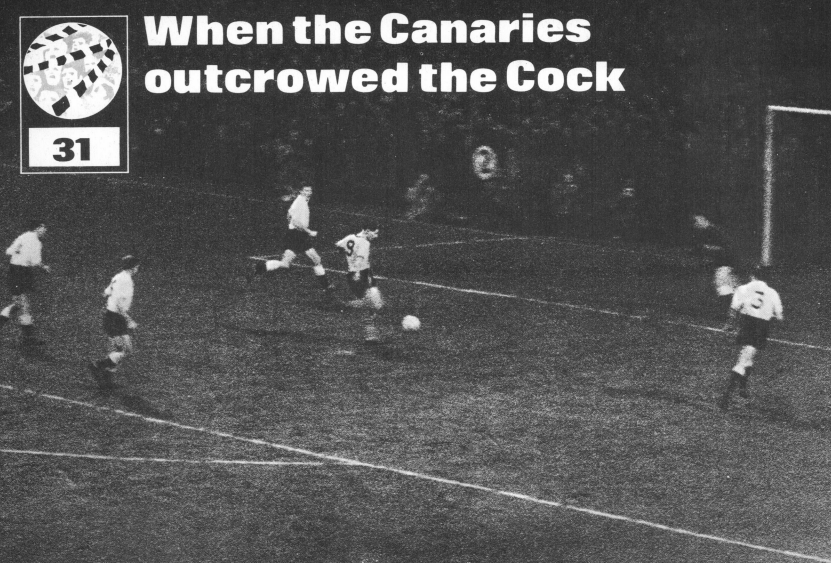

PATHÉ NEWS

'There's nothing to say,' snapped Spurs manager Bill Nicholson as he shouldered his way through a posse of eager reporters at Norwich in February 1959. 'You saw what happened. You saw us buried and that's what most of you came for anyway.'

Such resentment was not unusual in a losing manager when the circumstances brought fame to less distinguished opponents. But for Nicholson, in his first full season in charge at White Hart Lane, the defeat was even harder to take. The knowledge that another sensational Norwich Cup success assured dramatic headlines for the men who covered it merely amplified his irritation.

Norwich had become everybody's team. A middle-of-the-road Third Division club, they had come bursting out of nowhere to establish themselves as possibly the most accomplished giant-killers in the history of the FA Cup.

Three months earlier their manager, Archie Macaulay, a distinguished former Scottish international, was barricaded in his office while disillusioned supporters protested in the street outside. Macaulay was in trouble. Norwich were struggling to establish even respectability in the Third Division and a successful Cup run was the remotest of possibilities.

Indeed Norwich struggled to beat an amateur club, Ilford and were almost put out at Swindon. Not even the prospect of a home third-round tie against Manchester United could alter Norwich's stumbling mood as they sneaked through in a replay against Swindon with a goal from Peter Clelland, a reserve playing his first senior game.

Clelland's goal brought United to Carrow Road on 10 January but he played no further part in a campaign which was to take Norwich within one missed chance of being the first Third Division club to appear in an FA Cup Final.

United were admittedly still recovering from the awful tragedy which overtook them at Munich twelve months earlier. But no one could have foreseen the drama which unfolded at Carrow Road.

An ice-hardened surface aroused some apprehension among the United players and promoted the faint possibility of a shock result. Hard running and an abundance of courage in difficult conditions had been at the root of more than one sensational Cup result.

But although the uncertain footing undoubtedly contributed to United's defeat, there could be no denying the almost unbelievable quality of Norwich's football. They were a team transformed, and only outstanding goalkeeping by Harry Gregg prevented an overwhelming defeat.

'Overnight we had this conviction that we could beat anyone'

The most obvious Norwich hero was centre-forward Terry Bly who scored twice. But the whole team was seen to be blessed with skill and experience which only needed confidence to weld it all into a match-winning combination.

Macaulay arranged them cleverly. Ron Ashman with over 400 senior games behind him was converted into a solid, thinking full-back. Bobby Brennan's Irish skills were resurrected on the left wing at a time when most people felt he was finished.

Errol Crossan, a crew-cut Canadian, ran with paralysing directness along the opposite flank. Jimmy Hill, another little Irishman, brought craft to the middle of the field. Bly began to score consistently. Terry Allcock, Matt Crowe, Roy McCrohan, Barry Butler and Brian Thurlow began to make impressive contributions.

Skipper Ashman, later to manage the club before moving on to Scunthorpe, said: 'It's diffi-

cult to work out just what happened to us. One minute we were a struggling Third Division team lucky to be in the third round. Then overnight we had this conviction that we could beat anyone.

'You see it wasn't just that we had taken United to the cleaners. There were good players in the team. A lot of good players. We weren't a kick and rush side and it just needed something to set it all off.

'Beating United did that for us. We were on our way. Home advantage is a tremendous thing in the FA Cup, but as time went on we honestly believed we could win anywhere and against anyone.'

Cardiff City from the Second Division were next on Norwich's list of victims and then came Spurs. The draw had been unkind. White Hart Lane with its awesome atmosphere was a problem for the best and even though Spurs were battling through a difficult period it seemed as though the Norwich bubble was about to burst.

Over 20,000 fans, almost double the number who had stood and watched Norwich's ragged start to the season, travelled to cheer their team in London.

Norwich was gripped by a cup fever. Tickets were at a premium. Work schedules had gone haywire and there was not a citizen who could not repeat the mournful yet oddly inspiring lyric of the terrace anthem: 'On the Ball City'. Ten years later, hysteria was to be a recognized feature as support and loyalty intensified. In 1959, such public emotion as was seen in Norwich made front page news. The city lived for the next match. Exiles from the length of the country flocked back to Carrow Road to take part in the mass adulation of the 'Canaries'.

The fever was pitched even higher by the realization that Spurs had problems. Nicholson, taking over the previous autumn from Jimmy

Above left Terry Bly, clean away with Ashman's mis-kick, drives in the winner at Carrow Road.
Top Terry Allcock's (right) goal at White Hart Lane almost won Norwich the tie at the first attempt. Jones' equalizer came in the last minute.
Above Jubilation as Norwich move into Round 6.

Anderson, had begun with a fantastic 10-4 victory over Everton. But winter had come to undermine Spurs' confidence and threaten them with relegation. Within two years they were to emerge as the most dominant team in Britain winning the Championship and the FA Cup in the same season and playing with marvellous flair.

And yet in February 1959 the clouds hung low over the club. The famed Danny Blanchflower had lost his place. Cliff Jones, signed for a record fee from Swansea, looked more like an apprentice than the world-class winger he was to become. Dave Mackay, John White and Bill Brown, men who were to have a brilliant effect on Spurs in the months to come, had yet to be signed. There was discontent in the crowd and Norwich were in the mood to take advantage.

It was not a pretty game. Norwich, aware of the prize, shed some of their free style to confront Spurs with aggressive and often mean tackling. Ashman said: 'We felt that we had to keep things tight because Spurs had some outstanding individual players. They had to be pinned down and in a Cup-tie atmosphere you are bound to get rugged stuff. We needed a goal to settle us down.'

That goal came 25 minutes from time when Allcock drove them into the lead. Hill, shooting over from four yards, Allcock and Bly all had chances to make things safe, but with 40 seconds left Spurs looked gloomily resigned to defeat.

Jones, his murderous pace never evident, had wandered ineffectively along the left wing, barracked by the crowd and clearly conscious of

his poor form. Then with the game almost lost Spurs equalized. Dave Dunmore centred from the left and the Norwich defence, deceived by Bobby Smith's decision to let the ball fly through, could not get to Jones as he volleyed a fine goal.

Smith said later: 'We were finished you know. We were out of it. Cliff's call saved us. I was shaping to shoot when I heard him shout, "Leave it Bobby." I held back and Cliff stuck it away. I'm sure I wouldn't have scored.'

Norwich's one slip earns Spurs a replay at Carrow Road

Ashman, saddened by the manner of Spurs' survival, said: 'It was about the one defensive error we made. We never expected Dunmore to retrieve the ball after Jim Iley had sliced a shot away towards the touchline. But he did. I managed to get a hand to Cliff Jones' shot but I couldn't stop it.'

Norwich's disappointment was softened by the knowledge that Spurs would now have to contend with an atmosphere almost unique in British football. Back came Blanchflower to play as an inside-forward and inspire Spurs to an improved performance. But Spurs desperately needed a goal to quieten the intensity of noise.

Blanchflower was to say: 'I have played all round the world in some of the world's great stadiums. But I have never experienced an atmosphere like that. The crowd are worth a goal start to Norwich. The anthems, the cheers are always in your ears. There is no way that you can shut them out.'

Spurs went close and then Bobby Smith drove in the shot which might well have ended the Norwich story. But goalkeeper Ken Nethercott,

a veteran whose career would soon end with a shoulder injury in the sixth round at Sheffield United, launched himself into a superb save. 'At my age one good save a match is enough,' cracked Nethercott later. It was enough to fend off Spurs.

They were finally beaten in the 63rd minute when Bly proved yet again he had touched an unforgettable peak in his career.

Ashman chipped the ball forward, and later owned up to a mis-kick. But the ball fell for Bly. He drove it beneath goalkeeper John Hollowbread and 38,000 voices tore the night sky apart.

When it was over Ashman and his team were swamped by a delirious crowd, and Ashman himself was soon to dance an excited jig with a policeman for whom duty had taken second place to excitement.

Nicholson eventually pronounced a careful judgement on the match. 'Norwich are a good side and they kept coming at us all the time. Good luck to them in the next round.'

The story was far from over. Norwich hung on with Nethercott injured to draw in the sixth round at Sheffield United. The replay went their way on another astonishingly wild night at Carrow Road.

In the semi-finals they went back to White Hart Lane to face Luton. They might have won through to Wembley there and again in the replay at Birmingham the following Wednesday. But Hill missed a vital chance in the replay and Luton sneaked through 1-0. It was all over.

Norwich City: Nethercott, Thurlow, Ashman, McCrohan, Butler, Crowe, Crossan, Allcock, Bly, Hill, Brennan.
Tottenham Hotspur: Hollowbread, Baker, Hopkins, Dodge, Norman, Iley, Brooks (Medwin replay), Harmer (Blanchflower replay), Smith, Dunmore (Clayton replay), Jones.

32

Spurs lower th old gold standard

On a warm, sunny day in April 1960 Tottenham Hotspur came to Molineux and beat Wolverhampton Wanderers 3-1, winning with a fluent inventiveness that made the tactics of their opponents seem as dated as the Iron Age. The fact of Spurs' victory was important enough, for it prevented Wolves becoming the first team this century to achieve the double of League Championship and FA Cup but, as the seasons that immediately followed confirmed, the manner of it was of even greater significance for it marked the end of a decade dominated by the Midlands club and questioned a style of football which for long had been accepted as reflecting the true character of the English game.

Wolves were the most consistent force of the fifties; only the tragic Manchester United side, the Busby Babes lost in the Munich air crash in 1958, seriously challenged their reign.

Stan Cullis, who had spent his formative years under the autocratic influence of Major Frank Buckley, had taken over the managership at a relatively early age, 32, and while he was no dictator he shared his mentor's views in enforcing strict discipline both on and off the field. Cullis's teams were dedicated to the long-passing game, to a seven-man attack with thrust and pace on the wings and surging power through the middle. They beat on opposing defences like stormy seas on a harbour wall; the defences were frequently inundated.

Molineux's run of success lasted from 1949 to 1960, ending, as it had begun, with the winning of the FA Cup. The League Championship was won three times, in 1954, 1958 and 1959 and even when they were not winning something Wolves always netted shoals of goals. At the start of the 1955-56 season Cardiff City were routed 9-1 at Ninian Park (equalling the Division One record away victory) and for four seasons, from 1957-58 to 1960-61, Wolves teams topped a hundred goals in the First Division.

Wolves almost achieved the double but were already past their best

But by the spring of 1960, although the success of the club was assured and Cullis's position almost as secure as Matt Busby's, doubts were emerging. Most of the outstanding names of the previous decade had either retired, passed on to lesser clubs, or simply been dropped. Billy Wright had retired, to be replaced as captain first by the darkly destructive Eddie Stuart, then by the scholarly Bill Slater. Peter Broadbent, still turning beautifully with the ball, remained to give the side its measure of culture but with the departure of Swinbourne, Hancocks, Mullen and Wilshaw—perhaps the most exciting forward line in British post-War football—the team was no longer irresistible; often it looked ordinary.

Not that the 1959-60 season had been a failure; far from it. In their assault on the double Wolves had put six goals past the eventual champions, Burnley, nine past frail Fulham, had scored five at Luton, and had won a remarkable game against Manchester City 6-4 at Maine Road. Blackburn were much the less favoured of the Cup finalists. Admittedly, Wolves had been beaten 5-1 by Spurs at White Hart Lane before Christmas, a victory inspired by a hat-trick from Bobby Smith, but, in spite of the greater margin, lacking the compre-

hensiveness of the result at Molineux. Wolves, by their subsequent results, appeared to have shrugged that one off.

The side that faced Tottenham at Molineux still preserved the confidence and *esprit de corps* which had become the hallmarks of Cullis's teams. 'The team I had possibly didn't match the Spurs side which won the Championship in terms of skill,' he said later. 'But if we were deficient there, we made up for it with fitness and successful tactics.' The last part of that statement was debatable but there was no denying Wolves' fitness. Motivated as ever by Broadbent, they were heavily reliant on the steely application of Eddie Clamp and the elegant power of Ron Flowers, whose surging runs from deep positions and ability to score with low, powerful shots from beyond the penalty area had partly compensated the England side for the loss of Edwards.

But Wolves no longer enjoyed the absolute mastery of the wings which had been so essential to their earlier successes. Norman Deeley, a stocky 5ft 5in, had joined Wolves as a schoolboy in 1948 and though when Mullen and Hancocks departed Cullis bought heavily—Jackie Henderson from Portsmouth and Harry Hooper from West Ham—Deeley had seen both come and go. A persistent winger, his ability to get behind a defence and cross the ball quickly and accurately had brought Wolves a lot of goals, many of them scored by Murray who had made a passable job of succeeding Swinbourne. But Deeley was a comparatively lone threat after Mullen and Hancocks. Never a defensive side, Wolves were to concede twenty goals a season more than in their Championship years. Finlayson, the goalkeeper, suffered moments of ponderous fallibility. The side looked vulnerable.

Tottenham, in contrast to Wolves, had pottered through the fifties after winning the First Division title at the start of the decade. Their success in the 1959-60 season was surprising because of the side's brashness, invention and sheer entertainment value. Manchester United had developed an essentially skilful game which combined short and long passes and created space where none apparently existed; they relied less on brawn and stamina than on brain and wit. Now Spurs were to carry this idea forward, not through the painstaking process of building from youth but through the expediency of the cheque book. The wealthiest club in the land, they harnessed a series of outstanding signings to a number of fairly ordinary performers who became so caught up in the euphoria that they discovered in their play new depths of skill and imagination.

Tottenham were not a one-man team, far from it, but they owed the major part of their success to Blanchflower's flair for organizing tactics on the field to suit the fluctuating patterns and situations which develop throughout 90 minutes of football. He had joined Spurs from Aston Villa in 1954 for a fee of £30,000. Another club to show interest in him had been Wolves.

In a BBC discussion with George Noakes, Cullis's assistant and chief scout, Blanchflower had joked: 'Tell Stan that if I went to Wolves he and I would be so busy arguing with one another that I would never get the chance to play for him.' At White Hart Lane the joke became a reality. Signed by the ailing Arthur Rowe, Blanchflower could not persuade Rowe's successor, Jimmy Anderson, that the captain should organize

the side on the field. 'What's the point of me picking a team if Danny goes and changes it,' said Anderson, and Blanchflower was dropped.

Early in 1959 he was dropped again, by the next manager, Bill Nicholson, and spent a number of matches in the reserves, 'Visiting places I had never even heard of.' It was an odd position for the man who had established himself as a captain and midfield player of the highest international class when he led Northern Ireland to the quarter-finals of the World Cup in 1958. But before the end of that season he was back to help Tottenham avoid relegation with an ease which suggested much better things for North London in the autumn. So it proved. Nicholson had bought Dave Mackay from Hearts in March; Bill Brown, a goalkeeper with astonishing reflexes and powers of recovery, came from Dundee. The side began brilliantly and in October Nicholson signed John White from Falkirk to replace Tommy Harmer as schemer—Scottish waif for Cockney wisp. Then Les Allen came from Stamford Bridge to team up with another former Chelsea man, Bobby Smith.

Two Easter defeats at home ended Spurs' hopes of the Championship

They were expected to win the League title that season; everyone else, with the possible exception of Burnley, seemed so far behind in ideas. In fact they came to Molineux with the Championship no more than a faint hope having spent a fretful Easter losing two home matches to Manchester City and Chelsea.

So most of the crowd of 55,000, packed sweatily into the lopsided old ground, were optimistic. A win for Wolves would be an important, possibly decisive, step towards the first treble since the thirties. They led the First Division with 52 points from 40 matches; Tottenham were second with 49 from the same number; Burnley third with 48 from 38. If Wolves won, then they would need only to beat a muddled Chelsea team at Stamford Bridge to complete the first, and hardest, half of the double.

Spurs seemed unperturbed, so unperturbed that an hour before the kick-off they held a team meeting, not in the dressing room but in the centre of the pitch. Visiting sides frequently stroll on to the arena before an important match, testing the atmosphere and settling their nerves, but this was something new. Tottenham did not gaze at the sky or prod the turf with tentative feet, they simply gathered round Blanchflower, listened to what he had to say, then, their business done, walked off to change.

The crowd stirred, some hooted, most were perplexed. But no more perplexed than the Wolves defence, which was torn apart after only two minutes play. The movement began in orthodox fashion with Blanchflower and Cliff Jones, a darting, fearless winger, exchanging passes on the right. As Blanchflower collected the return and Jones ran on towards the corner flag, Wolves covered across, whereupon Blanchflower turned smartly inside, catching them on the wrong foot. His centre, stunningly accurate, was met superbly by Smith and Tottenham were ahead.

The goal had a deadening effect on Wolverhampton's movements. Clamp and Flowers struggled to achieve their familiar momentum but Blanchflower was always a thought, a pass and a bodyswerve ahead of them. Spurs had had to reorganize their side because of an injury to Les Allen: Mackay had moved up to inside-left and Tony Marchi came in to partner Blanchflower. Marchi's careful interceptions and studious use of the long, oblique pass provided the perfect complement to Blanchflower's endless flow of ideas. Tottenham were able to open up the flanks at will, unleashing Jones and Terry Dyson, the jockey's son who had just started to make his mark in the first team, to plague the Wolves defence.

Briefly Wolves recaptured the style that had made them such a successful club. Clamp, oddly

unchallenged by Mackay, carried the ball upfield and crossed to Broadbent, lurking in the penalty area. Brown could not hold his first shot and was beaten by his second. Molineux breathed more easily; now, surely, Wolves would impose their customary authority on the match. But before half-time they were back where they had started. Smith, wandering to the wing, collected Dyson's neat pass, centred, and Mackay headed Spurs back in front.

Wolves began the second half with typical voracity but without the ability to satisfy their appetite. As Tottenham divided and conquered Wolves' defensive cover the hapless Finlayson was frequently left exposed. Bravely he tipped away a drive from White; incredibly Jones hit first the left-hand post then the right with the goalkeeper as helpless as a knife-thrower's stooge. Again, briefly, Wolverhampton's hopes rose as Brown saved full-length from Murray but by now Cullis's men were resorting to long, high and hopeless lobs down the middle, giving Maurice Norman, Spurs' centre-half, few problems.

Spurs reduced Wolves' famous style of play to a crude parody

Molineux's pattern of success had become a parody. They were unable to dominate the midfield and lacked their traditional penetration down the wings where Deeley's influence was minimal. In contrast to Tottenham they had no alternative repertoire of ideas or skills with which they could deny Spurs' supremacy. When Tottenham scored again it was all over. Mackay sent Dyson away on the left and, as yet another cross evaded Finlayson and Slater, Jones launched himself full-length to head a goal which epitomized the flair and vitality that made him such an exciting player.

The crowd departed thoughtfully, full of praise for the excellence of Tottenham's performance but still not quite sure what had happened to Wolves. A week later Wolves won resoundingly, 5-1, at Chelsea, but Burnley made the most of their games in hand and took the Championship by a single point. At Wembley Wolves won the FA Cup by beating Blackburn 3-0 in a colourless game marred after Whelan, Rovers' left-back, broke a leg; no substitutes were allowed then.

The following season, as Spurs won the double, Wolves finished a creditable third in the League; but then 18th, 5th and 16th. Stan Cullis was dismissed peremptorily on 15 September 1964, and Wolves were relegated at the end of the season.

Tottenham's victory on that April day had been no fluke; an era had ended. Yet there were earlier portents of Wolves' imminent decline, particularly in European football. Wolves, the club famous for its prestigious victories over Moscow Spartak and Budapest Honved, had been quietly dismissed in the 1958-59 European Cup by Schalke 04, the German side. In the following season, after defeating Vorwaerts and Red Star Belgrade, they were sent reeling from the competition by Barcelona, who won 4-0 in Spain and 5-2 at Molineux. Wolves had been baffled by the immaculate control of Suarez, the speed and precision of Martinez and Villaverde. They had no answer to opponents who switched positions at will, changed pace with bewildering ease, rarely put a pass to an opponent and shot with ferocious accuracy; who could control the ball with chest and thigh as well as instep. Tottenham had also demonstrated the limitations of Wolves' style; it was not mere coincidence that they were the first English club to win a European trophy and the first club in the twentieth century to achieve what Wolves had so narrowly missed—the double of League Championship and FA Cup.

Top *The 55,000 Molineux crowd was expecting a Wolves' victory that would make their third successive Championship almost certain. But within two minutes Bobby Smith had headed in Blanchflower's centre for the first of Spurs' three goals.*

Centre *Wolves' equalizer: Bill Brown parried Peter Broadbent's first shot but Broadbent followed up to give Wolves their only goal.*
Above *At home, earlier, Spurs had defeated Wolves 5-1 and Bobby Smith had scored a hat-trick.*

Wolverhampton Wanderers: Finlayson, Showell, Harris, Clamp, Slater, Flowers, Mannion, Mason, Murray, Broadbent, Deeley.
Tottenham Hotspur: Brown, Baker, Henry, Blanchflower, Norman, Marchi, Jones, White, Smith, Mackay, Dyson.

33

Hampden acclaims the ultimate perfection

GLASGOW HERALD

Real Madrid pranced around the Hampden Park turf, parading the European Cup in a delirious lap of honour. The crowd acclaimed ecstatically; the occasion could have been a national victory over England, the object of such a tribute the Scottish team itself. Yet this was no manifestation of any narrow nationalism, but a natural reaction, on the part of the crowd, to the experience of seeing the sport they loved best played to what seemed to be its ultimate standards of perfection.

The Scottish fans knew they had seen one of the greatest ever games of club football; the only tinge of regret was that there was little hope of seeing its like again. They noted the day, 18 May 1960, and marked it as others had done Crispin's Day and counted themselves lucky to have been there.

As Real Madrid cavorted around the track, celebrating their 7-3 victory over Eintracht Frankfurt, champions of Germany, it seemed as if they had set out to expose as fallacy the old saying that familiarity breeds contempt. The Spanish club had indeed monopolized the trophy since the inception of the tournament and this was their fifth consecutive win in the final.

Above all were the goals—seven for Real and three for Eintracht

But if the occasion of victory was nothing new, the manner of this particular one certainly was. For even the greats can be stirred when all their skills are brought to bear at once; that in itself is the supreme sporting satisfaction. But Real's cup of joy was all the more complete for the presence of almost 130,000 Scottish football connoisseurs to testify to their achievement.

The great crowd had not just been entertained, they had been moved to flattering, awestruck appreciation. They had known about di Stefano, Puskas and Gento but to read about them and to see flashes of them on television was quite different to seeing them in the flesh, flaunting all that had made them incomparable. There were 127,621 present that night; they paid £55,000 for admission, at the time a record for any football match in Great Britain.

They grudged not a shilling of that total as they thrilled to the haughty generalship of di Stefano, the technical perfection, the ingenuity and the precise scoring of Puskas and the destroying pace of Gento. In contrast were the industry of Del Sol and the directness of Canario but above all in a great match were the goals, ten of them, and most of them memorable. There has never been such another final for it came in an era before the skills and the arts of the game of football were inhibited by cold method.

The honour that Eintracht took from the match was that they never ceased to be worthy opponents of the champions. Beforehand they had not been given much chance of being other than that. They had indeed toyed with Glasgow Rangers in the semi-final, winning 12-4 on aggregate, but they had had a miserable season in the German League. Their team manager, Ernst Berger, had himself admitted that Real Madrid were the finest team in the world. He could find nobody to argue with his assessment; recent history had proved it and recent form had confirmed it.

In both legs of the semi-final Real had outclassed Barcelona who had themselves previously

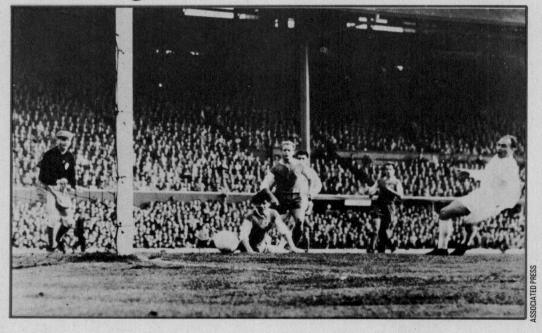

ASSOCIATED PRESS

humiliated Wolverhampton Wanderers, who had later emerged as FA Cup winners.

Real Madrid were of course no ordinary club side. They were a collector's team with treasures gathered from all over the football world. It was indicative of their great bank of talent that Didi, who had been outstanding in that exciting Brazilian team which won the World Cup in Sweden, could not even find a place in the party.

Their forwards were the envy of the whole football world, yet behind one of the finest group of forwards ever assembled by any club there was a firm, dependable defence. It was organized round that most formidable centre-half Santamaria and Dominguez, the Argentine international goalkeeper.

Real Madrid's problem was to select the eleven best from the best. In so doing they brought in another Brazilian, Canario, who had been a reserve for most of the season and gave him as his partner on the right-wing, Del Sol, the latest gem added to the Real treasures. But as usual there were di Stefano, the fittest 34-year-old in the game, Puskas, the Galloping Major, and Gento, whose speed has rarely been surpassed by any other winger.

Eintracht had not got a single international player in their team

The Real party had gone to Troon on the Ayrshire coast while a few miles along the beaches, in Skelmorlie, Eintracht settled to prepare for what was arguably the most difficult task ever set any team in a major final. They showed some apprehension. They had not a current

72

GLASGOW HERALD

clear of Santamaria and swept the ball into the net from six yards.

At last Real's urgency noticeably increased and they equalised in the 26th minute. It was a typical Real goal of simplicity and precision. Canario beat Hoefer on the right as if he were not there. His low cross eluded the defence but found di Stefano. He struck it past Loy with the cold stroke of a master. Just three minutes later the faultless positioning and alertness of di Stefano were made clear again when Canario's swerving shot spun from the diving body of the goalkeeper. The centre-forward had taken four steps and hooked the ball over the prostrate body of the goalkeeper before anybody else had moved. And so Real led.

Football of exciting quality flowed from them. Di Stefano was patrolling the centre of the field from penalty-spot to penalty-spot, demanding the ball, receiving it and then using it to the continual frustration of Eintracht. He strutted the field arrogantly, knowing he was master.

Eintracht's goal had a freakish escape when a shot from Vidal cannoned off a defender's back and struck a post before being cleared. Then one minute from the interval the great Puskas with his strutting little strides broke into the scene. He took a pass nonchalantly from the fluent feet of Del Sol, jockeyed for position near the bye-line and then, from a ridiculously narrow angle, struck a shot surely over the head of the goalkeeper. Only Puskas could do such things.

Again the mastery of Puskas brought roars of acclaim from the crowd

On Eintracht's right flank Lutz was taking no comfort from the fact that he was opposing one of the fastest wingers in the world and in the 54th minute he pushed Gento in a race for the ball. The referee, Jack Mowat, awarded Real a penalty-kick. Eintracht did not approve. It seemed pointless to ask Puskas to take the kick but he went through the motions and the score was 4-1.

In another six minutes it was five. For an instant Gento was in front of Lutz and then he was gone to appear out of a blur and cross accurately to his inside partner. Puskas bowed benignly to head the ball into the goal.

Again, in the 70th minute, the mastery of Puskas brought roars of acclaim. He reached back for a pass that was straying away from him, killed the ball and, pivoting with speed that was astonishing in one so portly, shot high into the net from 16 yards with his left foot.

Within two minutes Stein shot a good goal; although there was no chance of a fight back, the goal was welcomed as a fitting reward for the commendable efforts of the Germans. Then the difference in class between the two teams was seen in a goal that has rarely been bettered at Hampden. Di Stefano demanded the ball deep in his own defence, then in a straight run for the middle of the other goal he strung together at stirring speed a cluster of passes, sending defenders sprawling on various unrewarding paths before striking a lordly shot into Eintracht's net.

Fifteen minutes from the end Vidal mis-hit a pass to his keeper to show that the players of Real were indeed mortal and Stein was quick to the ball to round Dominguez and make the score 7-3. There were no more goals but every minute was football ecstasy. Di Stefano, unbending afterwards, said, 'It was one of our best games ever.' With a past as rich as that of Real, this was indeed a tribute to their performance.

Next day Real returned in triumph to Madrid but not without incident. At Prestwick airport their plane was delayed for four hours. It was almost as if Scotland did not want to allow them to go.

Real Madrid: Dominguez, Marquitos, Pachin, Vidal, Santamaria, Zarraga, Canario, Del Sol, di Stefano, Puskas, Gento.
Eintracht Frankfurt: Loy, Lutz, Hoefer, Well-baecher, Eigenbrodt, Stinka, Kress, Lindner, Stein, Pfaff, Meier.

PRESS ASSOCIATION

Above left Kress, the Eintracht right-winger sweeps the ball past Dominguez in the 20th minute for his side's first goal. Kress' shot was the culmination of a fine move in which the centre-forward Stein drew two defenders as he raced in along the bye-line before pushing the ball to Kress who had moved inside. In the early stages Eintracht did much to justify the warnings of those who had seen their 6-3 victory at Hampden over Glasgow Rangers.
Below left After the match di Stefano said that, even after Kress' goal, he felt Real would win. He could hardly have imagined that he would score three and Puskas four. Here he converts Canario's cross for the equaliser.
Above top Puskas has to be helped up after scoring his side's fifth goal and his own third.
Above Real parade the cup they had won for the fifth time in five years. They were to win it only once more during the sixties.

German international in the party and, although against Rangers they had shown strength and intelligence, those qualities fell far short of genius.

There was tension born of expectancy as the audience settled to enjoy the national game played as only foreigners could then play it. To begin with, however, the play was untidy as the players probed the opposition and sought to overcome the unfamiliarity of the ground.

There was some sympathy for the German underdogs and it was they who made the first breaks. Meier's swinging shot had Dominguez in trouble and the ball slapped against the crossbar. Kress and Pfaff raised exciting possibilities by showing they could make progress along Real's left flank.

With Stein and Pfaff in particular showing the same form that had devastated Rangers in the semi-final, it was clear that Real were not going to have it all their own way so soon, in spite of what had been expected of them.

Del Sol quickly showed what was likely to happen when, with a mesmeric flash of footwork, he had Loy sprawling at his feet, but Eintracht were nonetheless worrying Real by their ample exploitation of the gap on Real's left. Twice only

Worrying for Real was the gap on the left of their defence

desperate interceptions prevented a goal before, in the 20th minute, Eintracht finally took some dividends from their pressure on the left with a goal to give all the match needed as a contest. Stein raced along the bye-line, accelerated to break clear, then cut the ball sharply back. Kress leapt

34

No justice for the six-goal Law

If Denis Law is at all addicted to recurring nightmares then the one he would have most frequently could well be the third-round Cup-tie against Luton Town which began on Saturday 20 January 1961.

On that day, a day when the British rain seemed more like the monsoons of India, and the pitch looked as though someone had been clog-dancing on chocolate blancmange, Law rose above it all to score a double hat-trick.

All he earned from one of the most prolific day's work in his career was a record that didn't count as the first player to score six goals in a Cup-tie. But that was small consolation for City when, eventually, the seemingly impossible happened and they lost the tie.

In a match that had all the excitement and drama that the FA Cup can provide, Manchester City, thanks entirely to the brilliant opportunism of the fair-haired Law had built up a lead of 6-2 when the referee, K R Tuck of Chesterfield, abandoned play with 21 minutes remaining.

At half-time, with City leading 3-2, the game already looked doomed

It was not a controversial decision and even the most partisan supporters in the crowd of 23,727 were frankly surprised that the match was not abandoned earlier. A pitch that resembled a mudheap at the start, gradually churned up into a morass under the ceaseless onslaught of the torrential rain. And at half-time, when City had recovered from the shock of being two goals down in 18 minutes to lead 3-2, many thousands did not expect to see the start of the second half. With the mud deepening and spreading, the officials were finding it difficult to see the vital lines on the pitch, but no one could accuse Mr Tuck of not trying.

Finally, in the 69th minute after the exuberant, merciless Law had added his second hat-trick, the referee called his linesmen on to the pitch for a consultation.

By that time, the pitch had become completely waterlogged, and was even under water in places. It was completely impossible to move the ball with any accuracy at all. In fact, hundreds of rain-soaked spectators, correctly anticipating the verdict, had left the ground before the final decision to call off play was made.

Naturally, there were recriminations from Manchester City whose manager, Les McDowell, contended—with some logic—that the game had gone on so long in such appalling conditions, that it should have continued to its appointed end.

The Luton manager Sam Bartram, the famous ex-Charlton goalkeeper, was of course delighted at the reprieve. It could not have come at a better time for him since he was in his first months in charge and was facing up to the tough task of re-building a Luton team which had just been relegated from the First Division. As it happened, future events were to prove that Luton were at the start of the slide which became an avalanche and finally landed them into the Fourth Division. By then, though, Bartram had turned to the profession of journalism.

The only consolation for City was the thought that they could reverse their abysmal opening to the game. For, in that first match,

Top The man with the hollowest victory in football history—the 21-year-old Denis Law who scored a double hat-trick for Manchester City, six goals which didn't count.

Above His second goal in that ill-fated third-round Cup tie. At the time he was between his British record transfer fees between Manchester City (£55,000) and Turin (£100,000).

Above Law scores the third of his six goals in the first match against Luton. His score would have been a Cup record—but for the mud.
Right Law makes another goal in the second match of the tie (he worried the Luton defence so much that Bramwell (No 3) pushed the ball into his own net). Despite Law's efforts, City lost 3-1.

Luton produced a tearaway start for which they had become noted. Their lead could very well have been 3-0 before Law began to turn on his magic. For City's defence, not renowned for its quickness in those days, was excessively slow on the turn in the mud. And, apart from conceding two goals to the thrust of Alec Ashworth, they should have gone further into arrears when Scottish winger, Jim Fleming, whose finishing was always liable to be erratic, missed what was described at the time as the easiest chance that was likely to come his way in a match of such importance.

There can be no doubt that, had City not possessed a player of such flair and brilliance as Law, their Cup hopes could have been even more shortlived than they actually were.

Recognizing the source from which most danger was likely to come, Bartram had detailed Dave Pacey, a strong wing-half of sufficient ability to earn an England Under-23 cap, to shadow Law throughout the game. Undoubtedly Pacey's intentions were good, but they were never carried into effect because marking Law proved to be about as profitable as trying to grab a handful of quicksilver. Law's first goal came a minute after Ashworth's second, after which City were firmly in business, with Law gaining the freedom of the pitch and literally turning the game upside down.

His first hat-trick was completed with two spectacular headers which left the former Arsenal goalkeeper, Jim Standen, groping at thin air.

The momentum that Law had given City continued into the second half, with three more goals. The only one about which there was reasonable cause for doubt was the fifth which was credited in the first place to Joe Hayes whose shot appeared to go through unhindered and enter the net off the inside of a post. However, it was finally decided that Law somehow managed to get a touch, an unlucky decision for Hayes who had had so much to do with the destruction of the Luton defence with his fast, progressive play that often had Luton's Eire right-back, Brendan McNally, at a complete loss.

Next day, the newspapers raved about the game. 'What a pity it had to finish at all because, up to its untimely end, it was simply magnificent,' said one.

And another, 'Law's was a brilliant display in 69 minutes of soccer that will live for a long time in the minds of all who saw it. On a field that first resembled a beach with the tide just out, then in deep mud and then in a shallow lake, the men of City and Luton played a brand of football that soccer's new deal was made for.'

In view of what happened in the replay, the words of another Sunday newspaper could be regarded as prophetic: 'City look set to win Wednesday's game, but they will do well to remember the way in which their defence was pulled to pieces in the first 20 minutes. Had Luton accepted their chances, even the Law-inspired City would have been unable to get back into this game.'

Of course, the story cannot be complete without the sequel before a crowd of 15,583 which was probably bigger than Luton had dared hope for, considering the necessity for an afternoon kick-off. This was because City had refused to play the second match in the evening because they considered that Luton's floodlights were not good enough. The objection was commonly considered to have come from City's German-born keeper, Bert Trautmann, though a denial was issued at the time.

Naturally enough, City were unchanged, but Luton made five alterations, including a completely new half-back line which involved the recall of the experienced Bob Morton, who had seemed on the point of a transfer to Preston North End, and Terry Kelly, with Groves moving to left-half. Seamus Dunne came in at right-back for his fellow Eire international, McNally, and Alwyn McGuffie moved forward in place of Allan Brown, the Scottish cap.

This time, the ploy was not to follow Law everywhere, but to prevent his gaining possession by assuming more command in the middle of the field. In particular, Groves subdued the Irish international, little George Hannah, who had caused such destruction from midfield in the first meeting. Luton looked sounder all round.

Again Luton made a great start—but this time they kept the lead

Again, Luton had a great start with Ashworth, later to play for Preston at Wembley, putting them ahead after 20 minutes and Fleming atoning for his previous miss with a goal two minutes later.

When Law swooped to reduce the arrears on the stroke of half-time, many people wondered whether he could do it again.

However, City were not helped by an injury to Ken Barnes which left him limping on the left wing, and another goal for Ashworth after 64 minutes completed what was surely the biggest turnabout in football history.

The only feasible consolation for Law in defeat was the sure knowledge that no other player alive could have turned on the sort of display he gave in the first match. He was out in a class of his own and that match probably had much to do with persuading Turin to pay out a then record fee of £100,000 for him a few months later.

At the time, English football could ill afford to lose such as this Scottish genius, but the trend was for the big names to be tempted to Italy and Law's share of the fee, reported to be £10,000, was doubtless a considerable persuader in determining the decision.

Since then, of course, he has returned to continue to adorn the game over here, but it is doubtful whether he has ever regained the heights he reached in just over an hour of appalling conditions at Luton's Kenilworth Road on that cold, wet, dark Saturday afternoon.

Luton Town: (1st match) Standen, McNally, Bramwell, Pacey, Groves, McGuffie, Noake, Ashworth, Turner, Brown, Fleming.
Luton Town: (2nd match) Standen, Dunne, Bramwell, Morton, Kelly, Groves, Noake, Ashworth, Turner, McGuffie, Fleming.
Manchester City: (1st and 2nd matches) Trautmann, Leivers, Betts, Barnes, Plenderleith, Shawcross, Barlow, Hannah, Baker, Law, Hayes.

l p- ff 's day of tears

'We couldn't help but play well—they left us so many gaps. The continentals leave gaps too. Let's hope we find them in the World Cup.'

The speaker, on an April day in 1961, was Walter Winterbottom, manager of the England team, approaching as near delirium as anyone had ever seen him. Justifiably, for England had just massacred Scotland 9-3, the record win in the series between the countries, and Winterbottom was looking ahead to a bigger test in Chile in a year's time.

Sadly, his hopes of a similar performance were not borne out. Seven of the team who put Wembley on a par with Flodden and Culloden in the list of Scottish routs were on duty in South America, but six hours of labouring in four matches there produced only five goals (two of them penalties) compared with the nine put past the miserable Frank Haffey in 76 minutes.

The rout of the Scots was the fifth of eight impressive England displays in succession during that 1960-61 season. The team, who had won only once in seven starts the previous season, suddenly came alive with the switch to a fluid 4-2-4 system. In little more than a month, Ireland were beaten 5-2, Luxembourg 9-0, Spain 4-2—for all that inside trio of Suarez, di Stefano, del Sol—and Wales 5-1. Despite the five-month gap until the next match, the mood of inspiration was quickly caught again, as Scotland found to their shame. So too did Mexico, thrashed 8-0 soon afterwards.

The team did so well that Winterbottom did not want to change it

Then came a 1-1 draw with Portugal in Lisbon in a World Cup qualifier, a 3-2 win in Rome, and a defeat at last, 3-1 in Vienna. But England had good cause to be delighted with a record of seven wins and a draw in nine games, with 45 goals scored and 14 conceded.

This sort of form justified Winterbottom's determination to keep changes to a minimum. Johnny Haynes, Bobby Charlton, Bryan Douglas, Jimmy Armfield, Peter Swan, and Ron Flowers played in all the matches. Ron Springett, Mick McNeil, Bobby Robson and Jimmy Greaves missed only one, Bobby Smith three.

Allied to tactics and consistency, this was a team of considerable individual skill. Haynes was at his peak, a willing worker with superb judgment of a pass. He and Robson, equally inventive, were a near-perfect fulcrum for 4-2-4. Springett was not yet exposed in his later fallibility, Armfield was near world-class at full-back, and the muscular yet deft mixture that was Flowers suitably disguised the lingering doubts about Swan and McNeil.

In attack, the Matthews-style intricacies of Douglas contrasted well with Charlton's more direct approach, while Smith was a revelation. Despite much criticism, he carried his belligerent leadership of Tottenham's double-chasing attack into the England line, giving it strength through the centre that had been missing since Lofthouse stepped down.

Above all, there was the impish genius of Greaves. No other player had his flair for seeing and snatching the half-chance. With his speed, his control and his perception, he turned the forwards from a very good unit into one that was virtually unstoppable when the ball ran well. At this distance, it is hard to reconcile the Chelsea player's astounding ability with the fact that he was then merely 20 years old.

Scotland, as usual, had ample talent available for Wembley, despite some injuries. But, as so often before and since, they did not utilize it properly. After a short flirtation with team managers, the Scottish FA had reverted to government by committee, with all the lobbying that such a method involves. The traditional mistrust of 'Anglos' was as rife as ever, with the result that only two were chosen.

In contrast to Winterbottom's consistency, 22 players appeared in Scotland's three matches in the Home International series that season, with only Mackay, Caldow and Wilson playing in all three.

True, the injuries were costly. John White of

Spurs could not play ('What a great game to miss' was his comment afterwards), while two goal-keepers, Lawrie Leslie of Airdrie and White's club-mate, Bill Brown, were also ruled out. As a result, Celtic's Frank Haffey was brought in: the selectors had not absorbed the lesson of the previous year's Hampden clash.

Not so much Haffey's fault—more the fault of the team selectors

Injuries to two others gave Haffey his chance in that match, and he marked his debut by mishandling virtually one ball in two. He escaped from a 1-1 draw thinking his chance had gone, only to get another. Poor Haffey! The blame for his disastrous performance was not so much his, more that of the men who chose him.

Haffey was enormously popular in Scotland, with crowds and with players. He had a reputation as a comic and a 'character'—he later became a professional singer—and colleagues swore that no more pleasant personality had pulled on a jersey. But Haffey was cruelly exposed at Wembley. It was plainly too much for him: his nerves, twitching enough almost to be seen from the stands, betrayed him again and again.

Certain Scots, notably Law and Mackay, still hate to talk of this match. Another, not so reticent, blamed Haffey for four of the goals, 'and he might have stopped two more, an' all'.

Haffey, however, does not deserve all the blame. If his selection was curious, Scotland's tactics defied logic. Mackay, seemingly imbued with the desire to win the match alone, rampaged upfield and left gaps which a player only half as astute as Haynes could have exploited. McCann, the other wing-half, did much the same. The backs played both wide and square, leaving McNeill the middle man in a line of one. Even if the forwards defied shortage of height and weight, doing much that was good and a little that was brilliant, the inadequacies of the men behind gave them an impossible task.

Yet for all the problems Scotland faced through their selections and compounded by their tactics, the match *could* have been saved. Early in the second half, England had been pulled back from 3-0 to 3-2, and a surprise looked possible. The prompt reply, so effectively dousing the sudden Scottish fire, left much resentment, for the Scots claimed that Greaves had taken a free-kick several yards from the spot where the offence was committed. This was the start of a move ended by Douglas with England's fourth goal. From that point, Scotland did not merely collapse, they disintegrated.

Robson (9 minutes), Greaves (20 and 29) had given England their half-time lead: on another day, at another place, Haffey might have stopped all three. But the thousands who had travelled south on the 'whisky specials' had cause to cheer when Mackay's long-range drive flew past Springett (was he thinking of his daughter born just before the kick-off?) and when Wilson bravely dived to head a second.

Then came that Douglas goal, reducing the revived Scots to their previous panic and indecision. If the pattern of England's approach was often the same—a short ball from defence to Haynes or Robson, then a longer pass to the front—the transfers were so accurate, the positioning so astute, the speed so relentless, that the Scots were shattered.

Smith, groggy after an elbow on the head, reacted instinctively to a through ball from Haynes, beat McNeill, and shot past Haffey. That was in the 73rd minute; and in the space of 12 more, another four goals went in.

A reply from Quinn was an irrelevance, for Haynes scored twice in 90 seconds, Greaves completed his hat-trick, and Smith scored goal number nine. Wembley suited him: in four appearances there that season, three for country, one for club, he scored six times, all the goals in the net to the right of the royal box.

Haynes was carried away shoulder-high at the end, while the man dubbed as 'Slap-Haffey' stumbled away in tears.

Seven wins and one draw in eight matches—why didn't they win in Chile?

So England finished top of the Home Championship—the six games produced the remarkable total of 40 goals—but the World Cup was to prove a bitter anti-climax. Smith, beset by personal troubles, had lost his place, even at Tottenham, and his promising replacement, Hitchens, had followed Greaves to Italy. Both played in Chile, but were shadows of their best. Robson had dropped out, Haynes and Charlton were jaded, and Springett made some costly errors. In that mood, lacking inspiration, England went out to Brazil, the eventual winners, in the quarter-final.

As for Scotland, they failed to qualify for Chile. After finishing level in their group with the Czechs, the eventual defeated finalists, they lost the eliminator. Not surprisingly, Haffey did not play.

England: Springett, Armfield, McNeil, Robson, Swan, Flowers, Douglas, Greaves, Smith, Haynes, Charlton
Scotland: Haffey, Shearer, Caldow, Mackay, McNeill, McCann, McLeod, Law, St John, Quinn, Wilson

Nobody seemed to be able to stop England in season 1960-61, least of all the hapless Frank Haffey, Celtic and Scotland goalkeeper. This is how he let in the nine goals in Scotland's 9-3 defeat:
1 Haffey lunges in vain as Bobby Robson's 25-yard shot hits the back of the net.
2 He looks round in despair as the first of Greaves' hat-trick flies past him.
3 'Oh no, not again!' Haffey seems to be saying as Greaves follows his second goal into the net.
4 With despair in his eyes, Haffey watches Bryan Douglas's shot enter the net for the fourth goal.
5 In goes the fifth—put there by the big Spurs centre-forward Bobby Smith.
6 Haffey stares in disbelief at the sixth goal slammed in by England captain, Johnny Haynes.
7 Less than 90 seconds later, another Haynes shot flies past the man dubbed 'Slap-Haffey'.
8 Greaves completes his hat-trick to bring the total up to eight.
9 Smith makes it nine as Haffey raises his hand as if to say, 'No more.'

When Danny's blarney talked Spurs to victory

36

The sea mist which settled shroudlike along the Dutch coastline one evening in May 1963 was entirely in character with the mood of persistent gloom that surrounded Tottenham Hotspur as they prepared for the final of the European Cup Winners Cup.

For three years Spurs had not only been the most influential team in Britain but also the most appealing. In 1961 they achieved the 'impossible' when they won the League Championship and the FA Cup in the same season. The next year they won the Cup again, finished third in the First Division behind a remarkable Ipswich side and Burnley, and reached the semi-final of the European Cup before losing on aggregate to Benfica.

Great teams do not last for ever and Spurs were no exception. Yet they could still call on a battery of world-class players like Dave Mackay, John White, Jimmy Greaves and Cliff Jones. And Danny Blanchflower, although suffering from a niggling knee injury and nearing the end of his career, was still there to weave style, romance and blarney into their game. Indeed, Spurs in full flow were still gloriously attractive, displaying a brand of football that was an arousing mixture of elegant skill and savage finishing.

In the League they had scored over a hundred goals and in the Cup Winners Cup they had blossomed at White Hart Lane, giving two outstanding performances that echoed the form that had destroyed famed opponents in the European Cup the previous year.

When Spurs had begun their 1963 Cup Winners Cup campaign against Glasgow Rangers, it had been easy to recall the shattering defeats that they had inflicted on Gornik Zabrze of Poland and Dukla Prague of Czechoslovakia. Indeed, the same passionate atmosphere as had prevailed then was again apparent. The same stirring battle hymn 'Glory, glory, hallelujah' rolled over White Hart Lane as Spurs, inspired by the mercurial White, tore the Scottish Cup winners to pieces.

Rangers were carefully put aside in the second leg and Slovan Bratislava and OFK Belgrade were likewise dismissed as Spurs moved steadily on into the final.

Why then was it that, having successfully guided his team this far, Bill Nicholson wore a worried frown that was more than just a manifestation of natural foreboding? Why was it that every British newspaperman wrote off Spurs' chances of winning the final? What reason was there for this extraordinary lack of confidence in Spurs' ability to beat Atletico Madrid?

There were two reasons. Firstly, the edge had gone from their game. They had lost their way during the closing weeks of the League season, eventually finishing in second place to Everton by a margin of six points. Secondly, and of even greater significance, Dave Mackay was battling against injury.

Mackay was the very soul of Spurs, a magnificently skilful and aggressive footballer who played as though there was the skirl of a thousand pipes in his ears and a claymore clutched in his right hand. Yet now, with the final fast approaching, Mackay was trying to will himself to overcome the nagging, undermining pain of an abdominal injury. In the shadow of the Feyenoord Stadium in Rotter-

dam, scene of the final, Mackay, Spurs' greatest all round player, was struggling to get fit in time for the game. Perhaps only Mackay would have attempted to play in such circumstances. The grimace on his face and the reflex clutch at his abdomen was a clue to the pain he was prepared to endure.

It was this prospect of Mackay's absence which troubled Spurs most. With Mackay they were confident that they could regain their best form at a critical stage in their history. Without him, who knew? The team had doubts, and as 15 May, the day of the final, approached, the reporters had been quick to reflect those doubts in their forecasts.

Welshman Cliff Jones said as Mackay desperately tried to conquer his injury, 'With Dave in the team we feel we can beat anyone. He makes things happen. He makes us go. If he doesn't play tomorrow then the odds will change.'

The odds did change. Mackay did not make it, and Blanchflower, who equally might well have missed the match, rubbed the soreness from the cartilage scar around his right knee and prepared to give one more convincing performance in a notable career.

GERRY CRANHAM

Blanchflower's soft Irish charm and complicated philosophy had always complemented Nicholson's dogged refusal to be satisfied by anything short of perfection. And, although there had been occasional friction between them, there was also a mutual respect that was always to Spurs' advantage. Blanchflower was a part of the team yet curiously apart from it too. A loner, he now listened in silence as Nicholson conducted a team talk that was loaded with respect for the opposition.

Nicholson went through the Atletico players one by one, cataloguing their skills and potential. The Spanish centre-half was described as a giant who took no prisoners. Their midfield men were skilful, inventive players who would be difficult to contain. They had a winger—called Jones—who could touch even time.

Blanchflower listened carefully until Nicholson finished, then altered the entire mood of the meeting. Jimmy Greaves said later: 'In his way Bill was brilliant. You had to hand it to him. If he had passed around photographs of the Atletico players we couldn't have known them better. When Bill began they were a mystery to us. By the time he had finished they were like old friends.

'But he had also succeeded in worrying us. Were they as good as he suggested? That's when Danny came in. He looked around the room and the Irishisms flowed. He said that if their centre-half was big and ugly then ours, Maurice Norman, was even bigger and uglier. If they had a winger called Jones who could do even time then we had one, also called Jones, who could catch pigeons. Danny made us laugh away all our doubts.' And so it was under Blanchflower's leadership that Spurs prepared for battle in the Feyenoord Stadium.

On their way to the ground from the coastal hideaway where they had been preparing for the final, Spurs were reminded of their responsibility. For all his dourness and unsmiling professionalism, Nicholson had always been a far-seeing man eager to present appealing football. Now he told his team, 'Spurs are nothing unless we are in European football. We

GERRY CRANHAM

have got to be there next season and this is our last chance to ensure that we are.'

And suddenly an apparently tired and seemingly dispirited team found its touch again.

It was the Spurs wingers who really won the game for them. Cliff Jones, the spectacular Welshman with the destructive speed and hip-swaying swerve of a rugby three-quarter, ran the Spaniards ragged.

On the other side little Terry Dyson played the game of his life. In exalted company he had been seen as an ordinary player. But he was industrious and cheeky, and he scored vital goals. In this game, he scored twice to regain the initiative for Spurs when things turned

against them in the second half.

The early mood, however, was set in the 16th minute when Spurs created a fine goal. Nicholson had noticed that Atletico were suspect down the left side of their defence and the plan was to leave space into which Jones could gallop with the ball.

It worked perfectly. Bobby Smith, probably the most underrated forward of his time, resisted a butchering challenge by centre-half Griffa and set Jones free. The Welshman flew down the line, displaying the speed in possession that helped make him one of the most effective wingers in world football at that time. His cross came in low and Jimmy Greaves, following in among the panicking Spaniards, scored with devastating economy.

Spurs were now in full flow. In the 32nd minute they scored again. Jones to Dyson. Smith pulled back a pass from the bye-line and White drove the ball deliberately past goalkeeper Madinabeytia.

Two-nil down, the Spaniards began the second half in search of a quick goal. And they got one—after only a minute's play.

Spurs got themselves in a tangle. With goalkeeper Bill Brown beaten, full-back Ron Henry had to punch the ball away from under the crossbar and Atletico's left-winger Collar struck a successful penalty.

That goal brought a crisis for Spurs. They lost the composure that had highlighted their football in the first half as the Spaniards probed hungrily in search of an equalizer.

For twenty minutes Spurs' nerve was stretched. Goalkeeper Brown sprawled at Mendoza's feet to make a fine, courageous save. Then a shot from the suddenly activated Chuzo whistled by a post, and Ramiro was close with another. Atletico won four corners in the space of five minutes and the tension increased.

But suddenly, just when it seemed as though Spurs might crack under this tremendous pressure, they scored again.

There was no apparent danger as Dyson wormed free from Rivilla's lunging tackle and hung the ball above the Spanish crossbar. It was clearly an intended centre. But it became a memorable, if somewhat of a fluke, goal. Madinabeytia raised his hands, fumbled, the ball ran back off his knuckles and Dyson cavorted in triumph.

The Spaniards were broken. They had burnt themselves out and Spurs came at them with the killer instinct aroused by the scent of victory.

First Greaves volleyed a goal from Dyson's cross. Then Dyson wrote himself into football history. He took a pass from White, and ran thirty yards, dummying this way and that. In those seconds he was everybody and everything, a Pele, a Matthews, a Finney, a Puskas. Finally he checked and rifled a fine goal. It was the supreme moment of his career.

Nicholson said afterwards: 'Dyson played the game of his life, better than I have ever seen him play, better than I thought he could play. Maurice Norman and Tony Marchi were magnificent.

'But don't forget that it was a fluke goal that put things right for us in the second half. We had stopped winning the ball. But we took command again after that.

'I am tremendously proud for the players and my club to be manager of the first British team to win a European trophy.'

So Spurs went marching on. They did not know then that it was towards tragedy. Towards White's death, Mackay's savage and immobilizing injury, Norman's broken leg and the collapse of Smith's career. It was to be four years before they won another Cup final.

Tottenham Hotspur: Brown, Baker, Henry, Blanchflower, Norman, Marchi, Jones, White, Smith, Greaves, Dyson.

Atletico Madrid: Madinabeytia, Rivilla, Rodriguez, Ramiro, Griffa, Glaria, Jones, Adelardo, Chuzo, Mendoza, Collar.

Top left *Jimmy Greaves adopts the stance of a Piccadilly busker as he stabs home Terry Dyson's cross for Spurs' fourth goal. Greaves and Dyson scored two goals each in a game which was wide open until* **bottom right** *a speculative centre from Dyson was fumbled by the Spanish goalkeeper Madinabeytia and found its way into the net.*
Bottom left *Bill Nicholson said afterwards 'Dyson played the game of his life: better than I have seen him play, better than I thought he could play.' It was the highlight in the career of a winger who never bathed in the limelight accorded to some of his more celebrated contemporaries.*
Centre left *Dyson was, nevertheless, a man worthy to share the same dressing room as brilliant*

team-mates and fellow forwards Jimmy Greaves and Cliff Jones (left). It was Jones, the Welsh winger whom the Spurs manager rated the best in the world, who had instigated the first two Tottenham goals. Oddly enough the Spaniards also had a winger called Jones, but he was unable to match the destructive running and deceptive dummying of the Welshman, often more reminiscent of the rugby three-quarter he might have become than the soccer winger he was.
Top right *Tottenham Hotspur triumphant after becoming the first British side ever to win a European trophy. Standing: Greaves, Norman, Brown, White, Smith and Marchi; kneeling: Dyson, Henry, Blanchflower, Baker and Jones.*

37

Triumph—on the field where they nearly failed

The mood of the West Ham players in the coach taking them from their Hendon hotel to Wembley Stadium was subdued. It was a drive punctuated with long silences. The cause was something more than just the nervous apprehension that inevitably precedes a Wembley final. 'It was all sweaty palms and memories of the year before,' recalls left-back Jack Burkett.

The year before, West Ham had gone to Wembley for the FA Cup Final against Preston North End as the firmest favourites in years. And they won by 3 goals to 2, a win that gave them their ticket to the European Cup Winners Cup. But only after Preston, a team trying hard to escape from the Second Division, had led 2-1 and forced West Ham to football that was nervous, error-ridden and foreign to their usual flowing style.

Still, West Ham won, and they left Wembley with the Cup and made their way to London's Hilton Hotel to celebrate their victory. There was, however, to be a rude awakening.

Across the country, the next morning's newspapers were lavish with praise for Preston, cool in their appreciation of West Ham. It hurt West Ham's players—more deeply than they cared to admit at the time—to see Preston skipper Nobby Lawton quoted as saying: 'I suppose I'm expected to say we were beaten by a great side, but honestly I don't think they were great. They couldn't stop us from creating far more chances than they had.'

So West Ham found themselves robbed of the glory of winning the FA Cup. They accepted Preston had been the better team in the first half. But they believed Ron Boyce's injury-time winner was reward for the grip they got on the game later on. 'We expected to wake up the next day as heroes,' said goalkeeper Jim Standen. 'But Wembley, it seemed, belonged to the losers. It was a real sickener.'

Now, on the evening of 19 May 1965, they were back at Wembley . . . and the memory of their last visit lingered. This time it was for the final of the Cup Winners Cup—a trophy that Tottenham Hotspur had first won for England by defeating Atletico Madrid 5-1 in Rotterdam two years earlier.

West Ham had got to Wembley by beating—in two-leg ties—La Gantoise (Belgium), Sparta Prague (Czechoslovakia), Lausanne (Switzerland) and Real Zaragoza (Spain).

The opposition came from West Germany—Munich 1860, a powerful, well-organized team which included four full internationals.

Munich's path had taken them past Union (Luxembourg), Porto (Portugal), Legia Warsaw (Poland) and Torino (Italy).

Munich had just finished third in their highly competitive Bundesliga. And Max Merkel, their coach—the highest paid in Germany—vowed: 'We will complete a satisfactory season by beating this excellent West Ham side on their own English soil.'

In the West Ham dressing-room—the one they used a year and 17 days before against Preston—manager Ron Greenwood and trainer Bill Jenkins were calm and full of confidence. Greenwood reminded his players of some of the points in the dossier handed to each of them several days earlier, dossiers that contained a concise run-down on the Munich team, their strengths, weaknesses and expected tactics.

As the moment came for the teams to go out before 100,000 fans and millions more watching on television across Europe, he repeated what had become his sermon for the week: 'There is no glory in *getting* to Wembley. The achievement is in *winning*.'

Greenwood made four changes from the side that had appeared at Wembley a year earlier, to field a team nine of whom were discovered by chief scout Wally St Pier and groomed through youth and reserve sides. Joe Kirkup, who later moved on to Southampton after a spell with Chelsea, replaced the elegant but ageing John Bond at right-back. Martin Peters replaced Eddie Bovington in the midfield. The stocky striker Brian Dear took over from the injured Johnny Byrne, who would, it was felt, be badly missed. A fine target player and a reliable finisher, Byrne was at the peak of his career. And in what was to prove a match-winning position, Alan Sealey played on the right wing instead of Peter Brabrook.

Any fears that West Ham's flair for attacking football would be submerged were immediately dispelled as the final began.

Above *West Ham pose with the Cup and a huge mascot hammer after their Wembley triumph.*

Straightaway, West Ham produced marvellous open football which was to thrill the huge audience with its inventiveness and skill for 90 minutes. The lesson of the year before—that a Wembley final must be taken to the opposition—had been well learned. Munich, too, were interested only in winning. As a result, both teams played football that was bold and imaginative, making the action high-speed and frenetic.

'With both sides throwing players forward,' recalls right-back Kirkup, 'the score could have been 3-3 after 20 minutes if all the chances had been taken.'

West Ham pulled speedy left-winger John Sissons off his touchline—and with him came Munich right-back Wagner. Attackers were then pumped into the path which that tactic created. On the other flank, the power and the pace of Sealey added to Munich's problems. Several times, Munich left-back Kohlers resorted to body-checks in his increasingly difficult task of thwarting Sealey.

But as the West Ham theme song of 'Bubbles' rang out over Wembley in a continuous chorus from their thousands of dockland fans, the English side experienced a frustrating 45 minutes of missed opportunities. On the quarter-hour, Sissons sliced a shot wide of a post from five yards when only towering Munich keeper Peter Radenkovic stood between him and the first goal. Sissons put his hands to his head in disgust, and remembers thinking, 'Oh God, it's going to be one of those nights.' Radenkovic, from Yugoslavia, breathed with relief. The way Radenkovic commanded his penalty area, allowing shots to skim just wide of his goal—he watched one hit his goalpost—casually stooping to gather the ball, and using the length and width of his penalty area for precision-placed clearances, was a feature of Munich's display.

West Ham continued to swarm forward. Sealey and Dear slid to meet a centre from Sissons across the open Munich goal. Both missed it.

Munich, too, had their chances. Jim Standen's reflexes were stretched to the limit as he made two point-blank saves from Rudi Brunnenmeier, Munich's German international centre-forward and skipper. The way Brunnenmeier combined

'This is what winning at Wembley last year was all about...'

with inside-right Kuppers to create openings meant that West Ham dare not relax their vigilance at the back for one moment.

At half-time, in the West Ham dressing-room, manager Greenwood's order for the 45 minutes to come was short and to the point. 'Go out and play the way you did in the first half,' he said. 'Any doubts we had about the way the game was going disappeared at that point,' Sissons remembers. Across the stone corridor that separates the dressing rooms at the bottom end of the stadium, Munich's Merkel said much the same thing to his team.

And so the second half began with the same glorious football. Bena and Luttrop pushed Munich forward . . . the immaculate Bobby Moore and West Ham's determined defenders eased them back. Sissons relieved the siege with a quick break and a low shot that cannoned off the foot of the far post.

Then, in the 69th minute, the deadlock was broken. Ron Boyce, the midfield dynamo of West Ham's side, made the opening and Sealey struck the shot that sent the London team in front. Boyce recalls that first vital goal like this: 'I intercepted in midfield, and saw that it was two to one for Alan and myself against the goalkeeper. I thought Alan was better placed for a shot so I gave him the ball. He did the rest.'

Sealey had hardly regained his balance from turning a double somersault of joy when he scored West Ham's second goal—just 90 seconds later—that was to kill off Munich's brave and energetic challenge. A Moore free-kick was cleverly flicked on by Peters, and Sealey steadied himself to shoot in from two yards. 'I'd scored only three first-team goals the previous season. I remember being happy just to be in the side that evening,' said Sealey.

Sealey, who arrived at West Ham from Leyton Orient in a straight swap for Dave Dunmore, had been married only four days earlier, and his wife Janice was in the crowd that shared his excitement. It was quite a wedding present.

Sealey's night to remember was, however, to be followed by a nightmare. In a knock-about cricket match at the end of a training session before the following season, he tripped over a bench and broke an ankle. It was virtually to end his first-class career. But he could look back with satisfaction on his part in this match—a match that proved conclusively that Greenwood's way was the right way, the exciting, intelligent one of brain before brawn.

As the game drew to its fascinating finale, still poor Sissons could find no luck. A thundering 20-yard drive beat Radenkovic and almost broke his goal-post. West Ham's fans, and those who became honorary supporters for the night, were now singing 'Ee-Ay-Addio, We've Won The Cup'

Top *An Alan Sealey goal gives West Ham the lead.*
Left *Just 90 seconds later the Londoners' superiority is established with a second Sealey goal. These two goals won West Ham the Cup Winners Cup in what was a marvellously open contest. Afterwards manager Ron Greenwood said 'This game did not just happen. It was the result of four years' hard work.'*
Above *West Ham collect their reward for all that hard work.*

as Hungarian referee Istvan Zsolt signalled the end of the game.

Moore went up to the Royal Box to receive the cup and the stadium erupted in a deafening salvo of salute that seemed to know no end. It had been a triumph for West Ham, for Britain... and above all for football. It was described as a match in a million. Few who saw it would disagree.

As his players danced delightedly around the pitch with their trophy, Greenwood, the architect of it all, stood alone, looking up at the towering and packed stands echoing their salute. 'This is what winning here last year was all about,' he said.

Meanwhile, as the disappointment of defeat began to bite deep, the Munich dressing-room door stayed shut to sports writers, sympathizers and well-wishers. Merkel and his men wanted to be alone, out of all the commotion. By contrast,

happy West Ham soaked in baths where the champagne mixed with the water and anyone who came through the open door was welcomed as a friend. Soon afterwards, the two teams sat down side by side in the stadium for a meal. 'It was OK, but it wasn't what we wanted,' said West Ham's Kirkup. 'We wanted to be with our wives, but they were separated from us by a large partition. It took nearly two hours for our coach to get back to Upton Park, and it was the early hours of the following morning before we were really able to celebrate with them.'

The following morning, instead of the shattering criticism that had so spoiled West Ham's Wembley victory the year before, newspaper critics all across Europe filled endless columns in their praise of the superb spectacle they had seen. 'West Ham never at any time looked like

losing a splendid final,' wrote Rolph Gonther, of Abendzeitung Munich. 'Their wingers were undoubtedly the match winners.'

And when Munich got back to Germany, manager Merkel reflected: 'It was our privilege to take part in a memorable final. For us, only the result was wrong.'

For West Ham, 19 May 1965, was a high-water mark of achievement. Their football in the years that followed was sometimes as exciting, but never as successful.

West Ham United: Standen, Kirkup, Burkett, Peters, Brown, Moore, Sealey, Boyce, Hurst, Dear, Sissons.
Munich 1860: Radenkovic, Wagner, Kohlars, Bena, Reich, Luttrop, Heiss, Kuppers, Brunnenmeier, Grosser, Rebele.

When Scotland saw Naples and died

38

If it were ever necessary to nominate one match to illustrate all that has been wrong with Scottish international football, and all the wrongs that have been done to Scottish footballers, the 1965 defeat by Italy in Naples would surely be that game.

Aberrational planning, inadequate preparation, wilful hinderance by those best placed to help, selfishness, betrayal, obstinacy and arrogance—all the more infuriating characteristics of Scottish international football were to be observed in the circumstances of a defeat that left Scotland sullen and smouldering behind her borders the following summer when the 1966 World Cup was decided in England.

In the autumn of 1965 a place for Scotland in the last 16 for the World Cup finals seemed assured on three counts: One, Scotland had available an exceptionally fine current crop of players, men like Law and Baxter, Gilzean, St John, Mackay, Bremner, Greig and Murdoch were at or approaching their peak. Two, Scotland had well begun the task of qualifying, having beaten the group's outsiders, Finland, twice and having drawn away with Poland. And thirdly, Scotland's most perceptive and professional manager, Jock Stein, had just been appointed in charge of the team on an open-ended contract—'until Scotland are finished with the World Cup.'

It seemed then that Stein would be occupied until the following summer at least, for the tasks now facing Scotland were to beat Poland at home and then get the better of two matches with group favourites, Italy. The victory of the North Koreans over Italy in 1966 would prove in retrospect that the task was not impossible.

Things began to go wrong, wildly and improbably wrong, in October 1965, when Scotland were beaten at Hampden Park 2-1 by Poland. It was a strong Scottish team that was defeated but, more to the point, six of the side were 'Anglos' (Scots playing for English League clubs) and, almost as a reflex action, it was upon them that the critics' scorn and the selectors' blame instantly fell.

A day and a half to prepare for a match awaited for 4 years

For the next match, the home game with Italy, the Scottish pack was re-shuffled entirely. St John, the fine Liverpool forward, had ventured to criticize the national team's policies in public, and although he had already been pencilled in for the team, his name was erased by the unforgiving selectors and he never played for his country again. He was not the only notable absentee; Law, Crerand, Mackay, Stevenson and Yeats were also among the discards.

Perhaps, though, a clearer guide to the improvidence of the Scottish planning came with a remark by Jock Stein on the eve of the game when he paid tribute to 'the vast amount of thought and effort the players and officials have put into this important job since Sunday.' These last two words summed up the position with unconscious irony . . . 'since Sunday'.

A day and a half's earnest preparation for a task that had faced Scotland for four years, since they failed to win a play-off with the Czechs to qualify for the 1962 World Cup; a day and a half to weld together a team showing seven changes since the last match, a day and a half to work out ways to beat the most polished and professional defensive side in Europe.

The fault was not that of Stein or his players, but rather of a system that permitted Scottish players not much more than time for a round of hand-shakes and a brisk warm-up before playing vital games. So, after just 36 hours together, Scotland went out to play Italy with a side that included two new caps, Murdoch and McKinnon, one wing-half, Greig, at full-back, another, Bremner, at inside-forward, and captained by Baxter, a man rejected as 'too idle' for the previous game.

In the event Scotland muddled along a little further. Just 90 seconds before the end of a game that had seen the Scots, with typical bravery, assault a nine-man Italian defence that played with predictable composure, they scored to win. It was Greig, in an act of final desperation, who came racing upfield to take a return pass from Baxter and score with a low shot from just inside the penalty area.

Greig was already Scotland's man of the match, because of two goal-line saves after Italian shots had beaten the crippled Brown. But after his goal he was chaired around Hampden as the cheers of 101,000 fans beat down. Scottish hopes would at least see Naples before they died.

Amid this heady atmosphere it was only the neutrals, like observing English pressmen, and the professionals, like the cautious Stein, who were prepared to sound a note of warning: Scotland, they reminded the few who cared to listen, still had to beat Italy away or at least draw to force a play-off, and the best efforts of players and their employers would be needed to achieve that.

One by one the Anglos were hauled away to play in England

Stein was already brandishing carrots. The Scots had been promised an extra £100 bonus before their victory at Hampden and later the lure was raised to £250 a man for success in Italy. These were incredible amounts for the time, considering that an agreement existed placing a 'ceiling' of £60 on international fees for matches between the home countries—and considering that the FA was under pressure to REDUCE the match fee for England teams on the ground that excessive bonuses might lead to desperate action on the field.

But Stein could hardly afford to ignore any means of inspiring his squad, especially as the evidence accumulated that he was not going to get the help he needed from English clubs. In the 28 days between the two games with Italy, nothing went right for his planning.

For a start the Italians took a unilateral decision to shift that match from Rome to Naples, certain that the further south Scotland were made to travel the greater the problems would grow; the climate of Naples and the exciteability of the Neapolitan crowds were notorious.

Then, one by one, key players, skilled forwards Stein would need to overcome Italy, were injured or declared unavailable by their clubs. And a suggestion that all Scots selected should be released for special training sessions for a week before the match was rejected without hesitation.

It was a much-changed, much-weakened Scottish squad that Stein finally assembled in Largs the week before the match. And still his problems were only just beginning. It had been assumed that the players he had gathered were his for a week. Not so. On Friday, one by one, the Anglos took telephone calls at the hotel in Largs, and then muttering their apologies, departed south to play for their clubs in the English League. Of the seven clubs who had released players to Stein, only Leeds did not recall their men. And the 'guilty' managers included Tommy Docherty, Bill Shankly and Matt Busby—Scotsmen all.

Stein is forgiving about that black Friday. 'The fault is not with the managers, their first duty is to their clubs, but with the system. As manager of Celtic I can see the problem from the other side. In their position, with League matches to play on that Saturday, I might have had to do the same. But if you ask me why we can't organize our game so that there would have been opportunity to postpone League matches . . . well, that's something else.'

The consequences of the conflict between club and country were seen fully on Monday when Scotland left for Naples: of the team chosen by Stein, even after allowing for earlier injuries, five players were now forced to withdraw. Two, Law and Stevenson, had been hurt playing on Saturday, and a sixth, Rangers' Henderson, had suffered an injury which was finally to rule him out on the eve of the match.

The 48 hours in Naples before the game were, by Stein's own description, 'a nightmare . . . an absolute shambles.' By going down to Burnley on Saturday (a journey so hastily arranged he had to borrow Pat Crerand's car to get back to Scotland) he had at least found himself a goalkeeper, Adam Blacklaw, whose only previous caps had come three years earlier. But he had precious little else.

He had two left-backs (Provan eventually had to play on the right) two centre-halves (Yeats eventually was pressed in at nominal centre-forward) and he was without first-choice men like Mackay, Stevenson, Crerand, Law, Baxter, Gilzean, St John, Henderson and Johnstone.

Scotland's desperate solution in Naples— instant catenaccio

It was not, in fact, until the team walked out over the moat to face the derision of the Neapolitan crowd, that the shape of Stein's emergency team was known. He had elected, observers then saw, to gamble on playing the Italians at their own game —a 'sort of do-it-yourself catenaccio kit' as it was scornfully described, with provision for only two forwards, Cooke and Hughes, and the rest packed in defence to attempt the draw that could produce a play-off.

Given the circumstances there was probably little else to be done. But no watcher pretended that this was more than a hopeless gamble, for Scotland, after one training session and a one-hour briefing, were attempting to play the Italians at the game they knew better than anyone else in the world. The tactical formation—say 5-3-2—is not uncommon today, but teams who employ it do so through choice. Scotland had the style forced upon them by circumstance.

Yet for nearly half the match hope was permitted to linger on. Scotland, with Yeats and McKinnon performing marvellously at the centre of the defence and Cooke and Hughes raiding with desperate bravery in almost total isolation, fended off the persistent Italians. The precise and patient advances of Mazzola and Rivera, the swifter runs of Lodetti and Bulgarelli were turned into cul-de-sacs by the positional skill of Bremner and Murdoch, and there extinguished by fierce Scottish tackling.

Finally an error, just before half-time, brought Scotland down. Rivera broke into space on the left and centred high. McCreadie, anxious about the proven threat of Mazzola, was lured into the centre by the hanging pass, missed the ball and turned to see Pascutti volley a first goal past Blacklaw.

Scotland had been a team chosen to stop goals, but now they needed to score. In the second half Yeats took his number 9 shirt up where it belonged, Forrest and Bremner pushed forward to reinforce —and the gaps were created for the Italians to exploit with chilling ease. Facchetti strode forward to aim a half-clearance over Blacklaw's head from 30 yards for a second goal and with two minutes left Mora slid through to round off a move that owed everything to Rivera's now-freed genius.

At the end 70,000 Neapolitans went berserk with joy, the sky over the stadium was blackened with a rain of thrown cushions and with the smoke of firecrackers. Stein left to pack, muttering that he would never take over a Scottish team again—'Not in those circumstances—not for £10,000'—and he never has; and his players scattered to become sullen spectators of the 1966 World Cup, and of England's triumph.

Italy: Albertosi, Burgnich, Facchetti, Rosato, Salvadore, Lodetti, Mora, Bulgarelli, Mazzola, Rivera, Pascutti.
Scotland: Blacklaw, Provan, McCreadie, Murdoch, McKinnon, Greig, Forrest, Bremner, Yeats, Cooke, Hughes.

1 *Pascutti shoots, and his grin tells the whole story: Scotland's defiant rearguard action has ended with the Italians' first goal.*
2 *McCreadie, outlined against a background of jubilant Neapolitans, watches in dismay as Mora's shot slips past Blacklaw for the third goal.*
3 *Cartoonist Jon, of the* Daily Mail, *captured the essence of Scottish team-building problems.*
4 *Blacklaw goes up to field a centre from an Italian raid, and just to be sure Bremner's hands provide extra cover: so desperate was the Scottish situation no chances could be taken.*
5 *A glum-looking Jock Stein — the manager who described the national set-up as 'a shambles'.*

JON'S SPORTING TYPES

" I recognise most of the Italian team, but who are those chaps in blue shirts ? "

39

Ramsey unveils his plan to beat the world

Everyone knows that the match which won the World Cup for England was played at Wembley on a warm July afternoon in 1966. Comparatively few are aware that the formula which was to breed and bring that historic success was realized less than eight months earlier in the vividly contrasting setting of a bitterly cold December evening in Madrid: 8 December 1965, the night England beat Spain 2-0 in the Bernabeu Stadium.

During those ninety minutes the deep and sometimes devious mind of Alf Ramsey—he was not Sir Alf then—reached the firm conclusion that he had found and proved the system which could and, in the event, did, win the biggest prize in the game.

All the months and all the matches leading up to July 1966 were, of course, significant to Ramsey, if only because they provided the opportunity for players and plans to be tried—and discarded. But the match against Spain was to become undoubtedly, indisputably, the most significant of all.

For the previous eighteen months, with time running out, he had persisted mainly with a 4-2-4 system. It had produced some reasonable results but it failed to satisfy the demands he knew would have to be met in the future. Said Ramsey, 'A vital requisite for successful 4-2-4 is a pair of attacking wingers with the ability and speed to take on defenders, to get past them, take the ball to the goal-line and pull it back. This always presents the biggest problem for goalkeepers. It became apparent to me that we hadn't got the wingers who could give us the service we wanted because of the way defences had tightened up. If a winger did get past a full-back he was always confronted by another covering player. We had to think of something else.'

The 'something else' was 4-3-3—basically a back four of defenders, three midfield men and three strikers.

A commonly held and incorrect theory was that Ramsey had been influenced by the idea of 4-3-3 ever since an Argentine team had won a tournament in Brazil against opposition that included England during the summer of 1964.

The system could be devastating against those unprepared for it

Ramsey denied it. 'The Argentines usually played with at least five, and sometimes more, players crowding the middle of the field,' he said. 'Their object seemed mainly to avoid defeat. Mine has always been to win.' However, when Ramsey adopted the system in 1964 it was not entirely new. The Brazilians had flirted around the fringes of 4-3-3 in winning the World Cup in Sweden in 1958.

The first match an England team won using 4-3-3 tactics was in fact played in private, without a single outsider present. It took place at a training session at Lilleshall in January 1965, at a time when the clubs were prepared to accommodate even the most demanding claims of the national team. The England manager recalls, 'I played what amounted to a rather cruel trick on the younger players during a practice match between the seniors and the under-23s. I gave them no advance warning of the tactics the senior players had been instructed to employ. Normally these matches are difficult as a guide. The youngsters,

eager to impress, go flat out. The seniors will not give as much as they should, complacent in the knowledge that they are playing against opposition they feel they could overcome quickly and easily.

'In this particular match the instructions to the youngsters were to go out and play their normal game. The seniors, with three outstanding footballers in midfield—Bryan Douglas, Johnny Byrne and George Eastham—played 4-3-3 and ran riot against the young lads. They didn't know what it was all about.'

The game showed only too clearly the devastation the system could produce against opponents unprepared for it. The Spain match was to supply even more convincing proof.

Ramsey, naturally cautious, went half-way with 4-3-3 in two successful matches during the summer tour of 1965—victories by 1-0 over West Germany and 2-1 against Sweden. But each time the team had included orthodox wingers—Terry Paine and Derek Temple against the Germans, Paine and Connelly against the Swedes.

The scheme was shelved temporarily until patchy form later that year—a goalless draw against Wales, a defeat by Austria, a 2-1 win over Northern Ireland, all played with 4-2-4 tactics—forced a reappraisal.

Before the match against Spain, Ramsey, half-explaining and half-excusing the absence of any recognized wingers in his side, had said: 'The numbers these men will wear are nothing more than a means of identifying them for the spectators.' Those spectators will probably never forget them.

A back four that was to become internationally famous—George Cohen, Jack Charlton, Bobby Moore and Ray Wilson—wore an impregnable look from the start.

The middle three, George Eastham, Nobby Stiles and Bobby Charlton, combined artistry with efficiency in winning, receiving and working the ball. The front men, Alan Ball, Joe Baker and Roger Hunt compounded Spanish defensive confusion with harrassing, hounding and thrusting.

Even Ramsey himself could hardly have dared hope every man and every move would operate as superbly, smoothly and accurately as they did.

From the start of the match the Spaniards were chasing phantoms. They were attempting to play a marking game but with every England player working, running, switching bewilderingly, opponents spent most of their time failing even to find the individuals they were supposed to stop.

And the fact that the Spaniards themselves were fielding an experimental team without their ageing stars—centre-half Santamaria, winger Gento and the great general di Stefano—could not and did not diminish the exhilaration of it all.

The Spaniards were merely searching for a new team. England, by then Britain's only representatives in the World Cup—Scotland had been knocked out by Italy in Naples forty-eight hours earlier—were investigating a whole new strategy.

As Spanish manager Jose Villalonga said afterwards: 'They were phenomenal, far superior both in their experiment and their players.'

The Spanish full-backs in particular, with no wingers to mark, were consistently being lured out of position, creating situations for passes to be pushed into the gaps they left behind.

And increasingly often those gaps were filled by raids from men whose role has been most changed by modern football, the overlapping full-backs.

It was, for instance, Ray Wilson who hit the cross from which Joe Baker nipped in to score at the far post after only eight minutes. It was George Cohen who forced the Spanish goalkeeper Iribar to two of the many fine saves which made the victory margin less humiliating than the difference in quality. In contrast Gordon Banks in the England goal had to display his own impeccable reflexes in only two moments of desperate action during the whole affair.

Even the reshuffles after the substitution England were forced to make in the 39th minute, when Baker was injured challenging for another Cohen cross, hardly interrupted the flow of football.

Bobby Charlton worked just as well when he was pushed further forward. Norman Hunter, the substitute, originally brought into the midfield and then, in the second-half, moved into deeper defence to free Bobby Moore's greater creativity. On his first international experience, Hunter demonstrated the versatility that was to make him such a valuable recruit.

Moore, in fact, responded so joyously to the demands of a job that set him free from the inevitable restrictions of his normal responsibilities that in the end he rivalled Eastham as England's most constructive contributor.

England should have had three more goals in the final stages

It was Moore who combined with Cohen to set up the goal, scored by Roger Hunt, which made it completely safe for England after thirteen minutes of the second half.

A combination of the restive crowd, only 25,000 of them thinly sprinkled around the enormous grandstands that can hold four times as many, and the ignominy of it all, spurred the Spaniards into furious retaliation. Wounded pride drove them into too many harsh tackles, but since England have always been able to play that game too, roughness was countered with resolution and the game entered a memorable final phase.

It became one of the few occasions on a foreign field when an overseas crowd have swung themselves solidly behind an England side that was outclassing, toying with, their idols.

The fans even rejoiced when England played the possession game, greeting each accurate pass with enthusiastic 'Ole's' as the ball was swept from man to man and back again, around and through lunging, frustrated attempts to intercept.

Even the fact that England should have had at least three more goals via the openings that were created in this spell—Hunt missed two and Alan Ball, doing his 'Mr Everywhere' act, another—did not detract from the enjoyment of a night when the term 'wingless wonders' contained no hint of derision.

That night Ramsey had found his system and everyone stopped laughing at his most famous forecast—that England would win the 1966 World Cup.

Spain: Iribar, Reija, Sanchis, Glaria, Olivella, Zoco, Ufarte, Rodrigues, Ansola, Marcelino, Lapetra. (Names substituted for Lapetra.)
England: Banks, Cohen, Wilson, Stiles, J. Charlton, Moore, Ball, Hunt, Baker, Eastham, R. Charlton. (Hunter substituted for Baker.)

Right *Joe Baker scores from Ray Wilson's cross in the eighth minute. Baker's joy foreshadowed that of the England team after the World Cup triumph. The match against Spain convinced Alf Ramsey that his system would make England World Cup winners in 1966.*
Inset top right *The sparsely filled terraces of Madrid's Bernabeu Stadium held a mere 25,000 who were so enchanted with England's play that by the end they were cheering the visitors.*

Diddy men take on Eusebio

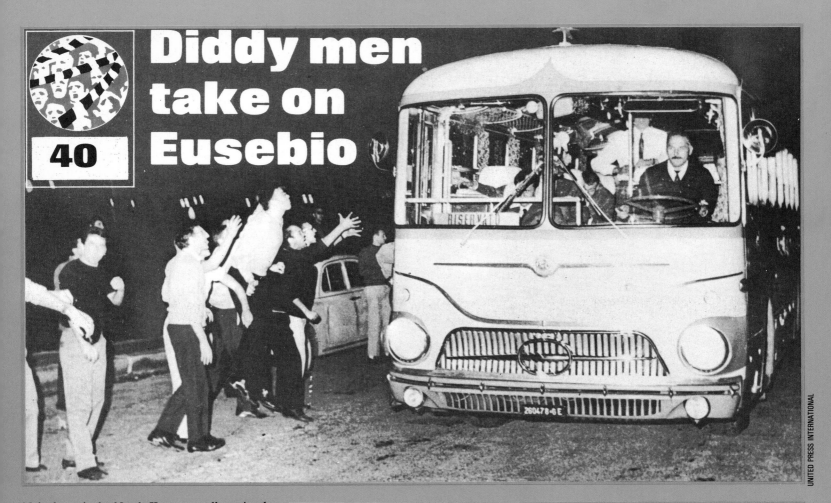

Nobody took the North Koreans really seriously in the summer of 1966. They had come to the World Cup finals unobserved and unknown. To those following the competition closely it seemed they had just a walk-on part like extras on a film-set, about to be cut down by John Wayne and the other big names.

Sir Stanley Rous, President of FIFA, warned: 'Do not under-estimate them. They could shock a lot of people.' However, the rest of the football world gave a discreet smile of indulgence and dismissed that statement as diplomacy.

The North Koreans had come to England by way of Australia. South Korea refused to take part in a qualifying round against their old enemies and so Australia and North Korea, both regarded as footballing small-fry, were left to fight it out for a place in the finals.

They met twice in Phnom Penh, Cambodia and the Australians went down 6-1 and 3-1. Their team manager was reported as saying: 'The North Koreans are outstanding footballers. I have never seen a team so well organized.'

But as Australia had not made even a pin-prick impact on international football, nobody listened. In England, the betting shops were offering odds of 1,000-1 if you wanted North Korea to carry your money in the World Cup.

The draw did nothing to excite confidence in the Koreans. Cynics claimed they were 'making up the numbers' in the north-east England group. For their opposition was to come from Russia, Italy and Chile, all established powers in world football.

Yet had anybody managed to peep behind the Bamboo Curtain two years earlier they would have been alerted to the fact that North Korea were planning their World Cup challenge like a military operation.

Forty specially selected footballers were drafted into the North Korean army. They were officially soldiers but the only shots they were required to fire were at goal. Club sides from East Germany, Russia, Poland and Bulgaria were brought in to test the Koreans. Finally, 22 players—all unmarried, non-smokers and tee-totallers—were selected for the carefully-prepared assault on the World Cup.

When they arrived at their Middlesbrough training centre, curious observers came from far and wide to see the Koreans in match practice, and they were instantly impressed—by their superb physical fitness, their speed and ball control and, above all, their tremendous enthusiasm. But with no player above 5ft 8in tall, everybody predicted their destruction from aerial attacks.

The doubts about the North Koreans were rather pointedly expressed by a Middlesbrough fan who shouted from the touchline during one training session: 'Ee, heck, you lads'll have to climb on each other's shoulders if you're going to stop the likes of our Jackie Charlton.'

The message may have lost something in its interpretation but such was the thoroughness of their preparation that the Koreans had undoubtedly considered the possibilities of such a tactic. However it was difficult to see what they could do to combat their marked deficiency in inches.

Indeed, that was proved conclusively in their first match. It was a lack of inches rather than skill that led to their 3-0 defeat by Russia. The Koreans, short, boney and slim, looked like pygmies alongside the husky giants from the Soviet Union.

Yet even in defeat there was something about the Koreans that demanded respect and admiration. They played to a flexible 4-2-4 formation, with all four front-runners ready to scurry back to help in defence at the peak of the Russian pressure. They hurried and harrassed the Russians into making elementary errors and worried them with buzzing, short passing movements that lacked only the final 'killer' touch.

Off the pitch, the Koreans were friendly, smiling people, and the Middlesbrough fans quickly adopted them as the team they most wanted to succeed. 'Kor-ree-aah, Kor-ree-aah'

Top left The Italians return home to a hail of abuse after their shock 1-0 defeat by North Korea.
Left As a result of that win, the Koreans met Portugal in the quarter-final, and astonishingly took a three-goal lead. Here, Li Dong Woon scores.
Above A typical Korean reaction to each goal.
Top It was left to Eusebio to repair the damage done to Portugal. Here, after thirty minutes, he scores the first of his four goals with a fierce shot.

was the continual chant from the Teessiders who were having great fun twisting their tongues round names like Shin Yung Kyoo, Pak Sueng Zin, Hang Bong Zin and Pak Doo Ik.

Somehow there was a rhythm in their names that came out in their play and next time out they hauled Chile back to a 1-1 draw after trailing at half-time. Pak Sueng Zin snatched the equalizer two minutes from the end, and the Koreans wept tears of triumph at the final whistle.

Mr Kim Eung Su, the polite Korean team manager, said: 'Today the sun shines on Korea and we thank the peoples of Middlesbrough for becoming part of our team. It is so lovely.'

It was even lovelier for the Koreans at Ayresome Park four days later. They beat Group favourites Italy 1-0 in the most astonishing World Cup upset since a rag-tag United States team conquered England at Belo Horizonte in 1950.

The Italian defence was riddled with uncer-tainty as the Koreans moved forward with ever-increasing momentum. Four minutes before half-time, Pak Doo Ik, the Korean centre-forward, fired the winning shot.

The Indians had upped and massacred John Wayne and his men.

The shamed Italians went home to be greeted by a hail of rotten tomatoes from their disgusted supporters. The North Koreans, unbelievably, were in the World Cup quarter-finals.

Waiting for them at Goodison Park were Portugal, impressive winners of the powerful north-west group. They had a 100 per cent record, having accounted for Hungary, Brazil (the defending champions) and Bulgaria. They also had Eusebio, the Black Panther from Mozambique, who already had emerged as the most lethal striker in the tournament.

North Korea's victory over the Italians was dismissed as a fluke by most people, and Portugal were the firmest of firm favourites before a ball had been kicked.

But the odds against Korea tumbled in the very first minute when Li Dong Woon hit a long pass to the heart of the Portuguese defence. The ball was deflected out to Han Bong Zin on the right wing who quickly transferred it inside to Pak Seung Zin as he came scampering through.

Seung Zin came backwards into the penalty area, screening the ball and acting as though he were preparing to lay it off to a colleague. He suddenly turned and, as he did so, fired a rising shot into the top left-hand corner of the net. The game was but a minute old and the Koreans were a goal up.

Merseyside bubbled with laughter. There was a Kop-like roar from the terraces of 'Come on the "Diddymen".' For the Koreans were still not being taken seriously. But while the crowd made fun, the Koreans got on with the job of dis-mantling a Portuguese defence that seemed too easily exposed to the perils of panic. Pak Doo Ik and Yang Sung Kook cleverly combined to make an opening for Li Dong Woon who coldly drilled the ball past shaky goalkeeper Pereira.

In the press box, Korean journalists were hugging and kissing each other like consenting adults. Portugal, it appeared, were about as unconcerned by Korea's flying start as the amused spectators. 'It may have looked that way, but to be honest we were completely stunned,' the magnificent Coluna was to say later. 'The Koreans took us by surprise. It was like trying to hold a cyclone.'

The game was 24 minutes old when, unbeliev-ably, Korea went three goals clear. Yang Sung Kook collected a short pass from Han Bong Zin, outwitted two defenders and launched a right foot shot high into the net as he crumpled under the weight of a late tackle.

Portugal 0, North Korea 3. And with that score-line, the fans at last stopped laughing. They cheered for the 'Diddymen' from the East with the sort of fervour reserved for Liverpool and Everton. Nor were the shock waves confined to Goodison. The news of the game, carried by pocket-radios, was greeted by bursts of astonished laughter and delight on the grounds where the other quarter-finals were being played. The entire country seemed to be cocking an ear to echoes from Liverpool.

Meanwhile, the pride of Benfica was suddenly beginning to dominate the tempo of the game. He was coming deep to collect the ball and then running straight at the Korean defenders as if wanting to be ambushed. Just as they com-mitted themselves, he would change direction to leave two, sometimes three Koreans kicking his shadow.

On the half-hour, Eusebio exchanged passes with Simoes and then sprinted across the face of the Korean defence before unleashing a shot that acrobatic goalkeeper Li Chan Myung could only wave at on its way into the net.

Eusebio carried on running right into the Korean net, picked up the ball and ran with it back to the centre-circle—a performance that was to become familiar during the next hour. 'I was impatient to get on with it,' Eusebio explained later. 'Every second was precious to us.'

Eusebio was retrieving the ball from the Korean goal again seconds before half-time. He had put it there from the penalty spot after the towering Torres had been tripped by Shin Yung Kyoo, the one really hard tackler in the Korean defence.

The Koreans began to crack like bamboo sticks in a hurricane

So at the interval it was Portugal 2, North Korea 3—the Koreans were starting to crack like bamboo sticks in a hurricane, a hurricane called 'Eusebio'.

The game was virtually decided 15 minutes into the second half—and, of course, it was a stroke of genius from Eusebio that did it. He sent Simoes racing clear down the left and met the return cross with just about the fiercest right-foot shot that had been seen at Goodison since the days of Dixie Dean. It was 3-3 with half-an-hour to go and the confused Koreans were now in a state of concussion.

They just did not know how to stop Eusebio. Moments later he came dancing through the left side of their defence and was tripped from behind as he shaped to shoot. He picked himself up, dusted himself off and coolly guided the penalty shot into the net.

There was time for Eusebio to have a prodi-gious 30-yard drive scrambled off the line and then to create an opening for Augusto to make it 5-3 in the closing minutes.

Then the match that belonged to Eusebio—North Korea and Eusebio—was over. Portugal were to go on to the semi-finals and ultimate defeat by England. The Koreans were to return home where there was a tumultuous welcome awaiting them.

'We have learned much,' said team manager, Mr Kim Eung Su. 'The game is growing in Korea and our performances here will have inspired and encouraged the youth of our country. Perhaps one day we shall return to the World Cup finals with bigger surprises.' There were many who agreed with Mr Kim Eung Su, who thought it likely the Koreans would return. But they doubted whether the Koreans could cause a bigger shock than they did in 1966.

Portugal: Pereira, Morais, Baptista, Lucas, Hilario, Graca, Coluna, Augusto, Eusebio, Torres, Simoes.
North Korea: Li Chan Myung, Lim Zoong Sun, Shin Yung Kyoo, Ha Jung Won, Oh Yoon Kyung, Pak Seung Zin, Im Seung Hwi, Han Bong Zin, Pak Doo Ik, Li Dong Woon, Yang Sung Kook.

When the kicking stopped and the football started

It is not often that Tass gets carried away. As the official Russian News Agency, its normal tone is cold and matter-of-fact, shunning the vivid phrase and rejecting the lyrical.

Yet on a July evening in 1966, the Tass man was up in the clouds. 'The match', he wrote, 'came like a spring of clear water breaking through the murky wave of dirty football which has flooded recent matches in the championship.'

Sir Alf Ramsey's normal tone also holds more than a touch of austerity, yet the hours after the game found him in similarly exuberant mood: 'There has never been anything like it', he said. 'This was the greatest England win since I became manager.'

But before investigating just what it was about this World Cup semi-final that moved Tass and Ramsey to such tribute, it is essential to look at the events which preceded England's meeting with Portugal in 1966.

Had the tournament been a West End show it could hardly have survived its opening night, England and Uruguay providing 90 minutes of defensive football which people remember with a wince and a yawn. It may have been inevitable that the competition should have opened with such a deplorable match. Uruguay were limited less by talent than by ambition, while England were burdened by expectations which were too great and an approach which was consequently too cautious.

Whatever the reasons for them, the pressures weighing upon players had been revealed and an unhappy tone had been established. And the defensive football was soon to be joined by an infinitely worse vice—that of physically destructive football.

Pele, as ever, Brazil's greatest hope, was first intimidated by the Bulgarians and then effectively kicked out of the tournament by the Portuguese defenders, Vicente and Morais. The Uruguayans went their unlovely way against Mexico and France before losing their heads, the match and two of their players, Troche and Silva, in an ugly quarter-final against West Germany.

The Germans themselves added a new dimension of unpleasantness to the whole affair by squeezing the last drop of dramatic effect from the mildest of offences. They were first suspected during the group match with Argentina when the Argentinian defender Albrecht was sent off. Suspicion grew with the Uruguayan game, and blossomed into total certainty in their semi-final with the normally impeccably behaved Russians, when Chislenko was sent from the field for aiming a kick which may have connected but which could never have caused the pain shown by Held.

By far the most endearing side was that of North Korea. Rumour alleged that the players had undergone years of monastic severity to prepare for the World Cup, but their football denied it. They brought off the shock of the tournament by defeating the homesick Italians, then took a 3-0 lead in an exhilarating quarter-final with Portugal before succumbing to four Eusebio goals and losing 5-3.

England, meanwhile, had improved upon their dreary opening, though only marginally. Certainly their rate of improvement never matched the antagonism which marked their progress and grew almost by the hour.

The target for most of that ill-feeling was a man who stood five feet five and a half inches, weighed a pound or so more than ten stone and had, in his short international career, acquired the kind of reputation most heavy-weight champions spend their fighting life trying to develop.

Nobby Stiles was England's ball-winner in mid-field. He applied himself to that task with a kind of frantic determination which, allied to his chronic short-sightedness, made a certain number of bad tackles inevitable.

It was one such tackle—a late and heavy affair on the Frenchman, Simon—which established forever his reputation. Stiles was cautioned during the game, but the FIFA disciplinary board, swayed perhaps by the general outrage, went further. They informed the FA that if Stiles were reported again 'either by the referee or by the Official Commissar for the match', serious action would be taken.

This threat seemed to legalize the anti-Stiles prejudice. More, it put his place in the competition at the mercy not only of a weak referee but also in the hands of an anonymous man in the crowd whose adverse report from a seat in the stands could finish him.

Ramsey, with one of the most important decisions of his career, stood by Stiles. He looked at Nobby's total of ten fouls in three matches, but decided he was indispensable—and picked him against Argentina.

Students of American Presidential elections, when they reflect upon a victorious campaign, can look with hindsight at a candidate's progress, point to a particular day or hour and say: 'That's when the whole thing caught fire; that's when it came alive.'

So it was with England's assault on the World Cup. Suddenly the public felt that success was possible. Suddenly they were sick of the sneers that Stiles, Ramsey and the rest were suffering. Suddenly it was 'Us' and 'Them'.

The match with Argentina reinforced prejudice on all sides. Those who believed that the whole competition was designed to ensure an English success pointed to the absurdly officious German referee Herr Kreitlein who sent off the Argentinian captain, Antonio Rattin, for disputing a decision just when it seemed that the South Americans' football might prove decisive. Those who believed in the English cause claimed that the Argentinians behaved like caricatures of South American players, kicking and spitting and gesticulating at an English team which refused retaliation.

But England went through with a goal from Hurst, playing in place of the injured Greaves, and the confrontation with Portugal was shaping up as a game which would lack nothing except uncommitted onlookers.

Portugal had acquired the image of the only remaining champions of pure football in the tournament. People had forgotten the brutality which crippled Pele; indeed, Vicente and Morais were out of the side. What mattered now was Eusebio, who had scored half of Portugal's 14 goals and had, by every account, captured the affection of a vast new football audience of middle-

Above For a moment the action is elsewhere, but Nobby Stiles and Jack Charlton closely police Eusebio. Before the match, Eusebio expressed fears that Stiles might deal roughly with him. In the event, he could have no complaints.
Top left Bobby Charlton turns in triumph having given England the lead. His team-mates are equally delighted to signal this important goal.
Top right Now, in the second half, Charlton puts England two up with a marvellous shot that earned the acclaim of the Portuguese side. He blasts a pass from Geoff Hurst past goalkeeper Jose Pereira. These two goals were enough to take England into the World Cup final, despite a successful penalty from Eusebio.
Right After the match, Eusebio wipes his tears with his shirt as his colleagues console him.

aged mothers; all of them beguiled by his little-boy aura which television managed to capture so well.

But Eusebio was worried about the pre-match publicity which presented the game as a personal duel between himself and Stiles: 'Stiles is a hard man,' he said. 'I am not afraid, but sometimes he does things and referees take no notice.'

If Nobby was reassured by that glimpse of Eusebio's anxiety, he could take little comfort from his own record in semi-finals. Six times he had played in semi-finals with Manchester United, both at home and in Europe. He had been successful just once.

An assessment of the two sides revealed that this was to be far more than a Stiles-Eusebio battle (in fact the English system of marking space ensured that they only rarely came into conflict). Portugal had an elderly side, but the wealth of top-class European experience, the confidence they carried and the fact that the backbone of the team (the 6ft 4in Torres, Coluna, Simoes and Jose Augusto) was drawn exclusively from the Benfica club provided adequate compensation for the high average age of the team.

England, entering the match with a more modest record, could offer the motivation of Ramsey and the sheer presence of Bobby Moore to complement the brainy, articulate play of Peters, the rapidly maturing Ball, the finest full-backs in the tournament in Cohen and Wilson. And Bobby Charlton.

They could also offer the Wembley crowd, which was acquiring a fervour more usually associated with Glasgow or Naples and had become a factor to the extent that many countries protested against England playing five consecutive matches at 'home'—as if the alternative, Goodison Park, would have been less fervent than Wembley.

Given the pressures of the warm July evening, the rewards at stake and the ultra-physical background of the competition, the first half of that semi-final was awaited with some anxiety. In the event it produced just three fouls—the first, for obstruction, not until the 27th minute—and the French referee M. Pierre Schwinte seemed as enthralled as the fans by the quality of the football.

'Great ref, that fellow,' Stiles was to say. 'I waved my arm once and he told me he was the only one who'd be lifting his arm that night. But he did it quietly, courteously, you know?'

That almost unblemished 45 minutes belonged largely to England, but it was fraught with fears caused by the three unaccepted chances which fell to Hurst (making 93,000 people think of the absent Greaves), and the half-chances which went to the Charltons, Jack and Bobby.

But the half-hour gave England the lead. The immaculate Wilson flung a long ball to the brink of the Portuguese area. Roger Hunt gave chase—he always gave chase, without thanks or praise—and drove his shot against the legs of goalkeeper Jose Pereira. It rebounded to the one player

England would have chosen to meet such a chance —and Bobby Charlton guided the ball into the Portuguese goal.

But Eusebio took over the rest of the half in the way great players can. An explosive volley flew from the arms of Gordon Banks and was smuggled from the line by Stiles. And a strong, swerving run, a marvel of control and changing pace, gave dire warning of what might lie ahead.

It was the 30 minutes which followed the interval, however, that yielded the football which has made a legend of the game.

Portugal swept forward massively, usually along the ground—seeking the quick, incisive pass which would release Eusebio—occasionally through the air, searching for the head of Torres. Always dangerously, purposefully.

England used Peters and Ball to work slavishly for midfield equality, trusting that Portugal's forward surge would render them vulnerable to the retaliation of Bobby Charlton's shooting. And the crowd managed to be both deafeningly partisan and totally absorbed by the skills of the struggle.

In the event, England's policy was the correct one. Twice Charlton drove savagely at square passes. Twice he was denied, the second time by inches. The third effort proved decisive.

Moore's deep cross-field pass sent George Cohen pounding up the right wing. The ball was played forward to Geoff Hurst and the big man, displaying both his strength and his appreciation of the moment, held off two challenges and delayed an impudent age before rolling the ball into the path of Charlton who accelerated into the chance and blasted England further into the lead.

The reaction of the crowd was almost frightening as Wembley shimmered with noise, but the reaction of the Portuguese was far more interesting. Jose Augusto actually extended his hand to congratulate the scorer while several of his colleagues applauded the goal. Was this really a life-or-death semi-final?

Indeed it was, and within two minutes Portugal had proved the point. The admirable Simoes swept over a long cross, Banks made his first mistake of the tournament, misreading it completely, and Jack Charlton's hand knocked Torres' header from the line.

Banks then made his second mistake, obeying an instinct to dive to his left for Eusebio's penalty which rolled into the right corner. Ramsey had instructed his goalkeeper to dive right for any penalty and the manager was furious that such a lapse had cost England her first goal of the competition.

But, despite the late efforts of Eusebio and Coluna, efforts which all but silenced the raging crowd, it was not to cost England the match. One last heart-catching moment when a penalty against Moore was demanded and refused, and England were through.

The English players fell upon each other, their relief at having survived mixed with a certainty that such football would be more than sufficient to overcome West Germany in the final.

The crowd, like sports crowds everywhere, stayed around to sing and chant and cheer, reluctant to leave the place where such deeds had been accomplished.

And Eusebio? He conformed to the little-boy image to the end, trudging from the Wembley pitch with shoulders jerking with sobs and socks sagging around his ankles. If the whole affair had been scripted, a shameless director would have made him wipe his eyes with the hem of his shirt.

He did just that, of course, and a million mums cried with him. They were to cry again a few days later, this time with a little man of five foot five and a half and ten stone something. But this time it was different. Nobby Stiles was to dance away from Wembley.

England: Banks, Cohen, Wilson, Stiles, Charlton (J), Moore, Ball, Hurst, Charlton (R), Hunt, Peters.
Portugal: Jose Pereira; Festa, Baptista, Carlos, Hilario, Graca, Coluna, Jose Augusto, Torres, Eusebio, Simoes.

42

The 5.15 winners at Hurst's park

It can take a long time to lay a ghost. It was thirteen years before English football laid its own particular bogey—the memory of the Hungarians in 1953. That was the year Hungary outclassed England at Wembley to prove that the home country was no longer master of the game it had introduced to the world. During the next thirteen years Tottenham and West Ham recovered some prestige by winning the Cup Winners Cup, but complete redemption, particularly in the World Cup, was not even approached never mind achieved.

1966 changed that. It raised the status of English football back to its earlier eminence and gave it a tremendous impetus for at least four years, during which all the major European club trophies were won. The interest in the tournament confounded all those who forecast that the public would resent the amount of football that was televised continuously. And the significance of that World Cup for the individuals directly involved in England's triumph was no less great. None of them has ever been the same since West Germany were defeated.

Success brought Alf Ramsey a knighthood, fame, a secure reputation and, for a time, a complete answer to his critics. His appointment in 1963 had been quite popular; it was felt that any man who could take Ipswich from the Third Division to the League Championship must be able to improve England. Yet by 1966 the public and the press were less enchanted; failures in attack did not seem to justify Ramsey's repeated assertion that England would win the World Cup. England's success put him beyond criticism.

The players were idolized, possibly because they did not have the responsibility of repeating that performance. The World Cup final made the fortunes of some of them. Conversely, those who did not win a place in that team, notably Jimmy Greaves, missed a supreme moment of glory.

Not all of them became rich though. Some are still playing, some have retired from football, one or two are hovering on the brink of retirement like gods reluctant to go down among the mortals. Generally, it was the younger ones who benefited most. For Moore, Hurst, Ball and Peters 1966 was the year they became part of football's rich and fashionable elite. In 1972 Moore and Hurst were able to regard with almost academic interest their successful legal battle against a belated tax demand on the £1,000 bonus they drew for winning the World Cup.

Geoff Hurst, then of West Ham, later of Stoke and still the only man ever to score a hat-trick in a World Cup final, knows exactly what beating West Germany at Wembley meant for him: 'Quite simply, it changed my life. Until that day I had been regarded as some sort of packhorse at West Ham. Appreciated within the club but hardly even noticed by the world outside. Oh I got a few goals, but I wasn't in the habit of scoring hat-tricks. I was the converted wing-half put up front to run about and take the weight off the real players. Or that's what everyone seemed to think, if they thought anything at all about me.

'Then, in one day, I became an international celebrity. An overnight star. Suddenly the world knew about Geoff Hurst. As far as earning capacity was concerned the sky became the limit. Nothing was ever the same again. Everywhere Judith and I went people wanted to know us, to wine and dine us. I became a better player for it. And that was a good job because everyone I played against now had a new respect for me. So it became a lot harder for me to play and to carry on scoring goals. That was not only the day of my life, but the day which made my life what it has become.'

By the time Hurst and his colleagues had reached the final a fine game against Portugal had eliminated the memory of less impressive performances against Uruguay, Mexico, France and Argentina. By now there was also a tide of national support that helped reconcile the public with Ramsey's unfamiliar, wingerless team. However, they still had to beat West Germany, a side well-suited to match England's own style.

A defender himself, Ramsey had built his side primarily on its rearguard. The team as a whole emphasized fitness and continuous hard work. But one of their major qualities was the faith in their own ability that Ramsey had instilled. They certainly needed it because the whole country was asking that they win the Jules Rimet Trophy; it was the only topic of conversation in England. But despite, or because of, the home advantage they were under a lot of pressure.

Once the paraphernalia had ended and the match at last begun, it was the Germans who took the initiative. Emmerich, Held and Haller had England on the rack. Two showers had put a treacherous sheen on the now sunlit Wembley turf and in a fraught 13th minute Ray Wilson, who had played impeccably throughout the tournament, made his first mistake when he headed a deep cross from Seeler to the deadly feet of the blond Haller. Those were the sort of chances he did not miss.

It was a disappointment but at least it ended

*Below England are only seconds away from their first World Cup triumph when **left** West Germany are awarded a free-kick and **right** despite Bobby Moore's protest Weber had equalized from it.*
***Centre** Martin Peters hugs his West Ham colleague Geoff Hurst who has just made it 4-2 for England with the last kick of the match and completed the first hat-trick in a World Cup final.*

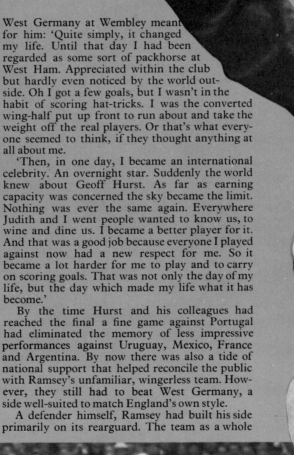

SYNDICATION INTERNATIONAL

the tension of waiting for the first goal and England's fans reassured themselves with the knowledge that not since 1938 had the team which scored first in a World Cup final won the trophy. (The English have always had a high regard for tradition.) It was also becoming clear that the Germans feared Bobby Charlton, whose World Cup was really the highlight of a very distinguished career. They were using, some said wasting, their best man, Beckenbauer, on the task of marking England's most famed footballer.

To popular relief England were level within six minutes, thanks to West Ham. Moore was fouled and his own swift 35 yard free-kick found Hurst running behind the German line for a headed equalizer right out of the Upton Park coaching manual. So it stayed to half-time, thanks in no small measure to Banks, who proved himself with point blank saves from Emmerich and Overath.

In the second half it was England's turn to be jubilant, thirteen minutes from the end, when they scored a second goal. Alan Ball, who must always be remembered for his performance that day, chased the ball down the right and forced a corner which he took himself. From it Hottges blocked a shot by Hurst, but no-one could stop Peters taking accurate advantage of the rebound.

Peters says: 'That remains my memory of the

final. Because Geoff went on to get a hat-trick people usually can't remember who got England's other goal. Yet without extra-time I might have been the man who won the World Cup for England.'

He might have been. But that would have deprived football of a dramatic climax in a tense, exhausting and testing extra-time that thoroughly vindicated Ramsey's values of fitness, effort and team-work. In the last minute referee Dienst judged that Jack Charlton had used Seeler's back for support and awarded a free-kick. Emmerich took it and the ball was played across the England penalty-area to Weber, who crept up on the blind side to equalize. There was a strong suspicion that Schnellinger had handled the ball but the goal stood and the trophy was snatched out of Bobby Moore's hands.

Charlton says now: 'I thought "Oh God, I'm going to be the one who lost the World Cup" . . . even though I knew I'd done nothing wrong. It still haunts me, that moment.' As it was, half an hour later Charlton was sinking to the Wembley turf to bury his head in his hands and cry tears of joy and relief. 'Once we'd won it I never even got round to thinking about my future. I've just gone on for another six years and loved every minute of it, with Leeds being involved in all the honours. That day opened the way for me to achieve everything I've wanted from the game as a player.'

Then 32, he may not have remained in the limelight if England had lost. But even six years later he was commanding a place in Leeds' first team. The 1966 World Cup made him one of the game's leading personalities.

It was at that critical moment, as the teams rested at the end of extra-time, that Ramsey made what was possibly his most decisive contribution to England's ultimate victory. Despite the immense pressure he walked onto the pitch with his usual calm and confident manner to reassure and inspire his players. 'You've won it once,' he said. 'You have proved you can win it. Now go out and win it again.' He pointed to the tired Germans and convinced his team that they had

no more resistance. England were ready to resume.

It was nearly halfway through extra-time, in the 100th minute, when England scored the goal they had been seeking. Stiles sent a long pass down the right for Ball. Once again he centred immediately and Hurst trapped the ball, pivoted and hit a mighty shot against the crossbar which rebounded down into the German goal. Or did it?

Television evidence has not proved conclusive because the keeper blocked the view. But the immediate reaction was that England had scored. Hunt, following up, turned round, arm raised in celebration and, with what was probably the most controversial decision in World Cup history, Tofik Bakhramov hoisted his flag to signal that Hurst's shot had bounced down just inside the line before Weber cleared.

From that moment England, coolly commanded by Bobby Moore (who was voted Player of Players after this game), settled in defence of their hard-earned lead. With great composure they absorbed the last, dying attacks of the very tired German team. Yet the drama was still not complete. In the very last minute Moore made a long, shrewd clearance to Geoff Hurst who, with the energy and determination that epitomized Ramsey's policies, raced away among the weary German defenders and scored with a 20-yard left foot drive that conclusively confirmed England's victory and gave him a unique hat-trick. It was the last kick of the 1966 World Cup and as it went in there were already several fans on the pitch.

To the acclaim of the nation Bobby Moore received the trophy from the Queen. It was fitting that Moore should accept the trophy for he had proved himself one of the world's best footballers, eliminating a tendency to make an occasional, drastic mistake.

Ramsey had created a team that he could rely upon and, almost dutifully, it won the World Cup. During their progress individual players, Hurst especially, attained new peaks of ability and fame. Some of them enhanced their new reputation afterwards, while others, such as George Cohen, Ray Wilson, Roger Hunt and Nobby Stiles, succumbed to injury, loss of form or age, to fade and soon drop out of the game. But none of them was ever the same again: they were the men who had won the World Cup.

Ramsey continued as England's manager, still enjoying the loyalty of his players although encountering increasing criticism of his selection. Gradually he seemed to be becoming the man who achieved nothing but the 1966 success rather than the optimist who fulfilled a remarkable promise. When he made that astonishing prophecy it was not mere braggadocio; it was more an expression of the man's almost immutable confidence. And that, most of all, was the quality he restored to English football.

England: Banks, Cohen, Wilson, Stiles, Charlton (J), Moore, Ball, Hunt, Charlton (R), Hurst, Peters.
West Germany: Tilkowski, Hottges, Schulz, Weber, Schnellinger, Haller, Beckenbauer, Overath, Seeler, Held, Emmerich.

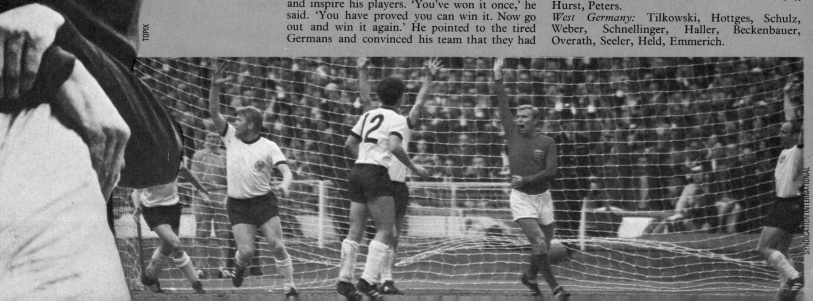

QPR lift the League Cup— and its status

43

Above This, the first of Clark's two goals, pointed to the easy WBA win everyone expected.
Above right Roger Morgan scored Rangers' first goal 18 minutes into the second half.
Right Lazarus scored QPR's winner after a collision between Hunt and goalkeeper Sheppard.
Below right Rodney Marsh, overcome after Rangers' victory, being consoled by Jimmy Langley, whose experience and composure prevented a complete first-half rout. At half-time manager Alec Stock told Marsh 'Go out and show the world you're the greatest'. His brilliant, solo equalizer after a run from the half-way line completely demoralized West Brom and inspired QPR to victory.

In the mind's eye of this footballing nation, it was to be just the Working Man's Wembley.

It seemed beneath the dignity of the great bowl of a stadium, the setting for so much wondrous football, to be staging the final of the Football League Cup—that grey, largely unwanted brainchild of League secretary Alan Hardaker. The cream of the clubs were still contesting the League Cup with about as much show of enthusiasm as a cat for cold water. At first they had not deigned to enter. Now they were under pressure to take part but under no obligation to win the wretched cup.

The result of that attitude was to throw up a first Wembley final of that competition which in prospect excited few people outside West Bromwich and London's Shepherd's Bush.

The world was not to know what a match of wild excitement was in store . . . or what a change that day, Saturday 4 March 1967, was to bring about in the Football League Cup.

The world, in fact, took so much convincing that even in the week of the match itself the League and Wembley officials were predicting a half-full stadium. In the event, Wembley was duly packed to its 100,000 capacity. And a raucous, down-to-earth atmosphere was guaranteed by the League's decision to give each competing club 30,000 tickets, 10,000 each more than the FA Cup finalists.

Contrary to every prediction and most expectations, the vast gallery of fans were to be most richly rewarded by the skills and graces of Queen's Park Rangers, the little Third Division team considered by most commentators to be at Wembley by default of the big guns and to give West Bromwich Albion somebody to play against.

But Rangers had in fact demolished First Division Leicester 4-2 in the fourth round and gone on to beat Second Division Birmingham in a two-match semi-final. They had gone to St Andrews and silenced the roar for an all-Midlands final straight away by winning 4-1, a score which included what Rodney Marsh still recalls as: 'My best ever header. I actually got up so high I nodded it *down* just under the crossbar.'

Marsh, supreme entertainer picked up for £15,000 from Fulham and later to be sold for £200,000 to Manchester City, was the inspiration behind this adventurous side which was climbing out of the Third Division as rapidly as it was heading for history. Marsh scored twice more in the 3-1 second leg home win at cramped Shepherd's

Bush to complete the triumph which made Rangers the first side from the Third Division to play in a final at Wembley.

Alec Stock—as much an impresario as a manager and as cute a box office judge as a reader of football—was in no doubt his team could win. The unbiased experts thought differently. Jimmy Hagan's Albion had played brilliantly in their semi-final as well, beating West Ham 4-0 at The Hawthorns and holding West Ham at their very best to a 2-2 draw at Upton Park.

Albion, said the world, were too wise in the ways of cup fighting and too full of First Division skill to let the upstart Rangers pull off the biggest upset of all. The Albion line-up was full of familiar names, including Jeff Astle, Tony Brown, Bobby Hope and John Kaye. QPR were, by contrast, a collection of youngsters, veterans like the aged Jim Langley, rejects and even, in Keith Sanderson, one part-timer. Of course they had Rodney Marsh who, for a long time yet was to be plagued by the mistaken opinion that his unusual gifts would only have an impact in the lower divisions.

Before the match Hagan thinks Marsh is strictly a Third Division star

Hagan said of Marsh the day before the great event: 'He is top scorer in the League (36 goals at the time) because he is the striker in a successful team at the top of a lower division and playing confidently. Anyone can get goals in those circumstances.' Hagan, later manager of Portuguese champions Benfica, is haunted by those words. Although for 45 minutes it seemed he was right.

In the first half the famous turf, the great crowd, the sense of occasion overpowered QPR much more than Albion's football. Their team were paralysed, the famous big drum which had thundered out the beat of Rangers' success down at the Bush was silent.

And in seven minutes the experts were preening themselves on a sound prediction. Bobby Cram sought out Doug Fraser. The Scotsman's through pass found Clive Clark—previously with QPR and later to return there. Chippy Clark launched into a familiar diagonal run from the left wing, cut in and scored at full speed with an accurate

right foot shot. Simple. And so it was again in the 36th minute, with the same sort of unmarked run, the same sort of right foot shot, this time from Tony Brown's pass.

It could, it should, have been more by half time. Only the redoubtable Langley—already in his 30s—summoned up the experience and the clarity of thinking to check the tide.

Peter Springett, Ron's younger goalkeeping brother, once came to the rescue with a leaping save from Astle. But at half-time the talk was not of who would win, but of the margin of Albion's victory.

That was the talk everywhere, that is, but in the Rangers dressing-room. It was reported in the frenzy after the match that Stock said: 'At half-time I just told the lads to play football and be a credit to the club and to the occasion.' Either Stock or the chroniclers did a master of psychology a grave disservice by an error of omission.

Rodney Marsh recalls: 'We were beaten. Our heads were down. Alec told us to be a credit alright. But he also told us we were the better side and all we had to do was show it.

'He told us we would win.'He told me: "Rodney, none of them can lace your boots. Go out and show them what good football, real football is all about. Go out and show the world you're the greatest".'

The change was instantly obvious. With nothing to lose, Rangers for the first time looked capable of playing. It took 18 minutes for the first tangible piece of evidence.

Mark Lazarus, who had played with many clubs and had been a great favourite with all their crowds, was beginning to run riot on the right wing. 'The Kosher Garrincha' they called him, with the memory of Brazil's World Cup exploits in England not yet a year old.

One vigorous Albion attempt to discourage Lazarus won Rangers a free-kick. Les Allen—formerly a member of the Spurs double side and later to briefly manage QPR—sent the ball high into the penalty area for Roger Morgan to climb above the straining ruck of defenders to head QPR back into the game.

It took only 12 more minutes and a piece of pure, vintage Rodney Marsh fantasy to make it 2-2 and send fear into every Albion heart. Marsh secured possession on the half-way line and embarked on an amazing zig-zagging run which left three fine defenders strewn in his wake. He

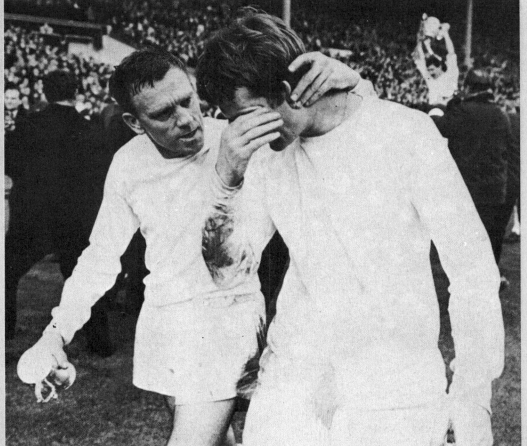

scored with a piercing, low right foot shot which went in off goalkeeper Sheppard's left-hand post.

It was more than a goal. It was a thrust deep into Albion's heart, an effort they knew they could never match, an act of total demoralization. One leading football writer was moved to comment: 'I have seen many great goals by many world class players at Wembley but none of them was in any way better than this extraordinary individual effort.'

The crowd said it more simply: 'Rod-nee, Rod-nee.' The war-cry of Shepherd's Bush rang out for their idol for the first time at Wembley.

Albion were beaten then. But not until eight minutes from the end did a controversial goal turn the truth of the situation into an unarguable statistic. Lazarus, having seen one glorious effort rebound from Sheppard's legs, was to be the scorer.

Sheppard had come out well to a through ball and appeared in possession although prostrate when Rangers centre-half Ron Hunt slithered into him at the end of his long forward run.

The centre-half's lunging leg both knocked out Sheppard and knocked the ball loose. Lazarus struck it back over the pair of them although he now reports: 'I had a film over my left eye from early in the second half. Everything was blurred after a ball bounced badly and hit me in the eye. But when that chance came to me I knew it was going into the net.'

But was it a goal? Albion raged with protest. Lancaster referee Walter Crossley would not be budged from awarding the winner. Hunt, he insisted, did not mean to hit Sheppard—and without foul intention the law says there can be no foul.

Hunt confirms: 'It was a 50-50 chance for Dick Sheppard and me. I kicked the ball, it rebounded off the keeper. And we collided quite hard as I went sliding on and we both went down.' No inquest ever altered a result. And none of the later pictorial evidence provided a telling argument for either side.

'I felt wonderful and gave them all Sunday morning off training'

For Rangers it was enough that Mike Keen climbed the steps to receive the League Cup from Sir Robert Bellinger, Lord Mayor of London and director of Arsenal, who was soon to see his own club suffer at the hands of Swindon the same humiliation which in that moment was enveloping West Bromwich.

In controversial and at one time unlikely defeat, Hagan was more generous than he had been before the match: 'I did not think at the time that two goals were enough. We should have gone for a third—especially against a side like Rangers. They finished the better side.'

Stock says: 'We just turned over in bed on the Sunday morning and read about that final in the papers. I felt wonderful and I gave them all Sunday morning off training.'

To Alec Stock, that was a generous gesture to his cup winners because they were due at Bournemouth on Tuesday to continue their successful pursuit of the second half of a remarkable double—the League Cup and the Third Division Championship. Queen's Park Rangers, and particularly Rodney Marsh, had arrived irresistibly and zestfully in the nation's eye.

So, too, had the League Cup. Even top First Division players envied Rangers their £220 a man bonuses and perks.

Also that year, for the first time, the League Cup winners were eligible for the Fairs Cup. That was QPR's only disappointment—entry was restricted to First Division clubs.

West Bromwich Albion: Sheppard, Cram, Williams, Collard, Clarke, Fraser, Brown, Astle, Kaye, Hope, Clark. Sub: Foggo.
Queen's Park Rangers: Springett, Hazell, Langley, Sibley, Hunt, Keen, Lazarus, Sanderson, Allen, Marsh, Morgan (R). Sub: Morgan (I).

Some gam , some goal, some finish

44

Really great matches are not easily compounded. They can emerge only in a great context, when the crowd is packed and expectant, when the players are tense and utterly committed, when there is some great prize to be gained.

After the sixth-round draw for the FA Cup was made in 1967 it was clear that such a game was in prospect, for Nottingham Forest had been drawn to play the Cup holders Everton at Trent Bridge. But few could have anticipated just how memorable the encounter would be. In 1967 Nottingham were being managed with gentle Irish charm by

Johnny Carey, who had been captain of Manchester United in 1948, and moulded by Tommy Cavanagh, a silver-haired sergeant-major of a Liverpudlian, who was their trainer-coach. Carey had inherited a predominantly pretty side, playing the neat football which had destroyed Luton Town in the early stages of the 1959 Cup Final, but vulnerable to the pressures of the long English season.

To counteract this Carey had bought Terry Hennessey, a stooping, spindly player from Birmingham City, and seldom can one signing have

had such a major effect on a side. Hennessey, with his acute positional sense, hard but eminently fair tackle, and his natural inclination to attack whenever the opportunity presented itself, had given Forest a broad and solid foundation on which to build a successful team.

The speed of their transformation proved yet again that although the ingredients of a good side can be bought or developed locally the blend which is essential to success will come and go of its own accord.

Most of the club's players were not outstanding individually. Never the wealthiest of clubs, Forest had to buy men below their best and coax something extra out of them or develop whatever talent they could find on their own doorstep. Cavanagh took much of the credit for this. The players worked for him willingly and with success came new assurance; their skills were blended so successfully that their shortcomings did not matter. John Barnwell, a former Arsenal forward, was the key figure in midfield, finding his men with chips, lobs and deflections; Frank Wignall was a mobile, easily-found target for the long, high passes of Winfield and Newton. Playing off Wignall, Forest had Joe Baker, another former Arsenal player, supposedly slowing down but

Inset left Jimmy Husband, a teenager with just a few weeks first team experience, scored both the Merseysiders' goals.
Inset right Ian Storey-Moore, who chose the sixth round clash between Forest and Everton for a memorable hat-trick.
Top left A clash of the generals; Henry Newton shows no mercy to Alan Ball, whom he was to join at Goodison Park three years later for a fee of £130,000.
Left Husband flicks the ball past Peter Grummitt's groping left hand for the only goal of the first half.
Above Alan Hinton (jumping) and Frank Wignall (on ground), who provided the ammunition for Moore to fire, challenge Rankin.

still capable of upsetting a defence with sudden bursts of acceleration through the middle. Most important of all, as it turned out, they had Ian Storey-Moore, a young forward whose penchant for scoring goals had begun to give the side a taste of greatness.

The Everton team to meet Forest bore little resemblance to the side that had won the Cup the previous year. Only Wright, Wilson, Labone, Harvey and Young had played at Wembley; the most important addition had been that of Alan Ball, signed from Blackpool for a British record of £110,000. With Ball in the side Everton's wealth of talent had at last begun to have some meaning. Previously the team had had much individual skill but lacked purpose; Ball, working with Colin Harvey, had given the side a backbone and it was obvious that if both or either could dominate the midfield against Forest then the game would be half won. More vital to the result, however, was the blow suffered by Everton at White Hart Lane on Easter Monday when Gordon West, their goalkeeper, broke a bone in his right hand. This left Andy Rankin, a willing but inexperienced understudy, to face the bustling Nottingham attack.

April 8 1967 was a typical Nottingham day.

The air was damp, the little shops in Arkwright Street glowed mistily in the gloom and the Trent flowed darkly past the City Ground. Inside, the keenest Nottingham supporters were packed into the Trent End, a narrow strip of terracing tucked between the goal and the river; the followers of Everton were massed, in a broad band of blue and white, opposite the main stand.

Yet no sooner had the game started than there was a threat of anti-climax. After only two minutes Baker set out on a typical sprint straight at the heart of the Everton defence. He was approaching the penalty area and was in the act of shooting when Labone, flinging himself feet first in a slithering tackle, blocked him. Baker rolled over and over in acute pain. He could hardly bend his left leg. Every kick, every tackle was agony yet he carried on for another half-hour before Alan Hinton, whose form that season had been erratic, took his place. Baker never recovered from that tackle, seemingly losing his most valuable asset – the courage for the telling sprint past the centre-back.

Forest's ebullient confidence was draining away with Baker's injury. Ball and Harvey were controlling the pace of the game to Everton's choosing and, while Nottingham were reorganizing themselves to accommodate Hinton, the Cup holders struck. Jimmy Husband ran on to a glorious lob from Ball to flick the ball wide of Grummitt's left hand. The sense of disappointment lasted into the second half. It was not so much the fact that Nottingham were losing or, indeed, that the quality of the football was poor, for Everton were displaying a cool mastery of the situation that looked likely to take them into the semi-finals. But Baker's injury appeared to have deprived the encounter of its classical context.

Suddenly, the spirit of the Cup was alive again. As if by a signal Nottingham were moving forward to greater purpose. As Everton, taken unawares, reeled back, Rankin faced his first test of the match—and failed. West would probably have held Wignall's shot but Rankin could only block it and Storey-Moore pounced on the rebound to bring the scores level after 66 minutes. Two minutes later everybody was on his feet. Again the Everton cover was swept aside, again Wignall played an essential part, nodding Hinton's cross down to the onrushing feet of Storey-Moore who gave Forest the lead with a superb shot squeezed through the narrowest of gaps.

It says much for Everton that they remained unshaken. They had made no attempt to close the game up after their first-half goal, continuing to come forward in a wave of blue that had occasionally threatened to swamp the Trent End and flow into the grey that was the wide river beyond. Husband and Morrissey were the vanguard, reacting like marionettes as Alan Ball pulled their strings with those lightning through passes that are always inconceivable until he seems to make them inevitable.

Frank Wignall—the ex-Everton reserve who deprived them of the Cup

But by half-time Forest were over the shock of the loss of their inspiration Baker and Frank Wignall, who had moved to Forest from Everton for a giveaway £20,000, chose the next 45 minutes to give perhaps his most memorable display.

The second half saw Labone increasingly pulled out of position. The Everton captain was suddenly unable to reach crosses he had cleared majestically before the teams changed ends. And, as Labone shrank, so Wignall grew. To his right Hinton—never a brave player, often retiring to the point of vapidity—was gaining confidence against another World Cup star, Ray Wilson, and all over the Everton half was a hyphenated star in the making as Storey-Moore rushed around trying to pick up the crumbs from Wignall's forehead.

After Forest went ahead the pace actually quickened. Neither side seemed to want a replay. But the momentum was now with Forest. In mid-

field Newton was tackling like a dumper truck, Barnwell was as delicate as ever—dropping balls for Hinton and Moore to run on to—and Hennessey and his forthright full-backs were content to pump long balls up front where Wignall, with all the grace of a runaway threshing-machine, was forcing Everton's back four to struggle for everything that came into their path.

But, as if at the whim of a playful deity, the game suddenly swung again and it was Everton who found the net next. Ball conjured a pass out of nothing to send Brown away on the right—where the ungainly Winfield had long been the chink in Forest's armour. Hennessey moved to cover, a body swerve, and Brown was gone. A second later so was the ball and there was Husband to turn it past the despairing Grummitt with a coolness that turned Forest's sunny spring into icy mid-winter.

In a moment the wheel had turned full-circle. Everton were now like a pack of hounds after the scent of Wembley turf. Grummitt tipped a marvellous shot from Morrissey over the bar, but Everton could not capitalize on the mood of the moment and, inexorably, Forest re-established their foothold. A rare excursion into the penalty area saw Bobby McKinlay put the ball past Rankin —only for Harvey to head off the line—and as the game crept to its fitting finale the crowd nervously consulted their watches. The climax came with less than 60 seconds left.

The most astonishing goal of the match—Moore has to shoot four times

Winfield sent a long, high centre into the penalty area and the omnipotent head of Wignall deflected the ball down to Storey-Moore, who proceeded to win the game for Forest in astonishing fashion. He kicked the ball against Hurst, hammered the rebound at Rankin, nodded Rankin's weak clearance against the bar and finally headed the ball over the goal-line.

Seldom can the dramatic course of a game have been plotted so perfectly. It was a fitting climax to a great game, to Forest's season and, in a sense, to the club's 100-year history. But that was not clear at the time—the climax was yet to come according to the 100,000 who queued all night for Forest's allocation of semi-final tickets. It would have taken a brave man to suggest to anyone in Nottingham that Forest would not win the double.

But the lace city was to be disappointed. At Hillsborough an imp who had long figured in Forest nightmares—one Jimmy Greaves— swayed a semi-final Forest should have won with a marvellous opportunist goal, and Terry Hennessey gave away a second to a voracious Frank Saul. In the League Forest could never catch Manchester United.

Forest had simply not been good enough. Like a surfer over-reaching himself they had been carried along on top of a wave of enthusiasm and a temporary blend which had reached its zenith on that April Saturday. Sadly it left them in the seasons to come. Bobby McKinlay had grown too old, John Barnwell suffered an injury which was finally to put him out of the game, the enthusiasm of the full-backs never again compensated for their shortcomings in ability. Cavanagh and Carey were unable to find the right men to fill the holes and the club wasted £100,000 in a moment of sheer madness—trying to replace Barnwell with a Jim Baxter patently past his best.

Just five seasons later only one—full-back Peter Hindley—of the twelve men who had represented Forest was still in their first-team. Eight of the other eleven had been sold, fetching an astonishing £600,000. And all Forest had to show for it was a place in the Second Division.

Nottingham Forest: Grummitt, Hindley, Winfield, Hennessey, McKinlay, Newton, Lyons, Barnwell, Baker, Wignall, Storey-Moore. Substitute: Hinton for Baker.
Everton: Rankin, Wright, Wilson, Hurst, Labone, Harvey, Young, Ball, Husband, Brown, Morrissey.

Scotland win their own world championship

45

Any account of what happened when England met Scotland at Wembley on 15 April, 1967, should begin with a brief indication of what happened on the eighteenth fairway at Chorlton Golf Club in Manchester late on the afternoon of 30 July, 1966. On that earlier occasion Denis Law, having lost £10 to his golfing partner, was squelching off the waterlogged course with a scowl black enough to make people believe all those Music Hall quips about the Aberdonian's love affair with money. The blond hair was plastered down by the rain, the thin shoulders were hunched high and altogether his aspect was about as welcoming as an electrified fence.

It was at this moment that someone approached with the historic news that England had just won the World Cup. 'They did the Germans 4-2 in extra time,' he called enthusiastically. Law threw down his clubs. 'Bastards', he said. 'That makes my day.'

Law's patriotism was not as serious as it sounded but that expression of it did reflect an element basic to his character and to that of nearly all Scots: a capacity for bringing theatrical, almost religious intensity to any situation that involves their pride. It can be an immensely tiresome trait, as anyone who has ever encountered it will testify, but in the context of sport it can be formidable and exciting, sometimes even moving. This combativeness is not related to a suspicion of their own inferiority but, as one found vividly on close examination of Ken Buchanan, the world lightweight champion, to a conviction that the rest of the world is conspiring to conceal how remarkable they really are. Law, Jim Baxter, Billy Bremner and the other outstanding Scottish footballers saw England's victory in the World Cup as contributing to that conspiracy.

'They're strengthening the World Cup final side to meet us'

It was, after all, the kind of achievement that might delude the gullible into believing that the English, not the Scots, were the best players of the game in Britain. Such a heresy had to be crushed and Law, Baxter and the rest went to Wembley on that warm and sunny April afternoon of 1967 determined to put the record right.

The Scots were convinced that they were taking on an even stronger England team than the one that had beaten West Germany for the Jules Rimet trophy, because the only change from that side was the inclusion of Jimmy Greaves in preference to Roger Hunt. 'They won the World Cup and now they're strengthening the team to meet us,' was the consensus in the Scottish party that set out for London under a new manager, Bobby Brown. 'At least they will have no excuse when we give them the treatment.'

In the event, England were provided with the most valid of excuses. After only 11 minutes' play Jack Charlton and Bobby Lennox raced for a ball on the Scottish left wing, the centre-half won it, but at great cost. At first Lennox seemed to be the more badly injured but within a minute it was evident that the damage to Charlton was much more severe. Prolonged treatment on the field did no good and as he was taken off he could hardly place the slightest weight on his right foot. He returned in the 26th minute and it said a great deal for his courage that he made

KEYSTONE

Above *Before the match one newspaper said, 'I doubt if there will be a repeat of England's 1961 9-3 win. I can see no way the Scots can score three goals.' Here Bobby Lennox (left) causes a few red faces in the press-box by increasing Scotland's lead to 2-0.*
Right *Denis Law, scorer of Scotland's first goal and a great player at his greatest that day, receives the uninhibited congratulations of one of the 30,000 Scots at Wembley.*

himself a menacing centre-forward, the most enterprising and persistent attacker England had. But he was sorely missed in the defence, where his strength and reliability had been fundamental to his country's success in the World Cup.

Charlton's injury, another affecting Greaves and a strain that took Ray Wilson well below his usual standard of excellence, entitled England to sympathy but certainly did not justify the suggestions that Scotland owed their win entirely to the opposition's bad luck. That analysis was about as comprehensive as saying the home side lost the Battle of Hastings on a cut-eye decision. The truth is that the Scots—inspired by the splendid, challenging arrogance of Law and Baxter and by the 30,000 of their countrymen on the terraces who had turned themselves into intimidating composites of Harry Lauder and a commercial for Alcoholics Anonymous—played like winners from the first kick of the ball. They attacked constantly with confident precision, making brilliant use of the natural 4-3-3 formation their variety of skills gave them. Greig was the defensive half-back, with Baxter, the central intelligence of the team, deployed slightly deeper than the other middle-men, Bremner and McCalliog. The side had been chosen with the prime objective of dominating the midfield. This was accomplished with an ease that was almost insulting.

Wallace, cooler and more ambitious than a late, emergency selection had any right to be, moved from wing to wing carrying danger to Wilson and Cohen in turn. Lennox, more orthodoxly direct, used his fierce pace sensibly. And at the heart of it, of course, there was Law, vibrantly aggressive, going after goals with a ruthless drive that would have frightened any army: a great player at his greatest. It is widely accepted that Law, with his murderous quickness and total bravery in the penalty box, is one of the very few forwards in the world who evoke special concern in Gordon Banks. This distinction was unlikely to be surrendered as the result of a performance in which besides stamping

his mark on every Scottish attack, he was to score the first all-important goal and stretch Banks to a save of astonishing athleticism.

The Scots never permitted their opponents to exploit the hustling game that had won the world championship. You cannot hustle to any great purpose without the ball and Baxter immediately impressed on those around him the advantages of relaxed, thoughtful football. He was quite happy to stand on the ball and wait for Bremner or McCalliog, Law or Lennox to set up the positions, make the runs he required. If an Englishman challenged he would be sidestepped contemptuously or beaten by a simple, well-aimed pass from the most controlled left foot in British football at the time. At such moments Baxter's demeanour was so provocatively assured that it was almost possible to see a cartoonist's balloon above his head with the words: 'Hey you with the World Cup medal. Come in here and I'll show you a thing or two.'

...Moore risked decapitation to head for a corner...

Clearly England's response to all this must have been more effective had Charlton remained fit. Without him the defence was unsure and ill-organized. Peters went back for a time to a central defensive position, marking Law, but the Scots soon appreciated that they were not being met with the same physical authority—though Moore attempted to compensate for one of his rare days of indifferent form by digging in hard and often—and the momentum they had established at the outset was steadily increased.

Hurst and Greaves were left isolated upfield, restricted to the odd hopeful pass from the harrassed men behind them. Ball scurried and harried as busily as ever but his industry

Above England players look dejected as they see their chance of remaining unbeaten World Champions slip away. Having pulled back to 2-1 with five minutes to go, they concede a third goal to the rampant Scots.

was not enough against so much skill and composure. There were occasional graceful runs from Bobby Charlton but in the main his promptings were ignored. An early exception to that pattern came when the Manchester United player's wonderful pass led to a brief opening for Hurst, and Simpson did well to beat down the shot. Scotland were too dominant to let that gesture go by without retaliation. They supplied it when Gemmell feinted to give the ball down the right, veered inside and shot violently. Moore risked decapitation to head for a corner. Soon afterwards Gemmell, having been brought down by Wilson, had to go off for treatment and while he was behind the English goal Scotland scored. From a free-kick on the left the ball travelled swiftly across the field to Wallace. His shot was blocked but Law, predictably, was following up. Law's first attempt was stopped by Banks but his reflexes were too sharp to allow interference with his second shot.

Scotland maintained a comfortable ascendency for the rest of the first half and those who criticized them for failing to score more goals, for contenting themselves with a leisurely exhibition of their talents, had not understood the psychology of Scottish football. A Scottish novelist, who is also a fanatical Sunday player, offered some clarification after the match: 'When the English are on top their natural expression of it is to hammer in goals. We'd love to score plenty, too, of course, but our instinctive way of showing we are in complete control is to go along the wing bouncing the ball on the instep, making an arse of anybody who comes in to tackle.' That is exaggeration, but it makes the point.

What is undeniable is that Scotland's domination of this international grew out of an insistence on using artistic flair to expose the limitations of scientific efficiency. Their aim was to discredit and disorganize England's high-powered football and that was something to be done principally in midfield. A big score in their favour was never likely; supremacy was to be expressed in the manner of the victory, not the extent of it. As it was, the score that emerged from the match flattered everything about England except their fighting heart.

Even that did not seem sufficient to keep them in the contest at the beginning of the second-half. Almost instantly Bremner was dispossessing Peters and his shot was only inches outside Banks' goal. Ball made a spirited counter-attack. His refusal to submit quietly had put him in frequent trouble with the referee but now he did something more admirable with a superb dribble down the left wing which stranded three Scots before he cut the ball back to Bobby Charlton. Finding his shot blocked, Charlton headed in the rebound only to see Simpson drop on the ball on the goal-line. The English players claimed angrily that it had gone over but they were frustrated then, as they were three times later: when Bobby Charlton beat two men and put the ball over the bar, when Greig headed off the line and when Simpson dived at Hurst's feet.

When the Scots struck it was with something better than near-misses

When the Scots struck, however, it was with something better than near-misses. They had never lost their verve or their cohesion and with 12 minutes left Lennox drove in a second thrilling goal. The English defence dealt inadequately with a loose ball and when a cross from the right reached Lennox on the edge of the penalty area he pivoted smartly and swung his right foot to send the ball briskly beyond Banks' left side.

Far from being the conclusive blow, that goal detonated a final explosion of excitement. Five minutes from the end Greaves, asserting himself at last, skilfully back-heeled ahead of Alan Ball and Ball's low centre was driven in off a post by Jack Charlton. Within seconds virtuosity was being answered with virtuosity as Law checked in mid-gallop to chip brilliantly over Banks and the goalkeeper lunged back to make an unforgettable save. Banks was ill-rewarded. Close, accurate passing took Wallace and McCalliog through the English defence and McCalliog completed the damage powerfully with his right foot. Now the match was a turmoil of incident. Before the celebrating Scottish supporters could be pushed back into the crowd England had scored again. Hurst's header to a cross from Bobby Charlton on the right soared in a lazy arc before dropping behind Simpson. His positioning here was, perhaps, the veteran Simpson's one blunder of the day.

It mattered little. Scotland's footballers had beaten England and now their followers defeated the London police. The Wembley pitch was completely overrun by hysterically jubilant thousands. Men danced in circles, rolled on the grass, tried to dig pieces out of the turf to carry home as souvenirs. Any among them who stopped to think for a moment probably suspected that the journey begun that sunlit afternoon—towards the European Nations' Cup finals of 1968—would not be completed. Some may even have guessed that Bobby Brown, the manager now being toasted, would soon be reviled and condemned to oblivion in this same stadium.

But all that was happily remote. For the moment what mattered was that the mind was full of memories and London was full of whisky. And who ever expects Scottish football to provide more than memories of great days and great players?

England: Banks, Cohen, Wilson, Stiles, Charlton J, Moore, Ball, Greaves, Charlton R, Hurst, Peters. *Scotland*: Simpson, Gemmell, McCreadie, Greig, McKinnon, Baxter, Wallace, Bremner, McCalliog, Law, Lennox.

When Lisbon belonged to Glasgow

46

It was in the 1972-73 season that a new item of jargon crept into British football: 'Total football'. It was intended to designate an all-out attacking style. Those susceptible to such things no doubt believed that this kind of style was something novel, something previously undreamed of. Others wondered what all the fuss was about. Had Real Madrid, then, played partial football? Had the Wolves of the fifties been dedicated to defence? Was there no aggression, no imagination, in the way Tottenham Hotspur had decorated the game at the turn of that decade? Above all, what were Celtic doing in Lisbon on 25 May 1967?

Celtic, particularly, because they did much more than become the first British club to win the European Cup. What they also did was to revive a wholly honourable fashion in football, and they did so with consummate timing. Indeed it could fairly be said that Celtic reversed a trend that had been threatening to ruin the European game.

Italian football had been dominating Europe. Its creed was craven defence, based on the assumption that if you didn't concede a goal, you couldn't lose. A rational but negative concept. It was a sterile business altogether, but it had been successful in Italy and clubs such as Inter and AC Milan had been threatening to monopolize the European Cup just as the Spaniards and the Portuguese had once done. In fact the trophy had gone to that city three times in four seasons.

Success, of course, is inevitably copied and the Italian style was successfuly translated abroad. Even in Britain this negative football was being watched with great interest, for it seemed to provide some sort of security for managers. In fact, and without exaggeration, football as a mass spectator sport was in jeopardy, simply because the Italians and their disciples had contrived to make it boring. There can be no question that Celtic came along just in time.

For the football played by Celtic was total, by any reasonable interpretation of that word. A French journalist once coined as good a description as any of the Celtic style. *L'orage*, he called them: 'The storm'. There was nothing particularly complex about their play, of course, nor did there have to be. Jock Stein worked on basic truths. He knew that people preferred adventurous, attacking football, and he also knew that it was his job to please as many fans as possible.

'The best place to defend is in the other team's penalty area'

Naturally, he had to ally all this aggression with efficiency, and this he did by making absolutely sure that no man would be allowed to wear a Celtic first-team jersey unless he was capable of lasting 90 energetic minutes. The man on the ball had to be supported by just about every other outfield player and this presupposed intelligent, perpetual running off the ball. The full-backs overlapped as a matter of course. Midfield men were always apt to race into a menacing attacking position. Wingers would be seen back in defence, harassing their opposite numbers.

Incredibly, Stein had been manager at Celtic Park for only one full season before that successful European Cup campaign. But that was quite long enough for him to blend his men into what is still recognized as the finest club side Scotland has ever known.

'The best place to defend', he was always fond of saying, 'is in the other team's penalty area.' It was a creed he followed to the best of his very considerable ability, and with few exceptions. 'The difference between a really good side and a great side', he had also said, 'can often be the touch of the unpredictable. Call it a flash of genius, if you like. Or flair.'

Celtic certainly had men with flair. Notably there was the incomparable Jimmy Johnstone, on his day quite irresistible. There was Bertie Auld, one of the architects of attack, a man with an exceptional ability to read the play and a great talent for distribution. There was Bobby Murdoch, a world-class blend of power, ferocious shooting, accurate passing from midfield, and delicate ball-control. There was also Tommy Gemmell, a full-back whose extrovert character was admirably suited to powerful runs down the wing which he finished off with marksmanship unusual in a defender. With such players Stein could prepare tactical plans so varied as to be unpredictable.

The road to Portugal's National Stadium had not been easy for either side. Celtic had beaten Zurich, Nantes, Vojvodina Novi Sad and Dukla Prague. Inter had disposed of Moscow Torpedo, Vasas Budapest, Real Madrid and CSKA Sofia. But Inter had the advantage of experience. This was, after all, their third European Cup final in four years. By comparison Celtic were innocents; it was the first time they had ever appeared in the European Cup. Little wonder then that most European football fans expected Inter to win even though they may have wished them to lose.

The exceptions, naturally enough, were at Parkhead, at the eastern end of Glasgow, where Jock Stein had been building up the morale of his men day by day, hour by hour, as the final approached. At the same time, he had been careful to emphasize the club's image. In the official Celtic magazine he wrote: 'It is important for Celtic's players to think they can win every match they play. But it is equally important for them to keep in mind that there is always the possibility of losing . . . if it should happen that we lose to Inter-Milan, we want to be remembered . . . for the football we have played.'

Jock Stein was not merely trying to pass the time when, at the team's pre-Lisbon training headquarters on the Ayrshire coast, he showed the players the film of that entrancing European Cup final of 1960 between Real Madrid and Eintracht Frankfurt. For he was showing them, in effect, the standards he wanted them to achieve. So, when Celtic at last faced Inter, they did so with the right attitude. As Stein says: 'The formation is not as important as the attitude. Attack should be in the mind.'

But, once the final had commenced, it was popular opinion that seemed to be vindicated. In the usual Italian opening burst Mazzola—possibly the most gifted player in the Inter side in the absence of the injured Suarez—had headed against the legs of Ronnie Simpson. Now, in the seventh minute, he started the move that produced the goal. He passed to Corso, who transferred the ball shrewdly to Cappellini, who found himself with only one green-and-white jersey barring the way to goal. The Italian was positioning himself for a shot when Jim Craig tackled heavily. The German referee, Herr Tschenscher, decided that the tackle warranted a penalty. Mazzola took the kick willingly and with confidence, leaving Simpson stranded at the wrong side of the goal.

It has been claimed that Celtic's officials were not really worried by that goal. If so, it was an impressive display of self-confidence for to the Italian mind the goal was perfectly timed to suit Inter's undeniable technical assets. It allowed them to employ all their defensive expertise to prevent Celtic scoring. After only seven minutes they retreated into packed but well-organized defence.

Yet Inter's tactics also suited their opponents. By conceding the initiative they exposed themselves to the full force of *l'orage*. Celtic, naturally and with the spur of a goal deficit, attacked incessantly. Inter's retreat into defence allowed Gemmel the freedom to move forward. Nor, without Suarez and Jair, who was also injured, did the Italian champions have the means of sudden, killing counter-attack.

However Inter, trained to weather such storms, did not yield immediately. In the Italian goal Sarti performed prodigies—he had to. His was among the greatest goalkeeping performances in the history of the European Cup and if he was helped by a generous quota of good fortune he deserved it. Bertie Auld and Tommy Gemmell both shot against the crossbar and every member of the Celtic forward-line—to say nothing of Murdoch —forced Sarti to saves, any one of which would have been memorable on its own. Celtic's captain, Billy McNeill, urged his team on tirelessly. Yet the Italian defence, inspired by the tremendous energy of Picchi, held on, encouraged by every passing minute.

'Celtic deserved to win . . . the match was a victory for sport'

Indeed an hour passed before Celtic managed to equalize. Appropriately, if one remembers their dedication to 'total football', the goal was created and executed by their full-backs. Craig carried the ball forcefully down the right and, as the defenders waited for a high centre to the far post, swept a square pass across the penalty area— right into the path of the racing Gemmell. From 20 yards Gemmell hit a shot that was too much even for Sarti.

If it had been a league match the Italians could have contented themselves with a draw, but in the circumstances they needed to break out of their own stronghold to recover their advantage. They could not. Already most people sensed Celtic's victory; they not only had territorial superiority but the wit and wisdom to use it to advantage.

And Inter were being run off their feet by this continuous, skilful pressure. They were being outplayed by the relatively unknown team from Scotland, desperately holding on in the hope of some unforeseen salvation. Six minutes from time Gemmell, again, passed to Murdoch who drove one more shot at goal. Sarti moved to cover, and was horrified as Steve Chalmers deflected the shot just enough to ruin his anticipation.

At last a British team had won the European Cup. On that brilliant day English football became British football once more as the whole nation praised the Scottish achievement. But any British victory would have been a triumph; it was the manner of Celtic's win that excited everyone.

The pitch was inevitably invaded by thousands of deliriously happy Scots and Celtic were applauded by the scarcely less delighted Portuguese—whose heroes Benfica had lost to Milan clubs in both 1963 and 1965. But the trophy itself hardly mattered. It was football that had triumphed. Even Helenio Herrera, Inter's controversial and successful manager, acknowledged that much: 'Celtic deserved to win,' he said. 'We lost, but the match was a victory for sport.'

Celtic: Simpson, Craig, Gemmell, Murdoch, McNeill, Clark, Johnstone, Wallace, Chalmers, Auld, Lennox.
Internatzionale Milan: Sarti, Burgnich, Facchetti, Bedin, Guarneri, Picchi, Domenghini, Bicicli, Mazzola, Cappellini, Corso.

Main picture *Facchetti deflects a shot by Lennox. After only seven minutes Mazzola scored a penalty and satisfied a personal ambition: it was on the same ground that his father played his last match before the Superga aircraft disaster. But after that goal it was Celtic who did all the attacking.*

Below left *Bobby Murdoch competing for the ball with Mario Corso to sustain Celtic's pressure.*

Below right *'We've won.' Chalmers (9) has just deflected Murdoch's shot for Celtic's second goal.*

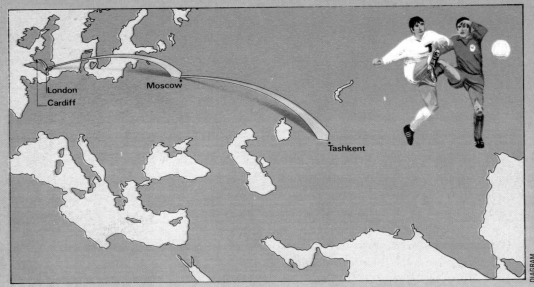

Cardiff's Asian adventure

47

Map, above and centre The worst problem of playing in Tashkent was the amount of time wasted in travelling and the interference with the team's normal routine. That Cardiff were able to overcome the problems of fatigue and boredom was a result of the meticulous preparations of manager Jimmy Scoular, the fascination of Tashkent, and the hospitality of the people. Hordes of local Uzbeks followed the Cardiff players—even observing them through the hotel windows.

Above right In the actual game Cardiff (dark shirts) defended in depth to protect their one goal lead from the first leg. They eventually lost 1-0 but won the replay in Augsburg, West Germany.

In March 1968 Cardiff City embarked on a footballing adventure that will stand for ever as one of the most bizarre ever experienced by a British club. The fact that Cardiff, then a lowly-placed Second Division side, survived it triumphantly adds a touch of poetry to the improbability of this soccer odyssey.

The competition was the European Cup Winners Cup, the continent's second most important tournament. The opposition was Moscow Torpedo, the representative side of the Soviet motor industry and among the most formidable of Russian teams. And the venue for the second leg was Tashkent, capital of Uzbekistan in Soviet Central Asia.

Wales, of course, had previously contributed some remarkable occasions to the history of the Cup Winners Cup. Its rules allowed the winners of the Welsh Cup the same right of entry as the FA Cup winners, and the Welsh revel in this loophole. In the early 1960s such unknown clubs as Bangor and Borough United bounded through it to compete with Europe's elite. As Wales' premier club, however, Cardiff rarely relinquished this unusual passport to glory and they have certainly not allowed Welsh interests in the competition to be regarded as a spot of light relief.

Cardiff had particularly distinguished themselves in the 1964-65 tournament by knocking out the holders, Sporting Lisbon, before losing narrowly to Real Zaragoza of Spain in the quarter-finals. Now once again, in 1967-68, Cardiff reached the quarter-finals after beating Shamrock Rovers and NAC Breda. With both Tottenham and Aberdeen eliminated before that stage Cardiff were the only British club left in the competition, and when they were paired with Moscow Torpedo they were naturally the centre of considerable interest.

That interest increased when the clubs began to negotiate dates and venues for their two matches. Torpedo were forced to apply for their home leg to be played at the Pakathor Stadium in Tashkent which, although well over 2,000 miles from Moscow, was the nearest suitable stadium not frozen by the harsh Russian winter.

Thus Cardiff were faced with a journey for the return leg of between 7,000 and 8,000 miles—and this during a vital period of a season when the club was perilously close to the Second Division relegation zone. Yet before he had time to concern himself with the sort of opposition Torpedo would provide, Jimmy Scoular, the Cardiff manager, had to figure out how to fit such an exhausting journey into an overcrowded fixture list. And that was only the first of his difficulties.

The dates arranged for the tie were 6 March for the first leg at Cardiff and 19 March for the second leg in Tashkent. This created problems for, on the previous Saturday, 16 March, Cardiff were due to play at Middlesbrough in a League match. In British football that is not exactly a short journey, so it was a little much to expect Cardiff to play in Middlesbrough on Saturday and then 4,000 miles away in Tashkent on the following Tuesday.

Could Cardiff play in Middlesbrough Saturday and Tashkent Tuesday?

But luckily, both Middlesbrough and Cardiff had been eliminated from the FA Cup and both therefore had no fixture on Saturday 9 March and Middlesbrough eventually agreed to rearrange the match for that date. Once the Tashkent journey had been accommodated in Cardiff's fixture list Scoular then had to ensure the long journey would not become dispiriting and futile—especially if Cardiff lost the first leg.

But before that he had to solve his team problems. Three of his regular first team were ineligible under EUFA's three-month qualification ruling. Goalkeeper Fred Davies, striker Brian Clark and forward Les Lea had each been signed less than three months previously. Scoular was also handicapped by his lack of knowledge about Torpedo and their style of play. No British side had played them recently and there was no question of a spying mission. So the Cardiff manager, a keen student of all opposition, had little other information than that every Torpedo player was a Russian international and that forward Eduard Streltsov was the current Soviet Player of the Year.

The little else he knew was that in the previous two rounds Torpedo had beaten Motor Zwickau of East Germany and the Czech side Spartak Trnava and, significantly, had won the away leg on both occasions. This evidence, plus Cardiff's apparent vulnerability, suggested that the Moscow team would attempt to win the first leg. But Torpedo's coach, Vladimir Zolotov, decided to abide by the almost traditional approach of an away side in the first leg of a cup-tie—that of deep and determined defence.

Cardiff could scarcely have requested better tactics from their opponents. All they had to do was contain the two lonely Torpedo front men, Streltsov and Pais, and they were virtually certain of keeping their goal intact. In the event they deservedly went one better, their Welsh international winger Barrie Jones heading a goal just before the interval.

Suddenly the prospect of the long journey became more bearable for Cardiff, although they still faced a footballing task even more formidable than the journey. A 3-2 win over Middlesbrough on the following Saturday did nothing to lessen the spirits of the Cardiff party of 16 players who assembled at Cardiff General Station on Thursday morning 14 March. Torpedo, muttering darkly, had gone to Tashkent the previous week. Cardiff intended flying from London to Moscow, staying two nights in the Russian capital and making a second long journey to Tashkent on Saturday.

Jimmy Scoular had thought of everything: tablets to ward off stomach trouble, canned food, a local student as personal interpreter and even a couple of gallons of orange juice. He refused to leave behind star defender Brian Harris who had injured his leg at Middlesbrough and was very doubtful. Portable heat pads were taken so that Harris could have treatment *en route*. In Moscow the temperature was an unwelcoming four degrees below freezing but that did not prevent Scoular arranging training facilities at the Lenin Stadium where Cardiff found their training companions were the Russian Olympic squad.

The warmth of the Russian hospitality, which included a night at the Bolshoi Ballet and conducted sightseeing, did not distract Cardiff minds from the purpose of their journey. Scoular saw to that, as he saw to it that the menu of the

giant Moscow hotel was changed to include prime steaks for his players. If morale ever slackened it was on the day Cardiff travelled on to Tashkent. After four hours stranded in a blizzard-bound airport and another four aloft the party's spirit and confidence was showing signs of wear and tear.

But in the Cotton Pickers Stadium during the second half of the match three days later it was definitely Moscow Torpedo who looked fed up and far from home as Cardiff broke into the sort of giant-killing mood more typical of the FA Cup than European competition.

What had happened was that the Cardiff players had reacted remarkably to the strangeness of their surroundings. Scoular had whipped them through tough training stints to overcome the effects of the travelling and the disturbance of their daily routine. And although they carefully discussed the approaching game from a tactical point of view, the Cardiff manager carefully maintained a light-hearted, good-humoured approach. The people of Tashkent took care of the rest.

Second Division players are not accustomed to being the centre of attraction outside their own environment. Here in Tashkent, where there were 250,000 applications for the 68,000 places in the all-seater stadium, Cardiff City could not have received more clamouring attention than if they had just landed from the Moon.

When they stepped, tired, from the Moscow plane, garlands of flowers were placed around their necks and when they boarded the coach to take them to their hotel it was the finest moment in the life of the coach driver who for the next three days drove wildly but well, with his fingers continually on the horn, waving the narrow streets clear with one hand and proudly drawing attention to his cargo with the other.

Ushered straight into the hotel dining room, where the spectators outnumbered the waiters by at least ten to one, the Cardiff party were delighted to see the tables ready laden with steak and chips. The delight was interrupted by the discovery that the meal was stone cold but a diplomatic incident was avoided when it was smilingly explained that cold steak and chips was in fact one of the local delicacies.

Tashkent, once the stamping ground of Ghengis Khan, was a fascinating blend of old and new worlds, of mud huts unchanged in design for centuries and modern apartment blocks specially constructed to withstand the earth tremors to which the city was frequently subject. The native Uzbeks, in their robes, shaven heads and square, embroidered skull caps, returned the curiosity of the visitors by following them around in hordes and maintaining a day-long watch for a glimpse of the players through the hotel windows.

In such a novel and stimulating environment the Cardiff team relaxed completely. Meanwhile Jimmy Scoular was working 16 hours a day preparing his plans and ensuring that all the match arrangements were to his liking. His experience in European football had taught him that every organizational detail was vital. From refusing to play with a continental-style, black-spotted ball because his players were not used to it, to his vehement insistence that the Welsh flag be flown at the stadium, Scoular did not miss a single opportunity to ensure that his team commenced on equal terms.

As was customary, neither side would release the details of its team until just before the kick-off, but not unexpectedly the roles of both teams had been switched from the first leg. Scoular had made one change. He left out Bryn Jones, a young reserve forward promoted for the first leg because of Clark's ineligibility, and brought in Norman Dean, normally a centre-forward, to play in the back four and allow Harris, who was by now fit, to act as sweeper.

What chance had Cardiff without three of their first team players?

It was difficult to see this side withstanding the power of Torpedo. Goalkeeper Bob Wilson was having only his second senior game of the year and apart from former Everton defender Harris and Welsh international Barrie Jones, Cardiff's team had little experience of such important occasions. Zolotov had dropped three of the Torpedo first leg side and among the newcomers was Mikhail Gershkovic, destined for prominence in the 1970 World Cup, but then an eager 20-year-old.

The uncovered tiers of the vast, oval stadium were crammed to capacity for this rare treat of international club competition, and the stadium had the ultimate in crowd barriers, the first two rows of the entire ground being occupied by soldiers of the Red Army.

It was to be expected that Cardiff would start carefully, unprepared to risk more than winger Ronnie Bird and the young, lanky centre-forward John Toshack out of defence. But their approach was far from timid. Their early task was to contain and harry, to disrupt Torpedo's pattern of attack before it formed.

Torpedo, strangely, did not attempt to overcome Cardiff with their so obviously superior skill. They battered City with long, high passes and shot from distant positions that provided more practice than peril for Wilson. It was highly significant that despite all Torpedo's first-half pressure Cardiff were forced to concede only two corners.

When Torpedo did score after 33 minutes it was unexpected and almost undeserved. The young Gershkovic, under pressure at the edge of the box, stabbed his foot under the ball to send a lob lazily curling over Wilson's head. If Torpedo were awaiting encouragement to win the tie there was no lack of it from the shrill voices of the wildly excited crowd. But still Cardiff would not be subdued. Streltsov, a player of immaculate skill

but less than dedicated application, only needed to extend himself a little more to destroy a slightly demoralized Cardiff defence, but neither he nor Torpedo could achieve the sort of command that conquers.

So Cardiff entered the second half unconvinced of their role as the besieged and, indeed, confident enough to start playing the ball upfield to Toshack and Bird more in hope of a goal than in search of a respite. In terms of control and composure, Cardiff had the better of the second half. Toshack, who had rejected a transfer to Fulham the previous week in favour of seeking European glory for Cardiff, nearly scored with a header that was only a foot wide of the far post. Cardiff's best chance of the game, however, fell to Bird, who unfortunately could not take advantage of as near an open goal a player receives in the quarter-final of a European competition.

But a 1-0 defeat, which meant a 1-1 draw on aggregate, was astoundingly good for Cardiff and humiliatingly bad for Torpedo who had been out-fought and out-thought by a team inferior in skill and experience. It was impossible to deny Cardiff their celebrations and the applause they received from hundreds of people outside their hotel. But eventually the celebrations had to cease for Cardiff were up at 4am the following morning to catch the Moscow flight which was to link up with the BEA Comet to London. Cardiff reached home in the early hours of Thursday 21 March after a 24-hour journey and the following evening had to turn out to face Hull City at Ninian Park and continue the more mundane but nevertheless essential task of avoiding relegation to the Third Division. Understandably, perhaps, they were beaten.

By the time Cardiff came to meet Torpedo in the play-off in Augsburg, Germany, on 3 April, relegation was a real threat on their minds. But it did not stop them defeating Torpedo 1-0. Strangely, it was Torpedo's best footballing performance of the three games but their appalling finishing and Cardiff's expected brave defiance prevented them scoring. Norman Dean, the reserve centre-forward turned defensive hero, scored the winning goal that brought to an end this amazing tie.

Cardiff's adventure in the Cup Winners Cup that season finally ended in Cardiff after drawing 1-1 in Hamburg. In the second leg of the semi-final Uwe Seeler scored a freak goal to give SV Hamburg a 3-2 victory. Perhaps an appearance in the final would have been too much to expect of a Second Division team that had already travelled to Central Asia for a European cup-tie.

Moscow Torpedo: Kavazashvili, Chumakov, Pakhomov, Yanets, Lenev, Shustikov, Stanichev, Streltsov, Scherbakov, Gershkovic, Pais.
Cardiff City: Wilson, Derrett, Ferguson, Clarke, Murray, Harris, Jones, Dean, King, Toshack, Bird.

48

Ten years after Munich

'We're professionals. We can't let emotion take over,' said Bobby Charlton a few days before the 1968 European Cup final. He was not fooling even himself. For this was one match where emotion overshadowed all else. Manchester United had only to beat Benfica to take the European Cup. But if the Portuguese side were to win, they would have to overcome far more than just Manchester United. The whole of Britain, and the sympathies of most of Europe too, were behind Matt Busby and his team, preparing to will them to victory and thus fulfil a dream that the Munich air disaster had shattered ten years before.

The trail which led Manchester United to Wembley in May 1968 had been frustratingly long and tortuous. Nobody wanted that journey to have been in vain; it had cost too much. It was Bobby Charlton who summed up everybody's sentiments: 'We've lived with it for so long. This time we must do it.' And as the day of the final, 29 May, drew near, all the players were gripped by the significance of the occasion.

Even Brian Kidd, 19 on the day of the match and the youngest member of the team, fully understood just how much victory meant to Matt Busby. 'I want us to win for the Boss,' he kept repeating, 'I want us to win for the Boss.'

It was 1956 when Matt Busby first took Manchester United into Europe. He had taken over as manager in 1945, and had dragged the club from the despondency created by a sizeable overdraft and a blitzed ground. He flexed his ambitions with an FA Cup win in 1948, and four years later guided his team to the League Championship. Now he began to look further, to the challenge of major European competition.

'I want us to win for the Boss. I want us to win for the Boss. I...'

When he finally took up that challenge in the 1956-57 European Cup, he did so in the face of fierce opposition from the Football League, who feared a congestion of fixtures. The previous year, the League had compelled Chelsea to withdraw from the competition. But Busby determinedly swept aside the League's fears of a fixture backlog. 'We have at least 18 players who can play in the first team without noticeably weakening it,' he boomed. And despite hints of disciplinary action, Busby and Manchester United went ahead; the League, eventually, backed down.

In their first venture into Europe, the Busby Babes (as the sportswriters tagged them), blazing a trail other British clubs would later follow, reached the semi-final of the competition, and were halted only by the redoubtable Real Madrid. The following year came Munich. Returning home from a successful quarter-final match against Red Star in Belgrade, the plane carrying the team crashed on take-off. Of the twenty-three people killed, eight were Manchester United players. The nucleus of Busby's young team was wiped out—Roger Byrne, Tommy Taylor, Mark Jones, David Pegg, Bill Whelan, Geoff Bent and Eddie Colman, and the greatest of them all, Duncan Edwards who seemed destined to become perhaps the finest wing-half of all time.

It took Matt Busby ten years to repair the damage. By that time, winning the European Cup was a driving force in all his work, so much so that he offered each of his players a £1000 bonus if they won the cup. Though they wanted victory for other reasons, the players were confident that they would earn their bonuses. Defeat? They did not consider it.

Bill Foulkes, the centre-half, who in the second leg of the semi-final had done a forward's job and scored the winning goal against Real Madrid, was convinced that if they were good enough to beat their old Spanish rivals, they could account for Benfica. After all, United had beaten them 5-1 in Lisbon two years earlier, and although Benfica were still a fine side, packed with internationals, Manchester United had the advantage of playing the final in England.

The team that played Benfica reflected the patience, planning and philosophy of Busby. Though he had spent money in hastily rebuilding the club after Munich, only two of the twelve players named for the final had come to Old Trafford for big fees—Alex Stepney and Pat Crerand. With Denis Law, Manchester United's £115,000 striker, watching the final on television from a hospital bed after a knee operation, it was basically a team fashioned from boys recruited when they left school. Those boys' skills Busby had patiently moulded until he considered them ready to face the demanding challenge of first-class football.

Under Busby's supervision, they had met this challenge well. But the younger players were still quite inexperienced, and with some of the team approaching the end of their careers, Denis Law's opportunist finishing was certain to be missed.

Unless, that was, George Best could compensate for Law's absence. Best was at his peak and had emerged as a world-class footballer, scoring 28 goals in 41 League appearances. Could Best reproduce some of the skills he had shown against Benfica in Lisbon two years before, when he scored two fine goals?

As part of his team's preparation for the final, Busby took them to a quiet hotel in Surrey to escape the building tension. Busby was worried that the frenzied public support which could uplift the team might rebound and overwhelm them. Spirits were high, but the pressure on the players was frightening.

It was a warm summer's evening as the two teams left behind them the relative calm of the Wembley dressing rooms and walked out on to the pitch. They were greeted by a shattering explosion of sound from the massed red and white ranks of their supporters. The noise did not let up for a moment, and the match started amidst this feverish din.

The first half was total anti-climax. With both teams playing fearful, uneasy football, there were 30 fouls in the first 45 minutes. Only Aston, the Manchester United winger, seemed able to settle to his game. He caused Adolfo all sorts of problems on the left flank, ghosting past him on one unstoppable run after another. But for all his jinking and darting, at half-time Manchester United had not scored. Indeed, they had missed several easy chances, Sadler being the chief culprit.

Benfica, too, had achieved little. Eusebio had hammered one 20-yard shot against the cross-

bar, but in the main he had been effectively, if sometimes crudely, marked by Nobby Stiles. Eusebio had told reporters before the match that he intended to ask the referee to keep a close watch on Stiles. But the referee found himself having to keep a closer watch on Eusebio's colleagues in defence, Humberto and Cruz, who had been meting out harsh treatment to Best.

By half-time it was clear to the packed crowd and the 250 million watching on television, that the pressure on Manchester United was disruptive. Their usual rhythm had been upset by an anxiety to win, urged on by the electric atmosphere in the stadium.

Nobody appreciated the danger of that situation more than Busby. He spoke to his team during the interval: 'Don't let the crowd get hold of you. Just keep playing your football. Play football.'

As the second half began, United seemed straight away to heed Matt Busby's advice. Sadler and Dunne had neatly worked the ball down the left wing before Sadler crossed it. Charlton, streaking into a gap, with a perfectly timed header glanced the ball into the net. One-nil to United, and the noise hit a crescendo. Bobby Charlton said afterwards that he thought the ball had skidded off his bald patch—but it gave United the lead they so desperately wanted.

Now they began to play with growing confidence. Aston left Adolfo stranded more and more as he produced a succession of brilliant runs which tantalized the Benfica defence, even if the chances he created were squandered. Once, Sadler slipped right through and had goalkeeper Henrique beaten, only to see the ball fly off his foot and over the bar.

Gradually it seemed that Charlton's goal, the brightest moment in what was still, for all the excitement, a match of poor quality, would be enough to take the cup to Old Trafford. It might not have been a great game, but it looked as though it had won them the cup. Then, with nine minutes to go...Graca equalized for Benfica. That was an appalling moment, leaving the United players stunned, the crowd horrified. For the first time it dawned on them all that Manchester United could still lose.

'Just a few minutes more and I'm sure Benfica would have won'

This fear grew as Benfica, their spirits renewed, surged forward. In the dying moments of the match, Eusebio, having shaken off Stiles, unleashed a tremendous point-blank shot. Stepney had come too far out of his goal. Yet, staggering as he frantically tried to get back into position, he saved. It was pure reflex action, but it enabled United to hang on until the end of normal time.

Stiles said afterwards that if the game had gone on without a break for a few minutes more Benfica would have won. 'For me it was like the World Cup final all over again,' he said.

Matt Busby strode quickly on to the pitch, his face not revealing the inner turmoil and frustration he really felt. For five fleeting minutes, he talked to his exhausted team. Faced with the demoralizing effects of that late Benfica goal, what could Busby say to avert the crisis? He simply told his men, 'You're throwing the game away with careless passing, instead of continuing with your football. You must start to hold the ball and play again.'

Some of the team were too spent to be roused even by Busby's words. Foulkes said later, 'I didn't want to listen. I didn't want to think. I just wanted to get it over with, one way or the other.' But from somewhere they summoned the extra energy to battle out the agonizing last 30 minutes.

Aston again led the offensive with a dazzling display which cut Benfica's right flank to

pieces. And then, quicker than anyone dared hope, United went ahead again.

It was no more than an everyday clearance when Stepney punted the ball upfield—but suddenly, the crowd started to roar. Kidd, stretching desperately, heads on to Best. Cruz, the Benfica watchdog, fails to hold his opponent, and Best tears away, evading one more desperate tackle. As Henrique races from his goal, Best glides around him and coolly chips the ball into the net.

That goal settled it. Manchester United, now in command again, soon consolidated their lead. Henrique could only push a header from Kidd onto the bar, and Kidd, flinging himself at the ball, made no mistake the second time. Charlton added a fourth goal with a typically graceful flourish, flicking Kidd's centre high into the Benfica goal. The uncertainty was over. United had won.

The crowd was deliriously happy. On the touchline, Busby and his colleagues danced, laughed and cried in a daze as they waited for the cup to be presented. Charlton, Foulkes and the rest of the Manchester United team tried to push Busby forward to receive it. 'No lads,' he said, 'this is your day.' But as he walked quietly off the pitch and into the tunnel, alone but for 100,000 pairs of eyes, it was not their day. It was his.

Manchester United: Stepney, Brennan, Foulkes, Stiles, Dunne, Crerand, Charlton, Sadler, Best, Kidd, Aston.
Benfica: Henrique, Adolfo, Humberto, Jacinto, Cruz, Graca, Coluna, Augusto, Torres, Eusebio, Simoes.

Left *The moment of truth for Benfica; George Best rounds goalkeeper Henrique to put Manchester United back into the lead during the first period of extra time. Two years earlier he had dazzled the Portuguese in their own 'Stadium of Light', scoring twice in a superb five goal display by United. On that occasion Matt Busby's first comment was 'I told them to play it defensive.' Benfica were forewarned but not forearmed. This time Best built the bridge between 100 minutes of rather dreary deadlock and a burst of inspired attacking talent. He is that rare footballing animal – the joker in the pack whose mood can win or lose even the most vital game. One goal proved the inspiration for two more, one from Brian Kidd on his 19th birthday and **below left** a second from Bobby Charlton. The United captain had run on to an astute square pass from Kidd and clipped the ball in a tantalizing parabola over Henrique's head for a remarkable goal.*
Below *The manager embraces his captain at the end of an 11-year trek across Europe.*

The disaster that led to triumph

49

The players jostle for the ball. With the pitch in a terrible state, they could not keep possession for long.

McLintock, then an attacking wing-half, to seal the gaps left by his surges upfield.

In retrospect, it seems logical, too, that Arsenal should from that defeat go on to do what they eventually did—search their own staff for replacements. The players thus discovered have blossomed—Charlie George, Ray Kennedy, Eddie Kelly, as well as that 'new' centre-half Frank McLintock.

But at the time it did not seem quite so obvious that Swindon might have done Arsenal a favour.

Certainly Arsenal's mood was hardly one of gratitude. Besides their horror at losing the match, they were rather bitter at the manner in which the events of the game were popularly misconstrued, even distorted. It is difficult not to sympathize with them.

For instance, it is not true that the game was ever viewed, could ever be viewed, as City Slickers v Country Bumpkins. Swindon's progress to the final had been hardly less impressive than Arsenal's. After disposing of Torquay and Bradford City in the early rounds, they had beaten Coventry and Burnley from the First Division, and Derby—eventually Division Two champions—and Blackburn from the Second.

In their own division Swindon were joint leaders at the time, on the way to the promotion their League Cup success was to boost. They had outstanding players in all departments. The defence was given a touch of class by the quick eye and keen tackling of Welsh international full-back Rod Thomas. The midfield had all the resourceful expertise of John Smith, the man who might have made a bigger name in his native London had his arrival on the scene not coincided with that of men such as Blanchflower, Mackay and Moore.

This was the match that changed the course of history for Arsenal

Up front Swindon had Don Rogers, the player whose talents had attracted half a dozen First Division clubs, all starting the bidding for him at £100,000. Swindon would not even quote a price for a winger whose acceleration, control and finishing confidence had already brought him five goals in the League Cup competition. The one reservation sometimes levelled against Rogers, that he might not have the temperament or the ambition to succeed away from the small town atmosphere of his club, was to be silenced permanently at Wembley.

Even before the match no one seriously felt Arsenal had any better individual players than these Swindon footballers. But the First Division club were obviously favourites. They were romantically depicted as being in specially determined mood to succeed because a year earlier in the final of the same competition they had been defeated by Leeds United, the team they had admitted to adopting as their model.

But this, instead, created its own extra difficulty for them. The adjectives they had been attracting as they inched their way grittily towards the final, beating Sunderland, Liverpool, Spurs, Blackpool and Scunthorpe, were all words that grudged them real praise—dogged, purposeful, disciplined, hard.

They wanted friends almost as much as they wanted trophies and everything that happened before the match conspired against them. Half the team were still suffering from the after-effects of a 'flu epidemic'. And the sight of the pitch at Wembley did nothing to lift the depressing, debilitating effect on their spirits. It was in a barely believable state, almost meriting postponement, ankle-deep in a mixture of sludge and sand left behind when thousands of gallons of rainwater had been pumped away. It was a setting designed for the simple brutality of basic Third Division football, a day for massed defences, thumped clearances, quick chases and breakaway goals.

Yet the fact that Arsenal sincerely tried

One match did more than any other to change the course of history for Arsenal. One match was the major influence in mapping the route that took this club out of the side-roads, diversions, and cul-de-sacs of the frustrating sixties on to the motorway of the seventies.

When Swindon, then in the Third Division, beat Arsenal 3-1 in extra time of the League Cup final at Wembley on 15 March 1969, that humiliating setback shoved the Highbury club into a situation where they had to re-examine and eventually revitalize their whole approach.

It may be a flagrant over-simplification to claim that the team and the tactics which were to win the Fairs Cup in 1970 and achieve the double of League Championship and FA Cup in 1971, were born out of the defeat of that day. It is much less of an exaggeration to state that in

the aftermath of that defeat, conception took place. For Bertie Mee, the Arsenal manager, and Don Howe, then the Arsenal coach, had both previously had doubts about whether the way they were going was right. After that shock Wembley defeat, their doubts hardened into conviction.

From this distance it is easy to see that among the many men Arsenal needed against Swindon at that time was a centre-half less violently committed than Ian Ure was always inclined to be; a midfield player sharper, more accurate, than David Court; a striker without the random vigour that made Bobby Gould both unpredictable and unreliable; and someone of individual flair to equal Swindon's Don Rogers.

From this distance it is also more obvious than it was then that a way had to be found of curbing the adventurous attitude of Frank

It was therefore ironic that his was the error that let Arsenal in for the equalizer. With just four minutes left he mistimed a dash from his line designed to foil a thrust from Bobby Gould, and Gould went on to tap the ball into an empty net.

It is equally ironic, however, that but for this equalizer a truer picture of the game would probably have remained in the memory, a picture of a cruelly unlucky Arsenal, beaten more by their own efforts than those of the opposition.

Don Rogers recalled that as he looked around before extra time he saw half a dozen rival players with their stockings rolled down and remembered thinking joyously: 'That'll do me.' His mood of soaring confidence was reflected in the brilliance of the contrasting goals he scored. The first, just before the end of the first half of extra time, can be validly compared with the one Puskas once scored against England at Wembley, controlling the ball with deft unconcern while surrounded and working it with one foot until he created the gap through which he could crack it into the net.

The second, just before the end, the inevitability of which had already been signalled by the despair in every Arsenal attitude, carried Rogers' own special characteristic. He burst from the halfway line, shoulders hunched, strides stretching and did not check until the swerve inside the penalty area which took him round Bob Wilson to make it 3-1.

Comments after the match from the two camps did little more than reveal once again how meaningless opinions harvested in heat can be. For Swindon manager Danny Williams it was 'A triumph of fitness and attacking football'—which overlooks that Arsenal had done far more of the attacking. To Don Howe it was 'A match that should have been over and won by us at half time. We won't take too much notice of it.' But that image of unconcern is something he subsequently drastically disproved.

After that shock defeat, the manager's doubts hardened into conviction

Even though Arsenal played well enough to have won, deeper reflections convinced the club that they could not expect to win more important trophies without considerable evolution.

Once again the result raised a familiar and slightly pointless speculation on the side issue of whether this Third Division success at Wembley to add to the one Queen's Park Rangers had achieved two seasons earlier, hinted at an imminent similar breakthrough in the FA Cup. Third Division managers are virtually unanimous in advocating the theory that it did. They understandably dislike attempts to have Swindon's and Rangers' successes cheapened by suggestions that First Division clubs do not try as hard as they should in the League Cup.

Because they do try as hard—in the later rounds. But in the early autumn when the League Cup begins, most First Division clubs cannot help being more conscious that the Championship race is still open, the FA Cup competition is still ahead. It tends to diminish the importance of the League Cup in their eyes—and changing that attitude could take many more years.

But a team that has reached the final is undoubtedly concerned with winning, and more so when the opposition is from a lower division. For no team likes to lose in the circumstances that Arsenal lost to Swindon. No club suffers happily the humiliation of losing to a team from two divisions below. But if such a defeat leads in the same way as Arsenal's to overwhelming successes, there may be some consolation in it.

Arsenal: Wilson, Storey, McNab, McLintock, Ure, Simpson, Radford, Sammels, Court, Gould, Armstrong. Sub: Graham.
Swindon: Downsborough, Thomas, Trollope, Butler, Burrows, Harland, Heath, Smart, Smith, Noble, Rogers. Sub: Penman.

Top Downsborough, Swindon's goalkeeper, magnificently kept Arsenal forwards at bay until the 86th minute.
Centre But Downsborough's first mistake allowed Bobby Gould to score a late equalizing goal for Arsenal.
Above Don Rogers' first extra-time goal so demoralized Arsenal that Swindon then took control of the game.

and deserved to succeed in playing attractive, attacking football throughout the first 90 minutes—and exhausted themselves doing it—received scant recognition.

Floating first to the surface of the memories of all those who saw the game and obscuring virtually everything else is the extra-time spectacular when Arsenal wilted and Swindon soared; when two marvellous goals from Rogers gave the game its ecstatic climax. That Arsenal controlled much, indeed most, of what had happened earlier is generally forgotten.

Even the Swindon goal in the 36th minute was largely the result of a tragi-comic error by Arsenal. Ure hit a back pass without the elementary precaution of first checking the

position of goalkeeper Bob Wilson to present Roger Smart with his scoring chance.

Before and after that lapse, with only brief breakaway interruptions by Swindon, Arsenal, right up until the 90-minute whistle, surged ceaselessly forward—and succeeded only in providing a back-cloth against which a Swindon player stole the centre of the stage.

Swindon's goalkeeper Peter Downsborough seemed to grow until he filled his goal-area with elastic invincibility. He made at least six saves that on any other day might have been too much to expect from any man. Nine times in ten minutes during the second half he plunged through panic in front of him, his defence scattered like confetti, to clear consecutive corners.

105

Magpies steal the silver

50

Above left *Bobby Moncur, who proved to be a match-winner in the Fairs Cup final, rises above everyone in the Ujpest penalty area at St James' Park. He scored United's first two goals in that match (Scott scored the third) to give Newcastle a healthy lead to take to Hungary.*

Above centre *The Ujpest goalkeeper stretches in vain: Newcastle have scored again. Bobby Moncur's goals were the first he had ever scored for club— after nine years.*

Above right *Ujpest almost rescued the final at home. They scored two goals in an exciting first-half but just after half-time Moncur scored again to inspire United to a 3-2 victory.*

When Newcastle returned to the First Division in 1965 they were eager for European football and the chance to recapture the glory previously associated with the club. Their chance came three seasons later when they squeezed into the Fairs Cup because of that competition's peculiar rule that no city was allowed to have more than one representative. It was a chance they took gratefully and with memorable style.

It was a tearaway, shattering, triumphant series for Newcastle. Being in the competition at all was exciting. The previous season there had been head-shaking about relegation, but a latish run took Newcastle to tenth place. With only one team from a city being allowed in, and if four English clubs were accepted, Newcastle would have European football. And so it happened, to Tyneside's delight. The six games at St James' Park between 11 September 1968 and 29 May 1969 had an attendance of over a third of a million, an average of 56,270.

46,300 welcomed Feyenoord of Rotterdam in the first round and roared with appreciation as Newcastle struck quickly and won 4-0. Jim Scott scored the important opening goal; Bryan Robson, emerging as a new star, dived forward for the second, and Tommy Gibb and Wyn Davies got the others. Geoff Allen, on the Newcastle left, had a sensationally good game, but injury forced him out of the team a few weeks later.

After that decisive, dramatic win, the Newcastle chairman, Lord Westwood, commented, 'We're daft enough to win this Cup.' Nearly 2,000 fans went to Rotterdam for the return but Newcastle, with the same side, were beaten 2-0.

Away to Sporting Club of Lisbon in the second round, torrential rain swept the Jose Alvalade Stadium and this probably helped Newcastle who played well before only 5,000 people. Scott scored again, and Bobby Moncur in defence showed the dominating authority which was to earn him the captaincy of Scotland. Sporting equalized near the end. There was only one goal in the second leg, but it inflamed the crowd of 53,650. Robson, in the air, volleyed the ball home.

The first leg of the third round was away to Real Zaragoza, twice finalists in the Fairs Cup, on New Year's Day. They were beaten 3-2 in Spain, but Robson scored again, and the brave Davies headed in Newcastle's crucial second before Miguel Planas got a fine winning goal. The return at St James' was watched by another large crowd of 56,200. Robson again scored a spectacular goal, from 30 yards. Tommy Gibb got a second, but Zaragoza came back well, scored and pressed. Newcastle's narrow 2-1 victory (4-4 on aggregate) meant that Newcastle went through on their away goals.

A third of a million fans cheered Newcastle to European cup glory

By this stage both manager Joe Harvey and Moncur preferred playing the first leg away. They were at home first, however, in the quarter-final to Vitoria Setubal. On an intensely cold night 57,602 enthusiastic fans turned up as snow was falling. Several players wore gloves and some of the Setubal players had not even seen snow—at least one of them had his hands wrapped in socks. The Portuguese had a miserable time and lost 5-1 to goals by Alan Foggon, Robson (2), Davies and Gibb. But Setubal's real form was displayed when they won the second leg 3-1—a return to the Jose Alvalade Stadium for Newcastle. Davies scored Newcastle's goal. Eight Newcastle players needed treatment but United

were through to the semi-finals against Glasgow Rangers.

Newcastle were now a formidable side, especially at home, and had matured during their cup progress. They were lucky to be drawn away for the first leg and their goalless draw at Ibrox was no surprise. But the second leg was perhaps the most frightening match ever played at St James'. Thousands of Scots made the short trip and there was some heavy drinking which helped to create an ominous atmosphere.

Rangers played well for a time and they looked the best Fairs Cup side seen at St James'. Then Newcastle settled down and came into the game. Suddenly a foul and a retaliation at the Gallowgate end, where the Rangers supporters were massed, made some of them erupt onto the field, and there was a short interruption.

But in the 54th minute Scott, running on to a ball from Gibb, scored with a terrific shot. Even then Rangers needed only an equalizing goal to go through to the final and play became tense and rough. Eleven minutes from the end, however, Jackie Sinclair scored Newcastle's second.

The mob violence started very shortly after that at the Gallowgate end. Bottles were thrown and the Rangers fans invaded the field. There were numerous scuffles with the police, and the players made for the dressing-rooms immediately. The pitch was eventually cleared only for the Scots to burst on to it again. That was when Newcastle fans approached them in line from the Leazes end and for some moments it looked as if a complete battle was going to be waged on the Park. Yet thankfully the two forces hesitated and the police intervened. After being off 18 minutes the players returned and finished the game.

So at last, after all these unprecedented adventures and problems, Newcastle were through

POPPERFOTO

UNITED PRESS INTERNATIONAL

to the final. A week later Ujpest Dozsa came to St James'. After the dour, cheerless semi-final there was a pleasant, relaxed atmosphere, even if United had to play the first leg at home.

The famous Hungarian side had had an easier journey through to the final with the exception of Leeds United whom they had twice beaten in the quarter-finals. Leeds judged them the best European team they had met. Furthermore, Ujpest had not lost a game, and drawn only one. Prior to the first leg ten of their players were in the Hungarian national squad; seven of them played against Czechoslovakia.

60,000 partisans saw Newcastle begin by probing and attacking. The well-built Hungarians defended competently, although their goalkeeper, Szentmihalyi, was lucky to be in line of a header from Robson. As half-time approached, Ujpest showed their own skill and began to take some control in midfield. Only a desperate save by Iam McFaul from Antal Dunai preserved Newcastle's equality.

After the interval Newcastle resumed their initiative but the hour passed without a goal. There were, however, signs that Ujpest were weakening; the Newcastle defence had tightened, and their high ball to Davies in the centre of Ujpest's defence were causing more and more trouble. Newcastle were able to move more men forward.

After 63 minutes Davies breasted down a free-kick from Gibb and shot hard. The ball rebounded off Szentimihalyi and Moncur, the centre-back of all people, lashed it into the net. Ujpest were now under even greater pressure and nine minutes later Moncur, amazingly, scored again. Seven minutes from the end Scott scored a triumphant third. Joe Harvey had hoped for a two goal lead—he had three. Ujpest had not had that number scored against them for two seasons. 'I think,' Harvey said, 'we have one hand on the Cup.'

The last game of the competition was in Budapest on 11 June 1969. By happy coincidence it was Joe Harvey's birthday. Newcastle were able to field the same side; as at St James' Foggon came on about three-quarter time. Ujpest were determined to show Newcastle their class and they produced a first-half display which alarmed every Briton there. There was even the odd occasion when only Davies was outside Newcastle's penalty box. The busy, dancing McFaul punched clear after Dunai was brought down; he touched round the post a swerving drive from Bankuti, and leaping to the corner he tipped a drive from Dunai

onto the bar.

The Hungarian pressure did not ease. Janos Gorocs, who had 58 caps, sped down the right-wing and flashed the ball across but somehow the players packed in the goalmouth all failed to get a touch to it. Luck was again with Newcastle when Dunai was brought down inside the box and a free-kick was given outside. But on the half-hour Ujpest at last achieved the reward they deserved. In the goalmouth, Dunai, seeing Ferenc Bene racing in, released a quick pass and Bene scored.

That goal worried an anxious Newcastle and another goal looked certain. It came near half-time. Gorocs, taking a long cross from the right, darted past Craig and then drove the ball between McFaul and the post. The crowd was frantic by now. The great Hungarian side has seemingly broken Newcastle. Everyone thought the equalizing goal had been scored immediately, but McFaul saved Newcastle by finger-tipping away a downward header from Dunai on half-time.

Were Newcastle's cup hopes saved by the half-time whistle?

The Ujpest players ran into their room excited, scenting victory, the crowd was exultant, Newcastle were shocked. The Fairs Cup, the seal of their efforts to force themselves up with the best, was slipping away from them. Fortunately, Joe Harvey remembered he still had one hand on it. McFaul's save on half-time, followed by the half-time break itself, gave Newcastle a chance to recover. Shrewd words in the dressing room rekindled the players' spirit. Newcastle had to lift themselves; they had to stop the Hungarians from dictating; they had, somehow, to wrench the

initiative. They did just that.

Straight from the kick-off, with Ujpest still geared for attacking, Newcastle won a corner. Sinclair took it. Davies and Szentimihalyi went for it together and the ball came back to Sinclair. He lifted it back and Moncur volleyed it home. It was the match-winner. His goal was a cruel blow to Ujpest; it changed their fortunes almost unbelievably. That quick goal after Ujpest's marvellous first-half performance, before most of their players had kicked the ball again, meant they were 4-2 behind on aggregate. They had to score three more goals not to be beaten. The game had swung into reverse.

The shocked Hungarians were never allowed to marshall their strength afterwards. Seven minutes later a shot from Scott came off Ede Dunai to Ben Arentoft and the little Dane drove the ball into the net. Newcastle were now dominating the midfield. Foggon, who came on for Scott, nearly scored immediately; with fourteen minutes left he raced past two men to shoot against the bar and score from the rebound.

It was Newcastle's only away win in the competition. With a refreshing willingness to attack they had beaten one of Europe's finest sides 6-2 on aggregate. Just as important, they had survived in Europe and proved that they were a major club once more. In their bus, returning through Budapest's streets, the players sang the Blaydon Races and Happy Birthday Joe Harvey. The North-East did not need to recall the fifties to savour the good days—they had returned.

Newcastle United: McFaul, Craig, Clark, Gibb, Burton, Moncur, Scott, Robson, Davies, Arentoft, Sinclair. Sub: Foggon.
Ujpest Dozsa: Szentimihalyi, Kapozsta, Solymosi, Bankuti, Nosko, Dunai (E), Fazekas, Gorocs, Bene, Dunai (A), Zambo.

The night Manchester belonged to City

51

In the 1969-70 season, for the first time, all 92 League clubs participated in the League Cup. Which was fortunate, for Manchester United, the only club not to participate the previous season, were competing again and their progress eventually produced an outstanding semi-final between United and Manchester City. It was also an important derby fixture for two clubs who were challenging fiercely for the status of being a city's top team and collecting a succession of major honours—including the European Cup, the League Championship and the FA Cup—in the process.

Manchester City had much the better of the draw for each round. They disposed of Southport easily enough at Haig Avenue, and then in succession they won at home against Liverpool, Everton, and Queen's Park Rangers. Manchester United began with a 1-0 victory at Old Trafford against Middlesbrough, familiar and difficult opponents in those years, and then won at home 2-0 against a plucky Wrexham side. In the fourth and fifth rounds respectively, they played goalless games at Burnley and Derby before winning the replays by the only goal. Then both Manchester teams were drawn against each other in the two-leg semi-finals, with the first leg at Maine Road on 3 December 1969.

A short time earlier, City had beaten United 4-0 in a league match at Maine Road, and with the same team available, City had no doubt that they could repeat that success if not the margin. Yet United were not prepared to allow City, of all teams, that satisfaction twice.

All sorts of conditions of men congregate for such confrontations. On this occasion, nearly 56,500 people squeezed into Maine Road among them a well known local clergyman who, when it was all over, sat in his seat and observed to nobody in particular, 'It was a helluva game.' It was a fair assessment.

'A game of two halves' is a popular football cliche but for once it was an accurate description of a match. Not often in their distinguished career

have United been so outplayed and so outclassed as they were in the first half. They should have been overwhelmed by City's superiority but they fought doggedly in an attempt to survive and, in the end, they had more reason to feel frustrated than disappointed. And City eventually were fortunate to win when by all logic they should have been home and dry before half-time. Yet the only tangible evidence of their first-half performance was a thirteenth minute goal by Bell after Lee had determinedly taken on United single handed.

For 45 minutes City's speed and precision confounded all except Stepney, and United were reduced to making tackles which seldom approached legality. Yet only Best was booked, and that was for showing dissent. Other more heinous misdemeanours went unpunished or unnoticed. Such forthright tactics certainly upset City, though, and prevented their accumulation of an unassailable lead. And when, after the interval, City were so anonymous in contrast to their first half skill and vitality, United got down to the business of playing football.

Two late City goals deprived United of a Wembley final

The teams had changed ends but the flow of the football was still surprisingly in the same direction. To the delight of the apprehensive United fans their team took control of the game. Best's fine appreciation of Charlton's immaculate distribution split City's defence which seemed likely to disintegrate under United's incessant pressure. When City did attempt to retaliate they were repelled by the United defenders, in particular by Dunne and Stiles, who shared the determination to secure an equalising goal, if not a winner, to take back to Old Trafford.

Stiles, without his teeth, presented a terrifying spectacle and gave an inspired performance. Occasionally his tackles were over-zealous and

increased the discontent of City's anxious supporters. But his tenacity was equalled by passing that could not have been bettered by the absent Law. Here was Stiles, hero and villain, *in excelsis*.

Inevitably, as City, the assured masters of the first half, were pressed back, United had to equalize as a climax to their sustained and exhilarating pressure. In the 66th minute Book, under heavy pressure, misdirected a header which Kidd gratefully received. He passed the ball astutely to Bobby Charlton who reliably drove it into the net.

Yet, with United apparently in control and with a chance of an unexpected victory, the game changed dramatically again in City's favour. With just two minutes left, and to the dismay of the exultant United fans, Ure brought down Lee in the penalty area. Despite the great tension Lee, with characteristic certainty, scored with the spot kick. So that United, having recovered so remarkably that victory seemed probable, suddenly discovered themselves defeated.

Few of the spectators seemed in a hurry to go home. Some seemed to think there would be extra time; others appeared to hope that the second leg match would begin as soon as the players had recovered their breath. Slowly, however, Manchester settled into an uneasy tension as it waited for the second leg at Old Trafford fourteen days later. Ominously, during this delay, United defeated Liverpool 4-1 at Anfield, the first visiting side to score four on that ground since Everton were there five years earlier.

But on the day of the second leg, 17 December, when a crowd of 63,418 descended on Old Trafford, United had made several changes from the side at Liverpool the previous Saturday. They opted for the experience of Law, Crerand and Stiles and left out Burns and Aston. For City only Bell was missing, replaced by Connor.

Unfortunately, the second leg match was sheer anti-climax, riddled with crudities and comedy. Towards the end when Law was limping and Stiles was receiving treatment on the field—in some ways he was fortunate to still be there at all —Kidd, United's substitute, began limbering up ready to take over from one of them. As Law went off Kidd walked on to take his place but was pushed off again by Stiles and Law. After a touchline conference Stiles and Law, both of whom had decided to see the thing through, carried on to the end and poor Kidd returned to his track suit muttering darkly about 'seeing the boss in the morning'.

This incident typified the confusion which betrayed United that night. Only Best was convincing in attack; only Edwards was consistent in defence. Ure was so aggravated that he had his name taken for a crude body check on Lee.

PRESS ASSOCIATION

City in their turn were as enigmatic as ever. In the absence of Bell, they did not appear to know whether to play for the draw that was sufficient or to capitalize on United's weakness. They missed countless chances at one end and presented United with similar opportunities at the other; if United had been in more recognizable form, they could have won. But they were not. City nevertheless took an inordinately long time to realize that this was not the United side which had given them such a difficult game at Maine Road.

Eventually City took the lead almost reluctantly in the 17th minute. After smart combination between Lee and Summerbee, Ure cleared off the line from Young. The ball ran loose to Bowyer who beat Stepney at the second attempt. Six minutes later, United equalized. Crerand recovered well after Charlton's pass had appeared to elude him, and gave the ball to Edwards who escaped from two would-be tacklers and drove the ball past Corrigan from just inside the penalty area.

With the second half fifteen minutes old, the crowd were treated to a glimpse of the vintage Best who wriggled in and out of the City defence before unleashing a shot of great power. Corrigan did well enough to stop the ball at all, but he let it drop at his feet and Law swiftly scored. United were 2-1 on the night and 3-3 on aggregate. Eight minutes from the end, however, Lee took an indirect free-kick which Stepney, for some inexplicable reason, attempted to save, but he could only push the ball out to Summerbee, moving in smartly, who scored at his leisure. Had Stepney just let the ball enter the net the eventual result might have been very different.

So City were through 4-3, and in the final they beat West Bromwich Albion and added the League Cup to the FA Challenge Cup they had won the previous season. The second leg was a disappointment after the splendid match at Maine Road, but the lesson was clear. The great United of the 1960s was no longer cock of the roost. City's chickens were well hatched.

Above Francis Lee's penalty, three minutes before the end of the game at Maine Road, robbed Manchester United of a well-deserved draw. Ian Ure, who conceded the penalty, disputed the goal: 'It was a diabolical decision. A terrible thing for the match to hinge on.' But City had a 2-1 lead. In the return at Old Trafford United fell 3-1 behind but equalised with goals by **below left** Edwards and **below centre** Law. Yet another late City goal—by Summerbee after Stepney had parried Lee's free-kick—ensured them of another Wembley final, in which they defeated West Bromwich Albion 2-1.

Manchester City: Corrigan, Book, Pardoe, Doyle, Booth, Oakes, Summerbee, Bell (Connor 2nd leg), Lee, Young, Bowyer.
Manchester United: Stepney, Edwards, Dunne, Burns (Stiles 2nd leg), Ure, Sadler, Best (Morgan 2nd leg), Kidd (Law 2nd leg), Charlton, Stiles (Crerand 2nd leg), Aston (Best 2nd leg).

52

When Celtic beat England's best

The elegant little Yorkshire town of Harrogate is better known for its spa waters and the high tax ratings of its inhabitants than for any special affinity to Association Football. Yet for a couple of days towards the end of March 1970, Harrogate was very much concerned with football, as host to one of the two best teams in Britain.

It was at Harrogate that Glasgow Celtic, champions of Scotland, were preparing to join battle with Leeds United, champions of England, in the semi-final of the European Cup. But there was much more at stake than simply a place in the European Cup final. As soon as the draw had been made the two-leg match was hailed as a contest for the British Championship. Indeed, it was this dual significance which made both legs of this match such memorable games for the millions who saw them.

There never has existed as such a competition to decide the Championship of Britain. There have been numerous inventions claimed to fit this bill, but most have presented fragile credentials and all have been unrecognized by the respective Football Associations.

This time it was different. This was a British Championship in everything but name. Here was a fully competitive game under official European jurisdiction. Celtic, 1967 winners of the European Cup, who had destroyed the myth of Italian invincibility, versus Leeds United, a team to which those well-worn adjectives —powerful, efficient, professional—could be applied without argument. Never before had the champions of England and Scotland been drawn together in such a contest.

In his Harrogate hotel, the night before the first leg of the tie, Jock Stein, Celtic's manager, was talking to the Press. 'Usually,' he said, 'we're favourites. We won't be favourites tomorrow, and that, gentlemen, doesn't worry us at all. It means that some of the burden is

lifted from our shoulders. Even people usually well disposed towards us think Leeds will beat us. Well, we'll soon see, won't we?'

Don Revie, manager of Leeds, made it clear that while he respected Celtic, he was confident that Leeds would deal with the Scottish champions.

The Press, on both sides of the border, were equally loyal. Wrote one English newspaper, 'Celtic have now won their extremely domestic title five times in a row, which merely establishes them as the biggest fish in surely the smallest pond ever dug . . . The Celtic fans obstinately refuse to recognize that England regards their rantings with only tolerant smiles. Now Celtic play Leeds in the European Cup and they had best look out—Revie's lads are not due to lose again until next Pancake Saturday.'

Scottish sports writers, not exactly noted for their lack of chauvinism, were of course well equipped to cater for comments like those. They showed a distinct indifference to what was popularly supposed in England to be the sad plight of the Leeds players before that first-leg game. In fact, the controversy in the build-up to the match was almost as entertaining as what was to happen eventually on the field.

It was a controversy fuelled by facts as well as prejudice. The facts were that the week before the match at Elland Road, Leeds had won a twice-drawn FA Cup semi-final against Manchester United. Then, on the Monday before meeting Celtic, Leeds United played Derby County with a side composed entirely of reserves. Asked by the Football League to explain this, Revie said that he had acted on medical advice. His first-team players, he said, were jaded, mentally and physically: they had played seven Cup-ties in 32 days, a daunting proposition for any side.

So the English Press said 'Poor old Leeds', though still forecasting a victory for them against Celtic. But the Scottish Press was cynical. They

asked pointedly whether all these jaded Leeds players would somehow recover in time to take part in the European Cup-tie. And they argued that Celtic had a right to be tired too. After all, they had played almost as many games as Leeds, and in Scotland, every game played by either Celtic or Rangers is like a cup-tie, because every other team in the Scottish League aspires to beat the Old Firm.

And so the arguments raged. It was obvious that the only way to resolve them was to look at the outcome of the match and the quality of the play at Elland Road on the night of 1 April 1970. And so the first leg began.

With the exception of Norman Hunter, who had been injured for some time, the Leeds side was the one established as the club's best; from the acrobatic Gary Sprake to captain Billy Bremner, to those superb strikers Mick Jones and Allan Clarke. And in an exceptionally exciting and dramatic game, Leeds made a formidable contribution. What they did not do was score a goal.

Of the 45,000 people crowded into Elland Road, many of them were from Glasgow. Before a minute had passed, the Scots, who had already been far from silent, erupted in ecstasy. Celtic had scored. Leeds had fallen victim to one of Jock Stein's most dangerous ploys—the fast, hammer-blow against a defence off its guard.

For Celtic attacked immediately, and from 20 yards, young George Connelly shot powerfully. A defender deflected the ball to the dismay of Sprake, and Celtic were in the lead.

Subsequent events owed nothing to any Celtic good fortune. Jackie Charlton, the Leeds centre-half and a man not given to extravagant praise of any member of another side, was to say later that the difference between Celtic and Leeds was represented in the person of one man— Jimmy Johnstone.

There was evidence for the claim. Johnstone proved quite unplayable. Terry Cooper, with a massive reputation as one of the world's finest full-backs, was unable to master him. Johnstone's twisting and turning on the ball, apparently in defiance of the natural laws of motion, demoralized first Cooper and then the rest of the Leeds defence for a good half-hour.

But Johnstone was magnificently supported by his midfield men, Bobby Murdoch and Bertie Auld. And in the second half, when Leeds launched attack after attack with all the very considerable pace and technique at their command, it was Billy McNeill who dominated a remarkable Celtic defence.

Had Leeds been able to devote their entire energies to attack, they would surely have

Left *Determined defence by Leeds thwarts a Celtic attack.* **Right** *After going for the ball, Celtic forward Hughes and Leeds goalkeeper Gary Sprake collided heavily.*

found a way through sooner or later. However, they were unable to do anything of the kind. Instead they had to keep a wary eye on the Celtic front-runners—notably Lennox, whose speed was the ideal complement to the long, cunning passes from defence of Murdoch and Auld.

And no matter how Bremner worked, no matter how Gray schemed, the Celtic tactics triumphed. It was a great match. And there was more to come.

The second leg was scheduled for Hampden Park on 15 April. The intervening two weeks produced yet more controversy. Celtic lost the Scottish Cup final to Aberdeen, together possibly with some of their morale. In the FA Cup Final at Wembley, Leeds drew, two goals each, with Chelsea. This match featured Leeds at their best, and this prompted high enthusiasm in England about their prospects of gaining revenge on Celtic in the second game—already guaranteed a crowd of 134,000. Billy McNeill had thrown off the effects of an injury, but Willie Wallace, less fortunate, was replaced by John Hughes. For Leeds, Paul Madeley replaced Paul Reaney at right-back who had broken a leg playing against West Ham two weeks before, and the destructive but gifted Norman Hunter was fit to go in at left-half.

Again both teams surpassed themselves. Bremner scored a memorable goal in the 13th minute, with a ferocious shot from outside the penalty area. Would the English champions at last take over? In the midfield, Bremner and Giles were working prodigiously. It was clear that Celtic

It was Murdoch and Auld against Bremner and Giles —and the Celtic men won

would lose if these two achieved control. But towards the end of the half, the battle for that vital area was being won not by Bremner and Giles, but by Murdoch and Auld. And with Johnstone continually threatening to leave their defence in ruins, Leeds were struggling.

Then, two minutes into the second half, Celtic's growing superiority was confirmed. Johnstone tapped a short corner-kick to Auld, who curved a cross over to the waiting Hughes. His header whipped past Sprake, and Celtic were level in the match, and 2-1 ahead on aggregate. Three minutes later, Sprake was hurt in a collision and was replaced by David Harvey. Harvey's first touch of the ball was to retrieve it from his net. For as soon as he had come on to the field, Johnstone set off on one of those devastating runs, leaving defenders in his wake. At precisely the right moment, Johnstone squared into the path of Murdoch, who smashed the ball into the net.

Celtic were in no serious danger after that. They were through, and convincingly, to another European Cup final, and they had established themselves as the best side in Britain.

It is a pity that such a mighty episode in British football should have had an unhappy aftermath, but maybe anti-climax was inevitable.

Leeds took on Chelsea in the FA Cup Final replay and lost 2-1 after extra time. A team that had promised to win everything sadly won nothing. Celtic went to Milan to meet Feyenoord of Holland in the European Cup final. They went as firm favourites, but too many of their players thought in their hearts the European Cup was won when Leeds were beaten. 'I believe Celtic lost the final before it began,' said Sir Robert Kelly, the club president. Far below form, Celtic also lost 2-1 after extra time. If the British title was won at Elland Road and at Hampden Park then there, also, the European title was surely lost.

Leeds: Sprake, Reaney, Cooper, Bremner, Charlton, Madeley, Lorimer, Clarke, Jones, Giles, Gray. (In the second match, Hunter came in for Reaney.)
Celtic: Williams, Hay, Gemmell, Murdoch, McNeill, Brogan, Johnstone, Connelly, Wallace, Auld, Lennox. (In the second match, Hughes replaced Wallace.)

Above *Despite treatment, Sprake left the field.* **Top** *Cock-a-hoop, Auld of Celtic flaunts his match souvenirs.*

CENTRAL PRESS

The day the best team lost

53

While Chelsea's players danced around the perimeter of the Old Trafford pitch on 29 April 1970, winners of the first FA Cup Final to be replayed since the competition was staged at Wembley, the Leeds players were locked, silent, shocked and disappointed in their dressing-room.

They were not even clutching the consolation of a loser's medal. They had not stayed for the presentation—and because of it became the victims of extra condemnation in a season which had already seen them suffer enough.

The inevitable story from their detractors was that they were bad losers, couldn't take it. Their manager Don Revie, a man who sometimes seems to take a perverse delight in believing that too few people honour his team's achievements, denies vehemently, in fact, that either version approaches the truth.

'What happened was that nothing seemed sufficiently organized. Fans were spilling on to the pitch where my players were standing. I felt they were in danger of being trampled. That is the only reason we did not stay to get the medals that were eventually sent on to us by parcel post the following month. But anyone who feels that Leeds players had no pride in accepting them should have been at our club party later in the summer. The presentation that took place then was the high-spot of the whole "do".'

Leeds' story overshadowed then and still obscures now the enormous credit Chelsea earned and deserved for the way they fought back to draw level three times in the two games before winning it in the ordeal-by-exhaustion of another extra half-hour.

Just a few weeks earlier the strides Leeds had been taking in the direction of the League Championship, the European Cup and the FA Cup had started to stutter.

Looking back on the way they went on to falter, stumble, fall and fail to win any of those trophies, there seems an inevitability about it all. Yet Leeds came to Wembley for the first match on 11 April 1970 in a mood that was almost one of euphoria.

Everton had raced away from them to take the League title. The mental pressure of three FA Cup semi-finals, extra matches they could have done without, had made it easier for Celtic to beat them at Elland Road in the first leg of the European Cup semi-final—lengthening the odds against Leeds that were to be justified with their exit in Glasgow the following week. International calls in a season already shortened because of the World Cup series in Mexico later in the summer had hardly helped.

And, finally, there had been the cruel blow nine days earlier when their England right-back Paul Reaney broke his leg in a League match at West Ham.

It might have made many teams tense, tight, cautious. It might have caused Leeds to revert to earlier tactics in their career, when their ruthless approach had made them perhaps the most unloved team in the land, and given them a reputation they took a long time to live down.

Instead, on the day, they played with the air of men determined not just to prove themselves but also to enjoy themselves, a mood and a motive made all the more admirable and memorable by a pitch that was a disgrace to the setting and the occasion.

Hundreds of tons of sand had transformed what had once been the most perfect playing surface in the world into a combination of swamp and beach, sandy, sticky, bumpy. 'You could feel the ground moving under your feet,' was the disgusted, valid comment of Leeds midfield player Johnny Giles. 'It was the worst I have ever known.' 'You didn't need boots, you needed hooves,' was the even more colourful description of Eddie McCreadie, the Chelsea left-back, one of the two men who suffered most harshly from the tricks it helped the ball to play.

In the 21st minute he was on his goal-line waiting for a header by Jack Charlton to bounce in front of him and be blocked. It didn't happen. The ball didn't bounce. It merely plopped and rolled under the boot poised to kill and clear it.

Leeds were however well worth that freak goal for the football they had played and went on playing; football of a quality seldom, if ever, matched in a Cup Final. And though Giles and Billy Bremner were the men behind the sweeping searching passes that constantly ripped and split Chelsea, their young left-winger Eddie Gray was the player who gave most of the moves a menacing purpose.

His control at speed hypnotised, tantalized and almost destroyed his 'sentry', Chelsea right-back David Webb. 'He murdered me,' said Webb after that first match. 'I kept lunging for the ball and suddenly there was nothing there any more. That game taught me that a defender should be careful about committing himself against a tricky forward.'

Chelsea won their way back into it with another goal that owed much to the pitch when, four minutes from half-time, Leeds goalkeeper Gary Sprake was beaten by a shot from winger Houseman so speculative it appeared to be hit in the direction of goal rather than at it.

But those who dismissed this as another of the terrible blunders to which Sprake is occasionally vulnerable, ignore that he had, as he explained afterwards, aimed his dive to cover the line of a shot rebounding from a true surface. Once again its trajectory was freakishly low and went beneath him.

Leeds went on creating chances at a ratio of at least three to one—including a shot from Gray that hit the bar—and it is relevant that the player voted overwhelmingly man of the match was Gray, with Chelsea goalkeeper Peter Bonetti the runner-up. That tells its own story of what was happening, how it was going.

There were just six minutes remaining when Leeds centre-forward Mick Jones scored what would surely have been the winner but for a lapse of concentration by centre-half Jack Charlton two minutes later. Leeds, in fact, seemed to have corporately lost their renowned professionalism for those few minutes. Don Revie said afterwards

that he had detected a sudden, fatal relaxation after Jones' goal.

The urgency and combative spirit of Chelsea striker Ian Hutchinson helped him to beat the Leeds centre-half to a ball in the air from the left that was no more than fifty-fifty. And Hutchinson's header dragged them level again.

They stayed that way through extra-time, despite an Allan Clarke shot that set the Chelsea crossbar twanging and a goal-line clearance of a Giles shot by Webb. At the time it seemed ample compensation for all this Chelsea defender's earlier ordeals but there was to be even greater compensation in the replay.

Webb figures in one of the two significant changes Chelsea made—a move to the centre of the defence leaving the more clinically ferocious marking of Ron Harris to quell Gray.

The other Chelsea change was one of attitude. At Wembley they had too often allowed themselves to be overawed by both the occasion and the opposition. Not this time. They were in a much meaner mood, reflected in a free kick count of eight against them before Leeds were awarded one.

Not that Leeds were subsequently guiltless afterwards on a night when referee Eric Jennings seemed too tolerant about the obvious undercurrent of ill-feeling. Bonetti for instance was hampered in his effort to get to the 35th-minute shot from Mick Jones that gave Leeds the lead yet again. He had been injured just earlier when Jones battered into him somewhat aggressively.

Then came the most spectacular goal of the whole series

The 'score' became one injury apiece when Gray, admittedly already much more subdued, winced and limped through the rest of it after a crippling foul by Harris. But if the game never approached the standards of the first meeting, the goal that turned it was the best of the series.

It came with just twelve minutes left and Leeds once again beginning to wear the look of men armoured by essential superiority. It was then that Chelsea's Charlie Cooke, playing so well in midfield that the continued absence through injury of Hudson became less serious than it might have been, made a marvellous run. The pass he hit was of killing perfection, aimed through the line of Leeds defenders, timed and hit precisely to bisect the path of Peter Osgood. The centre-forward, crouching as he reached the point of impact directed it carefully with a header out of reach of Leeds deputy goalkeeper David Harvey.

There was still a flicker of fight left in Leeds. Enough to provide a flurry of early attacks in extra time but not enough to survive the final shattering blow in the 104th minute of the match; the moment when David Webb put every ounce of his weight, every inch of his height, into a challenge.

Harvey seemed to have ample protection from a cluster of his own defenders when one of those awesomely long throws from Ian Hutchinson was flicked on across goal, yet Webb rose above them all, forced himself through them all to decide it finally.

Something died in Leeds right then. They had only the desperation of men suddenly as sad and as sick as any footballers have ever been. Those who criticized them afterwards for failing to come forward and take the losers medals might remember that—and show a little charity.

Chelsea (1st match): Bonetti, Webb, McCreadie, Hollins, Dempsey, Harris, Baldwin, Houseman, Osgood, Hutchinson, Cooke. Sub: Hinton.
Leeds United (1st match): Sprake, Madeley, Cooper, Bremner, Charlton, Hunter, Lorimer, Clarke, Jones, Giles, Gray. Sub: Bates (not used).
Chelsea (2nd match): Bonetti, Harris, McCreadie, Hollins, Dempsey, Webb, Baldwin, Cooke, Osgood, Hutchinson, Houseman. Sub: Hinton.
Leeds United (2nd match): Harvey, Madeley, Cooper, Bremner, Charlton, Hunter, Lorimer, Clarke, Jones, Giles, Gray. Sub: Bates (not used).

54

Laurels across Stanley Park

Most derby matches, particularly on Merseyside, are disappointments. The crowds expect too much and the players provide too little. This was particularly true after Liverpool's promotion to the First Division in 1962 sparked off the greatest period of rivalry the city had known; a decade of competition for football's top prizes. Liverpool rose as Second Division champions. In 1963 Everton were champions of the First. Then Liverpool won the League title, the FA Cup and the title again in successive seasons, with Everton adding the FA Cup for a Merseyside double in 1966. In 1970 Everton won the title again. The next season Liverpool were losing FA Cup finalists and in 1972 narrowly missed another League Championship.

Unfortunately, too many of the meetings between the two clubs from opposite sides of Stanley Park were little more than domestic squabbles, distinguished only by their pettiness. But on 21 November 1970, the 103rd Merseyside League derby between Liverpool and Everton produced an excellent game of football, fulfilling what people always hope for from a local derby. In fact it was only half a match that was memorable. The first half has long been forgotten—too much tension, too many fouls, not enough good football.

That first 45 minutes surprised no-one. The principle of avoiding defeat had long been established. To win was a bonus. Everton started the match as Football League champions. It was the first time since 1965 that they had gone above Liverpool in the First Division. When they held off Leeds' challenge to become such impressive champions they seemed set to rule not only Merseyside, but English football for years to come.

Everton, the struggling champions, against Shankly's new Liverpool

But Everton at the time were suffering the frequent reaction of title-winners in the season after their success. They had slipped down the First Division table but they still had a team capable of beating almost anyone on their day. It included three of England's Mexico World Cup squad—Alan Ball, Brian Labone and Tommy Wright—and had a fourth, Keith Newton, as substitute. They also had a £130,000 reinforcement after their early-season struggle—Henry Newton from Nottingham Forest.

Liverpool were young and inexperienced. Bill Shankly had finally broken up his great side of the sixties. Roger Hunt had departed for Bolton. Ron Yeats, Ian St John and Tommy Lawrence were now reserves. Shankly was building for the future. But as he reconstructed his team that season he had to face an injury crisis. Bobby Graham had a broken ankle and Ian Callaghan and Alun Evans had to have cartilage operations. On the morning of the match against Everton Peter Thompson failed a fitness test.

So Liverpool were now even more unfamiliar. Two weeks previously they had paid a club record transfer fee of £110,000 to Cardiff for John Toshack. They had also introduced university graduates Brian Hall and Steve Heighway. Utility man Ian Ross, wearing a number 11 jersey, was designated to shadow Alan Ball. In all they had seven men—Clemence, Lindsay, Lloyd, Hall, McLaughlin, Heighway and Toshack—in their first spell of regular First Division football. And Ross was but the ubiquitous replacement. Despite all this inexperience, Liverpool still had one factor in their favour—the tremendous Shankly spirit. It was to prove vital this day.

Everton were generally considered favourites even though Liverpool were three places ahead of Everton in the First Division. These meetings seldom took much notice of League form and Everton still recalled a visit to Anfield earlier that year when they had scored a fine 2-0 victory on their run-in to the Championship.

So it was the men in the royal blue of Everton who looked more confident and more likely winners in that poor first half. The young Liverpool side seemed to be gripped with a fear of losing. They were nervous and uncoordinated, rarely sustaining any penetrative attack on Everton's defence. Everton were not much better, but they appeared to have individuals capable of winning the match on their own. One of these was Joe Royle, the big young centre-forward who gave Larry Lloyd, Liverpool's new giant centre-half, a searching examination, particularly in the air.

In one of the rare exciting moments that broke the monotonous first half Royle leapt above Lloyd and powered a header for what seemed a certain goal. But Ray Clemence produced a spectacular

save. That one incident epitomized the half: Everton's forwards in deadlock with Liverpool's defenders. Half-time came as a welcome relief. After the interval the game resumed on the same low level. Then, suddenly, something unpredictable happened, a mistake created a goal and a tedious game was transformed into a classic. The turning-point was the 56th minute.

Amazingly, the mistake was made by the most dependable member of the defence that boasted the best record in the country. Liverpool captain Tommy Smith tried to dribble away from a position on the right deep inside his own half and was challenged by left-winger Johnny Morrissey, one of the few men to transfer between the two clubs when he moved across to Goodison Park eight years earlier.

Instead of hitting the ball away, Smith played it square across the face of his own penalty area. It was the perfect pass for Everton's sharp little striker Alan Whittle. He immediately intercepted the ball and, as Clemence moved out, delicately chipped it over his head.

Then eight minutes later Everton moved into that left-wing area again. Ball split the Liverpool defence with his first-time return pass to Morrissey. Smith and his colleagues looked in vain at the linesman and referee for offside. Morrissey moved in, pulling defenders towards him before delivering his centre over Lloyd and on to the head of Royle. The big centre-forward nodded. Clemence had no chance.

What could Liverpool's fans expect now? At best a 2-0 defeat or, much worse, an exhibition of pure football from Everton. To the despair of the home crowd Everton responded to the opportunity. Ball rubbed it in, performing all his party pieces. Was it going to be 0-3, 0-4 or even more?

Everton had already substituted the limping Howard Kendall with Keith Newton who went to left-back allowing Henry Newton to move forward into a more familiar midfield role. Liverpool pulled off the 18-year-old John McLaughlin, who looked out of his depth amid Everton's midfield, and

introduced Phil Boersma, one of their speedy forwards. Boersma did little directly to change the course of the match, but it was certainly speed that revived Liverpool.

In the 69th minute Smith hit a high ball away to the left. Steve Heighway, not long out of university and little more than a month into his First Division career, took the ball in his stride, rode a tackle from John Hurst and zig-zagged in from the left as the Everton defence wondered what he was going to do.

Until Heighway scored Everton had been in control of Anfield

Heighway, too, appeared to be wondering as he moved in at an angle with goalkeeper Andy Rankin coming across to the near post. Heighway looked up, made as if to pull the ball back with his left foot, then squeezed a right-foot shot into the far corner of the net. Heighway said later: 'Normally in a situation like this you would think "Well, we've pulled one back". But I think we all felt then that we would win the match.'

Seven minutes later a revitalized Liverpool equalized. Again it was Heighway who wrecked the Everton defence, dummying Tommy Wright to move on to the ball from a throw-in, moving down the left and then centring high into the penalty area. There was Toshack soaring above Labone to head a superb equalizer.

Even the Kop should have been satisfied. But they, like their team, sensed victory. They had to wait only another eight minutes. Alec Lindsay pushed forward from left-back to join the attack. He moved on to the ball and curled it across with his left foot. Toshack again got to it first with his head, but this time he did not aim for goal. He flicked it to one side and right-back Chris Lawler, scorer of so many important goals for Liverpool, sneaked in on the blind side of Keith Newton. Rankin had no chance as the ball was fired past

his right hand into the net.

In the last six minutes there was even more excitement as Everton tried to save the game they had seemed to have won. A shot by Keith Newton would have beaten many goalkeepers, though Clemence was equal to it.

But then it was over. A stunned Everton stayed in their dressing-room for an hour and could only shake their heads in disbelief as they left Anfield. Bill Shankly said: 'I have never been prouder of a Liverpool team than I was in this match.' It was a contest that had proved Shankly's judgement of the young players he had selected for the future.

Anfield was obviously unprepared to surrender any status to Everton just because the latter were League Champions. They were to demonstrate that point again that season—once more coming from behind to beat Everton in an FA Cup semi-final at Old Trafford. In the Final despite scoring the first goal, Liverpool were beaten 2-1 by new League Champions Arsenal after extra-time. Nevertheless, in Liverpool at least, it was early proof that the end of Liverpool's great team of the sixties was not to be the end of the club's high status in British football.

Liverpool: Clemence, Lawler, Lindsay, Smith, Lloyd, Hughes, Hall, McLaughlin, Heighway, Toshack, Ross. Sub: Boersma.
Everton: Rankin, Wright, Newton (H), Kendall, Labone, Harvey, Whittle, Ball, Royle, Hurst, Morrissey. Sub: Newton (K).

Opposite page *The first half: Clemence saves Liverpool by pushing the ball over the bar.*
Below left *The second half: Everton take a two-goal lead then Liverpool retaliate and it is Rankin who has to stretch to prevent a goal.*
Below right *Jubilation: Toshack has just equalized with less than 15 minutes left; the face of John Hurst (10) betrays Everton's dismay.*
Bottom *The winner: six minutes from time Chris Lawler sneaks in to complete Liverpool's recovery.*

The triumph of 'Grandad's Army'

55

From the moment Colchester were drawn from the depths of the Football League to face mighty Leeds in the fifth round of the 1971 FA Cup, the prophets were out in force. And it seemed quite safe for them to emerge. Obviously little Colchester would be utterly annihilated by the northern giants.

So, armed with logic and common sense, and clutching a wealth of statistics, the pundits pronounced at length on the obvious outcome of the match. To a man they dismissed Colchester as a spent side.

While all this was going on, Leeds remained silently aloof. They saw no need to join in the banter. Of course they were going to win—everybody knew that. Why bother to say so?

After the game, Leeds were still saying nothing. But it was a different kind of silence, awkward and solemn; it had lost its calm assurance.

As they flew back to Leeds on the evening of Saturday 13 February 1971, just one and a half hours after the match with Colchester had ended, the Leeds players were all wearing the same expression on their pale, set, unsmiling faces—not anger, or self-pity; not even disappointment. They were just blank and empty.

Manager Don Revie came closest to capturing the reason for what to a casual onlooker seemed a total absence of emotion when, long afterwards, he explained: 'They just didn't believe it had happened, that it could have happened. They were playing it all over again in their minds and still not accepting it.'

Perhaps only those who have closely observed victims of the effects of shock—a bad accident, a bereavement—will understand precisely what Revie meant. Leeds were suffering from what must rank as one of the greatest upsets in the long history of the FA Cup.

For Leeds went into that fifth round Cup match on the tight, tiny ground at Layer Road, Colchester not only as favourites to win the trophy—but also every other prize available. Their record indicates why.

In six completed seasons since promotion as Second Division champions, their achievements require a deep breath to say in one sentence. They had won the First Division Championship once and been runners-up three times, had reached the FA Cup Final twice and the semi-finals on another two occasions, had won the League Cup once, had won the Fairs Cup once and been beaten finalists, and had reached the semi-finals of the European Cup.

By common, even rapturous, consent they had become the perfect footballing machine, a marriage of talent and consistency. At the time of their game against Colchester they were once again setting the pace in the First Division, three points clear of everybody else, and looking as though, when the season ended, they would be in the thick of the battle for the League title.

Colchester's own contributions to the history of the game could, by comparison, be cruelly dismissed. The middle reaches of the Fourth Division seemed the appropriate environment for a club who had never done or won anything of significance—and who did not have the financial resources necessary if they were to improve their situation.

Their manager, Dick Graham, a controversial, unorthodox veteran who had gone grey in the game, refused to indulge in the traditional whistling in the dark that so often goes on when top opponents and unique opportunities are sent as a present from Lancaster Gate. He carefully refrained from the usual cliches about 'They're only eleven men, same as us,' recognizing that the rough and realistic translation of that comment is, 'I wish I had their eleven men and they had mine.'

The Colchester team was made up largely of veteran rejects—six of them were over thirty. Days before the game the side was being written off simply because of its average age. After the victory the players broke into spontaneous song—the current hit 'Grandad'—and in every conversation during the next week they proudly dubbed themselves 'Grandad's Army'. 'In my position', Graham expanded, 'I have to resurrect players. I look around to find men who have been discarded before their time and give them a new lease of life.'

Graham was prepared to make only two pre-match promises about his players' performances. One was that they would be as hard and fit as his famous insistence on intensive, hard-driving preparation could achieve. The other was that his psychological attitude towards each individual—coaxing one, bullying another

On the day, the meagre capacity of 16,000 did arrive, but there was no noticeable surge to pay black market prices for tickets and little genuine hope of success in the atmosphere before the match—more a cheerful determination to enjoy the execution. It all tended to make what was to happen a drama that stretched sporting credibility to its limits.

The immediately obvious reason for the Colchester victory was the burly Crawford's explosive contribution. He harassed Jack Charlton into a morass of wild errors. He scored two goals. He received ecstatic, hysterical acclaim at the time and in all the next day's reports.

His first goal, in the 18th minute, was brilliant. He timed his run to perfection and bisected the path of a long, dropping free-kick from his winger Brian Lewis—the sort his old Ipswich partner Jimmy Leadbetter used to hit—and glanced it with sweet satisfaction from the bone of his brow into the roof of the net.

But his second had an element of the freakish about it. Swivelling on his behind in a tangle with Leeds right-back Paul Reaney, he managed to scramble the ball in a slow, rolling arc past poor Gary Sprake, who seemed transfixed.

The Welsh international goalkeeper was bang in the middle of a spell of disastrous errors, his temperament and his talent temporarily left in shreds by the barracking of his own fans. It could, and did, only make his performance worse. Sprake was blatantly at fault when Colchester went further in front ten minutes after the half-time score that had been a sensation all over the country with its news. He was trapped, off his line, in a torment of hesitation, moving neither forward to challenge nor back for a salvaging dive as inside-right Dave Simmons hurtled to head another Lewis lob past him.

But a failure as immense as this one by Leeds

—would have them in the mood on the day to make any result a possibility.

Only one Colchester man was prepared to go further, feet first into an attitude of outrageous optimism. Ray Crawford, the 34-year-old former England centre-forward, rescued from non-League football by Graham, recalled the days of his pomp in the First Division with Ipswich. 'I always play well against Leeds', he said. 'I always score goals against Jack Charlton.' Crawford's remarks were dismissed as an attempt to whip up enthusiastic support in a town that too often failed to provide more than 5,000 fans at Colchester matches.

can never be deposited on the shoulders of individuals. There was so much more wrong with the favourites on this day. They had been warned beforehand by Revie that they would be harassed mercilessly. They were ordered to reject any temptations to mix it, and were cautioned that they must maintain their rhythm. Yet instead of trying to ride out the crashing, tackling storm of the early minutes, they fed it with illegalities and follies of their own, careering into reckless tackles and smashing the ball without thought.

The famous, formidable Leeds defence had seldom in its long time together crumbled as

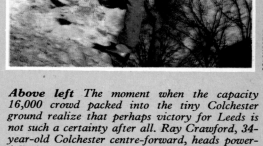

Above left *The moment when the capacity 16,000 crowd packed into the tiny Colchester ground realize that perhaps victory for Leeds is not such a certainty after all. Ray Crawford, 34-year-old Colchester centre-forward, heads powerfully into the roof of the net with Leeds full-backs Cooper and Reaney helpless to prevent a goal.*
Below, far left *Bewildered Leeds slip further behind. Again it is Crawford who does the damage, justifying his pre-match boast that he would score at least one goal against the northerners. With the desperate Leeds defence in a tangle, Crawford manages to prod the ball into the net.*
Below left *Soon after half-time, Colchester went three up when Simmons headed past Sprake to the astonishment and delight of the crowd. Here Crawford and Simmons savour what turns out to be the winning goal.*
Above *Before the match, Colchester manager Dick Graham told reporters that he would climb the walls of Colchester castle if his team succeeded in beating the Cup favourites. A few days after Colchester had sent Leeds reeling, Graham was only too happy to keep his word and scale the crumbling walls.*

'It was the most controlled demonstration of pure football I've ever seen in such circumstances' was the generous tribute afterwards from Dick Graham, unashamedly wet-eyed at the time.

It enabled Leeds to pull back two goals, in the 61st minute by Norman Hunter, and by Giles a quarter of an hour from the end. It restricted exhausted Colchester, all their confidence visibly draining, to brief breakaways—in one of which Crawford confessed he was 'just too bloody tired to kick the ball that should have given me my hat-trick'.

It gave the game a climax it did not really need to remain totally, marvellously memorable. Just three minutes from time Leeds centre-forward Mick Jones connected perfectly to deflect a cross from Peter Lorimer far out of the reach of most goalkeepers. Even though it hit Colchester's centre-half Brian Garvey on its way to the goal, Colchester's Graham Smith managed to see it in enough time to change direction, drop on it and hold it. Colchester had beaten Leeds United.

Order was restored three weeks later when Everton put five past the Essex lads at Goodison in the next round of the Cup. Colchester returned to their bid for promotion, Leeds to their assault on the championship. Both failed. The former suffered from a reaction to short-lived success, the latter, perhaps, from a reaction to all too familiar failure. For Colchester it was to be the magnificent highlight of a mundane existence; for Leeds one more sad entry in a diary of frustration.

Colchester: Smith, Hall, Cram, Gilchrist, Garvey, Kurila, Lewis, Simmons, Mahon, Crawford, Gibbs.
Leeds: Sprake, Reaney, Cooper, Bates, Charlton, Hunter, Lorimer, Clarke, Jones, Giles, Madeley.

disastrously as it did while the damage was done. The midfield, too, had not often failed so miserably to function efficiently. Johnny Giles, the man who was expected to dominate the centre, compounded the effect of absence through injury of his partner Billy Bremner by pursuing pointless feuds with the tough little man marking him, wing-half John Gilchrist.

Gilchrist afterwards helped partly to explain Giles' belligerent display. 'Right at the start Terry Cooper miscued this clearance up into the stand. "Blimey," I thought, "What sort of effort was that from an England full-back?" Trouble was, I must have said it aloud. And

Giles overheard. "Never mind Cooper, how many caps have *you* got?" he shouted back. I couldn't let it go at that, so I told him, "None. . . . but then I wasn't born in Ireland, where they give away caps with packets of cornflakes." Looking back, I think I'd have been better keeping my trap shut. He's small, is Giles, but he can be bloody hard. I'll be carrying the marks from this match long after it has been forgotten.'

The irony of it all was that having lost their heads, their cool and the game, Leeds should suddenly but belatedly remember who they were and what their name was supposed to mean.

56

Arsenal lock out Leeds at Tottenham

It has been estimated that more than 150,000 people set off from their homes on Monday 3 May 1971 hoping to see the season's final First Division match between Tottenham Hotspur and Arsenal at White Hart Lane. Around 100,000 of them were still pushing and shoving their way to nowhere outside the ground when the gates locked 51,192 lucky fans inside.

They had all been attracted by a unique derby match that would decide the League Championship. There were only two clubs in the race:

Leeds United and Arsenal. The third club, Tottenham in fact, finished over ten points behind. But Leeds, football's perennial bridesmaid, had completed their fixtures and could only wait and see if their 64 points would be enough. Arsenal, on 63 points, needed only a scoreless draw to win the championship for a record eighth time by 0.013 of a goal. But a defeat, or a goal-scoring draw would concede the Championship to Leeds.

A more climactic conclusion to the arduous

League programme would have been difficult to devise. Next to Leeds themselves Spurs were about the last team Arsenal wished to visit, particularly as Arsenal's six defeats had all been away from home. The two North London clubs—like most football neighbours—had always had their own private championship. During the sixties it was Tottenham who had proved that they were the top team in North London. But at last Arsenal had a wonderful chance to eclipse their rivals: if they could survive at White Hart Lane they would have accomplished one half of the coveted and elusive double, a feat accomplished only once in the twentieth century, in 1960-61, by Spurs.

With so much prestige at stake there was no possibility of any connivance in Arsenal's triumph. Yet there was a widespread suspicion that Tottenham would hand the title to Arsenal.

Alan Mullery, Spurs skipper, expressed Tottenham's viewpoint. 'Listen,' he told newsmen, 'Arsenal have got as much chance of being handed the title by Spurs as I have of being given the Crown Jewels. They are the *last* people we want winning the Championship. Everybody is on about the great season Arsenal are having. Well, we're not doing too badly. We have won the League Cup and reached the sixth round of the FA Cup. Now we mean to round off our season by beating Arsenal—and that will put us third in the table. That can't be bad.'

Mullery's sentiments were echoed by Bill Nicholson. 'We are tremendously proud of our double achievement,' he said. 'I suppose some other club has got to do it again sometime but we will be doing our best to see it isn't Arsenal. My instructions to the Tottenham players will be to go out to try to win.'

If all this was not enough incentive to beat Arsenal, Spurs also had the prospect of a £400 per man position bonus if they won.

Yet if there was tension in London, it was a night of torture in Yorkshire. 'We have done all we can and now we are helpless,' said Leeds manager Don Revie. 'My players have been magnificent all season. I would hate to see them pipped on the post again. We have got 64 points and there have never been runners-up with a collection as big as that. We are not going to sit around waiting for the result of the match at Tottenham. The lads are playing in Chris Chilton's testimonial match at Hull and I'll be there watching them. It is now up to Tottenham.'

There were a lot of people that night who hoped Arsenal would be defeated. The North was hoping for a double triumph: Leeds to win the League and Bill Shankly's Liverpool to defeat Arsenal at Wembley in the FA Cup Final five days later. Even London was divided although the capital's first Championship for a decade was at stake.

But it was very nearly the great game that did not start. The streets surrounding White Hart Lane were jammed solid with human bodies and worried police were working overtime to control them. Traffic was at a standstill—including the Arsenal team coach. 'I honestly didn't think we were going to make it to the ground,' said captain Frank McLintock. 'Our coach was travelling at about a mile an hour. We finally made it to a side-entrance and the coach had to mount the pavement so that we could get to the gate. I have never seen anything like it. The wonder is nobody was killed in the crush.'

This was an aspect of that match which was overlooked in the week's excitement. Another major disaster could have occurred that night, only four months after the tragedy at Ibrox.

One man remembers that night at White Hart Lane even more vividly than most—referee

Top left Arsenal needed a goalless draw or victory. Radford watches Kennedy's header win the match and the title three minutes from time.
Left Earlier in the game Spurs had forced their North London neighbours to defend desperately. Wilson saves from Peters and Gilzean.
Right Frank McLintock, wearing a Leeds United scarf, being chaired off the pitch. Arsenal had just deprived Leeds of the title by a single point.

Kevin Howley. 'It was the last League match of my career,' he recalls. 'What a way to go out. It was a superb finale and a match that was a credit to British football.'

The atmosphere inside the ground would have affected a stone statue. It seemed that most of the crowd were there to urge the team to greatness. 'I was a bag of nerves and kept shouting advice and instructions to try and keep on top of things,' says Frank McLintock. 'But I might as well have been talking to myself. You just couldn't hear a thing out there. The noise was deafening.'

Charlie George, the young exhibitionist who provided Arsenal with necessary moments of brilliance, his shoulder-length hair flapping at his back like a string curtain, almost snatched the lead in the opening seconds. Right-back Pat Rice made a deep incursion into Tottenham's left flank before striking a pass into the path of George who powerfully struck an instant shot. But goalkeeper Pat Jennings took off like an Olympic diver attempting a high-tariff dive and turned the ball over the bar.

Arsenal's Championship dilemma—to defend and hope or play to win

That proved Tottenham were in no mood to give their neighbours any favours. Instead they started linking some fast-flowing moves and Arsenal's nerves were apparent—they could not afford to concede a single goal in those taut circumstances. Martin Peters stopped their hearts with a swerving shot that clipped the top of the Arsenal bar with goalkeeper Bob Wilson stranded.

Arsenal looked perilously close to a nervous collapse, their side unused to the pressures of being at the top, but McLintock began to pump confidence into them from the back with the sort of inspiring captaincy that earned him the Footballer of the Year title.

Arsenal needed such leadership. They were missing the biting tackles of midfield anchorman Peter Storey who had failed a fitness test that afternoon. Eddie Kelly had been drafted into the side and gradually came more and more into the action as the game grew older. George Armstrong was, as usual, covering marathon distances at sprinter's speed. 'With a worker like Geordie in the team we are able to play a 4-3-4 formation,' said coach Don Howe. 'He covers enough ground for two men.'

Tottenham's defenders were stretched in the last 15 minutes of a frantic first half. McLintock had a shot hooked off the line by Peter Collins and then the ball was swinging across the Spurs goalmouth as Arsenal forced four corners inside two minutes.

During the second half, however, as Tottenham composed some stunning movements of their own, the tension became almost unendurable. Goalkeeper Bob Wilson was injured diving at the feet of raiding right-back Joe Kinnear and there was a brief explosion of bad temper as Arsenal defender Bob McNab moved in to protect his goalkeeper. Then Arsenal had a fright when Cyril Knowles pushed over a low cross that gave Alan Gilzean a clear sight of goal. 'That should have been it,' Gilzean said later, 'but I was so busy looking for a place to put it that I took my eye off the ball and missed connecting by no more than an inch.'

The game was now ticking into its final minutes and it looked as if Arsenal's dilemma of playing for a goalless draw or for victory had resolved itself.

Then, with three minutes to go, Charlie George—flourishing all his precocious skills—cut in dangerously towards goal. Goalkeeper Pat Jennings covered his near post ready for a shot that never came.

George transferred the ball at shoulder height into the middle and John Radford powered a header that looked a certain goal until the acrobatic Jennings intervened, catapulting to his right to push the ball away. Tottenham's confused defenders were still regrouping when Armstrong calmly lofted the ball back into the goalmouth and Ray Kennedy stepped forward to head high into the net off the bar.

There was an explosive roar as Arsenal fans prematurely celebrated winning the Championship. But there were still three minutes to go and a Tottenham equalizer would have tugged the title away from Arsenal and given it to Leeds. 'That was the longest three minutes I have ever known,' said Kennedy, who was having an incredible first full season in League football. 'I remember thinking to myself as Tottenham came back at us that perhaps it might have been better had my header not gone into the net.'

And Tottenham did strive to equalize. For Arsenal to win the Championship would diminish their own considerable success of that season; to lose at home would leave no doubt about Arsenal's superiority. There were 10 red-shirted defenders stretched across the Arsenal goalmouth in a last-ditch defence of their lead and the title.

In the last minute it looked as if they would be overrun as the ball became lost under a flurry of feet just two yards off the Arsenal goal-line. But Bob Wilson dived bravely in among the blur of boots to clear this last moment of danger. Then Arsenal were relieved by referee Howley's final whistle of his League career. The title was Arsenal's. The grief belonged to Leeds.

'I'm going out to get drunk out of my mind,' said centre-half Jackie Charlton when the result was relayed to Hull. 'Arsenal owe it all to Spurs. They beat us at Elland Road and now this . . . .'

Back at White Hart Lane Arsenal's fans had taken over the ground and they danced in untidy delight across their neighbours' plot of land. Charlie George had leapt into the arms of coach Don Howe who said: 'This is only the start. Next season we are going to win the European Cup.'

Howe was already looking beyond Saturday's Cup Final. Yet by the time 'next season' had arrived Don Howe had departed for West Bromwich and the challenge of managership.

Before he left, however, Arsenal added the FA Cup to their League Championship. It was a tremendous achievement but it is tempting to ask whether Arsenal would have beaten Liverpool 2-1 in extra-time if they had not had the huge psychological benefit of winning the League title.

Such questions are unanswerable. But what is certain is that no team in the League's history has become Champions so narrowly, by a matter of minutes. It was a most dramatic way to win the title, the most cruel way for Leeds to lose it.

Tottenham: Jennings, Kinnear, Knowles, Mullery, Collins, Beal, Gilzean, Perryman, Chivers, Peters, Neighbour. Sub: Pearce.
Arsenal: Wilson, Rice, McNab, Kelly, McLintock, Simpson, Armstrong, Graham, Radford, Kennedy, George. Sub: Sammels.

57

When 4-1 against Partick meant 4-1 against Celtic

In the autumn of 1971, yet another chant, new in content if not form, was added to the extensive repertoire in Scottish football: 'Thistle 4, Celtic 1, Hallelujah!' It was sung with particular relish on the terraces of Ibrox Park, where any discomfiture of Celtic is celebrated with a fervour normally reserved for Hogmanay, Burns' night or a Rangers' triumph.

The chant referred, of course, to the historic proceedings at Hampden Park on Saturday, 23 October 1971 when, in their most remarkable achievement for half a century, Partick Thistle beat Celtic by four goals to one and so won the Scottish League Cup.

It was a result which all of Britain found hard to believe. The television half-time results service repeated it—4-0 at the time—for the benefit of the incredulous public. A good many jokes were made at the expense of the officials whose job it was to compose the half-time scoreboards at Scottish football grounds. Somebody, the chant on the terraces went, had got it the wrong way round.

A careful examination of the background to this match will show why it ranks amongst the biggest surprises football has known since the defeat of Arsenal by Walsall in 1933. For a start, the name Partick Thistle is not normally associated with the winning of football trophies. It is part of the club's tradition that they should entertain, that they should be completely unpredictable, that they should win or lose with grace and good sportsmanship. But it is fair to say that the possibility of winning a major trophy barely registers in the minds of even their most ardent supporters.

Around Maryhill, where the club has its headquarters, there is a deep affection for Partick Thistle. Nor is this affection limited to that particular part of Glasgow. Like Queen's Park and Hearts, Thistle have their devotees all over Scotland. For they have come to stand for a romantic aspect of what has come to be a ruthlessly professional game. It is a friendly club, run by friendly people. On a Saturday afternoon, it is a good place to go if you like your football to be fun—and non-sectarian.

Something changed at Firhill Park after that League Cup final

After the League Cup final of 1971, all of these qualities remained at Firhill Park. But something had changed, inevitably so. Partick Thistle had won a major trophy at last. They had become accepted as one of the more powerful members of the soccer community. The change of status was not unwelcome to their fans, players and, above all, to their manager, Dave McParland.

It was McParland who moulded the victorious Thistle side. Himself a former Thistle player of repute, he had taken them out of the Second Division at the end of season 1970-71 and he had done so in style, five points ahead of the runners-up, East Fife. Most newly promoted clubs, most newly successful managers, would have been content to stay discreetly out of the way in the First Division, to consolidate.

Partick Thistle, bold as ever, were content with nothing of the sort. From the start, they showed an eagerness to challenge for everything in sight. The average age of their players was

22, but this did not deter them in the slightest. What they lacked in experience, they balanced in enthusiasm, attacking spirit and considerable, genuine skill. Even so, and in spite of finishing at the top of a tough League Cup section, they were not really expected to reach the final, much less win it. The bubble had to burst—that, at any rate, was the public reaction to their initial success.

Thus, in the week preceding the League Cup final, it was possible to get odds of 4-1 against Thistle; the figures were to seem symbolic. The Glasgow bookmakers, who know all about such matters, were happier to take bets on Thistle than Celtic, for they had come to regard an investment with Celtic—at long odds on—as a short-term loan at high interest.

The respective managers were both careful and wary. Jock Stein, who would never write off even a non-League side, said he believed it would be a hard game. He was not disposed to comment much further. Dave McParland struck a hopeful rather than optimistic note—'We will have a real go,' he said. As more than one Glasgow wag pointed out, the same sentiments could have been expressed by the Christians before they encountered the lions.

Perhaps the easiest way to understand the extent of the shock-waves that were to engulf Scottish football is to glance at the names in the Celtic side.

There were Bobby Murdoch, threatening to regain the form that had once made him arguably the finest midfield man in Britain, Tommy Gemmell, flamboyant, highly-skilled defender with a habit of scoring goals on important occasions, David Hay, probably the best Scottish full-back to emerge in a decade, Jimmy Johnstone, world-class and just about unplayable when approaching his true form, Kenny Dalglish, a boy of remarkable gifts both in midfield and in the striking positions.

By no stretch of imagination could the Thistle players stand comparison with such names—not before the game, anyway. Their recent record had begun and ended with the Second Division championship. Celtic had won everything worth winning except the World Club Championship, and they came close to that, too. Now here were the champions competing in their eighth successive League Cup Final.

In the 62,740 crowd, the Thistle fans were well represented. Yet, it was a good-tempered assembly, and the mood was almost one of holiday. To Celtic fans, naturally, it was to be a Roman-style holiday. They argued only about how many goals the champions would score.

Now it has long been taken for granted in Scottish football that the best way to play Celtic is to try to match them at their own game. That is, to attack—or, if you like, 'to have a go', as Dave McParland had promised. It is a tactic that certainly fails more often than it succeeds, but at least it is thought to be an honourable one, and it has usually been responsible for any successes that have been won against Celtic.

In the event, Partick Thistle and Davie McParland kept their promise. It had undoubtedly been the intention of Celtic to settle down into their familiar smooth rhythm, and to put Thistle in their place, as a matter of course. But there was nothing smooth, nothing rhythmic about Celtic in that first, incredible 45-minute spell. Their defence was shattered by the double-spear-

Above The traditional scenes of jubilation when your team wins the cup—in this case the Scottish League Cup. But tradition had been turned upside down that day, 23 October 1971. Little Partick Thistle, before then known for their good-natured if unsuccessful style of play, had taken on and hammered mighty Celtic, who might have been forgiven if they had loaded the cup on to their coach before the match. Holding the cup is Thistle captain Alex Rae, the man who started the rot with the first goal after nine minutes. Thistle were to score another three in the first half to make the final score an unbelievable 4-1. **1** *Goal number three is seconds away as Denis McQuade with the ball at his feet has all the time in the world to pick his spot at the back of the net.* **2** *McQuade and Jimmy Bone run back to the centre-spot as the Thistle fans in a still bemused stadium erupt with joy.* **3** *While the Celtic defence dithered, Bone beat them all to score the fourth goal.* **4** *His triumph was shared by every Thistle supporter—the team that had walked out determined only 'to have a go' had triumphed.*

head of Frank Coulston and Jimmy Bone. Their flanks were turned by the fast, determined raids of wingers Denis McQuade and Bobby Lawrie. And, all the while, they were not only held, but surpassed, in the crucial midfield area.

It took time before the fans could understand what was going on

Yet it was some time before the fans could understand, and appreciate, what was going on. Thistle's first goal came in nine minutes when, following a corner-kick, their captain, Alex Rae, sent a first-time lob high into the top corner of the net. That was a surprise, but few interpreted it as a serious blow for Celtic. The second goal arrived six minutes later, when Lawrie neatly finished off a move created by McQuade and Bone yet, still, the fans regarded this as little more than an inconvenience to Celtic. Inevitably, Celtic launched their counter-attack, but with McQuade dropping back to midfield reinforced tactics were still unable to control the centre of the park. Jimmy Johnstone had to go off, injured, and was replaced by Jim Craig, who went to full-back, with David Hay moving forward. That was in the 17th minute, and doubtless Celtic were affected by the switch. Thistle, though, were not inclined to extend sympathy.

They continued to play football that was as exciting as it was effective, and in the 28th minute McQuade was up—again at a corner-kick—to score a third goal deflected off a defender. Eight minutes later, soon after Thistle had missed at least one excellent chance, Bone exploited a most embarrassing moment of indecision in the Celtic defence to make it 4-0.

It was a splendid compliment to Celtic that their chances of recovery in the second half were not written off at the interval. But although that second half was indeed a story of Celtic versus the Partick defence—sometimes a ten-man defence—Thistle remained courageous and composed in this role, and also contrived to cause plenty of trouble on the break. Glavin was hurt—and it merely gave Gibson an opportunity to join the stars. He took it well.

Could Celtic take advantage of their clear superiority in midfield?

Bobby Murdoch was playing magnificently now and, at last, Celtic had a clear advantage in midfield. Yet they were unable to convert their midfield superiority into goals. If their forwards weren't missing chances, Alan Rough was performing prodigies in the Thistle goal. There were only 20 minutes left when Dalglish did get one past him but, by that time, the Scottish League Cup was obviously bound for Firhill.

Many theories have been expounded since as to the reason for Thistle's triumph. The Celtic defence unquestionably suffered from the absence of their injured captain, Billy McNeill. Then there was the early injury to Johnstone. It is also quite possible that Celtic went into the game with the wrong attitude, that—like almost everybody else—they thought it would be too easy. All of these may well be contributory factors. But the chief factor must be that, on that unforgettable day, Partick Thistle earned just reward for glorious football. And with their victory, Scottish football itself was given new zest and encouragement. Monopolies are bad for the game—a point made before the final, and since, by no less a person than Jock Stein—and Thistle had indeed provided further promise of the break-up of the Old Firm's dominance.

Celtic: Williams, Hay, Gemmell, Murdoch, Connolly, Brogan, Johnstone, Dalglish, Hood, Callaghan, Macari. Sub: Craig.
Partick Thistle: Rough, Henson, Forsyth, Glavin, Campbell, Strachan, McQuade, Coulston, Bone, Rae, Lawrie. Sub: Gibson.

Eastham, scourge of West Ham

58

1 John Ritchie's goal at Upton Park cancelled the 2-1 lead West Ham gained at Stoke when Geoff Hurst scored a penalty. But **2** only a marvellous save by Gordon Banks in the last minutes of extra time deprived Hurst of another penalty goal and West Ham of a place at Wembley. **3** Whatever Stoke manager Tony Waddington said to Peter Dobing at the end of normal time he was not planning Banks' save. **4** Bobby Moore almost emulated Banks in the second replay after Bobby Ferguson had been injured. But he could only parry Mike Bernard's penalty and **5** the Stoke player followed up to give City a 1-0 lead. They went on to win 3-2 and 5-4 on aggregate.

George Eastham, a frail-looking Peter Pan of football, was not so much surprised that Stoke City won the 1972 League Cup final at Wembley as that they did it without need of a replay.

'I knew we would win the Cup,' said Eastham. 'The only thing I could not have predicted is that we managed to do it in 90 minutes. I was convinced we would at least need extra-time to overcome Chelsea. It was just something I felt in my bones.'

The thousands of fans who had followed Stoke's marathon trail to Wembley probably shared Eastham's feelings. Oxford United had taken them to a third-round replay and they then had to play three matches before mastering Manchester United in the fourth round.

Yet this was merely a warm-up for one of the classic Soccer serials of all time—Stoke City versus West Ham United.

It started at Stoke's Victoria Ground on 8 December 1971 and finished four matches later at Old Trafford, Manchester, on 26 January 1972 after a full seven hours of fascinating football intense with drama and emotion.

The first leg of their semi-final was played before an audience of 36,400. West Ham started slight favourites, having eliminated Leeds, Liverpool and Sheffield United in the previous three rounds. There was quite understandably a strong feeling in London that the League Cup was going to stay in the capital. Tottenham, the holders, were meeting Chelsea in the other semi-final.

This mood of confidence was strengthened when Hammers eased to a 2-1 victory after trailing to a goal by Stoke skipper Peter Dobing.

Geoff Hurst had cancelled out the Dobing goal with a disputed penalty. He powered the ball to the right of his England team-mate Gordon Banks at shoulder height and it smacked hard into the back of the net.

The West Ham players later marvelled at Banks having managed to get his finger-tips to the ball on its way into the net. 'Gordon knows exactly where I put them,' said Hurst. 'But if you connect properly no goalkeeper should have a chance of saving a penalty—not even Gordon Banks.' That remark was to be dramatically significant a week later.

It was Bermudan Clyde Best who gave West Ham a healthy 2-1 lead to take back to Upton Park for the second leg. Harry Redknapp fired over a shin-high centre from the right and Best rifled a volley past the anchored Banks. The West Ham players celebrated this magnificent goal as if it was a passport to Wembley.

'Not even Gordon Banks should have a chance of saving a penalty'

Stoke came out fighting for round two at Upton Park on December 15 in front of a 38,771 Cockney crowd that had come to cheer Hammers into the final. Too many people considered it a formality.

But Stoke had too much skill, too much stamina to be counted out until the final whistle. They reduced Hammers to a neurotic condition as, in midfield, Dobing and Eastham probed with passes that would have caused problems in the tightest defence and John Ritchie, always a towering menace to West Ham, struck a cleverly constructed goal to make it 2-2 on aggregate.

Stoke were running rings around West Ham as they strove for their first major honour in the club's 109-year history.

A gripping game overlapped into extra-time and officials from both sides were asking where the replay venue would be when another penalty was given, against Gordon Banks, just three minutes from the end.

Banks had rugby-tackled Harry Redknapp during a goalmouth skirmish and his frantic pleas that he had been impeded first were stonily ignored. For the second time in seven days, it was Banks v Hurst—like an action replay of a High Noon duel with the odds in Hurst's favour.

Hurst took his usual eight yard run-up and thrashed the ball mightily with his right foot, again to the right of Banks. The world's greatest goalkeeper made a panther-like spring, going almost too far, but somehow recovering to spread his hands under the ball and push it high up into the air and over the bar. Hurst stood staring in total disbelief as Stoke players pounded past him and started parading Banks around the penalty area as if he was the League Cup.

Four West Ham players had crouched down with their backs to the Stoke goal as Hurst took the penalty. They had missed one of the most stunning saves ever made. Hurst was inconsolable afterwards. Bobby Moore summed it up: 'That wasn't a penalty *miss*—that was a penalty *save*. Only Gordon could have done it.'

Suddenly West Ham, Wembley favourites when they won at Stoke, were the underdogs. Fate and Stoke City seemed to conspire to deny West Ham victory.

Round three was staged at Hillsborough on January 5 and the crowd was swollen to 46,916 by neutral Yorkshiremen who had heard that this serial was something special. They were not dis-

appointed. The only thing missing from this replay was goals. It was a marvellous match that featured some spectacular saves by goalkeepers Bobby Ferguson and, of course, Gordon Banks. But, above all, there was a magnificent performance from Bobby Moore, whose skill dominated the game.

Hammers manager Ron Greenwood lost the toss for the second-replay venue. It went to Old Trafford and meant another long, expensive journey for the West Ham fans. 'I knew I would lose the toss,' groaned Greenwood. 'We have had one of those nights when just about everything has gone wrong. Nobody will believe it when I say our team coach hit six cars on the way to the ground. The only consolation we have is that we are still in the Cup and we like playing at Old Trafford. The pitch suits us nicely.'

By now, the semi-final series had captured the imagination of the country and 49,247 fans gathered at Old Trafford for the fourth meeting. It meant a total 171,334 people had seen the exciting sequence of matches and West Ham and Stoke were both more than £50,000 better off for the experience.

This final contest was packed with pathos, high emotion, stunning soccer, triumph and suspense —everything that makes football a great game.

The match was just 13 minutes old when Stoke striker Terry Conroy trailed a leg as he leapt over the grounded Bobby Ferguson and accidentally caught him on the side of the head. Ferguson tottered off the pitch for emergency treatment and his rubber legs told their own sorry tale of his concussion.

Manager Greenwood came on to the pitch to join in the goalmouth discussion to decide who should take over from Ferguson. Clyde Best, the

usual deputy, declined. He did not fancy being shot at in front-line conditions like these.

Then Bobby Moore was surprisingly nominated and accepted the role. It seemed Hammers were sacrificing the best of their defenders for the job of fishing the ball out of the net. But Moore, as ever, proved his sense of occasion by managing to look and play the part of a competent goalkeeper.

However, West Ham, playing with ten men, were disorganized and right-back John McDowell, propelled by panic, sabotaged West Ham's big-hearted performance when he recklessly conceded a penalty. Moore incredibly managed to smother the spot-kick but Mike Bernard followed up fast to slam the loose ball into the net.

When an England captain almost saved a penalty in a cup semi-final

Then the Hammers showed they were a team of character as well as class by overcoming this setback. Refusing to submit they began to dominate the play and Stoke seemed thrown out of their smooth stride by having to face 10 men, everyone of whom was putting in the effort of two players.

Billy Bonds, the heart of the Hammers, was monopolising the midfield and equalised with a strong shot that was deflected wide of the diving Banks. West Ham, not content to defend, maintained their pressure and Trevor Brooking was rewarded for his enterprise and effort with a cleverly-created goal that demoralized Stoke. Suddenly, George Eastham looked every one of his 35 years. The steam had gone out of Peter Dobing. Terry Conroy and Jimmy Greenhoff

were running nowhere fast and John Ritchie was cold and miserable.

But when Bobby Ferguson came back into the West Ham goal, Stoke sensed that their one-goal deficit was only temporary. Ferguson looked as dazed as a fighter who has taken too many punches and Stoke began to follow the obvious tactic of shooting on sight to test West Ham's vulnerability. Peter Dobing sprinted to steal the equaliser and it was Terry Conroy who finally settled this marathon contest. He smashed in a second-half long-range shot that Ferguson could only wave at on its way into the net.

West Ham tried bravely to salvage the situation; to recover the single goal that would give them another chance of winning the semi-final even if it required extra-time or another replay. The heroic Hurst flapped his arms in frustration when the advantage rule was played after he had been fouled inside the penalty area. But Stoke had at last won their place in the final. It was 5-4 on aggregate.

It was as if fate as much as football had finally decided the outcome of this epic serial, though Ron Greenwood later angrily suggested that Stoke had deliberately exploited Ferguson's handicap. But Ferguson could only say: 'I don't remember a thing about it. I couldn't tell you what happened in the game.'

For everybody else, it was unforgettable.

Stoke City: Banks, Marsh, Pejic, Bernard, Bloor, Jump (Skeels 2nd leg, Smith 1st and 2nd replays), Conroy, Greenhoff (sub Skeels 1st replay), Dobing, Ritchie, Eastham (sub Mahoney 2nd leg).
West Ham United: Ferguson, McDowell, Lampard, Bonds, Taylor, Moore, Redknapp (sub Eustace 2nd replay), Best, Hurst, Brooking, Robson.

59

Hereford's triumph, Newcastle's loss, Barrow's demise

On Saturday 5 February 1972 the ice which had gripped Hereford for 10 days suddenly began to melt, and to this day there are those who insist that this was caused not by a change in the weather but by the temperature generated by a town gripped with FA Cup fever.

In any event suddenly, after half a dozen postponements due to the weather, now the FA Cup third round replay between the local team of part-timers and Newcastle United of the First Division, was on.

In Hereford the event was seen as more than just a football match: another creditable performance against high-class opposition would be convincing evidence in support of their claim for election to the Football League. The Press Box at Hereford's compact Edgar Street ground, which normally housed four Press men and one photographer for Southern League matches, was inundated by 60 reporters, 35 photographers and television crews hoping to bring the world news of a sensation.

What had initially aroused such interest and stimulated dreams of a great Cup triumph was

Hereford's brave performance at St James' Park 12 days before when they had snatched a 2-2 draw after taking the lead in two minutes. Could they now beat Newcastle at Hereford?

For Newcastle, though less vital, the match was important because their restoration to Division One had not, in six seasons, produced the success Tyneside hoped for and a long Cup run would do something to restore their momentum. But Newcastle were obviously uneasy.

Their Cup record was poor since the palmy days of the early fifties when they won the trophy three times in five years, and there were a remarkable number of Third and Fourth Division clubs whose main claim to fame was having beaten Newcastle United in the Cup. A week's delay waiting cooped-up in an hotel while the game was repeatedly postponed had not helped their nerves. The players had to have extra clothes sent from Newcastle and organized darts and domino competitions to relieve the boredom.

Also, they were without centre-half Ollie Burton who had badly damaged a knee in Newcastle's 0-0 draw at Huddersfield the Saturday before. In fact

Burton was never to play again. His injury made way for the return of skipper Bob Moncur after a calf injury which had threatened his career and had kept him out of football for several months.

Newcastle also had £180,000 Malcolm Macdonald, who was to become Newcastle's first full England international in 16 years, and £150,000 Scottish midfield star Tony Green. In comparison Hereford were composed of ex-League players now finishing their careers in the Southern League and young men who, as yet, were unknown.

The tension was acute as Hereford began on the defensive. Newcastle, desperately wanting to assert their nominal superiority, attacked the non-Leaguers throughout the first-half and, naturally, exposed some flaws in the defence of a side which, judged solely on pedigree, should not have been on the same pitch as the First Division club.

Newcastle attacked from the start, anxious to avoid humiliation

But Macdonald had failed to show the finishing ability Newcastle had paid so much for. He scored 23 goals for Newcastle in his first season in Division One, but in the Cup replay with Hereford he twice went round the keeper and then missed an open goal. And Hereford goal-keeper Fred Potter, a part-timer after a League career with Aston Villa and Doncaster, pulled off several first-class saves to keep the score 0-0 at the interval.

As the second-half began to drift on with Newcastle throwing away chances like confetti at a wedding, the Hereford players and the crowd

realized that the First Division team, for all their efforts, were not assured of victory. Newcastle could be beaten—especially as their confidence was waning under the constant strain. Dudley Tyler, a pencil-slim inside-forward who had a hole-in-the-heart operation as a child, began to probe and worry Newcastle when Hereford broke out of defence. His ability was obviously far above Southern League standards. He was the man to inspire Hereford.

Yet it looked a predictable result eight minutes from the end of normal time when Newcastle at last took the lead. Viv Busby, on loan from Luton Town, lofted a high cross from the right-wing and Macdonald, close to goal, headed sharply past the helpless Potter. That should have been the end. The crowd sighed and prepared for an honourable defeat. It would take something out of the ordinary to revive little Hereford now with Newcastle prepared to retreat and defend their lead until referee Turner's final whistle.

Incredibly that something was to happen. With only four minutes remaining Ron Radford, a carpenter, became a hero when he won the ball in a tackle, got up, played a short one-two with Owen and shot from 30 yards past Iam McFaul with such immense power and accuracy that it won him BBC's 'Goal of the Year' award. The tension of this Cup replay, increased by so many postponements, was heightened even further. And no longer was the apparent problem, 'Could Hereford beat Newcastle?' but, 'Could Newcastle beat Hereford?' With one goal each the teams went on to play extra-time.

Lifted by a delirious crowd Hereford, socks down and arms pumping, threw themselves at a panicing Newcastle. It amazed no-one when the part-timers scored again, the final goal coming from Hereford's substitute, Ricky George, on for injured right-back Roger Griffiths. One hundred and three minutes after the kick-off George received the ball from Tyler in the right-hand corner of the penalty area, turned and, as Moncur came forward, swung a shot across McFaul and into the net. For the second time the pitch was flooded by banner-waving Hereford fans.

Hereford's victory was as bitter for Newcastle as their 2-1 home defeat by Bedford Town in 1964. For Hereford, it was the first defeat of a First Division side by a non-League club since Yeovil put out Sunderland in 1949.

After Radford's 'Goal of the Year' the Southern League team had to win

Moncur admits: 'I was close to tears at the finish. After months of worrying if my career was finished I had to come back in this match and be labelled as the skipper of the first First Division side to be humiliated in 23 years. The upsetting thing is that, looking back, we had only ourselves to blame. We wasted so many good chances throughout. And after Hereford equalized we went to pieces.'

Colin Addison, Hereford's player-manager, had always believed that after the 2-2 draw at Newcastle his side had a great chance and when United failed to take control early in the replay he decided it must be Hereford's day. He drove his players on and once Radford equalized he felt certain of victory.

The game had consequences for both clubs. Hereford's claim to League status was justified by that victory and strengthened by their fourth round tie with West Ham, which they lost in a replay at Upton Park. This memorable progress in the Cup was the most valuable publicity they could have had, and it was a popular—though in the event extremely close—decision to elect them to the Fourth Division in place of Barrow at the end of the season. Dudley Tyler, who played so well in both ties against the First Division clubs, gained Hereford £25,000 from West Ham, a record fee paid to a non-League club. At the beginning of the next season he was playing First Division football.

But if that second match against Newcastle had made Tyler's career it might have ruined Viv Busby's. Busby, who had only months before been playing with Wycombe Wanderers and who had created what could have been Newcastle's winning goal eight minutes from the end of normal time, was likely to have stayed on Tyneside if Newcastle had won. But the despondent Geordies returned him to Luton Town.

For Hereford the game was the key to their League career. For Newcastle it was one they could only forget as soon as possible.

Hereford: Potter, Griffiths, Mallender, Jones, McLaughlin, Addison, Gough, Tyler, Meadows, Owen, Radford. Sub: George.
Newcastle United: McFaul, Craig, Clark, Nattrass, Howard, Moncur, Busby, Green, Macdonald, Tudor, Hibbitt.

Below left One of Fred Potter's many fine saves that prevented Newcastle from dominating Hereford United in the Cup replay at Edgar Street.
Below centre Macdonald finally seemed to have relieved Newcastle's mounting anxiety with this headed goal only eight minutes from time.
Below right But one goal was not enough. Four minutes later Radford equalized and in extra-time this shot by George won the match for Hereford.

The day the magic lived again

60

A young redhead called Horswill was in tears. A hefty centre-forward of Hungarian extraction called Halom held his hands in prayer, his eyes skyward. And a tiny Scot called Kerr wiped his hands on his red-white shirt before taking the Cup from the Duchess of Kent.

Sunderland from the backwaters of the Second Division had won an unforgettable victory. They had beaten Leeds United, the perfect product of an era that had equated success with cynicism, more commonly known as 'professionalism'. They had laid waste a side who fielded 11 full internationals. They had become the first Second Division side to win the Cup for 42 years. They had, on their way, defeated three of the previous four Cup winners. Above all, they had fashioned a victory that breathed new life into an area of economic depression and, perhaps, into the very game itself at the end of the most depressed season in decades.

To those from the North East with long memories it was a win with an ironic twist. The decline of Sunderland as a worthwhile force coincided with a rush of spending that earned the club a 'Bank of England' tag. Now its renaissance had come on the cheap as the club mirrored its environment with a shortage of funds. But the real significance was earlier that season, when sufficient cash *was* available to strengthen the club as it tottered towards Division Three.

The sole redeeming feature of the most depressing season ever?

That money went to Blackpool, but not for a player. It bought a manager, and a man with the dual love of football and the North East. Bob Stokoe had performed with stature for Newcastle United in the fifties.

As a manager he had seen as many downs as ups on a tour through the less prestigious areas of Bury, Carlisle, Charlton and Rochdale. Yet he arrived home with an effect rarely equalled by the US Cavalry at the crucial stage of a western.

Immediately League results improved as he injected confidence and stability into his staff. The nightmare of the Third Division football at Roker Park stopped recurring. And the new vitality he had brought began to express itself in the Cup. With replay wins over Notts County and Reading, Sunderland found themselves in the fifth round.

Character and resolution that had been missing for so long earned a draw on Manchester City's Maine Road ground and ensured a packed Roker Park. There Stokoe's side showed just what ability they had when it was allied to confidence. On a breathtaking night City were torn apart, particularly by a virtuoso performance from Billy Hughes.

Luton Town crumbled in front of the awakened Sunderland crowd in the sixth round. And Hillsborough, the semi-final venue, was too far north to be neutral. Arsenal's players felt the pressure enough to make elementary mistakes—as when Blockley's weak back pass let in Halom to put Sunderland in front—and the remarkable reserves which had caused them to twice resist Stoke City in the two previous semi-finals were

nowhere in evidence as the tiny Billy Hughes headed Sunderland's second. Incredibly Bob Stokoe was to lead Sunderland out at Wembley, where West Bromwich Albion had been the last non-First Division side to win the Cup way back in 1931.

Every ounce of common sense demanded that there the fun would stop. Though Leeds United had made a habit of coming second, the Empire Stadium was their second home. Most of the side had played in the 2-2 draw there in the 1970 Final and in the win over Arsenal two years later. Madeley, Hunter, Clarke were regular gladiators for Sir Alf Ramsey and England. The likes of Lorimer, Bremner, Giles, Yorath and the others had played internationals in that unique atmosphere. Some of Stokoe's squad had never been there—even to watch a game.

Though their names meant little away from Wearside, Stokoe had some competent players. The veteran Montgomery, perhaps the best known, had served at Roker for 13 years and his name had been on Ramsey's lists. Dave Watson, with something of the John Charles about him, had come from Rotherham for £100,000 as an aggressive centre-forward. It was typical of Stokoe that one of his first tactical moves was to switch Watson from attack to the heart of the defence. The big man, who had been finding goals desperately hard to come by as a centre-forward, immediately started to score coming from the back, as well as being the focal point of the defence.

Kerr, the skipper, had twice recovered from broken legs without impairing his creative talents. The precocious, abrasive, Horswill blended easily with him in midfield. Dennis Tueart and Hughes had the pace and aggression to commit defenders. Porterfield, a sweet left foot.

Throughout the country these qualities were thrust forward, brave efforts at logic by everyone outside Leeds, suddenly becoming fanatic about the side which had captured their imagination. But in the vernacular of the day on the lush green turf of Wembley, there was no way.

Even Stokoe could not hold a candle to the achievements of Don Revie, the arch-motivator who had taken Leeds to nine finals in as many seasons. More than almost any other man, Revie would be aware of the dangers of over-confidence, the only obvious danger to his side.

The Final took place on a day that belonged to April rather than May. Heavy early morning showers made the pitch slippery, too much so for the following patches of bright sunshine to dry it. And the showers were to continue throughout the afternoon. If the neutrals needed any more convincing where their hearts were they got it when Stokoe, his craggy face wreathed in smiles, led out his men dressed in the same red tracksuit. The ranks were symbolically closed.

Revie, in his lucky grey suit, had Eddie Gray, fit again after a bout of injury, in the file behind him. That in itself was even more ominous for the underdogs. Yet as the match got underway, it was Sunderland's awareness of Gray's threat which gave them an early psychological thrust. As soon as the Scottish international, his shoulders hunched to feed out his bewildering dummies, received the ball, Kerr dropped back to support the tall, threatened Malone. Gray would slip one, but never both, and each time he lost

the ball a little of his confidence ebbed away with it. There were no David Webbs this time.

Leeds' opening had an ominous pitch to it. Clarke twice could not pull the trigger when the goal was in his sights as first Watson and then Pitt produced rescuing tackles. Stokoe had admitted that he feared an early goal, but a plucky shot from Horswill that slithered past Harvey's right-hand post after twenty minutes announced that the preliminaries were past without any losses.

There was just time to reflect that Sunderland had survived a third of the game when they scored. Kerr's long ball into the Leeds goal area had all the makings of a mis-hit cross when Harvey, sensibly aware of the greasiness of the ball, elected to turn it over his crossbar rather than catch it.

Hughes struck the left-wing corner deep to the far post, probably aiming for the powerful forehead of the dangerous Watson. Certainly that was what the Leeds defenders thought because two of them leapt with the centre-half as he flung himself upwards to reach the ball. The cross was too strong, though, as it flew beyond Watson towards Halom.

The first Second Division Cup winners for over forty years

Under pressure he managed to divert it back across goal with his knee. Porterfield arrived into the space vacated by one of the Leeds players who had been pre-occupied with Watson at the same time as the ball. He cushioned it on his left thigh and then volleyed over Harvey with his right boot. It was the darts player landing double top with his wrong hand. Porterfield, as he said later, usually uses that right foot just to stand on.

The lead stood until half-time, but had they the legs to repeat the show in the second half? On a yielding Wembley pitch the odds seemed against them.

The expected assault soon began. But Watson and Pitt showed a mastery of Jones and Clarke in the air that any First Division defence would have envied. Kerr and Malone curbed Gray so well that Revie pulled him off. Horswill snapped away in front of the back four. And Sunderland survived.

Just twice did the defence and composure wane. And from either occasion Leeds, as Revie said after the game, would have won if they had scored. First Watson made his only blatant error appearing to trip Bremner in the area. Mr. Burns, close at hand, gestured play on. Then and more significantly Jim Montgomery produced a double save that made him say later; 'When I die I shall have my left hand embalmed.'

He reacted magnificently at the near post to push out Cherry's close-range diving header, but all seemed lost as the ball rolled invitingly towards Lorimer's famed right foot. From just five yards arguably the hardest shot of the era sent it solidly towards an unguarded goal, only for Montgomery to dive blindly into its path and turn it on to the bar off his left wrist. Lorimer will never believe it: 'I turned away. I was certain I'd scored.'

Somehow, everyone knew in that unbelievable fraction of a second that Leeds were beaten, that those were right who said that the team who had won, as Sunderland had done, in '37 were fated to succeed in '73. Sunderland continued to withstand as the seconds ticked slowly away. Dennis Tueart summed it up: 'I looked up at the bench and they held up five fingers. Five minutes to go. So I played on for another hour, then looked up, again. They held up three fingers.' And then Stokoe was sprinting on to the pitch to reach Montgomery, not yet far outside his penalty area, and embrace him. Kerr, dazed with the effort, fell down the first few steps of the royal box as he went to lift the Cup.

The despair of Leeds and their fans was equalled only by that of the bookies, who lost

millions of pounds. Everyone else shared in the pleasure of an underdog's success. For Leeds it was, perhaps, cathartic. They had come second yet again. Revie despaired, feeling that he could do no more for the club, and packed his bags for Everton—only to be eventually persuaded to stay and try once more. And at the start of the next season Leeds came out playing the best football since the Spurs double side of 1961.

And yet the day really belonged to the North East. It proved once again that football in the United Kingdom is really about provincialism. And, perhaps most important of all, it was a perfectly timed saving grace after the most depressing season of modern times. Gates had dropped dramatically, the game was overexposed on television, and fans talked wearily of the predictability and tedium of a defensively obsessed League. Even George Best, symbol of a magical age, announced unconvincingly that he

Above *The save of the season as Jim Montgomery parries Peter Lorimer's shot.*
Below *The goal of the season. Ian Porterfield leans back on his 'shooting' foot and makes Sunderland the biggest upsets since the War.*
Left *Captain and messianic manager.*

was giving the whole thing up.

And suddenly there was a fairy tale. A saviour returned, the underdogs succeeded in the least likely of all settings. There was still some romance left. Bob Stokoe could not have timed it better.

Leeds United: Harvey, Reaney, Madeley, Hunter, Cherry, Bremner, Giles, Gray (sub Yorath), Lorimer, Jones, Clarke.
Sunderland: Montgomery, Malone, Watson, Pitt, Guthrie, Kerr, Horswill, Porterfield, Hughes, Halom, Tueart.